WOMEN AND THE JUDICIARY
IN THE ASIA-PACIFIC

Courts can play an important role in addressing issues of inequality, discrimination and gender injustice for women. The feminisation of the judiciary – both in its thin meaning of women's entrance into the profession, as well as its thicker forms of realising gender justice – is a core part of the agenda for gender equality. This volume acknowledges both the diversity of meanings of the feminisation of the judiciary, as well as the complexity of the social and cultural realisation of gender equality. Containing original empirical studies, this book demonstrates the past and present challenges women face to entering the judiciary and progressing their career, as well as when and why they advocate for women's issues while on the bench. From stories of pioneering women to sector-wide institutional studies of the gender composition of the judiciary, this book reflects on the feminisation of the judiciary in the Asia-Pacific.

MELISSA CROUCH is Professor at the University of New South Wales (UNSW). She is the author of *The Constitution of Myanmar* (2019) and *Law and Religion in Indonesia* (2013). Melissa is the Vice President of the Asian Studies Association of Australia. She was awarded a major grant by the Australian Research Council to study constitutional change in authoritarian regimes. Her book, *The Constitution of Myanmar*, was shortlisted for the Australian Legal Research Awards 2020.

WOMEN AND THE JUDICIARY IN THE ASIA-PACIFIC

Edited by

MELISSA CROUCH

University of New South Wales

Shaftesbury Road, Cambridge CB2 8EA, United Kingdom

One Liberty Plaza, 20th Floor, New York, NY 10006, USA

477 Williamstown Road, Port Melbourne, VIC 3207, Australia

314–321, 3rd Floor, Plot 3, Splendor Forum, Jasola District Centre, New Delhi – 110025, India

103 Penang Road, #05–06/07, Visioncrest Commercial, Singapore 238467

Cambridge University Press is part of Cambridge University Press & Assessment, a department of the University of Cambridge.

We share the University's mission to contribute to society through the pursuit of education, learning and research at the highest international levels of excellence.

www.cambridge.org
Information on this title: www.cambridge.org/9781108999878

DOI: 10.1017/9781009000208

First published 2022
First paperback edition 2023

A catalogue record for this publication is available from the British Library

Library of Congress Cataloging-in-Publication data
Names: Crouch, Melissa, editor.
Title: Women and the judiciary in the Asia-Pacific / edited by Melissa Crouch, University of New South Wales, Sydney.
Description: Cambridge, United Kingdom ; New York, NY : Cambridge University Press, 2021. | Includes bibliographical references and index.
Identifiers: LCCN 2021024791 (print) | LCCN 2021024792 (ebook) | ISBN 9781316518328 (hardback) | ISBN 9781108999878 (paperback) | ISBN 9781009000208 (epub)
Subjects: LCSH: Women judges–Asia. | Women judges–Pacific Area. | Sex discrimination against women–Law and legislation–Asia. | Sex discrimination against women–Law and legislation–Pacific Area. | Women–Legal status, laws, etc.–Asia. | Women–Legal status, laws, etc.–Pacific Area. | BISAC: LAW / General
Classification: LCC KNC51 .W66 2021 (print) | LCC KNC51 (ebook) | DDC 347.5/014082–dc23
LC record available at https://lccn.loc.gov/2021024791
LC ebook record available at https://lccn.loc.gov/2021024792

ISBN   978-1-316-51832-8   Hardback
ISBN   978-1-108-99987-8   Paperback

CONTENTS

FIGURES

TABLES

PREFACE

This volume is the result of the Women in Asia Conference 2019 based on the theme 'Women in an Era of Anti-elitism in Asia'. The conference is an initiative of the Women in Asia Forum, which began in 1978 and is affiliated with the Asian Studies Association of Australia. In 1981, the first Women in Asia Conference was held at the University of New South Wales (UNSW) and the return of the conference to UNSW marked the thirteenth anniversary of the conference. I hosted the Women in Asia Conference together with Louise Edwards, Tanya Jakimow, Felix Tan, Carmen Leong and Minako Sakai.

We were delighted to welcome speakers from over fifteen countries in Asia, including India, Indonesia, Singapore, Japan, Sri Lanka, Thailand, the Philippines, Malaysia, Hong Kong, Bangladesh, China, Iran and Korea. The speakers were drawn from over thirty universities in Asia. The Women in Asia Conference provides a supportive and engaged intellectual environment to explore issues of gender and feminism theoretically, conceptually, politically and practically.

The theme, 'Women in an Era of Anti-elitism', addressed the challenges populism poses for gender equality. Many scholars often refer to the 'anti-establishment' or 'anti-elitist' element to populism, which is certainly one aspect of it. But populism, as Jan Werner Muller identifies, is also inherently anti-pluralist. Populism is a particularly exclusive and exclusionary form of identity politics. Populism understood as anti-pluralism is a threat to democracy. Populism poses a threat to rule of law, a threat to inclusivity and pluralism, and a threat to social and economic equality. While populism understood in this way is certainly a cause for concern, I am encouraged to see the various forms of resistance that have emerged and that were discussed and debated at the conference. Where there is populism, there is also resistance to populism. This age of populism contains a central paradox because populism not only poses a threat to gender equality but at the same time leads to new forms of resistance and efforts to enhance gender equality. This volume on women and judges in the Asia-Pacific is set against the rise of populism, which has also had an impact on the judiciary.

As part of the Women in Asia Conference, I convened a stream on 'Women in the Legal Profession and the Judiciary'. The speakers were funded to attend the conference by the Rule of Law Programme Asia of Konrad Adenauer Stiftung (KAS). I would like to thank and acknowledge the generosity and contribution of Gisela Elsner and Susan Chan from KAS. I would also like to thank the Gilbert & Tobin Centre for Public Law and the Institute for Global Development at UNSW for their support. Special thanks go to Kayla Lochner and Michael Burnside, who went above and beyond to facilitate and organise an outstanding event.

The opening and closing sessions of the stream on Women in the Legal Profession and the Judiciary featured contributions from Judge Selma Alaras, the Presiding Judge of the Regional Trial Court, Makati City, the Philippines, and Judge Saitip Sukatipan, Presiding Judge of the chamber, Nakorn Si Thammarat Administrative Court of Thailand. Their practitioner perspective helped to ground our discussions at the conference in the social, political and economic realities faced by women judges in the region.

Finally, I note that this volume presumes the reader has some basic information about the legal and judicial systems covered. We would refer readers in need of further background information on the courts of these jurisdictions to introductory texts such as Ann Black and Gary Bell's *Law and Legal Institutions of Asia: Traditions, Adaptations and Innovations*, or HP Lee and Marilyn Pittard's *Asia-Pacific Judiciaries: Independence Impartiality and Integrity*.[1]

---

[1] Ann Black and Gary Bell (eds.) (2011) *Law and Legal Institutions of Asia: Traditions, Adaptations and Innovations.* Cambridge University Press; HP Lee and Marilyn Pittard (eds.) (2018) *Asia-Pacific Judiciaries: Independence Impartiality and Integrity.* Cambridge University Press.

Sarah Bishop LLB (Hons), BAsSt (Thai) (Hons) is a PhD candidate at the ANU College of Law, Australian National University, Canberra. Her primary area of research is Asian law, with a focus on Thai law. Her doctoral thesis explores rights-based litigation in Thai courts under the 1997, 2006 and 2007 Thai Constitutions. Her previous publications include 'Challenging the Judicial Coup Myth: Thai Constitutional Courts and Political Crises' in Pavin Chachavalpongpun (ed.) *Coup, King, Crisis: A Critical Interregnum in Thailand* (Yale University Southeast Asia Studies, 2020); and 'The Criminal Justice Process of Thailand' and 'Yaowalak Anuphan, Thai Lawyers for Human Rights, Bangkok', both co-authored with Mark Nolan and published in Jane Goodman Delahunty and Dilip K. Das (eds.) *Trends in Legal Advocacy* (CRC Press/Taylor and Francis Group, 2017). She has also published three invited peer-reviewed opinion pieces with East Asia Forum. Bishop has taught courses in law, Asian studies and human rights and peace studies in Australia, Thailand and Japan.

Simashree Bora teaches sociology at Cotton University, Guwahati Assam. She has received her PhD in sociology from Jawaharlal Nehru University New Delhi. She completed her PhD thesis on 'A Sociological Study of Island Ecology and Vaishnavite Institutions in Majuli, Assam'. She was also appointed as visiting faculty at Maharashtra National Law University, Mumbai and South Asian University, New Delhi. She has published in journals such as the *Indian Journal of Gender Studies* and *Indian Anthropologist*. Her latest research project was on 'Revisiting the Past and Unveiling a Gendered Legacy: The History and Representation of Women in Neo-Vaishnavism in Assam', published and funded by Zubaan-Sasakawa Peace Foundation Research Grants. Her interests lie in gender studies, sociology of religion, ecology and environment and north-east India.

Melissa Crouch is professor and Associate Dean of Research at the Faculty of Law and Justice, University of New South Wales, Sydney. She leads the Southeast Asia Law & Policy Forum at UNSW Law. Crouch is the author of *Law and Religion in Indonesia: Conflict and the Courts in West Java* (Routledge, 2014) and *The Constitution of Myanmar* (Hart Publishing, 2019). She has published in a range of peer-reviewed journals including the *Law & Society Review, International Journal of Constitutional Law* and *Oxford Journal of Legal Studies*. She is the editor of several volumes including *The Politics of Courts: Judicial Reform and Legal Culture in Indonesia* (Cambridge University Press, 2019); *Islam and the State in Myanmar: Muslim-Buddhist Relations and the Politics of Belonging* (Oxford University Press, 2016); and *The Business of Transition: Law, Development and Economics in Myanmar* (Cambridge University Press, 2017).

Imelda Deinla is a fellow at the School of Regulation and Global Governance, College of Asia Pacific, Australian National University, Canberra. Her research interests focus on comparative studies on rule of law in Southeast Asia and ASEAN, as well as on legal pluralism, hybrid justice and women and peacebuilding in Mindanao, Philippines. She also works on issues of trust and legitimacy, the role of civil society and the interaction of political actors in post-conflict settings. She holds a concurrent role as project director of the ANU Philippines Project, a policy-engaged research initiative on the Philippines between the Australian and Philippine academic and policy community. Deinla is the author of *The Development of the Rule of Law in ASEAN: The State and Regional Integration* (Cambridge University Press, 2017) and the editor of *From Aquino II to Duterte (2010–2018): Change, Continuity—and Rupture* (ISEAS Publishing, 2019, with Bjorn Dressel). In addition, she has authored many articles and book chapters on peacebuilding, legal pluralism and the rule of law in the Philippines.

Gauri Dhakal is a retired justice of the Supreme Court of Nepal. She completed her MA, BL and BA education at Tribhuvan University, Kathmandu. Dhakal is active in the International Association for Women Judges and in 1989 received the Judge of the Year Award from the Association. She is the current vice president of the Nepalese Women Judges Forum. Since retiring, she is undertaking research on the judiciary, and is active in philanthrophic work.

Subas P. Dhakal is a senior lecturer at the University of New England (Armidale) in New South Wales, Australia. He has expertise on the theory and practices of sustainable development and published in the area of the future of education and employment. He is a co-editor of two volumes on graduate work-readiness across the Asia and Pacific region, published by Routledge (2018) and Springer (2019). He also serves as an Editorial Review Board Member of the journal *Equality, Diversity and Inclusion*.

Anna Dziedzic is a global academic fellow at the Faculty of Law at the University of Hong Kong. She completed her PhD at Melbourne Law School in 2019, with a thesis on the use of foreign judges in Pacific Island states. She also holds an MA in human rights from University College London and first-class honours degrees in arts and law from the Australian National University. She researches across the field of comparative constitutional law, with a particular interest in the constitutional systems of the Asia-Pacific region. Dziedzic has published articles and book chapters on a range of issues, including constitution-making, federalism, parliamentary sovereignty, foreign judges and Indigenous constitutions. She has particular expertise in the constitutional systems of Pacific Island states and has worked with government agencies, international organisations and non-governmental organisations in the Pacific region on gender issues, peacebuilding and constitution making. As co-convenor of the Constitution Transformation Network, she organises the annual Melbourne Forum on Constitution Building in Asia and the Pacific (with International IDEA) and has contributed to comparative, country-specific and thematic policy papers and reports on conceptual and practical issues in constitutional transformation.

Natasha Naidu is a BA/LLB (Hons I) graduate from the University of New South Wales, Australia. Her research interest focuses on the rule of law in South and Southeast Asia. Naidu has previously interned at the Extraordinary Chambers in the Courts of Cambodia (ECCC) and been a member of the editorial board of the *University of New South Wales Law Journal*. She has published journal articles on political interference at the ECCC. She is a research assistant at UNSW Law and a case analyst at the *Oxford Reports on International Law*.

Dinesha Samararatne, LLB (Hons) (Colombo), LLM (Harvard), PhD (Colombo), is an academic attached to the Department of Public &

International Law, Faculty of Law of the University of Colombo, Sri Lanka. She is a convenor of the Constitution Transformation Network (CTN) of the Melbourne Law School, a co-editor of the blog of the International Association for Constitutional Law (IACL) and an articles editor for the *Indian Law Review*. From 2019 to 2020, she was a postdoctoral fellow of the Laureate Program in Comparative Constitutional Law at the Melbourne Law School. Her research expertise lies in the fields of constitutional law, administrative law and human rights law. Her publications have featured in the *Asian Journal of Comparative Law*, *Indian Law Review*, *Journal of Asian Studies*, *Journal of Law and Society* and *Asian Journal of Law and Society*.

Ulrike Schultz is a professor at the University of Hagen, Germany. She is an expert on women and the legal profession and is editor of the following volumes: *Women in the Judiciary* (edited together with Gisela Shaw, 2012); *Gender and Judging* (edited together with Gisela Shaw, Routledge, 2013); and *Gender and Judicial Education* (edited together with Gisela Shaw and Brettel Dawson, Routledge, 2016).

Sharada Shrestha is a retired justice of the Supreme Court of Nepal. She obtained her LLM qualification from Lucknow University, India, and completed her BL and BSc education at Tribhuvan University in Nepal. In 1966, Shrestha became the first woman judge in the country when she was appointed as judge to the Land Reform Special Court. She is the current president of the Nepalese Women Judges Forum and a member of the International Association of Women Judges. Since retiring, she has been active in social work in Nepal.

Kerstin Steiner is an associate professor at the La Trobe Law School, La Trobe University, Melbourne. She is also a senior associate at the Centre for Indonesian Law, Islam and Society (CILIS) and an associate at the Asian Law Centre (ALC), both at the University of Melbourne. She is specialising in Southeast Asian legal studies, researching the intersection of law, politics, economics and society, especially with regard to Islam. Steiner has held numerous visiting positions and presented her research extensively at a range of highly prestigious national and international institutions. She has numerous publications in the area of Islam, law and human rights, including two forthcoming 'The Challenges for Human Rights in Asia: Islam and the Patchwork System for Freedom of Religion in Malaysia' in Bernd Kannowski and Kerstin Steiner (eds) Nomos

Verlag (forthcoming) and 'Access to Justice and Legal Aid in the Syariah Courts in Malaysia: A Colourful but threadbare System' in Helena Whalen-Bridge (ed) *The Role of Lawyers in Access to Justice: Asian and Comparative Perspectives*, Cambridge University Press. Other publications include 'Islam, Law and Human Rights of Women in Malaysia' in Niamh Reilly (ed.) *International Human Rights: Human Rights of Women* (Springer, 2019) and two volumes, one on Singapore and one on Malaysia and Brunei, in the series 'Islam, Law and the State in Southeast Asia' (with Tim Lindsey, I. B. Taurus, 2012). She is guest editor with Dominik Mueller of the special issue 'The Bureaucratisation of Islam in Southeast Asia: Transdisciplinary Perspectives' in the *Journal of Current Southeast Asian Affairs* (2018). She has provided expert advice on Islamic family law for a United Nations Convention on the Elimination of Discrimination against Women report on Malaysia (2014) and for a comparative study on Islamic family law (2016–2017).

ABBREVIATIONS

CA	Court of Appeals
CEDAW	Convention on the Elimination of Discrimination against Women
COMELEC	Commission on Elections
COVID-19	coronavirus disease
CTA	Court of Tax Appeals
EDSA	Epifanio delos Santos Avenue (road in Manila, Philippines)
IAWJ	International Association of Women Judges
IBP	Integrated Bar Association of the Philippines
ICESCR	International Covenant on Economic, Social and Cultural Rights
ICTR	International Criminal Tribunal for Rwanda
ICTY	International Criminal Tribunal for the former Yugoslavia
JBC	Judicial and Bar Council
JIM	Jemaah Islah Malaysia
JSC	Judicial Services Commission
LDCs	least developed countries
LGUs	local government units
LTTE	Liberation Tigers of Tamil Ealam
MCTC	Municipal Circuit Trial Courts
MeTC	Metropolitan Trial Courts
MTC	Municipal Trial Courts
NGOs	non-governmental organisations
NLC	Nepal Law College
OECD	Organisation for Economic Co-operation and Development
PacLII	Pacific Legal Information Institute
PAO	Public Attorney's Office
PJDP	Pacific Judicial Development Programme
PNG	Papua New Guinea

PTC	Philippine Truth Commission
SDGs	Sustainable Development Goals
SPLA	South Pacific Lawyers Association
UAE	United Arab Emirates
UCPPR	International Covenant on Civil and Political Rights
UK	United Kingdom
UMNO	United Malays National Organisation
UN Women	United Nations Entity for Gender Equality and the Empowerment of Women
UP	University of the Philippines
UPNG	University of Papua New Guinea
USA	United States of America
USP	University of the South Pacific
WEF	World Economic Forum
WLB	Women's Legal Bureau Inc. (now the Women's Legal and Human Rights Bureau)

The Feminisation of the Judiciary in the Asia-Pacific

The Challenges of Formal and Substantive Equality

MELISSA CROUCH AND NATASHA NAIDU

In 2018, senior advocate Indira Jaising appeared before the Supreme Court of India on behalf of petitioners to challenge a ban against women between the ages of ten and fifty (the ages of menstruation) entering the Sabarimala temple as unconstitutional (Jain 2019). The Sabarimala temple in Kerala is a site of worship for the Hindu deity Lord Ayyappa and attracts millions of pilgrims each year, making it one of the world's largest sites of annual pilgrimage. The traditional view is that young women are not permitted to offer worship in the temple because the deity must not be tempted to deviate from their vow of celibacy.[1] In 1991, in an earlier legal challenge, the Kerala High Court had upheld the restriction on women entering the temple.

Prior to the hearing of the case, the petitioners in the Sabarimala case submitted a plea requesting a judicial bench with equal numbers of male and female judges. Instead, only one female judge was appointed to the five-judge bench (PTI 2018), although this is not for a lack of women judges who could have sat on the case. Nevertheless, the majority judgment ruled in favour of the petitioners and held that the ban on women entering the temple was unconstitutional because it infringed the right to equality. This landmark decision paved the way for women to enter and worship at the temple.

Yet the sole dissent in the court case was issued by the female judge, Justice Indu Malhotra. Justice Malhotra held that the ban on women was not unconstitutional as the temple had a right to manage its own internal affairs. On this basis, Justice Malhotra would have dismissed the case.

The decision in the Sabarimala temple case raises a number of complex questions about women judges in India and in the Asia-Pacific at

---

[1] *Sabarimala* [10] (Misra CJI).

large. What role do courts play in promoting gender equality? What difference, if any, do women judges make? When and why do women judges advance gender equality? How do we hold in tension both the promise and paradox of women judges, as embodied in the dissent of women judges like Justice Malhotra?

While women judges may be champions for gender equality, in reality judicial figures like Justice Indu Malhotra demonstrate that some women judges may also be barriers to equality. Justice Indu Malhotra is herself the only female to have been appointed to the bench from the bar and only the second woman to be appointed as senior advocate by the Supreme Court of India. Yet in the Sabarimala decision, a complex set of factors intersect with gender, including religion.

Controversies like this reveal the contemporary struggles of the women's movement and the role that courts play in the Asia-Pacific. The incident highlights the central role that judges can potentially play in the struggle for gender equality. In this case, the petitioners deliberately sought a gender equal bench, although this was not granted. The outcome of the case shows that advances in gender equality through the courts is possible, although translating that decision into accepted social practice remains difficult.

This case raises questions about the position and influence of women judges across the Asia-Pacific that have been underexplored to date. To what extent are women able to enter the judiciary and under what conditions? How do women fare in terms of mobility within the judiciary? To what extent can we identify the feminisation of the judiciary in the Asia-Pacific and what does this look like? Does the place of women in the judiciary in the Asia-Pacific depart from, or mirror, the place of women within society? Are experiences of judging in Asia gendered? What is distinctive about professional identity formation for women in the judiciary in the Asia-Pacific?

The purpose of this book is to offer in-depth reflections on the feminisation of the judiciary in the Asia-Pacific, grounded in original empirical studies. This volume aims to capture the historical trajectory and contemporary impact of the role of women in the judiciary in the Asia-Pacific.[2] Our study of women judges in the Asia-Pacific acknowledges the diversity and complexity of the region – including the differences between civil law, socialist and common law systems; differences

---

[2] The regional coverage in this book is intended to be illustrative rather than comprehensive.

between liberal democracies and illiberal authoritarian regimes that affect the independence of the courts and the relative distance of the legal profession from the regime in power; differences in conceptions of work and family that affect the role of women in the workplace; and differences in the social, economic and historical trajectories of the state, particularly the growing inequality between the rich and the poor worldwide.

In this chapter, we identify and explore core themes that emerge from the literature through the lens of thick and thin conceptions of the feminisation of the judiciary. We define the feminisation of the judiciary as the growing presence and influence of women judges in the courts in support of gender equality. This view of the feminisation of the judiciary does not presume all women judges support an agenda for equality, but rather that women judges have a potentially significant role to play in support of gender equality. We suggest that a thin conception of the feminisation of the judiciary is concerned with the entrance of women into the judiciary and their career progression. This view of feminisation focuses on trailblazing women, the barriers women face to enter the judiciary, and the factors that explain when, how and why women enter the judiciary. These histories and stories are important and deserve greater recognition. Yet a focus on the feminisation of the judiciary must go far beyond the issue of entrance to the profession.

A thicker, and more contested, concept of the feminisation of the judiciary focuses on the diverse range of challenges women judges face in the judiciary. This includes issues with career progression and substantive aspects of judicial practice, such as how women judges decide cases and whether they do so in ways that advance gender equality.

This volume takes up the call to chart an agenda for the study of women in the judiciary in the Global South.[3] In this chapter we consider debates over the feminisation of the judiciary and the findings of studies that consider both its thin and thick meanings in the Global North and beyond to the Asia-Pacific. This volume extends the geographic scope of studies on women judges beyond the geographic focus of the existing literature on East Asia, particularly China, Korea and Japan.

Entrance to the judiciary is clearly a preliminary first step, and many of the chapters in this volume tell this story. We highlight the ongoing historic milestones achieved in terms of women's appointments to positions of high judicial office and the resulting political tensions across the

---

[3] Ulrike Schultz (2003: xxv) notes that a study of women in the judiciary in 'underdeveloped or in developing countries' remains to be written.

Asia-Pacific. We also capture the growth in professional organisations for women in the law across the past two decades, which we suggest is one demonstration of the feminisation of the legal and judicial profession in the Asia-Pacific.

Thin Feminisiation: Entrance to the Judiciary

A major area of scholarly debate centres on what constitutes the femi-nisation of the judiciary and how, or to what extent, feminisation has in fact occurred. Some scholars have adopted a thin version of feminisation akin to entrance to the judiciary or legal profession. It is now well established that feminist assumptions of the need for a critical mass of women on the bench alone is not sufficient to guarantee gender equality. The literature is clear that adding women to a male-dominated judiciary does not necessarily ensure substantive equality. However, the entrance of women into the judiciary across the Asia-Pacific remains a necessary and symbolic first step in the struggle for substantive equality.

Given the relationship between the courts and the wider legal profes-sion, studying women judges needs to begin with studies of women, although these studies primarily focus on the Global North. The litera-ture offers a conceptual starting point for studies of women in the legal sector in the Asia-Pacific, but it is also a necessary point of departure given the social, economic and historical differences of the judiciary and society in the Global South.

The first major and ongoing preoccupation of studies of women in law is when, how and under what conditions women have entered the profession. Studies of women in the legal profession in the United States and the Global North more broadly were brought to the fore with Cynthia Epstein's landmark book, *Women in Law* (1981). Epstein's pioneering study traces the increase in the entry of women into the legal profession from the mid-1960s to the late 1970s. This trend was enabled by the dramatic increase in the number of women entering law school, affirming the interconnected nature of entrance to legal education and the legal profession. Epstein's work has in turn led to studies on the extent to which female graduates enter the legal profession or judiciary in similar numbers to male graduates, often identifying the additional barriers that women face to gaining entry to the legal sector. Kay and Gorman (2008, 302) suggest that in the Global North, women are more likely than men to be recruited into less remunerative or prestigious practice areas (Kay and Gorman 2008, 302). Women law graduates report taking their first jobs outside the legal sector more frequently than male graduates, and women are less likely to hold prestigious judicial clerkships (Kay and Gorman 2008, 303).

This has led to a debate about whether the entrance of women into the legal profession and judiciary displaces the position of men. In the context of the United States, this has not occurred because, from the 1970s–80s, major growth in the size of the legal profession occurred at the same time as women entered the profession in increasing numbers (Menkel-Meadow 1989). This may also be true in some jurisdictions in the Asia-Pacific that have seen an expansion of the judiciary in the late twentieth and early twenty-first century. Countries such as Indonesia have gone through a process of democratisation that has included major judicial reform (Crouch 2019b) and therefore an expansion in the number of judicial positions available.

The literature specifically on women and judicial appointments is concerned with the first women judges, the challenges they faced in entering the profession and the extent to which they were 'trailblazers' and role models for other women to follow (Norgren 2018). Studies of judicial appointments identify and explain the increase in the number of female judges in the profession over time (Valdini and Shortell 2016). The concern with identifying and overcoming barriers to career entry for women in the courts resonates in some countries in the Asia-Pacific that have low numbers of women in the profession and need to address issues of entry to the judiciary, such as India and South Korea.

However, the existing literature has yet to pay sufficient attention to women in the legal sector in the Asia-Pacific, where women may constitute the majority of legal professionals. For example, in Myanmar, the majority of judges, lawyers, legal academics and public prosecutors are women (Crouch 2020). In such contexts, an important preliminary question to ask is why and how women constitute the majority of the profession in the first place. Historically, under colonial rule and the early decades of independence, the legal profession was entirely male. In Myanmar, the shift to law as a women's profession began during the socialist era of the 1960s, as the legal profession began to diminish in political importance, public status and influence.[4] During the socialist regime, law as a profession was co-opted by the regime, depoliticised and suffered a decline in prestige as it came to be closely associated with the socialist-military

---

[4] This is like other socialist contexts such as East Germany, where Markovits (1995) notes that 50 per cent of the legal profession were women.

administration (Crouch 2019b). Given a range of countries in the region that are either socialist or formerly socialist (including China, Vietnam, North Korea, Laos, Myanmar and Cambodia), we need studies of women in the judiciary in the Asia-Pacific that appropriately acknowledge and consider the influence of the wider political and social context.

Further, rethinking what the literature means by a 'profession' when we study the judiciary is crucial. We need to remain open to alternative conceptions of the judiciary and ways the role of the judicial branch may perform different roles in illiberal regimes. For example, in contexts like Myanmar the judiciary is better understood as an administrative body that is part of the bureaucracy (Crouch 2019a). The high numbers of women in the legal profession in Myanmar contrasts with the relative absence of women from positions of leadership in the highest courts, such as the Supreme Court. There has never been a female judge on the Supreme Court of Myanmar since it began operation in 1948. There have been women on the Constitutional Tribunal, although this court was only established in 2011; it is a marginal institution because it hears very few cases (Crouch 2018). There is a need to interrogate the social and cultural factors that influence how the minority of men within the judicial system come to occupy the most important positions. This compels us to consider the relationship between the judiciary and other institutions such as the military, because for many decades entry into the military was a more secure and potentially lucrative profession for men (Crouch 2019a), and was not a pathway generally open to women.

The question of how women gain entrance to the judiciary is also related to access to the legal profession and legal education in the Asia-Pacific. There is an emerging scholarly focus on gender composition in legal education, corporate firms, the bar and the judiciary in the Asia-Pacific, with studies of Korea, India, Japan and Pakistan. A first point of inquiry regarding entrance to the legal profession and judiciary has been legal education (see Steele and Taylor 2010). While legal education is one important step towards women entering the judiciary, it constitutes only one of the challenges for women to enter the profession. For example, since the 1980s in Taiwan, women have studied law in roughly equal numbers to male students, although access to the legal profession remains exclusive in part due to difficult entrance exams (Tay Sheng-Wang 2010). In Chapter 3 of this volume, Dinesha Samararatne explains that 80 per cent of law graduates are women, and this growth corresponds with increasing numbers of women at the bar and in the Attorney General's department. Likewise, in Myanmar, one of the reasons that women are a significant percent of all aspects of the legal professions is that women make up an estimated 90 per cent of undergraduates studying law.

Likewise, there is emerging literature on the entry of women to the bar in the Asia-Pacific. For example, in Japan, while the entry of women to the profession has increased, a glass ceiling on gender balance at the bar exists, with women representing no more than 18.5 per cent of the bar (Levin 2019). In the context of Thailand, in 2007, Siampukdee (n.d.) documents that women make up just over 5 per cent of the police force; 17 per cent of prosecutors; and 22 per cent of judges. While this represents an increase in women's representation since the 1980s, Siampukdee notes the ongoing challenges for women in terms of promotion and aspiring to higher office and positions of leadership.

The path to enter the judiciary diverges between jurisdictions with career judges and non-career judges, which generally corresponds to the difference between civil law and common law systems. Across the Asia-Pacific, common law jurisdictions usually require graduates to first become lawyers and build a successful career as a lawyer before potentially being appointed as a judge. In contrast, civil law and socialist or former socialist countries usually offer law graduates the choice of taking an entrance exam in order to become a career judge. These judges may be classified as civil servants.

Some jurisdictions in the Asia-Pacific, however, have mixed approaches to judicial appointments. For example, even though the government in Myanmar claims its legal system is based on the common law, entrance to the judiciary is similar to a career-based civil law style path, with graduates able to take an entrance exam to become a judge (Crouch 2020). In another mixed setting, Indonesia's remarkable strategy of specialised courts since 1998 has led to the proliferation of ad hoc judicial positions, usually for a set term of five years (Crouch 2019b). This is even though civil law systems usually have career judges. Another point of difference is the representation of women in constitutional courts as these institutions have emerged around the world in the past three decades. Again in Indonesia, appointments to the Constitutional Court are direct and do not require a candidate to have a background as a judge, with candidates often coming from academia. In this regard, the study of women in the judiciary often depends upon whether the focus is on the lower courts or the apex court. Susan Silbey (1981) has pointed out that studies of law and courts often focus on the apex courts and overlook the lower courts, which is where people are more likely to come into contact with judicial institutions. Many of the chapters in this volume take up Silbey's call and consider women's representation and influence in both the apex courts and the lower courts.

Statistics on the numbers of women across the legal sector and particularly in the judiciary are documented in the chapters in this volume. One point of distinction from studies of the Global North is that the authors in this volume do not necessarily assume the validity of official statistics, and in fact in some cases are quick to question them (see Chapter 8). Official statistics are not necessarily accurate and may be open to interpretation. Further, for other jurisdictions, the size and scale of the population and the relationship between judges and society, including the relative importance or lack of importance of the courts, need to be kept in mind. For example, Cambodia has a population of 16 million and a judiciary of only 258 judges. Of these judges, only 37 are women, which means that 6 of the 24 first instance courts have no female judges at all.[5]

In some jurisdictions, the entrance of women has increased in certain areas of legal practice; this is the case in Pakistan, where the increase of women in the family courts from 2009 now means women constitute more than a third of these judges (Holden 2018). In India, despite the stagnation of female representation in the legal sector at just 5 per cent, some parts of the legal profession break with this pattern, such as commercial law firms. Ballakrishnen's (2017, 2021) important empirical work on Indian commercial law firms since the 1990s considers the large numbers of women in these workspaces, in comparison to other areas of legal work. She suggests that these commercial law firms, as a new institutional type in that context, do not carry the same structural barriers to entry that is evident in other legal institutions in India.

The literature specifically on women judges in the Asia-Pacific is also concerned with judicial appointments because the appointment of women judges is still a historic development in many jurisdictions. In their study of judges in China, Zheng, Ai and Liu (2017, 174) identify that the literature on judicial appointments in the Global North does not pay sufficient attention to the 'social processes by which women's judicial careers are structured, particularly in terms of promotion and attrition'. They examine why judicial career paths for women stagnate at the mid-career level. To explain both the mobility and glass ceiling for women judges, they identify two processes: reverse attrition, where men can leave

---

[5] I would like to thank Chhunvoleak Srun, judge of the Appellate Court of Cambodia, for this information.

for more prestigious positions and women take their place; and dual-track promotion, in which women judges are promoted in their 'professional track' based on an evaluation of their expertise and work performance but not in their 'political track' based on their social capital and political connections, or lack thereof. This process limits the promotion of women judges to mid-level positions. This is an important example of theory-building from the Global South.

The entrance of women to the judiciary has been illuminated by biographies of key pioneering women in the field, often using oral history to explore how women enter the profession. Some scholars have explored how and why judicial appointments are made by focusing on rich life biographies of the first woman lawyers and judges, such as Kim's (2003) study of Lee Tai-young, the first woman lawyer in Korea and Mossman et al.'s (2006) study of Cornelia Sorabji, the first woman lawyer in India. The interest in the lives of the first women lawyers and judges is instructive for understanding the challenges women face to entering the judiciary, and the role of pioneers in paving a way for other women. The chapters in this volume expand on and offer new accounts. The histories of women in the judiciary in some parts of the Asia-Pacific upend standard assumptions in the literature on the Global North about when and where women first gained entry to the judiciary. We need to reconsider the assertion that countries in Asia fail to exhibit feminisation at a rate comparable to the global average (e.g. Michelson 2013, 1075), and also to challenge the relevance of this comparison as a meaningful indicator of feminisation of the legal sector more broadly. For example, Indonesia had a female judge in its apex court many years before the United States did. In the 1960s, the first female judge, Sri Widojati Notoprojo, was appointed to the Indonesian Supreme Court. However, it was not until two decades later in 1981 that the US Supreme Court had its first female judge, Sandra Day O'Connor (Lev 1996, 191). These alternative stories challenge the assumption that women in the Asia-Pacific entered the profession at a later point in time than women in the Global North.

Thick Feminisation: What Difference Do Women Judges Make?

The literature has debated whether the profession can be considered feminised simply by the increased number of women or whether the profession is feminised when changed or influenced by women within the profession (Menkel-Meadow 1986, 898). It is essential to consider a thicker definition of feminisation of the judiciary beyond the entrance of women in the courts. The chapters in this volume are concerned with how feminisation is defined and contested, and how it can be measured or studied.

In the 1980s, Menkel-Meadow energised the debate on feminisation by arguing that the profession could not be considered feminised simply by the increase in the number of women in legal education. An increased number of women studying the law did not necessarily equate with feminisation of the study and practice of law or of the legal profession. Instead, a thicker conception of feminisation of the profession calls for inquiries such as whether or how the profession has been changed or influenced by women. This is more difficult to identify and study but provides a wide opportunity for future empirical research. This thicker conception of feminisation of the judiciary and legal profession more broadly in the Asia-Pacific is one the chapters in this volume take up.

Studies of women judges are often concerned with the relationship between women judges and judicial decision-making. Kay and Gorman (2008, 320) identify that the literature on judicial decision-making by women is grounded in certain assumptions of female judging: 'that women lawyers and judges have a stronger feminist consciousness or that they think about legal issues using a different moral voice'. Menkel-Meadow (1985, 59) argues that women judges may pay more attention to mercy than male judges and suggests that this may affect the process of judging.

Empirical research provides some support for the feminist conscious-ness view. Martin (1990) suggests that lawyers draw on their background experiences differently as women and men in approaching their role as a lawyer. For example, Martin (1990) found that women judges in the United States were more likely to have experienced sex discrimination than men and suggested that this might influence the 'decisional output' of a woman judge in a case involving sex discrimination. In a survey of Florida attorneys and judges, Martin et al. (2002) found that women more frequently reported gender disparagement and sexual harassment than men. Some scholars suggest that women judges may be more likely to reject stereotypes of women and legal presumptions in favour of men, for example when hearing cases involving domestic violence or the allocation of property during divorce (Kay and Gorman 2008, 321). Studies conflict as to whether women judges are more likely to make decisions that favour women; however, some studies suggest that women judges are more likely to support the woman's position in cases including discrimination, child support, property settlement and sexual assault (Kay and Gorman 2008, 321). The issue of whether women judges decide differently is underexplored in the literature on the Asia-Pacific.

The entry of women into the judiciary has prompted a related set of debates into whether female judges have a unique approach to decision-making, or whether they change the nature of substantive law or the practice of the law. Why is it important to increase the number of women judges in courts around the world? That is, is female judging distinctive in some way and, if so, how? These questions have not yet been a major focus of inquiry in the Asia-Pacific.

There is a small but growing scholarly interest in how, or to what extent, women in the profession or the judiciary influence the profession itself. In China, Shui Wei and Xin Xin (2013) find that women judges reject stereotypical female characteristics and follow settlement strategies in divorce mediations to show that they do not differ between genders. In Pakistan, Mehdi (2017) concludes that women judges are more inclined to pay attention to local customs and the way local customs can adversely affect women. However, this does not mean that women judges readily side with the female litigant. Indeed, Mehdi (2017, 219) reports that women judges would often 'do their utmost' to prevent the end of a marriage in divorce proceedings brought by a female litigant. In a separate study of Pakistan, Livia Holden (2017) explores the correlation between women judges and feminist judging concerning the protection of women's rights. Holden (2017, 766) concludes that women judges tend to recognise a significant role of Islam as 'infusing' an awareness of women's rights. The literature on women in the legal profession and the judiciary serves as a starting point for analysis, but studies of women lawyers and judges in Asia will need to go beyond the limits of these theories. There is significant scope to consider how women judges approach their role and use their powers of interpretation and decision-making, and whether there is a distinctly female approach to judging in the Asia-Pacific.

As women have entered the judiciary, the literature has turned to focus on the structural and cultural barriers that women face within the profession. The income gap between male and female lawyers, and the prevalence of sexual harassment in the workplace is well documented (Kay and Gorman 2008, 308–312). The literature also shows concern with the different opportunities that women have compared to men in promotion and attrition during career development. For example, studies have demonstrated that women are severely under-represented as partners in law firms and that having children has a positive impact on promotion chances for men but not for women (Kay and Gorman 2008, 308–311). Scholars have also pointed out the reality of occupational segregation (Menkel-Meadow 1989, 218), for example, women in the legal profession tend to work in areas such as family law, government law and public interest work rather than corporate law (Epstein 1981, 380–386).

Scholars have taken interest in the challenges that women face being promoted to higher ranking positions within the judiciary, especially to the office of the chief justice (or equivalent) (Valdini and Shortell 2016). However, there are limited studies of structural and cultural barriers that women in the legal profession in the Asia-Pacific face, except for China. Xiaonan Liu identifies multiple challenges that women lawyers and judges face specific to the Chinese context, which affects promotion opportunities (see also Liu 2013, 2015; Zheng, Ai and Liu 2017). For example, Xionan Liu (2013) discusses how women in Chinese legal education are still not perceived as 'true legal practitioners' and Xionan Liu (2015) explores how women judges in China are still subject to harmful gendered stereotypes. The privatisation of the bar in China raises a particular set of challenges for women lawyers, for example, Michelson (2009, 364–365) finds that it has had a negative impact on women's opportunities to practice law. Women lawyers earned less than their male counterparts and had fewer chances at making partner. This culminated in a significant career longevity gap identified by Michelson, where women lawyers left the profession without accumulating the work experience needed for greater professional rewards. In Anqui Shen's (2017) work on women lawyers and judges in China, she argues that Chinese women have never been expressly excluded from the legal world, nor has the Chinese judiciary ever been considered a male occupation. Therefore, in her view, feminisation is not an accurate depiction of the changing composition of the Chinese judiciary. Further, Shen argues that what women judges do in court differs little from what men do and that their position as men's equal in the judicial system is recognised and promoted. However, Shen finds that women do face barriers in reaching the upper echelons of judgeship. In Korea, Kim argues that family responsibilities and a male-oriented workplace structure will continue to present obstacles for women in the profession (Kim 2015).

Local legal contexts are inevitably intertwined with global developments and the literature on gender and the judiciary reflects a focus on the extent of compliance with international commitments and treaties, such as the Convention on the Elimination of Discrimination against Women (CEDAW), as well as compliance with domestic laws and constitutional commitments to gender equality.

One way in which the struggles of women in the judiciary in the Asia-Pacific have been studied is through the intersection of gender and religion. In two majority-Muslim countries, Indonesia and Pakistan, Rubya Mehdi (2017) and Euis Nurlaelawati and Arskal Salim (2017) explore the way that religion shapes and influences the experiences of woman judges, as well as how the emergence of women judges signifies a shift away from the idea in Islam that women cannot be judges. In Malaysia, Najibah Mohd Zin (2017) demonstrates the conflict between gendered and legal interpretations of whether women should be allowed to judge in Shari'a courts according to Shari'a law.

Although there has been a focus on the relationship between gender and religion in Muslim countries, there has not yet been studies of women in the judiciary in relation to other religions such as Buddhism, Hinduism and Catholicism in the Asia-Pacific. There is one study of Myanmar that demonstrates how male legal professionals created a system of Burmese Buddhist law favourable to men but with exceptions and considerations for second wives and their children in polygamous arrangements (Crouch 2016). There is also the possibility for studies on Islam and women in non-state judicial forums (Redding 2020), as well as the need to consider women in the law among Muslim-minority communities in countries such as India or Sri Lanka. To return to the story with which we began this chapter, the judgment of Justice Malhotra in the Sabarimala case, where devotees who worshipped at the temple belonged to a Hindu sect, demonstrates the need to consider how gender and religion also intersect beyond majority-Muslim countries in the Asia-Pacific.

Women Judges in High Office and Professional Associations

The feminisation of the judiciary has been furthered by the establishment of professional associations that advocate for women within the profession and within the legal system more broadly. This includes the formation and growth of women's bar associations and women's judicial associations. As mentioned, some jurisdictions, such as Indonesia, had female judicial appointments to the highest court well before some jurisdictions of the Global North such as the United States. But overall, there are still many contemporary milestones in terms of trailblazing women who have not only entered the profession but progressed to leadership positions in various tiers of the judicial profession in the Asia-Pacific.

There continues to be progress on the appointment of women to high-level positions of leadership within the judiciary across the region. In 1999, Nazhat Shameem was appointed as the first woman judge to the High Court of Fiji (see Chapter 2). In Pakistan, in 2013, Mrs Ashraf Jehan, was appointed the first female judge in the Federal Shariat Court, although five years later there were still no women judges at the higher level of the judiciary in the Supreme Court (Holden 2018). In Thailand, in October 2018, Ubonrat Luiwikkai became the first woman to be appointed to the position of president of the Thai Court of Appeal (see Chapter 4). In Malaysia, in 2019, a Muslim Malay woman, Tengku Maimun, was appointed as the first female chief justice of the Federal Court (Yi 2019), which is the highest court in the Malaysian legal system. These examples of historic judicial appointments for women, pioneers in female leadership within the judiciary, are symbolically significant.

Yet women judges in positions of high office and influence have come under attack in the region due to political opposition and the rise of populism. One example is the backlash and legal consequences faced by former Chief Justice Maria Lourdes Sereno of the Philippines. Sereno is a vocal critic of President Rodrigo Duterte's war on drugs and questioned the validity of his list of public officials deemed to be drug suspects. She also disagrees with other aspects of Duterte's policies, such as the imposition of martial law in the southern Philippines (Villamor 2018). In April 2018, Duterte publicly named Sereno as an 'enemy' (Curato 2019, 265). Just a month later, Sereno was put on trial based on a quo warranto petition, although many claim this petition was politically motivated (Mogato 2018; Chapter 6). The Supreme Court voted eight against six to remove Sereno from office on allegations that she had failed to fully disclose her wealth (Curato 2019, 265). The quo warranto trial was a means of removing Sereno from office despite the failure to initiate impeachment proceedings, as many suggest would have been the more appropriate response.

While individual women in high-level positions can shape public debate and perceptions on the role of women in law, the collectivisation of women and advocacy efforts are also important. One indication of the emergence of collective action by women in the legal sector is the proliferation of women lawyers and judges' associations in the Asia-Pacific over the past two decades. The formation of professional

Table 1.1 *Women lawyers' associations in Asia*

Association	Established
National Women Lawyers Society, Pakistan	2018
Women in Law Japan	2017
Korean Women Lawyers Association	2017
Women in Law Hong Kong	2015
Supreme Court Women's Lawyers Association, India	2013
Society of Women Lawyers, India	2010
All India Federation of Women Lawyers	2007
Singapore Association of Women Lawyers	2005
Association of Asian Women Lawyers	2001
Association of Women Lawyers, Malaysia	1983
Bangladesh National Women Lawyers Association	1979
Hong Kong Federation of Women Lawyers Limited	1975
Women Lawyers Forum, Bar Association of India	1960
Sri Lanka Women Lawyers' Association	1960
Japan Women's Bar Association	1950
Women Lawyers Association of Thailand	Unknown

associations and societies specifically for women focuses attention on their presence within the profession. It adds collective strength to demands women have within the profession to be treated without discrimination and ensures that there is advocacy within the profession for issues concerning gender and women.

There are at least twenty-four lawyers and judges' associations specifically for women in the Asia-Pacific (see Table 1.1). Of these twenty-four associations, sixteen are women lawyers' associations and the remaining eight are women judges' associations. Many of the women judges' associations were originally established as country-specific chapters of the International Association of Women Judges (IAWJ) and later developed into autonomous associations. The IAWJ was established in the early 1990s to support and foster the role of women in the judiciary and address issues of discrimination against women in the law more broadly. Another regional-level association is the Association of Asian Women Lawyers, established in 2001 with the primary goals of promoting equality, encouraging entrants to the legal profession from all backgrounds and offering support and guidance. The formation of country-specific women's judicial organisations suggests that collective action at the international level can be a significant catalyst and support for collective professional solidarity at the domestic level.

The emergence of different kinds of women's professional organisations suggests a widening conception of professional solidarity. For example, in 1950 the Japan Women's Bar Association was established as a network for women practising at Japan's bar. Almost seventy years later, in 2017, a group known as Women in Law Japan was established as a networking platform for women in the law in Japan inclusive of counsel, judges, prosecutors, paralegals and law students.

Of the sixteen women lawyers' associations in the Asia-Pacific, nine were established between 2000 and 2020. The other six associations were established periodically between 1950 and 1999, a much slower rate of establishment compared to the proliferation post 2000.[6] One reason that not all countries in the region have a separate women's organisation could be that some established bar associations or legal or judicial institutes may have a women's division or representative within the association.

The main aims of these women lawyers' associations can be grouped into three broad themes. First, these associations provide a network for support of women lawyers through networking activities, online platforms and mentoring programs. In recent times, associations such as Women in Law Hong Kong and Women in Law Japan have created innovative online platforms for women lawyers to connect. Second, the associations advocate for gender equality within the legal profession. For example, the National Women Lawyers Society in Pakistan aims to promote the advancement of women in the legal profession through conferences and practitioner training courses. The Sri Lanka Women Lawyers' Association advances similar aims through conferences, trips and meetings. Third, these associations advocate for and contribute to law reform and policy changes on issues to do with gender. For example, the Bangladesh National Women Lawyers Association and the All India Federation of Women Lawyers hold annual conferences and workshops on, as well as engage in, forms of activism such as initiating public interest litigation on issues of gender equality. One such example is the public interest litigation initiated by the Bangladesh National Women Lawyers Association demanding anti–workplace harassment legislation, which we discuss shortly.

---

[6] The date of establishment of one lawyers' association was unknown.

Table 1.2 *Women judges' associations in Asia*

Association	Established
Nepalese Women Judges Forum	2014
Korean Chapter of the IAWJ	2006
Korean Association of Women Judges	2000
China Women Judges Association	1994
Japanese National Association of Women Judges	1992
Bangladesh Women Judges Association	1989
Philippine Women Judges Association	1987
Chinese Taipei Chapter of the IAWJ, Taiwan	Unknown

Compared to women lawyers' associations, there are fewer women judges' associations. All of the women judges' associations in the Asia-Pacific have emerged since the late 1980s (see Table 1.2) and are primarily concentrated in East Asia and South Asia. Some of the countries that have a judges' association have strong ties to the United States, including South Korea, Japan, Taiwan and the Philippines. However, there are also women judges' associations in Nepal and Bangladesh. At the international level, the International Association of Women Judges has a chapter in Taiwan, Taipei and South Korea. The Association is also represented outside the Asia-Pacific with chapters in Canada, South Africa, Haiti and beyond.

The main aims and activities of these women judges' associations can also be grouped thematically. First, the women judges' associations are active in promoting gender equality. For example, the Nepalese Women Judges Forum conducted an awareness training on sexual harassment for high school girls in 2014. The Philippine Women Judges Association similarly conducts a variety of outreach programs. A notable point of departure from the women lawyers' associations is that the judges' associations do not advocate for law reform on issues relating to gender to the same degree, likely because of the requirement of impartiality imposed on judges. Second, women judges' associations provide a network of support and solidarity among women in the judiciary. For example, in June 2020, the Chinese Taipei Chapter of the IAWJ hosted a discussion on their experiences of remote hearings during the COVID-19 pandemic. Third, women judges' associations advocate for gender equality and reform within the judiciary itself. For example, the Bangladesh Women Judges Association holds discussions and round tables seeking to improve and advance the position of women in the judicial system.

Women judges are also active in countries yet to establish a discreet women judges' association. For example, following a two-day workshop hosted by the International Commission of Jurists and UN Women about applying a gendered perspective to cases, women judges in Indonesia took the lead in establishing guidance on gender and judging under the direction of Justice Teresita de Castro (chief justice of the Supreme Court of the Philippines 2008–18). This culminated in the publication of the Bangkok General Guidance for Judges on Applying a Gender Perspective in Southeast Asia (2016). The guidance promotes a gendered approach to judging and offers recommendations to courts on how they can be more gender sensitive

Where generalist bar or judicial associations exist, one challenge lies in mainstreaming women into the generalist associations, including opening positions of leadership to women. For example, in Malaysia, while the Bar Council's 18,000 strong membership is over 50 per cent female, there have only been two female presidents since the Bar Council was established in 1947 (Koshy 2018). In the 2018 Bar Council elections, only six women stood for election to the thirty-eight-member council, and all were from the Kuala Lumpur Bar, representing a highly urbanised context.

These women's lawyers and judges' associations play a range of roles, but some initiatives have been particularly prominent through the use of online platforms in the wake of the #MeToo movement. The #MeToo movement has had a profound impact on the legal profession and judiciary globally as allegations have emerged against leading lawyers and judges. One such example are the allegations against Dyson Heydon, former justice of the High Court of Australia. An internal inquiry at the High Court of Australia resulted in a statement by Chief Justice Susan Kiefel that the accounts of the complainants 'have been believed' (Kiefel 2020). In India, the first allegations of sexual harassment emerged against Junior Foreign Minister MJ Akbar. Lawyer Rutuja Shinde offered pro bono support to the victims of sexual harassment via Twitter and other women lawyers were quick to join the offer. A petition to provide pro bono support to survivors gained the support of over eighty women lawyers (Hemery and Singh 2019).

Similarly, in Bangladesh, the courts became the forum for cases of sexual discrimination and harassment in light of the #MeToo movement. The Bangladesh National Women Lawyers' Association filed a public interest litigation case requesting the High Court to order the government to pass legislation aimed at preventing sexual harassment in the workplace. This case resulted in the court issuing guidelines against sexual harassment in places of work and academic institutions across the country, in the absence of a formal law (Hemery and Singh 2019). Also in the region, in Pakistan, women lawyers have mobilised through an online platform launched by the Digital Rights Foundation. Lawyers can register to provide pro bono legal support for cases concerning the sexual harassment of women (Hemery and Singh 2019). Here the power of technology is harnessed to advance the #MeToo movement and address concerns to end sexual harassment more broadly.

Despite developments in these places, the #MeToo movement has had mixed reactions or little impact in other countries in the Asia-Pacific. Indonesia has seen a backlash against women who report cases of sexual harassment. In 2018, for example, an administrator at a high school in Mataram, Baiq Nuril Maknun, found herself subject to sexual harassment from the principal of the school (Cahaya 2018; see Chapter 5). She decided to record one of his lurid telephone calls about his sex life as evidence of his behaviour. Instead, the principal was successful in a case against Baiq Nuril Maknun, who was charged under the Information Technology and Electronic Transactions Law 2008. While the court case against her was not successful at first instance, in 2018 the Supreme Court agreed with the appeal by the principal and convicted the woman.[7] This caused significant social outcry particularly from women's rights groups in Indonesia, and it was only at that point that the president pardoned the woman. Defamation cases have also been brought against women who speak out about sexual harassment in India and China.

The growth of associations for women in the legal sector is important and deserves further study to better understand how and to what extent these groups influence their profession and work towards broader goals of women's empowerment and equality. Overall, as one indicator of a thick feminisation of the judiciary, progress on women judges in leadership and the impact of women's professional associations is clearly mixed across the region.

---

[7] District Court of Mataram Decision No 265/Pid.Sus/2017/PN Mtr, 26 Juli 2017; Supreme Court Decision No 574/Pid.Sus/2018.

Women in the Judiciary in an Era of Anti-elitism

The chapters in this volume consider whether and to what extent we can speak of the feminisation of the judiciary in the Asia-Pacific. These chapters are united in offering rich, empirical findings that open a path for distinct theoretical and empirical studies of women in the judiciary in the Asia-Pacific. The chapters navigate the twin difficulties of offering contextual description and empirical newness, with the challenge of applying and adapting approaches to understanding the feminisation of the judiciary in the Global South. The authors do not presume that women judges make a difference, but rather seek to open critical debate on the role women judges can and do play. The chapters are alert to the intersectionality of women judges, and that entrance to the judiciary for some women is influenced by their family connections in the profession, their ethnicity, religion or socio-economic status.

In Chapter 2, Anna Dzeidzic provides a historical and comparative analysis of the appointment of women judges in the Pacific with a focus on nine independent Commonwealth states: Fiji, Kiribati, Nauru, Papua New Guinea, Samoa, Solomon Islands, Tonga, Tuvalu and Vanuatu. Dzeidzic presents empirical data on the composition of the superior courts in these states, including judges' gender and professional background. She also examines how the criteria and processes of judicial appointment affect the appointment of women to the judiciary. She offers two main reasons why women are under-represented in the Pacific judiciaries: historical and continuing gender stereotyping which prevents women being regarded as of equal merit to men; and how the processes for judicial appointment, including the distinctive practice of appointing foreign judges, affects the appointment of women. Dziedzic considers why it matters whether women are included in Pacific judiciaries. Adopting a thicker conception of feminisation of the judiciary, she identifies ways that women judges in the Pacific have contributed to gender equality and explores how women judges on the superior courts of the Pacific can be a powerful expression of gender equality. At the same time, she is critical of the claim that women judges can contribute to substantive gender justice from the confines of their role as judges. While drawing parallels to the other Asian contexts discussed throughout the volume, Dzeidzic also identifies key features that distinguish the Pacific Islands context, for example by noting that the distinctive use of foreign judges in Pacific Island judiciaries also affects the appointment of women to the judiciary.

In Chapter 3, Dinesha Samararatne undertakes a jurisprudential analysis of nine cases before the courts in Sri Lanka to ask the 'woman question' of judicial decision-making in Sri Lanka. That is, through the jurisprudence, she examines the question of whether woman judges speak in a different voice. In doing so, Samararatne implicitly rejects a thinner conception of feminisation of the judiciary and instead seeks to challenge assumptions inherent to a thicker conception of feminisation – that women judges speak with a different voice. She embeds Sri Lanka's experience in its context, characterised as one of patriarchy, ethnic overdetermination, executive overreach, politicisation of public institutions and corruption. Samararatne's thoughtful analysis arrives at the conclusion that a feminist consciousness of law must go beyond the goal of increasing the number of women on the bench, as a thinner conception of feminisation would suggest. Instead, she advocates for the development of a feminist consciousness that demands reform to laws that discriminate against women, and the development of a legal culture in which there is recognition and sensitivity to the discrimination and exclusion experienced by women.

In Chapter 4, Sarah Bishop traces the shift in Thailand where women were not able to become judges, to the appointment of Ubonrat Luiwikkai, the first woman in Thailand to be appointed to the position of president of the Thai Court of Appeal. Bishop examines the trends in employment of women in the judiciary in Thailand more broadly and considers the remaining obstacles to women's progression in the judiciary. Among them, she finds that women judges are prevented from entering the judiciary due to family responsibilities, gender stereotypes and scrutiny over how women judges conduct themselves. Her examination of women judges entering the judiciary in Thailand resonates with those of Steiner, Dhakal and Dziedzic (Chapters 2, 7 and 8) who also examine the challenges and obstacles facing women's entry into the judiciary. Together they provide a rich comparative context to consider the success and challenges of women entering the judiciary in the Asia-Pacific and the future for women in the judiciary in the Asia-Pacific at large.

Chapter 5 by Melissa Crouch considers to what extent we can speak of the feminisation of the judiciary in Indonesia. She identifies that the literature on law in Indonesia is largely silent on the existence, role and challenges female judges face. Crouch offers an analysis of the one female judge on the Indonesian Constitutional Court, Ibu Maria Farida Indrati, and argues that she was a 'model minority judge' for both her legal formalism and her professional ethics. Crouch suggests that a model minority judge is one who is perceived to be part of a minority community (whether religious, ethnic, cultural or otherwise) and whose conduct while in judicial office is considered to be exemplary in terms of ethics, integrity, intellect and professionalism. Crouch offers a brief outline of the entrance of women judges to the Supreme Court and lower courts, profiling Justice Albertina Ho as another model minority judge. While these model minority women judges were clearly trailblazers and role models, the paradox is that other women who have entered the judiciary have perpetuated gender inequality. Crouch concludes by suggesting that an agenda for research on the feminisation of the legal profession in Indonesia needs to hold in tension this paradox.

Turning to the Philippines, Chapter 6 by Imelda Deinla asks how women judges perceive their role in protecting judicial independence. In this way, Deinla seeks to test theoretic propositions about a thicker conception of feminisation in a real-world context. Deinla asks whether women judges in the Philippines see and act differently in terms of their appreciation of the role, in comparison to men judges. Are there experiences peculiar to women judges in the issues and challenges of judicial independence? How do women judges in the Philippines handle or manage external political pressures as well as influences from their peers, particularly from higher courts? In asking these questions, Deinla considers the extent to which Philippine women judges advance judicial independence and the way they overcome political and institutional challenges. In undertaking this enquiry, she takes as a case study the value of judicial independence and asks whether there is a feminist method of judging and what that would entail. This grounds some of the conceptual discussion on feminist judging from the surrounding chapters in the real-world context.

Chapter 7 by Kerstin Steiner builds a narrative of the long and rocky road for women judges in the Malaysian judiciary. She complements the existing literature on women judges in Syariah courts by detailing the significant challenges women have overcome to enter the bench in the face of a national fatwa (Islamic legal opinion) that prohibits women from being appointed as judges. Steiner's analysis considers the intersection between gender and religion for women judges in the Asia-Pacific. Steiner's account connects with the key themes of women's access to the judiciary and the barriers that women face in entering the judiciary. In particular, her analysis of the extent to which the fatwa prevents women from being appointed as judges is illustrative of the influence religious leaders may have over legal practice and the challenges women judges face given the confluence of gender, law and religion in the Asia-Pacific.

In Chapter 8, on the situation for women judges in Nepal, Subas Dhakal, together with Justice Gauri Dhakal and Justice Sharada Shrestha, take as their starting point the nexus between women's empowerment and sustainable development to pose the question: what policy and practice insights can be generated from the current state of women in the judiciary in post-conflict and post-disaster Nepal? They first seek to answer this question through the theoretic framework of motility capital, that is, the capacity of actors to be mobile in social settings based on three factors of access, ability and appropriation. Second, their exploratory research approach utilises statistics on higher education enrolment and interviews with aspiring, sitting and retired judges as well as other stakeholders in judicial services. In doing so, they find that while student enrolment in legal education is encouraging, four specific systemic problems exist in advancing the prospect for women in the judiciary in Nepal: governance; the glass wall; the path of broken glass; and the glass ceiling. In other words, corruption, entry barriers, career hurdles and policy misappropriation have an adverse impact on the motility of women judges in Nepal. They conclude with two main policy and practice insights. First, if women's representation in the judiciary is to be increased, the relevance of legal education and the employability of graduates from various law schools needs serious attention. Second, it is vital to implement good governance within the judiciary by setting up independent institutional mechanisms to keep it free from political interference.

In Chapter 9, also focused on South Asia, Simashree Bora takes as her starting point the immobility of women in India's Supreme Court and High Courts and examines the hierarchy, representation and institutional processes involved in the judiciary in India. Bora also looks at the idea of gendered objectivity and its interconnectedness with changes in gender discourse within the system. Importantly, Bora interrogates gender objectivity in Indian Supreme Court jurisprudence. In doing so, she finds that the idea of an objective judgment is predetermined by a gendered interpretation that is biased against women and is deeply rooted in a patriarchal system. Bora concludes that women judges can bring to the bench a perspective that is not dominated by patriarchal attitudes, which is essential for the protection of constitutional rights and to support an approach to legal interpretation that is unbiased by gender norms.

Conclusion

While women's entrance to the judiciary remains a key preliminary step in the feminisation of the judiciary, the chapters in this volume differ in what might constitute the feminisation of the judiciary in their respective jurisdiction. What the chapters share in common is that the feminisation of the judiciary in the Asia-Pacific is connected to wider issues of recognition, equality and non-discrimination for women in society. The chapters are realistic, avoiding essentialist views of women in the judiciary, and do not assume that the mere presence of women in the judiciary will lead to substantive equality. The role of women in the judiciary in the Asia-Pacific, as in much of the Global South, is influenced by religious, traditional and customary values and practices, as well as postcolonial realities of corruption, inequality and violence.

To return to the story with which we began this chapter, the Sabarimala temple decision should have paved the way for women to enter and worship at the temple. Yet the decision was met with protests and resistance. Women who attempted to enter the temple after the Supreme Court decision were physically blocked and assaulted. In January 2019, five months after the decision was handed down, two women managed to enter the temple. Yet after that the temple was closed and a cleansing ritual conducted. Debate remains over the decision and women still cannot easily enter the temple. In light of Justice Malhotra's dissent, the enduring debate and tension further agitates the questions raised in this chapter about the influence and role of women judges in the Asia-Pacific.

The Asia-Pacific offers a compelling place from which to interrogate the role and status of women judges in society more broadly. To take these contexts seriously often requires us to start with a different set of questions and assumptions than is present in the existing literature on the Global North, whether it is the small island context of the Pacific, the post-conflict context of Nepal or the post-socialist legal profession of Myanmar. Our questions must acknowledge and embrace the diversity and complexity of the Asia-Pacific region and the challenges that women face in the judiciary in postcolonial contexts.

Many of the chapters in this volume illustrate the bravery and tenacity of women judges in the region. The chapters differ in whether the presence of women judges is an expression of gender equality, with Dziedzic arguing that this is the case in the Pacific, while Bishop problematises this idea and suggests the presence of women may be more tokenistic in Thailand.

The chapters also draw attention to the need to account for the differences between liberal democracies and illiberal authoritarian regimes; the differences in the career pathways of judges in civil and common law systems; and the differences in social and historical trajectories of the state, which have not necessarily been made explicit in studies of women in the judiciary. This volume serves as a starting point for future scholars to examine. The rich comparative analysis and original empirical research is an invitation for readers to consider the role of women in the judiciary and the challenge of gender equality in the Global South more broadly.

References

Ballakrishnen, Swethaa S (2021) *Accidental Feminism: Gender Parity and Selective Mobility among India's Professional Elite*. Princeton, NJ: Princeton University Press.

(2017) 'Women in India's Global Law Firms, Comparative Gender Frames and the Advantage of New Organizations' in David B. Wilkins, Vikramaditya S. Khanna, and David M. Trubek (eds.), *The Indian Legal Profession in the Age of Globalization: The Rise of the Corporate Legal Sector and Its Impact on Lawyers and Society*. Cambridge: Cambridge University Press.

Cahaya, Gemma Holliani (2018) 'Defamation Convict Allegedly Harassed Multiple Times by Superior', 15 November, *The Jakarta Post*, www.thejakartapost.com/news/2018/11/15/defamation-convict-allegedly-harassed-multiple-times-by-superior.html.

Crouch, Melissa (2020) 'Myanmar: Law as a Lucrative and Dangerous Legal Profession' in Richard Abel et al. (eds.), *Lawyers in Society*, 2nd ed., Oxford: Hart Publishing, pp. 775–787.

(2019a) *The Constitution of Myanmar: A Contextual Analysis*. Oxford: Hart Publishing.

(2019b) 'The Judicial Reform Landscape in Indonesia' in Melissa Crouch (ed.), *The Politics of Court Reform: Judicial Change and Legal Culture in Indonesia*. Cambridge: Cambridge University Press, pp. 1–28.

(2018) 'Democrats, Dictators and Constitutional Dialogue: Myanmar's Constitutional Tribunal' 16(2) *International Journal of Constitutional Law* 421.

(2016) 'Polygyny and the Power of Revenge: The Past and Future of Burmese Buddhist Law in Myanmar' 3(1) *Asian Journal of Law & Society* 85.

Curato, Nicole, (2019) 'Toxic Democracy? The Philippines in 2018' *Southeast Asian Affairs* 261.

Epstein, Cynthia Fuchs (1981) *Women in Law*. New York: Basic Books.

Hemery, Sophie and Gayeti Singh (2019) 'Feminist Lawyers of South Asia Tally to Aid of #MeToo Survivors', 4 May, *The Guardian*, www.theguardian.com/world/2019/may/04/feminist-lawyers-south-asia-rally-to-support-of-metoo-survivors.

Holden, Livia (2018) 'Women Judges in Pakistan' 26(1) *International Journal of the Legal Profession* 9.

(2017) 'Women Judges and Women's Rights in Pakistan' 7(4) *Onati Socio-Legal Series* 752.

Jain, Mehal (2019) 'Sabarimala: Purification Ritual Goes to the Heart of the Constitution, It Shows Untouchability: Jaising', 6 February, *Live Law*, www .livelaw.in/top-stories/sabarimala-purification-untouchabilty-jaising–142693.

Kay, Fiona and Elizabeth Gorman (2008) 'Women in the Legal Profession' 4 *Annual Review of Law and Social Science* 299.

Kiefel, Susan A C (2020) 'Statement of the Hon Susan Kiefel AC, Chief Justice of the High Court of Australia', 22 June, https://cdn.hcourt.gov.au/assets/news/ Statement%20by%20Chief%20Justice%20Susan%20Kiefel%20AC.pdf

Kim, Haesook (2015) 'Changes in Gender Composition and the Future of Gender Balance in the Legal Profession in Korea' in Setsuo Miyazawa et al. (eds.), *East Asia's Renewed Respect for the Rule of Law in the 21st Century: The Future of the Legal and Judicial Landscape in East Asia*. Leiden: Brill.

(2003) 'Lee Tai-Young (1914–1998): The Pioneer Woman Lawyer of South Korea' in Ulrike Schultz and Gisela Shaw (eds.), *Women in the World's Legal Professions*. Oxford: Hart Publishing, p. 451.

Koshy, Shaila (2018) 'Waiting for a Wetoo Moment', 25 November, *The Star*, www .thestar.com.my/news/nation/2018/11/25/waiting-for-a-wetoo-moment-the-bar-council-elections-are-on-but-are-women-lawyers-present-and-ready.

Lev, Daniel S (1996) 'On the Other Hand' in Laurie Sears (ed.), *Fantasizing the Feminine in Indonesia*. Durham, NC: Duke University Press.

(1972) *Islamic Courts in Indonesia*. Berkeley: University of California Press.

(1965) 'The Politics of Judicial Development in Indonesia', *Comparative Studies in Society and History* (January).

Levin, Mark A (2020) 'Gender and Law Scholarship in the Law in Japan Field' 21 *Asian-Pacific Law and Policy Journal* 2.

Liu, Xiaonan (2015) 'Gender, Law and Legal Professions in China' in Setsuo Miyazawa et al. (eds.), *East Asia's Renewed Respect for the Rule of Law in the 21st Century: The Future of the Legal and Judicial Landscape in East Asia*. Leiden: Brill.

(2013) 'Chinese Women in Legal Education' 20(2) *Indiana Journal of Global Legal Studies* 1311.

Markovits, Inga (1995) *Imperfect Justice: An East-West German Diary*. Oxford: Clarendon Press.

Mehdi, Rubya (2017) 'Lady Judges of Pakistan: Embodying the Changing Living Tradition of Islam' in Nadia Sonneveld and Monika Lindbekk (eds.), *Women Judges in the Muslim World: A Comparative Study of Discourse and Practice*. Leiden: Brill, p. 204.

Martin, E (1990) 'Men and Women on the Bench: Vive la Difference?' 73(4) *Judicature* 204.

Martin, P, J Reynolds and S Keith (2002) 'Gender Bias and Feminist Consciousness among Judges and Attorneys: A Standpoint Theory Analysis' 27(3) *Signs* 665.

Menkel-Meadow, Carrie (1989) 'Exploring a Research Agenda of the Feminisation of the Legal Profession: Theories of Gender and Social Change' 14(2) *Law & Social Inquiry* 289.

(1986) 'The Comparative Sociology of Women Lawyers: The "Feminisation" of the Legal Profession' 24(4) *Osgoode Hall Law Journal* 897.

(1985) 'Portia in a Different Voice: Speculations on a Women's Lawyering Process 1 *Berkley Women's Law Journal* 39.

Michelson, Ethan (2009) 'Gender Inequality in the Chinese Legal Profession' in Lisa Keister (ed.), *Work and Organizations in China after Thirty Years of Transition*. Emerald Group Insight.

Mogato, Manuel (2018) 'Philippine Supreme Court Removes Duterte "Enemy" Judge', 11 May, *Reuters*, https://in.reuters.com/article/philippines-judiciary/philippine-supreme-court-removes-duterte-enemy-judge-idINKBN1IC0EG.

Mossman, Mary Jane et al. (2006) 'The Empire and British India: The First Indian Women "In Law"' in Claus Dieterhlermann and Isabela Atanasiu (eds.), *The First Women Lawyers: A Comparative Study of Gender, Law and the Legal Professions*. Oxford: Bloomsbury Publishing.

Najibah Mohd Zin (2017) 'Female Judges in Malaysian *Shari`a* Courts: A Problem of Gender or Legal Interpretation?' in Nadia Sonneveld and Monika Lindbekk (eds.), *Women Judges in the Muslim World: A Comparative Study of Discourse and Practice*. Leiden: Brill, p. 53.

Norgren, Julian (2018) *Stories of Trailblazing Women Lawyers: Lives in the Law* New York: New York University Press.

Nurlaelawati, Euis and Arskal Salim (2017) 'Female Judges at Indonesian Religious Courtrooms: Opportunities and Challenges to Gender Equality' in Nadia Sonneveld and Monika Lindbekk (eds.), *Women Judges in the Muslim World: Comparative Study of Discourse and Practice*. Leiden: Brill.

PTI (2018) 'Sabarimala Temple Verdict: A Chronology of Events', 28 September, *The Indian Express*, https://indianexpress.com/article/india/sabarimala-temple-verdict-a-chronology-of-events-5378198.

Redding, Jeff A (2020) *The Rule and Role of Islamic Law: Constituting Secular Law and Governance in Contemporary India*. Seattle: University of Washington Press.

Samararatne, Dinesha (2020) 'Gendering the Legal Complex: Women in Sri Lanka's Legal Profession' 47(4) *International Journal of the Legal Profession* 666–693.

Schultz, Ulrike (2013) 'Introduction: Women in the World's Legal Professions' in Ulrike Schultz and Gisela Shaw (eds.), *Gender and Judging*. Oxford: Hart Publishing.

Shen, Anqi (2017) *Women Judges in Contemporary China: Gender, Judging and Living*. London: Palgrave Macmillan.

Siampukdee, Usamard 'Status of Women Profession: Gender Equality of Judicial Occupation in Thailand'. Institute of The Humanities, Human and Social Sciences. Japan.

Silbey, Susan (1981) 'Making Sense of the Lower Courts' 6(1) *Justice Systems Journal* 13.

Sonneveld, Nadia and Monika Lindbekk (2017) *Women Judges in the Muslim World: A Comparative Study of Discourse and Practice*. Leiden: Brill.

Stewart, Ann (2013) 'Gender and Judicial Education in India' in Ulrike Schultz and Gisela Shaw (eds.), *Gender and Judging*. Oxford: Hart Publishing, p. 523.

Tay Sheng-Wang (2010) 'The Development of Legal Education in Taiwan' in Stacey Steele and Kathryn Taylor (eds.), *Legal Education in Asia: Globalisation, Change and Contexts*. London: Routledge.

Valdini, Melody E and Christopher Shortell (2016) 'Women's Representation in the Highest Court: A Comparative Analysis of the Appointment of Female Justices' 69(4) *Political Research Quarterly* 865.

Villamor, Felipe (2018) 'Philippines' Top Judge Took On Duterte: Now, She's Out', 11 May, *New York Times*, www.nytimes.com/2018/05/11/world/asia/philip pines-chief-justice-rodrigo-duterte.html.

Wei, Shuai and Xin Xin (2013) 'Does Gender Play a Role in Divorce Mediation? Working Pattern of Women Judges in China' 18 *Asian Journal of Women's Studies* 149.

Yi, Beh Lih (2019) 'Malaysia's First Female Top Judge Is "Big Step" for Women's Justice', 3 May, *Thomson Reuters Foundation News*, http://news.trust.org/item/20190503085417-640d.

Zheng, Chunyan, Jiahui Ai and Sida Liu (2017) 'The Elastic Ceiling: Gender and Professional Career in Chinese Courts' 51(1) *Law & Society Review* 1.

Court Decisions

Indonesia (in Bahasa Indonesia)
District Court of Mataram No. 265/Pid.Sus/2017/PN Mtr, 26 July 2017
Supreme Court (Mahkamah Agung) Decision No. 574/Pid.Sus/2018.

India

Indian Young Lawyers Association *v.* The State of Kerala et al. (Writ Petition (Civil) No. 376 of 2006) ('*Sabarimala*').

2

'To Join the Bench and Be Decision-Makers'

Women Judges in Pacific Island Judiciaries

ANNA DZIEDZIC *

Looking down, at the sea of lawyers
Black and white, with black gowns all over
Hundreds of them, but mostly males, that superior gender
I stretched my neck, and strained my eyes
Searching for a female, far and nigh
They were less, much, much lesser
Drowned in the sea, of that superior gender

They all bowed, meekly, before me
Addressing me, sweetly, as 'Your Honour'
Culturally, this would have been impossible
For intelligent males, to show respect and be so humble

That sense of fulfilment, of hope and faith replenished
That new surge of courage, one I'd always cherish
To finally realise, that a mighty barrier had shattered
Like glass, into a thousand pieces it had scattered
Paving the way, for aspiring female lawyers
To join the Bench and be Decision-Makers

Wendy Jerome, 'Women Can Always Match the Stride'[1]

There have been concerted efforts in recent times to increase the number of women in positions of leadership across the Pacific region. These efforts have focused mainly on increasing the number of women elected to parliaments and, to a lesser extent, women in positions of leadership in

---

* With many thanks to all participants of the Women in Law in Asia panel at the Women in Asia Conference held at the University of New South Wales, 22–23 June 2019, and particular thanks to Melissa Crouch and Balawyn Jones for their comments on earlier drafts of this chapter.
[1] Extract from a poem by Papua New Guinean lawyer Wendy Jerome, published in *My Walk to Equality: Essays, Stories and Poetry by Papua New Guinean Women*. The poem is used in this chapter with the permission of the editor of the anthology, Rashmii Amoah Bell.

the public sector and civil society. Judicial office is also a forum for leadership, albeit of a different kind. Women judges recognise this: Nazhat Shameem, the first woman to be appointed a judge in Fiji, said that 'as a High Court judge I am in a position of leadership', a 'position to forge social and legal changes' (Soroptimists Club 2008). Judges are leaders because they communicate and enforce the values of the law to the wider community and shape and develop the law to meet social needs.

Leadership is also an expression of gender equality. This aspect of judicial service is vividly portrayed in Wendy Jerome's poem, 'Women Can Always Match the Stride', extracted in part at the beginning of this chapter, and from which the title to this chapter is drawn (Jerome 2017). Dedicated to the memory of Justice Catherine Davani, the first Papua New Guinean woman judge, the poem describes the personal reflections of a woman judge in a male-dominated profession and patriarchal society. It imagines a woman sitting on the bench, who has made sacrifices, overcome her fears, 'shattered like glass' the 'mighty barriers' that keep women from leadership and demonstrated that women *can* 'join the bench and be decision makers'. The 'mighty barriers' are the social gender roles that cast men as the 'superior gender' in all things, and public decision-making and leadership in particular. The poem shows how the presence of women in the judiciary can make a significant contribution to gender equality by challenging social stereotypes about the role of women in Pacific societies.

This chapter examines the position of women judges on superior courts in nine Pacific island states: Fiji, Kiribati, Papua New Guinea (PNG), Nauru, Samoa, Solomon Islands, Tonga, Tuvalu and Vanuatu. It presents the findings of an empirical investigation into the number and proportion of women judges on courts in the region, and suggests some reasons why women are under-represented on Pacific judiciaries. Moving beyond the numbers, this chapter also considers the contributions that women judges make to gender equality, exploring the significance of the presence of women in Pacific judiciaries and their substantive contribution to the law.

In contrast to the attention paid to women in other positions of leadership, there has been no comprehensive study of the number and proportion of women judges in the Pacific. This chapter seeks to redress this, utilising a new data set on the composition of the superior courts in nine Pacific states. The data, set out in Part II, shows that women judges are under-represented on Pacific island courts. To date, there have been no women judges in Kiribati and Tonga, only one each in Nauru and

Tuvalu, two in Vanuatu and three in Solomon Islands. In Fiji, Papua New Guinea and Samoa women judges have been appointed in greater number, but only in Samoa is there a trend towards gender parity.

Part III considers some of the reasons why there are so few women judges in the Pacific region. It argues that a core reason for the under-representation of women on Pacific courts is historical and continuing gender stereotyping, which prevents women being regarded as of equal ability – or 'merit' – to men. In addition, this part examines how the criteria and processes for judicial appointment, including the practice of appointing foreign judges to Pacific courts, affects the appointment of women to the judiciary. It highlights the factors that enable the appointment of women, as well as barriers to their appointment in greater number.

Part IV considers why it matters whether women are included on Pacific judiciaries. Drawing on reflections by women who have served as judges in the region, as well as scholarship on law and gender in the Pacific and other common law jurisdictions, this part identifies ways in which women judges in the Pacific contribute to gender equality. It explores how women judges are celebrated as role models for other women, but also how the visible embodiment of women in leadership positions can work to counter harmful stereotypes that cast women as incapable or unauthorised to exercise public power. It also critically examines the claim that women judges can contribute to substantive gender justice, albeit from within the confines of their role as judges, taking laws and practices relating to discrimination and violence against women as an example. This part also highlights the ways in which distinctive practices in the Pacific, such as the use of foreign judges, shed light on the intersectionality of gender with other identity attributes and its effect on perceptions of judges and their role.

This chapter begins, however, with a brief description of the legal systems of the nine Pacific states included in this study and the position of women within these states.

Part I: Women in Pacific Legal Systems

Pacific Courts and Legal Systems

The Pacific presents a distinctive regional context to explore the position of women in national judiciaries. As in many countries around the world, male judges outnumber female judges. However, the context in which Pacific judiciaries operate, informed by the history of colonisation and

characteristics of smallness and legal pluralism, shape the legal systems
and the experiences of women judges in distinctive ways.

Each of the nine Pacific states inherited common law legal systems
from British, Australian and New Zealand colonial administrations.[2]
Colonisers also introduced court systems modelled on those in their
own jurisdictions. Upon independence, the Pacific states maintained
these judicial structures, adapting them to the requirements of independent statehood, for example by replacing regional courts of appeal and the
Judicial Committee of the Privy Council with their own national courts.[3]

The nine states studied here are classified as small island developing
states. They have small populations, in some cases dispersed across
islands in large ocean territories. Papua New Guinea is by far the most
populous state in the region with just over eight and a half million
people, while the other states have far smaller populations.[4] Small populations, geographic isolation and limited resources affect the structure
and capacity of law and government institutions, including judiciaries
(Briguglio 1995, 1615–1618; Veenendaal 2015, 22–23). In several states,
there is insufficient demand to justify a full-time superior court or court
of appeal. As a result, all courts of appeal in the region are part time and
in the smallest states of Nauru and Tuvalu the superior courts also sit
part time. Small populations and relatively young national legal professions also mean that there are insufficient numbers of qualified local
candidates available and willing to fill the required judicial positions. As a
result, Pacific judiciaries rely on lawyers and judges from overseas. From
2000 to 2018, three-quarters of the judges on the superior courts in the
nine Pacific states were foreign judges, recruited from other common law
jurisdictions such as Australia, New Zealand, the United Kingdom, the
Gambia, Nigeria and Sri Lanka (Dziedzic 2021, chapter 2).

---

[2] Tonga was never formally colonised. However, as a protectorate from 1900 to 1970, the
British government assumed responsibility for defence, foreign affairs and some judicial
proceedings. Tonga's Constitution, made in 1875, was influenced by the constitutional
structures of Hawaii, the United Kingdom and the United States.

[3] Not all states were in a position to establish national judiciaries at the date of independence. Until the mid-1980s, Kiribati, Solomon Islands and Tuvalu extended the arrangements made during colonial times, when courts based in Fiji served the Western Pacific
region. Nauru continued to use the High Court of Australia as its final court of appeal
until 2018. Kiribati and Tuvalu retain appeals to the Judicial Committee of the Privy
Council, but no appeals have ever been taken.

[4] The populations of each state in 2018 were as follows: Tuvalu 10,200; Nauru 11,000; Tonga
100,300; Kiribati 120,100; Samoa 196,700; Vanuatu 304,500; Solomon Islands 682,500; Fiji
888,400, Papua New Guinea 8,558,800 (Pacific Community 2018).

Prior to colonisation, the peoples of the Pacific were governed according to custom. The region contains a great diversity of custom, reflected in different legal systems, laws and languages, across and within what are now state borders. In all states, custom continues to operate, as a recognised part of the law or as an alternative to the formal legal system for the resolution of disputes (New Zealand Law Commission 2006, 35–36; Corrin 2014; Forsyth 2009; Va'ai 1997).

Women in the Pacific

Women were marginalised in the western legal system and customary legal systems as they developed and operated during colonial times and independence. In precolonial times, gender relations varied across Pacific societies. Some societies valued complementarity, with women and men contributing differently, but equally, to the community (Slatter 2010, 94). Some Melanesian and Micronesian societies were and continue to be matrilineal, in which women exercise substantial powers over land and their communities (Sirivi and Havini 2004; Wale 2004, 11). In Polynesian societies, rank and genealogical connections could be more important than gender and Polynesian history features women who held considerable political power (O'Brien 2014, 289–292).

Social relations, including gender, were affected by the 'civilising' mission of Christianity and the disruptions of European exploration, exploitation and colonisation. While the dynamics are different across societies within the region, the broad effect of this history was to confine women largely to subordinate and domestic social roles, while men exercised public power through 'chiefly' systems institutionalised by colonial administrations and the introduced systems of government (Huffer 2006, 33; Monson 2017; Slatter 2010, 95–98). Women's subsistence work and their role in the extended family once meant women had significant status in their communities, however this work was devalued as cash generation became more important (Wale 2004, 12). The shift from extended families to the nuclear family marginalised the work of women as men came to be seen as the 'head' of the family (Wale 2004, 13).

As a region, the Pacific has one of the highest rates of violence against women compared to global averages (Pacific Women Shaping Pacific Development 2017b, 14). This is influenced by social norms and unequal gender relations, in which men's right to control and exert power over women, particularly within the family, is 'justified and culturally accepted' (Pacific Women Shaping Pacific Development 2017a, 14; Fiji Women's Crisis Centre 2013, chapter 6). Across the region, women are under-represented in national parliaments: in 2017, there were only thirty women parliamentarians, a regional average of just over 6 per cent (Baker 2018, 542). In this too, disparities in the treatment of women and men are informed and reinforced by harmful stereotypes and social beliefs about women and men, which are sometimes problematically justified by reference to custom, Christianity and the law (Corrin Care 2006; Slatter 2010, 105). While wide-ranging efforts across the fields of education, health, law reform and governance are being made regionally, within countries and within communities, to address discrimination and violence against women, social beliefs are intransigent and progress slow.

Part II: Gender and the Composition of Pacific Judiciaries

There have been two regional studies of the number of women in Pacific judiciaries. In 2012, the South Pacific Lawyers Association (SPLA) conducted a survey of its constituent member states[5] to gather demographic data on women in the legal profession. It concluded that women were under-represented in the judiciaries of the region but had insufficient data to determine the exact figures. In 2011, the Pacific Judicial Development Programme (PJDP) began to collate data from court annual reports on the gender distribution of judges and magistrates in fourteen Pacific states.[6] The PJDP Reports provided an indication of the proportion of women judges in each jurisdiction, but did not cover all superior courts. After producing three reports, the PJDP came to an end in 2015. Because accurate data on the total numbers of judges serving on Pacific courts is not readily available, in neither study was it possible to compare the proportion of women judges across the jurisdictions or changes over time.

This study presents more comprehensive data on the number and proportion of women judges in Pacific island states. To facilitate comparison across jurisdictions, this study draws on 'most similar cases', that is, those Pacific states that share a common law legal system and are

---

[5] Cook Islands, Fiji, Kiribati, Nauru, Niue, Norfolk Island, Papua New Guinea, Samoa, Solomon Islands, Tonga, Tuvalu and Vanuatu.

[6] Cook Islands, Federated States of Micronesia, Kiribati, Marshall Islands, Nauru, Niue, Palau, Papua New Guinea, Samoa, Solomon Islands, Tokelau, Tonga, Tuvalu and Vanuatu.

independent states.[7] The study therefore covers the nine independent Commonwealth member states in the region: Fiji, Kiribati, Nauru, Papua New Guinea, Samoa, Solomon Islands, Tonga, Tuvalu and Vanuatu.

This study focuses only on the composition of the superior courts of each state. A superior court is a court of unlimited jurisdiction in civil and criminal matters. Superior courts may be distinguished from customary courts which exercise jurisdiction based on customary law,[8] and lower courts (District or Magistrates Courts) with jurisdictions limited to civil cases involving a specified maximum monetary amount and less serious criminal offences. In Kiribati, Samoa, Solomon Islands, Tonga, Tuvalu and Vanuatu, the superior courts are the Supreme or High Court and the Court of Appeal. In Papua New Guinea, they are the National Court and the Supreme Court. Fiji's court system includes three superior courts: the High Court, the Court of Appeal and the Supreme Court, which is the court of final appeal. In Nauru until 2018 there was just the one superior court, the Supreme Court. Between 1976 and 2017, the High Court of Australia served as Nauru's court of final appeal before Nauru established its own court of appeal in 2018. The decision to focus on the superior courts reflects the accessibility of the data (discussed further shortly), the distinctive leadership position exercised by judges on the highest domestic courts and the impact that women in that position can have on the application and development of the law.

One reason for the limited data on the number and proportion of women judges is the difficulty in accessing and collecting information on the composition of courts in the Pacific region. There are no publicly available, comprehensive lists of the judges of each Pacific court for each year over the past decades. Nor do courts in the region consistently produce annual reports or law reports which list judges. In order to collect data on the composition of the relevant courts, I conducted an audit of judgments published by the Pacific Legal Information Institute (PacLII), an open-access online database of legal materials from Pacific jurisdictions. Not every decision of every court is provided to PacLII for publication and as a result the database is not exhaustive. It is however

---

[7] Thereby excluding Cook Islands and Niue (in free association with New Zealand); the Federated States of Micronesia, Marshall Islands and Palau (in free association with the United States); and territories of France, the United States and United Kingdom.

[8] In several states there are specialised courts to deal with customary matters such as land and titles. Local authorities may also have jurisdiction to adjudicate disputes according to custom.

sufficiently comprehensive to indicate the names of the judges who produced written judgments in each year. This information was verified, where possible, by reference to official notices of judicial appointment, published biographies and media reports. With information on the name and background of each judge, it was possible to then identify the women judges sitting on each court.

Since the establishment of national courts in each state to the end of 2019, a total of twenty-nine women have served as judges on the superior courts across the nine Pacific states, and they are listed in Table 2.1.

Kiribati and Tonga do not appear in Table 2.1 because no women have ever been appointed as judges of a superior court in those states.

In order to gain an insight into the proportion of women judges in each state and trends and progress in the appointment of women to Pacific judiciaries, I analysed the membership of each of the relevant courts for every calendar year from 2000 to 2019. During this period, twenty-eight women judges served with 274 male judges, which means women comprise only 9 per cent of all judges across the region. Taking the most recent year, 2019, alone, this figure remained at 9 per cent. This regional figure is lower than the global average of women on high courts, which in 2014 stood at 22 per cent (Escobar-Lemmon et al. 2019, 201). It is also lower than the proportion of women judges on superior courts in other Commonwealth jurisdictions in the region. In Australia, figures from 2013 indicate that women make up between 25 and 45 per cent of the members of the superior courts in the Commonwealth, states and territories (Kiefel and Saunders 2015, 53). In 2015, women comprised 30 per cent of the New Zealand judiciary (Adlam 2015). It is, however, slightly better than the regional average proportion of women in national parliaments in the Pacific region, which stood at 6.1 per cent in 2017 (Baker 2018).

The limited number of women judges means that tracking changes over time is meaningful only in Fiji, Papua New Guinea and Samoa. Figures 2.1–2.3 show the percentage of women judges in each state from 2000 to 2018. In all three states, judges from the lower courts are ex officio members of the higher courts where they sit with judges who are appointed solely as appellate judges.[9] In the case of Fiji and Samoa, the membership of the trial and appellate courts is sufficiently distinct and to reflect this Figures 2.1 and 2.3 separate out the membership of the

---

[9] *Constitution of Fiji 2013* s 98(2), 99(2); *Constitution of Fiji 1997* ss 127, 128; *Constitution of Papua New Guinea 1975* s 161(1); *Constitution of Samoa 1960* s 75(2)(a).

Table 2.1 *Women judges who have served on Pacific courts (to December 2019)*

State	Judge	Court(s)	Years of Service	Nationality
FIJI	Nazhat Shameem	High Court, Court of Appeal	1999–2009	Fiji
	Sian Elias	Supreme Court	2002–2003	New Zealand
	Mere Pulea	High Court	2004–2007	Fiji
	Gwen Philips	High Court	2006–2009	Fiji
	Jocelynne Scutt	High Court, Court of Appeal	2007–2009	Australia
	Anjala Wati	High Court, Court of Appeal, Supreme Court	2009–current	Fiji
	Dias Wickramasinghe	High Court	2010–2012	Sri Lanka
	Chandra Ekanayake	Supreme Court	2012–current	Sri Lanka
	Farzana Jameel	Court of Appeal	2017–2019	Sri Lanka
NAURU	Jane E Crulci (formerly Hamilton-White)	Supreme Court	2014–2017	Australia
PNG	Teresa Doherty	National and Supreme Court	1988–1997	United Kingdom
	Catherine Davani	National and Supreme Court	2001–2016	PNG
	Berna Collier	National and Supreme Court	2011–current	Australia
	Jacinta Murray	National and Supreme Court	2011–current	PNG
	Leka Nama Nablu	National and Supreme Court	2014–2019	PNG
	Hitelai Polume-Kiele	National and Supreme Court	2015–current	PNG
	Royale Thomson	National and Supreme Court	2018–current	Australia
	Teresa Berrigan	National and Supreme Court	2018–current	Australia
SAMOA	Anne E Gaskell	Supreme Court	2004	New Zealand
	Ida Malosi	Supreme Court	2013–2014	New Zealand
	Elizabeth Aitken	Supreme Court, Court of Appeal	2015	New Zealand
	Mata Tuatagaloa	Supreme Court, Court of Appeal	2015–current	Samoa

Table 2.1 *(cont.)*

State	Judge	Court(s)	Years of Service	Nationality
	Leilani Tuala Warren	Supreme Court, Court of Appeal	2016–current	Samoa
SOLOMON	Nkemdilim Amelia Izuako	High Court	2008–2009	Nigeria
ISLANDS	Margaret Wilson	Court of Appeal	2014–current	Australia
	Maelyn Bird	High Court	2019–current	Solomon Islands
TUVALU	Judith Potter	Court of Appeal	2014	New Zealand
VANUATU	Mary Sey	Supreme Court, Court of Appeal	2012–2017	Gambia
	Viran Molisa Trief	Supreme Court	2019–current	Vanuatu

different courts. For example, a judge appointed to the High Court of Fiji who sometimes sits on the Fiji Court of Appeal, is recorded in the total membership of both courts in a given year. In Papua New Guinea, judges are appointed as Judges of the National and Supreme Courts and in many cases serve concurrently on both courts. As a result, the composition of the two levels overlaps to a large degree each year and for this reason, the membership of the two courts has been combined for the purposes of this study.

For much of the case study period, women judges made up less than 20 per cent of the total number of judges on the relevant courts of Fiji, Papua New Guinea and Samoa. The precise percentages change over time as new judges are appointed and other judges come to the end of their appointments. Notably, however, there are periods in Fiji and Samoa where the proportion of women judges has exceeded this figure, and been as high as 27 per cent in Fiji in 2006 and 50 per cent in Samoa in 2016.

In Papua New Guinea and Samoa, there is an upward trend in the number of women appointed as judges, beginning in 2010 in Papua New Guinea and 2013 in Samoa. The trend is most marked in Samoa, which in part reflects the fact that its judiciary is much smaller than Papua New Guinea's. Samoa's Supreme Court had gender parity in 2016, when it comprised three women and three men judges. In contrast, the highest number of women on Papua New Guinea's courts was in 2018, when the

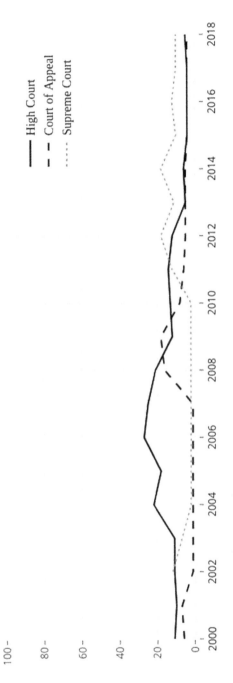

Figure 2.1 Percentage of women judges in Fiji

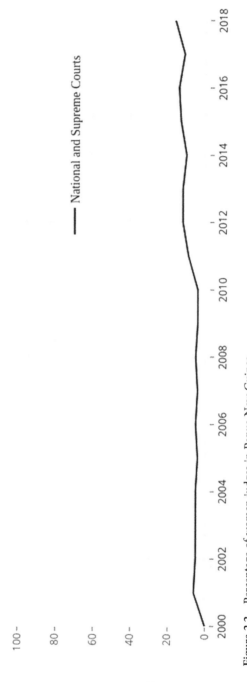

Figure 2.2 Percentage of women judges in Papua New Guinea

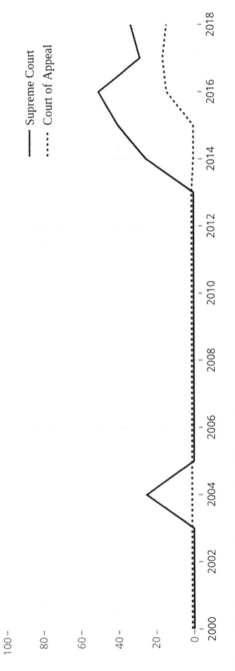

Figure 2.3 Percentage of women judges in Samoa

judiciary included six women judges, representing 16 per cent of the thirty-seven-member court.

In contrast, the proportion of women judges on Fiji's superior courts reached its peak in 2006, when three of the eleven judges of the High Court were Fijian women. In 2018, the proportion of women judges on all three Fijian superior courts was roughly the same as in 2000. One reason for the decline might relate to political events. The years 2007 to 2009 marked a period of upheaval for Fiji's judiciary, following a military coup in December 2006. In April 2009, the Court of Appeal ruled that the actions of the interim government established after the coup were unconstitutional. In response, the president abrogated the Constitution and revoked all judicial appointments. After this, only some judges were reappointed and the three Fijian women on the High Court in 2006 did not sit after 2009. Fiji's judiciary now includes a large number of foreign judges, who (as discussed in the next section) are overwhelmingly male.

Overall, the data shows that women are under-represented – and at times not represented at all – on the superior courts of the Pacific. While there has been some progress, with a significant number of 'first' women judges, it is still more likely than not that a judge of a superior court will be male. Only in Papua New Guinea and Samoa does there appear to be a sustained trend of increasing the number and proportion of women.

Part III: Why So Few Women Judges?

The lack of gender diversity and slow pace of change in Pacific courts can be attributed to a range of factors. This part examines three: the impact of gender stereotypes; the inclusion of women in the labour pools from which Pacific judges are recruited; and the procedures by which judges are selected.

Stereotypes about Women as a Barrier to Judicial Appointment

An inescapable explanation for the under-representation of women in Pacific judiciaries is the pervasive stereotypes about women's abilities and their role in society. Gender stereotypes are generalised social preconceptions about the attributes and characteristics that are, or ought to be, possessed by women and men (Cook and Cusack 2010). Gender stereotypes may be deeply entrenched in social norms that restrict women's choices and opportunities to enter public life, including the judiciary.

Nazhat Shameem, Fiji's first woman judge, has written about how the law, drawing on social cues, stereotypes women – victims, offenders and legal professionals – by assigning them to one of two categories: a 'protective' stereotype, which casts women as weak and emotional; and an 'evil' stereotype, which casts women as manipulative and devious (Shameem 2012, 2).[10] Stereotyped assumptions are also made about women judges. Teresa Doherty recalls claims that 'women on the bench or at the bar are too emotional or inconsistent' (International Development Law Organization 2018). Nazhat Shameem writes that 'appointing agencies, Judicial Services Commissions, and government bodies often believe that women will not make good judges because they are either too weak, or that they lack objectivity' (Shameem 2012, 6–7). She recalls how, when women were first appointed to the bench in Fiji, applications were made in rape cases for their recusal, on the basis that women could not hear rape cases objectively (Shameem 2012, 7).

Doherty and Shameem and other 'first' women judges observe that women need to prove their competence. Shameem said that '[w]omen still experience a testing time in court when they are first appointed on the Bench. There is no doubt that every woman who is appointed as the first woman on any Bench, has to prove her ability and her competence' (Shameem 2012, 7). Doherty advises women to 'really prepare before you take on any work. They will watch women to see if they make a mistake more than they will watch a man' (International Development Law Organization 2018). Catherine Davani, the first female Papua New Guinean judge, said that her appointment in 2001 'came with a lot of challenges. It wasn't easy at first, especially being a female among all males ... These challenges made me stronger but also taught me a thing or two – we can earn the respect of a man at the workplace if we show that we are very good at our job' (Kenneth 2016).

Stereotypes that cast women as inconsistent, emotional and weak stand in direct contrast to the ideal qualities of a judge, such as impartiality, rationality and authority (Rackley 2013, chapter 4). Pervasive gender stereotypes of this kind contribute to the 'default' image of a judge as male. Women judges therefore disrupt social expectations of both

---

[10] In this Shameem echoes feminist studies of law, for example Graycar and Morgan 2002; Jalal 1998.

women and judges. It is for this reason that women judges in the Pacific report having to work hard to prove their competence. This work involves more than women simply proving their professional credentials, it requires women judges to also actively disprove negative stereotypes about women's capacity and suitability for judicial office.

Such stereotypes are a barrier to the appointment of more women judges, because they influence the decisions of the authorities responsible for appointing judges. They can also work to prevent women even imagining that they might ever hold judicial office. As discussed in Part IV, the appointment of more women judges to Pacific courts is itself a partial solution to this problem, as the presence of women judges demonstrates women's capacity for judicial office and leadership, both to women and girls aspiring to a legal career and to the wider community.

The Pools for Recruitment

In each of the Pacific states, the qualifications for appointment to judicial office typically require candidates to have a minimum period of judicial or legal experience, either in the state itself or in countries with a comparable legal system.[11] This permits the appointment of both local and foreign judges. Because they are drawn from different labour pools, this section discusses local and foreign judges separately.

Local Judges

In the Pacific states, local judges tend to be recruited from private legal practice or from legal offices within government. As increasing numbers of Pacific women joined the legal profession, it was expected that more women would gradually hold judicial positions (Huffer 2006, 25). This section examines the participation of Pacific women in legal education and the legal profession as pathways to judicial office.

Access to legal education is a prerequisite to entry into the legal profession and the judiciary. The Pacific region has three law schools. The University of Papua New Guinea (UPNG) Law School was

---

[11] *Constitution of Fiji 2013* s 105; *Constitution of Fiji 1997* s 130; *Constitution of Kiribati 1979* ss 81(3), 91(1)(b); *Constitution of Nauru 1968* s 49(3); *National Court Act 1975* c 38 (PNG) ss 1, 2; *Constitution of Samoa 1960* s 65(5); *Constitution of Solomon Islands 1978* ss 78(3), 86(3); *Constitution of Tonga 1875* ss 85(1), 86(1); *Constitution of Tuvalu 1986* s 124; *Constitution of Vanuatu 1980* s 49(4).

established in 1965, while the School of Law of the University of the South Pacific (USP), which serves twelve member countries,[12] was established in 1994. The Fiji National University awarded its first law degrees in 2018. Given that the UPNG Law School has a longer history, it might be expected that, to date, more judges studied there. The educational background of Pacific women judges bears this out. All of the four Papua New Guinean women judges studied law at UPNG.[13] From the other Pacific jurisdictions, only one – Anjala Wati – is a graduate of USP. The other Pacific women who became judges all obtained their law degrees from institutions in Australia, New Zealand or the United Kingdom.[14] Several have postgraduate qualifications, also obtained overseas.[15] This might be expected to change in the future, as up to 80 per cent of the legal profession in Pacific states other than Papua New Guinea are graduates of USP (Bilimoria 2017, 247) and in 2010 over 50 per cent of enrolled law students were women (SPLA 2014, 4).

The number of women lawyers has increased over time. In 1995, only 13 per cent of lawyers in the Pacific were women (Jalal 1998, 543) but by 2012 this had increased to 34 per cent (SPLA 2014, 10). In Samoa, the only country in this study to have briefly achieved gender parity on a superior court, there is a much higher proportion of women lawyers, with figures from 2011 showing that 58 per cent of all lawyers in Samoa were women (Betham-Annandale 2014). In 2011, there was only one woman judge serving on the District Court, but in the years since several more women have been appointed to the District Court and from there to the Supreme Court (Betham-Annandale 2014).

Across the region, the proportion of women lawyers in government is higher than the proportion of women in private practice (SPLA 2014, 11–14). The appointment of women judges is therefore assisted by the criteria for judicial appointment, which in Pacific states recognises legal

---

[12] Cook Islands, Fiji Islands, Kiribati, Marshall Islands, Nauru, Niue, Samoa, Solomon Islands, Tonga, Tokelau, Tuvalu and Vanuatu.

[13] Justices Catherine Davani, Jacinta Murray, Leka Nablu and Hitelai Polume-Kiele.

[14] Mere Pulea (Lincoln's Inn, London); Nazhat Shameem (University of Sussex and University of Cambridge); Gwen Phillips and Viran Moisa Trief (Victoria University Wellington); Mata Tuatagaloa (University of New South Wales); Leilani Tuala Warren (University of Waikato). Public information on the educational background of Maelyn Bird could not be obtained.

[15] E.g. Justices Nazhat Shameem (MPhil Cambridge); Catherine Davani and Leka Nablu (LLM University of Sydney); Hitelai Polume-Kiele (LLM Melbourne Law School); Mata Tuatagaloa (Australian National University); Leilani Tuala Warren (LLM University of Waikato).

experience in government agencies as well as private practice. Six of the Pacific women judges had previously worked in public institutions,[16] while three were in private practice.[17]

The increasing numbers of women undertaking legal study and entering the legal profession suggest that the number of Pacific Islander women appointed to judicial office is likely to increase over time. However, generational change is no guarantee of future gender balance on the bench. Studying law in the Pacific takes a great deal of personal commitment and financial support. For many, higher education is possible with scholarships and other financial assistance. Law is taught in English, which is a second or third language for many students. Law schools are often located far away from home, and in many cases overseas (Bilimoria 2017, 248). Studies from other parts of the world show that women often face structural barriers to entry and promotion in the legal profession, such as the costs borne by women for maternity leave and childcare, or from sexual harassment and unsafe working conditions (Kay and Gorman 2008). The SPLA Survey identified the need for research on the extent to which issues of these kinds affect women lawyers in the Pacific (SPLA 2014, 7). For example, in writing about women's participation in public leadership, some have noted that the burden of balancing family responsibilities and work might be more manageable for women in the Pacific because of the support provided by extended family (Corbett and Liki 2015, 335–336). Unless the structural barriers in education and the legal profession in the Pacific are identified and addressed, it may be that Pacific women will still be under-represented on the bench long into the future.

Foreign Judges

Pacific states have a long-standing practice of recruiting candidates for judicial appointment from overseas. Of the twenty-nine women judges who have served in the Pacific, seventeen (58 per cent) have been foreign, in that they serve as a judge in a state in which they do not hold

---

[16] Nazhat Shameem (Director of Public Prosecutions); Viran Molisa Trief (Solicitor General); Gwen Phillips (Attorney General's Department); Leilani Tuala Warren (Samoa Law Reform Commission); Leka Nablu (Internal Revenue Commission), Hitelai Polume-Kiele (Department of Justice and Attorney-General). Prior to her appointment as a judge, Mere Pulea was a professor at USP.

[17] Jacinta Murray, Mata Tuatagaloa, Anjala Wati. Prior to their judicial appointments, Catherine Davani and Maelyn Bird had worked in both public and private legal practice.

citizenship, and typically in which they did not receive their legal education or engage in legal practice. There are, however, several examples of women judges who challenge the simple equation of citizenship with foreignness. Ida Malosi, for example, is a member of the Pacific diaspora, born to Samoan parents in New Zealand (Mafileo 2018). In 2002, when she was appointed a judge of the New Zealand Family Court, she was described as the 'first Pacific Island woman judge' in New Zealand. In examples of a different kind, Australians Royale Thompson and Teresa Berrigan worked as lawyers in Papua New Guinea prior to their appointments as judges in 2018, while Jane Crulci had professional legal experience in several Pacific countries prior to her appointment to the Supreme Court of Nauru. On the other hand, as noted, many Pacific Islander women judges received their legal education overseas, further blurring points of distinction between citizen and non-citizen judges.

The use of foreign judges gives Pacific states access to a wider and more diverse pool of candidates for judicial appointment. However, it appears that access to foreign candidates has not significantly benefitted the gender balance on Pacific courts. The *first* women judges of Nauru, Papua New Guinea, Samoa, Solomon Islands, Tuvalu and Vanuatu were foreign judges. However, of the 225 foreign judges who served on the superior courts of the Pacific from 2000 to 2019, only sixteen – 7 per cent – were women. In this, the proportion of local judges who are women is higher. Over the same period, twelve of ninety-two – or 13 per cent – of the local judges serving in the Pacific were women

The low proportion of women in the cohort of foreign judges is, in part, a reflection of a lack of diversity within the pools from which foreign judges are recruited. Foreign judges serving in the Pacific are usually sitting judges in their home jurisdiction, retired judges or senior lawyers (Dziedzic 2021, chapter 2). The cohort of foreign judges therefore tends to reflect the demographics of the judiciaries and legal professions of their home countries. The majority of foreign judges are recruited from Australia, New Zealand and Sri Lanka. In all three states, the number of women law graduates now exceeds that of men, while the number of women lawyers has increased to the point where women outnumber men in some sectors, although not in senior positions (Law Council of Australia 2017; New Zealand Law Society n.d.; Samararatne, Chapter 3). Despite this, women are under-represented on the judiciaries in all three states (Adlam 2015; Samararatne Chapter 3). This in turn affects the diversity of the pool from which foreign judges are recruited. The use of retired judges in particular extends the effect of historical under-representation of women on the courts of Australia, New Zealand and Sri Lanka into the Pacific.

Choices at Selection

The methods for recruiting candidates for judicial office and choices made at selection also affect the gender composition of Pacific judiciaries. Pacific states have made international and regional commitments to increase the proportion of women in leadership positions. International efforts initially focused on increasing the number of women in parliament. With the Sustainable Development Goals, however, this has expanded to ensuring women's 'full and effective participation and equal opportunities for leadership at all levels of decision making in political, economic and public life' (SDG Target 5.5). In 2012, Pacific Leaders committed to improving the position of women by signing the 'Gender Equality Declaration'. The revised Pacific Platform for Action on Advancement of Women and Gender Equality includes the goal of 'equal participation by women and men in public life' to be achieved through an 'increase in the number of women appointed and elected to public office' (Huffer 2006, 6).

These international and regional commitments have not been translated into laws and policies devoted to improved gender balance in Pacific judiciaries. There are, however, two historical precedents from the region. First, section 134 of the now repealed Constitution of Fiji 1997 set out the principle that the 'composition of the judiciary should, as far as possible, reflect the ethnic and gender balance of the community'. Second, in 2000, the Papua New Guinea parliament passed legislation to require at least one woman magistrate be appointed to every Village Court by 2005 (McLeod 2015, 11). This target was not reached: in 2007 there were just ten female village court magistrates from a total of 7,000 (Rau 2011). However, by 2013 there were approximately 900, representing about 8 per cent of all village court magistrates (Neill 2013). So while the quota did not immediately work, it perhaps paved the way for other efforts – supported by foreign development aid – to train and support women to become magistrates (Neill 2013; Rosenbaum 2014). These laws from Fiji and Papua New Guinea are no longer in force, and across the region there are no current requirements in policy or law for those responsible for judicial appointments to consider gender as a relevant criterion.

Studies from other legal systems have suggested that transparent procedures for judicial appointments would foster greater diversity, by breaking the informal processes whereby recommendations for judicial appointments are made by existing judges and other elites who are entrenched in the current system and its culture (Irving 2008, 137–138). All but two of the Pacific states utilise a Judicial Services Commission (JSC) or equivalent to recommend or directly make judicial appointments.[18] Some judicial positions are advertised, but others, particularly for foreign judges, are filled by informal means, through recommendations from other judges or as a result of personal connections made through judicial networks. There is some evidence that advertising judicial positions might increase women's chances of judicial appointment in the Pacific. For example, Mary Sey and Nkemdilim Izuako were both recruited through the Commonwealth Fund for Technical Cooperation, becoming the first female judges in Vanuatu and Solomon Islands respectively. It is unlikely that either would have been selected by those states' JSCs without the global advertising and recruitment process conducted by the Commonwealth Secretariat.

It seems unlikely that Pacific states will adopt affirmative action policies or laws to increase the number of women judges. Advocacy for special measures such as quotas to improve the representation of women in parliaments across the region has so far met with limited success (Baker 2019). Some women judges have spoken against gender quotas, concerned about the risk that they will be perceived as 'token' women. Mata Tuatagaloa, the first Samoan woman appointed to that country's Supreme Court, said that her 'first question to the Chief Justice when being approached to be a judge was, if you're appointing me because I'm a woman, I won't accept it, but if you're appointing me on my merit, then I will gladly accept it' (Samoa Observer 2019). Teresa Doherty recalls how 'soon after I was appointed in Papua New Guinea, the then Chief Justice said, "now they've got a woman judge, I hope they'll stop harping on at me about appointing a woman" (International Development Law Organization 2018). In a similar vein to Justice Tuatagaloa, Doherty says

> I don't like this term 'token women'. To me it carries an implication of insult, as if the woman is being appointed purely because there is a policy

---

[18] *Constitution of Fiji 2013* s 106; *Constitution of Kiribati 1979* ss 81(2), 91(1)(b); *Constitution of Papua New Guinea 1975* s 170(2); *Constitution of Samoa 1960* ss 72(3), 75(2)(b); *Constitution of Solomon Islands 1978* ss 78(1), 78(2), 86(1), 86(2); *Constitution of Tonga 1875* ss 85, 86; *Constitution of Vanuatu 1980* s 47(2). In Nauru and Tuvalu, judicial appointments are in the hands of the executive alone: *Constitution of Nauru 1968* s 49(2); *Constitution of Tuvalu 1986* s 123.

that demands a female appointee. It implies that the person is not being
put there on their own merit, that they're just going to be ticking the box
for female representation

(International Development Law Organization 2018).

The importance of 'merit' is often invoked to counter proposals for
express consideration of gender balance in judicial appointments. The
claim is that the best and most qualified person, regardless of gender,
should be appointed. Feminist scholars have, however, argued that merit
is itself a socially constructed and gendered concept. As discussed, the
qualities that are understood to make a 'good judge' have developed to
mirror the kind of judges we already have, and reflect attributes that are
stereotypically ascribed on a gendered basis to men and denied to women
(Thornton 2007).

In this, the barriers to the appointment of women judges circle back to
the core issue of gender stereotyping. Affirmative action to increase the
number of women law graduates and lawyers, transparent processes or
an express requirement to consider gender balance when making judicial
appointments might go some way to recognising and addressing structural barriers to the greater representation of women on Pacific judiciaries. However, shifting gendered stereotypes – about women and about
judges – is key to significant change.

Part IV: Do Women Judges Make a Difference?

Clearly, women are under-represented on Pacific judiciaries. But why
should it matter whether there are more women, or none at all, in judicial
office? Scholars examining other common law jurisdictions have identified a range of reasons why gender balance in the judiciary is important
(Rackley 2013, 24–28; Hunter 2015).

One set of arguments focuses on the relationship between the composition of the court and public confidence in the judiciary. It argues that
the community will vest greater trust in a judiciary that reflects the
society it serves (Barmes and Malleson 2018). This is particularly important when the judiciary is entrusted with safeguarding constitutional
rights, including gender equality. As United States Judge Chen asks,
'how can the public have confidence if the communities it is supposed
to protect are excluded from its ranks?' (Graham 2004, 156). The presence of women on the bench can reassure women litigants, witnesses and
advocates that they will be fairly heard.

Another set of arguments focuses on equal opportunity and the inclusion of women in public leadership roles. The presence of women in high judicial office demonstrates that women are equally qualified and as competent as men to be judges and that there is no gender discrimination in judicial appointments. Women on the bench also provide role models to other women who aspire to be judges, and mentoring and support to their peers in the judiciary and the legal profession, thereby encouraging other women in legal careers (Hunter 2015, 123).

A final set of arguments is that women bring a different perspective to adjudication and judicial decision-making. This claim is made in different ways, but all share the idea that judges, at least sometimes, must make decisions not on the mechanical application of predetermined rules, but guided by their own sense of the values and principles of law. One view focuses on the benefits of judges bringing diverse perspectives and values to solving difficult legal problems: as Lady Hale, former president of the United Kingdom Supreme Court, has said, 'in disputed points you need a variety of perspectives and life experiences to get the best possible results' (United Kingdom Parliament Constitution Committee 2012, paragraph 90). The claim becomes more controversial, however, when it moves towards the idea that women bring *particular* values or that women judges *represent* or *speak for* women. Such claims must be carefully made. One important consideration is to avoid essentialism, that is, casting the experiences of all women as the same, thereby fixing particular characteristics as inherently feminine such that one woman can speak for all. With these concerns in mind, Carrie Menkel-Meadow proposes that women in the law do bring different perspectives to men, and that these differences are socially constructed by women's shared experience of exclusion, oppression and learned attention to caring roles and relationships (Menkel-Meadow 1989, 312–313). Sometimes this different perspective is described as a 'gendered sensibility' (Hunter 2015, 124) which makes women more attuned to claims of women and others who are marginalised by law and social norms.

One objection to claims that women 'decide cases differently' is that this is incompatible with the judicial obligation of impartiality. Feminist scholars have made compelling arguments that legal understandings of 'impartiality' are not themselves objective, but rather constructed from a male perspective (Graycar 2008). Others argue that impartiality ought not be seen as an objective 'view from nowhere' but rather a 'view from everywhere' informed by the experiences of all members of the community (Phillips 1995, 187). The idea that judges might have different views,

informed in part by their individual backgrounds and experiences has
come, over time, to counter the outdated notion that common law judges
mechanically and 'impartially' apply the law to facts (Etherton 2010;
Rackley 2013, 164).

The literature summarised here was developed predominantly by
scholars writing about the Australian, British and North American legal
systems. As such, their claims should not be automatically transposed to
the Pacific context, where the law and legal profession are shaped by the
distinctive context of small island states, a multitude of indigenous legal
systems, and the impact of colonisation.

Using published interviews and writings by women who have served as
judges on Pacific courts and gender analyses of Pacific law and jurisprudence, this part seeks to better understand whether and how the women
judges on *Pacific* courts might make a difference to Pacific legal systems
and the communities in which they operate. It suggests that two of the
arguments in support of women in the judiciary resonate in the Pacific.
The first is that the presence of women judges counters harmful
stereotypes about gender that constrain women in public office. The
second is the degree to which women judges understand and use their
role to bring about substantive gender justice for women.

Women Judges as Leaders

It is common for women judges – especially 'first' women judges – to
express a hope that their appointments will inspire more women to seek
senior positions in the judiciary, legal profession and public service. Jane
Crulci, the first woman appointed to Nauru's Supreme Court stated that
'it would be wonderful breaking that barrier that more women in Nauru
saw careers in the judicial fields and basically the law and justice sector. It
would be something that one would aspire to leave that kind of legacy'
(Government of Nauru 2014, 3). Leilani Tuala Warren, a judge of the
Supreme Court of Samoa said that 'I hope that what I have achieved
will set and continue to set a good example to students in Samoa,
especially young women who are interested in the law' (University of
Waikato n.d.).

Politicians and lawyers have expressed similar sentiments on the
announcement of the appointment of women judges. Speaking of the
legacy left by Catherine Davani, the first female Papua New Guinean
judge, Prime Minister Peter O'Neill said that '[g]irls all around the nation
can look to the example she set and aspire to breakthrough barriers and

be everything they want to be in their careers' (Pacific Islands Law Officers' Network 2017). The Registrar of the Solomon Islands High Court, Nelson Laurere, commented that the appointment of Justice Nkemdilim Izuako was 'an opportunity for female lawyers in this jurisdiction, newly graduated, maybe few are already experienced to give them some competence in trying to make it to the bench as well' (Radio New Zealand 2008).

The examples provided cast women judges as role models and inspiration for girls and women seeking a career in public office. However, there is another, different, sense in which the appointment of women as judges sends a message, not just to women, but to the wider Pacific community. Prevalent gender stereotypes affect the extent to which women judges are seen as capable and authorised to exercise the public powers of judicial office to resolve disputes and punish wrongdoing, including wrongdoing by men who themselves hold public power. A young female lawyer working in Tuvalu reported that 'while no restrictions are placed on practice by female lawyers, cultural barriers exist in that mediation and arbitration are traditionally not seen as women's roles' (Bilimoria 2017, 248). In 1997, a government minister, who later became the prime minister of Vanuatu, called for the repeal of the Ombudsman Act because it contradicted the 'traditional practices' of Vanuatu by allowing the female Ombudsman to criticise male leaders. He said on his island, 'men could not be criticised by women' (Slatter 2010, 105).

Wendy Jerome's poem 'Women Can Always Match the Stride', extracted at the beginning of this chapter, speaks to the way in which the presence of a woman judge disrupts social gender roles. In the Papua New Guinean courtroom described in Jerome's poem, the mostly male lawyers in the courtroom address the judge 'sweetly, as "Your Honour"'. This 'culturally impossible' expression of deference by a man to a woman becomes not only possible, but the expected behaviour of those before the court.

The appointment of women to positions of leadership works to counter stereotypes about women's capacity for leadership and their right to participate in public life. The Solomon Islands Women's Council welcomed the appointment of Justice Izuako, saying it had 'reflected a lot of things to this country because she is a woman and in the Solomon Islands for a very, very long time it's been regarded as a field only for men. It's been very, very difficult for a woman to get that kind of position' (Radio New Zealand 2008). Similarly, Catherine Davani's appointment to Papua

New Guinea's judiciary was seen as a 'recognition that PNG women lawyers can contribute meaningfully to the administration of law and justice' (Daia-Bore 2011).

Such sentiments however are put to the test when women judges determine highly political, sensitive or controversial cases, or, to use the Vanuatu minister's phrase, when women criticise men. Such a situation arose in 2015, when Vanuatu's first and, at the time, only female judge, Mary Mam Yassin Sey, tried and convicted fifteen members of parliament for bribery and sentenced most to terms of imprisonment. The acts of bribery involved the members of parliament, all of whom were men, receiving money in return for switching their allegiances ahead of a vote of no confidence. The case was unprecedented in many ways, from the pursuit of sitting parliamentarians through the criminal justice system, to the respect shown by the executive and legislature to the judge's rulings in the case.[19] Justice Sey's decision disrupted 'political business as usual' (McDonnell 2015). There was a risk that Justice Sey, the woman judge who had held male politicians to account in a way they had never been before, would face criticism and backlash. She did receive threats (Dawuni 2018) and government ministers discussed deporting her before she could deliver sentences in the case (Forsyth and Batley 2016, 272–273). However, Justice Sey's decision – and the rule of law more generally – were publicly supported by leaders in the justice system, including the Director General of Justice, the Public Prosecutor, and the judiciary, making it difficult for critics to isolate and target the judge (Forsyth and Batley 2016, 266–267). There was a sense among the public that 'justice had been done' (Brennan 2015). Even some of those convicted made public statements about the importance of the independence of the judiciary (Forsyth and Batley 2016, 272). Bal Kama notes the significance that a judgment of this kind was made by a woman, saying that the challenge to Melanesian perceptions of women in leadership will perhaps help to forge a new precedent across the region (Kama 2016).

Women Judges as Law Reformers

The characterisation of women judges as role models who challenge and overcome prevalent gender stereotypes about women in leadership

---

[19] An attempt by the acting president to pardon the convicted members of parliament (including himself) was revoked by the president and held unconstitutional by the Supreme Court and Court of Appeal.

features fairly regularly in media reports about women judges in the Pacific. The idea that the inclusion of women in the judiciary is important because they bring a different perspective to judging appears more in the academic literature. This section examines the extent to which women judges in the Pacific are understood to use their position as judges to bring about substantive changes to law and legal procedures.

Features of Pacific legal systems might lend support to the idea that women judges are, to quote Nazhat Shameem, 'in a position to forge social and legal changes' (Soroptimists Club 2008). Upon independence, Pacific states inherited laws and legal systems from western colonial sources which require adaptation – and sometimes wholesale reform – to ensure they are appropriate for the particular context and needs of Pacific states. Often, such reforms are made by legislation, but as common law legal systems, judges too have the opportunity to shape and develop legal principles in the course of adjudication. Papua New Guinea's Constitution even gives judges express authority to develop the underlying law appropriate to the circumstances of Papua New Guinea.[20] Further, as states with small populations and customary forums for dispute resolution, there is less litigation and case law, and a single judge can have a significant impact by establishing long-lasting precedents.

This section draws together secondary literature and insights from women judges themselves on the significance of the gender of judges to substantive legal change, using as an example the law's response to gender-based violence and discrimination. Across the Pacific, there are high levels of violence against women, including intimate partner violence, violence within families, rape and sexual assault, sexual exploitation and trafficking and harmful practices against women such as accusations of sorcery (Pacific Women Shaping Pacific Development 2017b). Laws and customary practices in relation to family law, succession and property may discriminate against women (Farran 2009, chapter 5; Jivan and Forster 2007; Jalal 1998). Statutory and common law rules, developed in common law countries and adopted by Pacific states, contain many gender-biased elements. Examples in the law of sexual assault include the immunity for marital rape, the requirement for evidence of physical harm to prove non-consent and the requirement that a victim's evidence be corroborated.

---

[20] Constitution of Papua New Guinea 1975 schedule 2, part 3.

Law reform in states across the region has addressed some of these issues. However, the attitudes of the judges on the superior courts are also important in implementing legal reforms and, at times, in initiating such reforms themselves. In her study of the approach of Papua New Guinea's courts to sentencing men convicted of rape, Jean Zorn shows how the courts are 'ambivalent' about rape; on the one hand reciting statements about the unacceptable prevalence of rape in the country, but on the other hand fixing sentences for rape at very low levels (Zorn 2012, 164). Zorn argues that this ambivalence stems from women's subordinated status in Papua New Guinean society and in the law. Noting that 'almost every case is decided by a man, and a man writes the decision' (Zorn 2012, 165), she traces the evidence of male bias in the sentencing decisions of many (but not all) judges, who, she argues, lack the ability to empathise with the violence of rape and the pain experienced by victims, in short to understand that 'women are human beings just like men'.[21]

However, judges can also reform the law by developing new doctrines of common law, interpreting statutes and applying law to facts. In another study of the use made by Pacific courts of the Convention for the Elimination of Discrimination against Women (CEDAW), Jean Zorn identifies the ways in which judges – both male and female – on courts across the Pacific have overturned, amended and ameliorated discriminatory laws by drawing on the principles of gender equality enshrined in CEDAW (Zorn 2016). Such law reform is not the sole purview of women judges. However, women judges can contribute to what Nazhat Shameem describes as a 'gender competent bench', in which judges recognise and understand their own culturally driven perceptions about male and female roles and attributes (Shameem 2012, 1). Women judges bring a different perspective, informed by their own experiences. In the case of gender-based violence, the different perspectives and experiences of women can challenge the assumptions of other judges, as well as the assumptions on which legal rules are based. Teresa Doherty describes how women judges contribute to breaking down preconceived ideas 'that men bring to the bench and to the courts':

> In Papua New Guinea, I had to overcome vague, unsubstantiated attitudes that women who suffer abuse cannot give evidence in court because they

---

[21] This quote is taken from a judgment by Injia J in 1994. Zorn describes this comment as a 'revolutionary notion in a society whose deepest structures are predicated on the oppositional differences of the genders' (Zorn 2012, 189).

are too emotional, ashamed or don't want to relive the trauma. That is not true. It was important to show that women want justice and are equally capable of giving evidence

(International Development Law Organization 2018).

Women judges have also taken a different approach to court procedures. The Vanuatu Women's Centre praised the 'gender-sensitive' approach of Vanuatu's only female judge at the time, Justice Mary Sey, who resolved a disputed divorce proceeding through case management, rather than make the wife go to trial to prove her allegations of violence and the breakdown of the marriage (Vanuatu Women's Centre 2012, 35–36). Where a trial is necessary, the presence of women on the bench, as well as other parts of the legal profession, might also encourage women to come forward, describe the harms of gender-based violence and seek redress, allowing the diverse experiences of women to inform the development of the law (Farran 2009, 183).

The presence of women judges does not automatically guarantee that the law will change to better protect women. All judges, including women judges, bring their own assumptions and beliefs to the bench, informed by their own background and education. On this, Nazhat Shameem has sounded a note of caution:

For the women on the Bench, because you come from a privileged class of people, and because you yourselves may be the victims of abuse, for which you do not complain because of the class and gender pressure, you may be more judgmental of other women who have complained. Unconsciously, you may judge other women harshly for daring to do what you have not, because it is not, in your mind, what a lady does

(Shameem 2012, 5).

As Nazhat Shameem notes, gender balance 'does not guarantee a gender competent bench' and 'every judge must work to recognise gender bias and objectivity' (Shameem 2012, 7). In this, it would seem that the discourse in the Pacific about the difference that women judges make to the law aligns most clearly with the literature on the value of bringing different perspectives to bear on judicial understandings of the law and its operation in society, noting that deeply entrenched gender norms affect the perspectives of both women and men.

The experiences of women judges in the Pacific also highlight the importance of intersectionality, that is, the interconnectedness of social understandings of gender with other identity characteristics, such as race, class and nationality. In some ways, women judges in the Pacific share this experience with women judges across Asia (as highlighted in Chapter 3 by Samararatne). The peoples of the Pacific are diverse in language and cultures, in age, religion and sexuality. Characteristics such as race, age, religion and status might all contribute to how a judge understands the values of law and justice. Intersecting identities – and stereotypical views about them – also affect how judges are perceived by the communities they serve. For example, Nazhat Shameem has said that 'I am a Muslim, Indo-Fijian woman, and the combination of my race, religion and gender is very hard for many people to stomach' (Soroptimists Club 2008).

The use of foreign judges introduces an understudied point of difference and intersectionality. 'Foreignness' is a relative concept, defined against what is domestic or familiar. It can have negative connotations – of being different and not belonging – as well as positive connotations of impartiality, new experiences and novel insight (Honig 2001, chapter 1; Saunders 2003, chapter 1).

The prevalent use of foreign judges across the Pacific might mean that the only woman judge is also the only judge of a particular nationality, race or ethnic background. For example, Justice Mary Sey was not just the 'only' and 'first' woman judge on the Supreme Court of Vanuatu. She was also the only African judge on a court in which the majority of foreign judges are drawn from Australia and New Zealand. Justice Sey has spoken of how being at the intersection of multiple identities affected her work as a judge, and how, as a foreign 'outsider' she was criticised and threatened with deportation after her decision in the corruption case that led to the conviction of several members of parliament (Dawuni 2018).

Foreignness is also associated with positive values. Foreign judges can bring expert legal knowledge and new insights to the Pacific. For example, Jocelynne Scutt, an Australian lawyer who served as a judge on the High Court of Fiji, is an internationally recognised expert in law and gender.[22] Zorn explains how Justice Scutt developed Fijian jurisprudence on the legality of arranged marriages over her tenure. In a series of five cases, Justice Scutt changed the interpretation of the law so that 'duress' or 'coercion' into marriage did not require a woman to prove she

---

[22] Scutt is the author of, among other works, *The Incredible Woman: Power and Sexual Politics* (Artemis 1997).

was physically assaulted. Rather, she held that an arranged marriage is, in itself, coercive, especially for young people burdened with the weight of social and family expectations (Zorn 2016, 254; see also Scutt 2014). This is an example of a woman judge leading legal and social change to promote gender equality. There are some risks, however, when foreign judges seek to develop the law in ways that disrupt the values held by at least some in the wider society. The fact that a judge is an outsider to the Pacific state and its culture can undermine the extent to which the judge is able to 'speak for' Pacific women and adapt the laws of a community to which they do not belong (Dziedzic 2021, chapter 7). Law reform led by a foreign judge can also feed into a discourse in some parts of the Pacific that women's rights are foreign imports, and women's rights advocates are alienated from local culture and corrupted by Western thinking (Slatter 2010, 98; Farran 2009, 164). The intersection of gender and nationality can therefore restrict the extent to which women judges in the Pacific can engage in law reform.

It appears that in the Pacific, scholars, lawyers and judges themselves take a cautious approach to the difference that women judges might make to substantive law. They recognise that the presence of women judges cannot, in itself, shift the deeply embedded, gendered attitudes of law. Once women do achieve high office, in itself a rare and difficult achievement, there are limits on what they, as judges, can do, within the paradigms of the law, and against the stereotypes that shape how gender, as well as other identity characteristics, are perceived. Education, law reform, judicial training, legal advocacy and civil society movements all play a part in addressing the gender biases of the law, and in society generally.

Conclusion

The Pacific, while part of the 'Asia-Pacific' region, differs in significant ways from the Asian jurisdictions explored in this collection. Pacific states are small states and they are islands, geographically isolated in a large ocean. However, many of the issues arising in the Pacific – the under-representation of women at the higher levels of the judiciary; the barriers that stand in the way of women attaining positions of public leadership; and the challenge of overcoming, or better still changing, social gender norms – resonate with experiences in Asian jurisdictions described in other chapters.

The analysis in this chapter suggests that the appointment of women judges to Pacific judiciaries cannot, in and of itself, correct all the harmful gender biases in law and society. However, the appointment of women judges in greater number would counter some of the harmful stereotypes about women that persist in Pacific societies and contribute to work across a range of sectors in Pacific states to ensure that the law meets the needs of women and affirms gender justice. The presence of women judges on the superior courts of the Pacific is particularly powerful as an expression of gender equality. Their presence is a visible demonstration that women are of equal 'merit' and ability to men – in Jerome's words, that 'women can always match the stride' – in judicial office and in public leadership, countering prevalent stereotypes about the capacity and authority of women to participate in public life.

However, while many Pacific judiciaries celebrate the appointment of their first women judges – foreign and local – the proportion of women judges on Pacific courts across the region remains low at 9 per cent. As noted by Pacific feminist lawyer Imrana Jalal: '[i]f women want a more gender-conscious legal system, they need more female involvement in the system to hasten the process ... There must be a sufficient number of women in the law, as court officials, lawyers, magistrates and judges, to make a difference' (Jalal 1998, 542). This will be achieved when the regular appointment of women to Pacific judiciaries is the norm, rather than the exception.

The discussion identified a range of potential mechanisms to increase the number of women judges on Pacific courts, including increasing the representation of women in the labour pools from which judges are recruited; providing guidance to those responsible for judicial appointments to consider gender balance; the introduction of quotas; and transparent selection processes. At the heart of significant change, however, is challenging the gender stereotypes that flow into so many aspects of the law and justice systems in Pacific Island states.

There are, however, reasons to be hopeful. Pacific women are graduating from law school and entering the legal profession in far greater number than in the past. Trailblazing women judges from Pacific Island states and abroad have shown that women deserve equal opportunity to hold judicial office. In 2019, five states – Fiji, Papua New Guinea, Samoa, Solomon Islands and Vanuatu – had local women judges serving full time on their superior courts. Finally, the example of the Supreme Court of Samoa in 2016 shows that gender parity is not a distant aspiration for Pacific island states but is now possible.

References

Adlam, Geoff. 2015. 'New Zealand's Judiciary and Gender', 11 November, *New Zealand Law Society*, www.lawsociety.org.nz/practice-resources/research-and-insight/practice-trends-and-statistics/new-zealands-judiciary-and-gender.

Baker, Kerryn. 2019. *Pacific Women in Politics: Gender Quota Campaigns in the Pacific Islands*. Honolulu: University of Hawai'i Press.

2018. 'Great Expectations: Gender and Political Representation in the Pacific Islands'. *Government and Opposition* 53(3): 542–568.

Barmes, Lizzie and Kate Malleson. 2018. 'Lifting the Judicial Identity Blackout'. *Oxford Journal of Legal Studies* 38(2): 357–381.

Betham-Annandale, Mareva. 2014. 'A Word From . . .'. 9 *newSPLAsh: Women in Law in the South Pacific* 2.

Bilimoria, Nilesh N. 2017. 'Choices for the South Pacific Region's Bar Associations and Law Societies?' In *Small States in a Legal World*, edited by Petra Butler and Caroline Morris, 247. Cham: Springer International Publishing.

Brennan, Bridget. 2015. 'Vanuatu MPs Sent to Jail on Bribery Charges', 22 October, *ABC Radio*, PM program, www.abc.net.au/pm/content/2015/s4337030.htm.

Briguglio, Lino. 1995. 'Small Island Developing States and Their Economic Vulnerabilities'. *World Development* 23(9): 1615.

Cook, Rebecca J. and Simone Cusack. 2010. *Gender Stereotyping: Transnational Legal Perspectives*. Philadelphia: University of Pennsylvania Press.

Corbett, Jack and Asenati Liki. 2015. 'Intersecting Identities, Divergent Views: Interpreting the Experiences of Women Politicians in the Pacific Islands'. *Politics & Gender* 11(2): 320.

Corrin, Jennifer. 2014. 'Getting Down to Business: Developing the Underlying Law in Papua New Guinea'. *The Journal of Legal Pluralism and Unofficial Law* 46(2): 155.

Corrin Care, Jennifer. 2006. 'Negotiating the Constitutional Conundrum: Balancing Constitutional Identity with Principles of Gender Equality in Post-Colonial South Pacific Societies'. *Indigenous Law Journal* 5: 51.

Daia-Bore, Julia. 2011. 'Papua New Guinea's Davani Is First Local Woman National Judge', 7 February, *The National*, www.pireport.org/articles/2001/02/08/papua-new-guineas-davani-first-local-woman-national-judge.

Dawuni, Josephina Jarpa. 2018. 'Achieving Gender Parity in International Courts and Bodies: Does Diversity Matter?', 3 February, *IntLawGrrls*, https://ilg2.org/2018/02/03/achieving-gender-parity-in-international-courts-and-bodies-does-diversity-matter.

Dziedzic, Anna. 2021. *Foreign Judges in the Pacific*. Oxford: Hart Publishing.

Escobar-Lemmon, Maria C., Valerie Hoekstra, Alice J. Kang and Miki Caul Kittilson. 2019. 'Appointing Women to High Courts'. In *Research Handbook on Law and Courts*, edited by Susan M. Sterett and Lee Demetrius Walker, 200. Cheltenham: Edward Elgar.

Etherton, Terence. 2010. 'Liberty, the Archetype and Diversity: A Philosophy of Judging'. *Public Law* [2010]: 727.

Farran, Susan. 2009. *Human Rights in the South Pacific: Challenges and Changes*. London: Routledge-Cavendish.

Fiji Women's Crisis Centre. 2013. *Somebody's Life, Everybody's Business*. Suva: Fiji Women's Crisis Centre.

Forsyth, Miranda. 2009. *A Bird That Flies with Two Wings: The Kastom and State Justice Systems in Vanuatu*. Canberra: ANU Press.

Forsyth, Miranda and James Batley. 2016. 'What the Political Corruption Scandal of 2015 Reveals about Checks and Balances in Vanuatu Governance'. *Journal of Pacific History* 51(3): 255.

Government of Nauru. 2014. 'Nauru Supreme Court Resumes Proceedings', 18 September, *Nauru Bulletin* 2.

Graham, Barbara L. 2004. 'Toward an Understanding of Judicial Diversity in American Courts'. *Michigan Journal of Race & Law* 10: 153.

Graycar, Reg. 2008. 'Gender, Race, Bias and Perspective: OR, How Otherness Colours Your Judgment'. *International Journal of the Legal Profession* 15(1–2): 73.

Graycar, Regina and Jenny Morgan. 2002. *The Hidden Gender of Law*, 2nd ed. Annandale: Federation Press.

Honig, Bonnie. 2001. *Democracy and the Foreigner*. Princeton, NJ: Princeton University Press.

Huffer, Elise. 2006. 'A Woman's Place Is in the House – The House of Parliament'. In *Report 1: Desk Review of the Factors Which Enable and Constrain the Advancement of Women's Political Representation in Forum Island Countries*. Suva: Pacific Islands Forum Secretariat.

Hunter, Rosemary. 2015. 'More Than Just a Different Face? Judicial Diversity and Decision-Making'. *Current Legal Problems* 68(1): 119.

International Development Law Organization. 2018. 'Advice from Justice Doherty to Women: "Take Any Chance You Get"', www.idlo.int/news/highlights/advice-justice-doherty-women-take-any-chance.

Irving, Helen. 2008. *Gender and the Constitution: Equity and Agency in Comparative Constitutional Design*. Cambridge: Cambridge University Press.

Jalal, P. Imrana. 1998. *Law for Pacific Women: A Legal Rights Handbook*. Suva: Fiji Women's Rights Movement.

Jerome, Wendy. 2017. 'Women Can Always Match the Stride'. In *My Walk to Equality: Essays, Stories and Poetry by Papua New Guinean Women*, edited by Rashmii Amoah Bell, 167. Hervey Bay: Pukpuk Publications.

Jivan, Vedna and Christine Forster. 2007. *Translating CEDAW into Law: CEDAW Legislative Compliance in Nine Pacific Island Countries*. Suva: UNDP Pacific Centre and UNIFEM Pacific Regional Office.

Kama, Bal. 2016. 'Understanding Judicial Responses to Political Stability: A Case Study of Vanuatu and Papua New Guinea', 23 November, presented at the Pacific Constitutions Research Network Conference: Port Vila, www.paclii .org/pcn/publications2.html.

Kay, Fiona and Elizabeth Gorman. 2008. 'Women in the Legal Profession'. *Annual Review of Law and Social Science* 4: 299.

Kenneth, Gorethy. 2016. 'Tribute to Justice Catherine Davani', 15 November, *Post Courier*, https://postcourier.com.pg/tribute-to-justice-catherine-davani.

Kiefel, Susan and Cheryl Saunders. 2015. 'Concepts of Representation in Their Application to the Judiciary in Australia'. In *Fair Reflection of Society in Judicial Systems: A Comparative Study*, edited by Sophie Turenne, 41. Cham: Springer International Publishing.

Law Council of Australia. 2017. 'Women Outnumber Men in the Legal Profession for the First Time – but Not in Senior Ranks', 19 July, www.lawcouncil.asn .au/media/news/women-outnumber-men-in-the-legal-profession-for-the-first-time-but-not-in-senior-ranks.

Mafileo, Vea. (director) 2018. 'Daughters of the Migration: Judge Ida Malosi', *Coconet TV*, www.thecoconet.tv/coco-series/im:10801/daughters-of-the-migration-judge-ida-malosi.

McDonnell, Siobhan. 2015. 'Dirty Politics in Vanuatu', 14 October, *ANU College of Asia & the Pacific*, http://asiapacific.anu.edu.au/news-events/all-stories/dirty-politics-vanuatu.

McLeod, Abby. 2015. *Women's Leadership in the Pacific*. Birmingham: Developmental Leadership Program.

Menkel-Meadow, Carrie. 1989. 'Exploring a Research Agenda of the Feminization of the Legal Profession: Theories of Gender and Social Change'. *Law and Social Inquiry* 14(2): 289.

Monson. Rebecca. 2017. 'The Politics of Property: Gender, Land and Political Authority in Solomon Islands'. In *Kastom, Property and Ideology: Land Transformations in Melanesia*, edited by Siobhan McDonnell, Matthew G Allen and Colin Filer, 383. Canberra: ANU Press

Neill, Rosemary. 2013. 'Ladies Dispense Tough Justice', 29 June, *The Australian*, www.theaustralian.com.au/news/inquirer/ladies-dispense-tough-justice/news-story/4e2158624d94591a036020a011b54ccf.

New Zealand Law Commission. 2006. Converging Currents: Custom and Human Rights in the Pacific, Study Paper No. SP17.

New Zealand Law Society. Undated. 'By the Numbers', www.lawsociety.org.nz/law-society-services/women-in-the-legal-profession/by-the-numbers.

O'Brien, Patricia. 2014. 'Gender'. In *Pacific Histories: Ocean, Land, People*, edited by David Armitage and Alison Bashford, 282. Basingstoke: Palgrave Macmillan.

Pacific Community. 2018. 'PRISM 2018 Pocket Summary', https://prism.spc.int.

Pacific Islands Law Officers' Network. 2017. 'Obituary: Justice Catherine Davani'. *Talanoa* 7: 11.

Pacific Judicial Development Programme. 2015. *2014 Court Trend Report* (Federal Court of Australia and New Zealand Ministry of Foreign Affairs and Trade).

—— 2013. *2012 Court Trend Report* (Federal Court of Australia and New Zealand Ministry of Foreign Affairs and Trade).

—— 2012. *2011 Court Baseline Report* (Federal Court of Australia and New Zealand Ministry of Foreign Affairs and Trade).

Pacific Women Shaping Pacific Development. 2017a. 'Ending Violence against Women: Roadmap Synthesis Report', https://pacificwomen.org/key-pacific-women-resources/pacific-women-ending-violence-women-roadmap-synthesis-report.

—— 2017b. 'Ending Violence against Women', https://pacificwomen.org/our-work/focus-areas/ending-violence-against-women.

Phillips, Anne. 1995. *The Politics of Presence*. Oxford: Clarendon Press.

Rackley, Erika. 2013. *Women, Judging and the Judiciary: From Difference to Diversity*. Abingdon: Routledge.

Radio New Zealand. 2008. 'Solomons First Woman Judge Seen as Role Model', 19 June, www.rnz.co.nz/international/pacific-news/177803/solomons-first-woman-judge-seen-as-role-model.

Rau, Linda. 2011. 'Village Courts in PNG', 26–28 October, presented at the State Supported Community Justice Workshop: Honiaria, http://siteresources.worldbank.org/INTJUSFORPOOR/Resources/LRau.pdf.

Rosenbaum, Alana. 2014. 'The Women of Papua New Guinea's Village Courts', *The Monthly*, www.themonthly.com.au/issue/2014/august/1406815200/alana-rosenbaum/women-papua-new-guinea%E2%80%99s-village-courts.

Samoa Observer. 2019. 'Justice Tuatagaloa: NZ Prime Minister's Fellow', 8 February, www.samoaobserver.ws/category/samoa/34622.

Saunders, Rebecca. 2003. *The Concept of the Foreign: An Interdisciplinary Dialogue*. Lanham, MD: Lexington Books.

Scutt, Jocelynne. 2014. 'Human Rights, "Arranged" Marriages and Family Law: Should Culture Override or Inform Fraud and Duress?' *Denning Law Journal* 26: 62.

Sirivi, Josephine Tankunani and Marilyn Taleo Havini. 2004. *As Mothers of the Land: The Birth of the Bougainville Women for Peace and Freedom*. Sydney: Pandanus.

Slatter, Claire. 2010. 'Gender and Custom in the South Pacific'. *Yearbook of New Zealand Jurisprudence* 13 & 14: 89.

Shameem, Nazhat. 2012. 'Gender, Justice, and Judges', 14 June, speech to the Fiji Judiciary Criminal Law Workshop for Judges and Magistrates, www .leadershipforwomen.com.au/nazhat-shameem-2.

Soroptimists Club. 2008. 'Interview with Justice Nazhat Shameem', 10 May, Lautoka, http://intelligentsiya.blogspot.com/2012/02/nazhat-shameems-icc-dreams-finally.html.

South Pacific Lawyers Association (SPLA). 2014. *Women in the Law in the South Pacific: Survey Report.*

Thornton, Margaret. 2007. 'Otherness on the Bench: How Merit Is Gendered', *Sydney Law Review* 29: 391.

United Kingdom Parliament Constitution Committee. 2012. *25th Report: Judicial Appointments*, 7 March.

United Nations. 2015, *World Population Prospects: The 2015 Revision.* Department of Economic and Social Affairs, Population Division, http://esa.un.org/unpd/wpp.

University of Waikato. Undated. 'A New Judge in Samoa', *Alumni @ Waikato.* https://alumni.waikato.ac.nz/profiles/a-new-judge-in-samoa.

Va'ai, Asiata. 1997. 'The Idea of Law: A Pacific Perspective'. *Journal of Pacific Studies* 21: 225.

Vanuatu Women's Centre. 2012. *Program against Violence against Women: Progress Report 1*, https://dfat.gov.au/about-us/publications/Documents/vanuatu-womens-centre-progress-report-1.pdf.

Veenendaal, Wouter. 2015. *Politics and Democracy in Microstates.* Abingdon: Routledge.

Wale, Rose. 2004. *Solomon Islands: Status of Women, 2002–2003.* Suva: Pacific Foundation for the Advancement of Women.

Zorn, Jean. 2016. 'Translating and Internalising International Human Rights Law: The Courts of Melanesia Confront Gendered Violence'. In *Gender Violence & Human Rights: Seeking Justice in Fiji. Papua New Guinea & Vanuatu*, edited by Aletta Biersack, Margaret Jolly and Martha Macintyre, 229. Canberra: ANU Press.

2012. 'Engendering Violence in the Papua New Guinea Courts: Sentencing in Rape Trials'. In *Engendering Violence in Papua New Guinea*, edited by Margaret Jolly, Christine Stewart and Carolyn Brewer 263. Canberra: ANU Press.

3

Reframing Feminist Imperatives in Adjudication through a Reading of Sri Lankan Jurisprudence

DINESHA SAMARARATNE[*]

> ... it is as if, after a long period of dormancy, women's consciousness has suddenly come alive again (Jayawardena 2009, 259)

> ... with a few exceptions, the women worked within the boundaries laid down by men (Jayawardena 2009, 259)

> Further, on a reading of the judgement, it would appear that the learned trial Judge had been misled and dazzled by some wrong notion of gender inequality.
>
> *Addararachchi v. the State* 2000, 411

What does the study of the exercise of judicial discretion by judges reveal about advancing gender justice through adjudication? Some feminist scholars in the Global North have responded to this question through an examination of the inclusion and representation of women in the judiciary. Some others, more recently, have responded through feminist critiques of jurisprudence in a range of jurisdictions. In this chapter, I claim that in jurisdictions of the Global South, the question cannot be limited to a study of judges or jurisprudence. The focus must extend beyond the study of individual judges and/or their judgments to a study of the system of adjudication – the laws, legal institutions and the legal and political culture within which they operate. To that extent, I seek to reframe the feminist imperatives in the ongoing debates about advancing gender justice through adjudication.

[*] I thank Justice Saleem Marsoof, Neloufer de Mel, Chulani Kodikara, Visakesa Chandrasekaram, Yanitra Kumaraguru, Thiagi Piyadasa, Dinushika Dissanayake, Sankhitha Guneratne and Melissa Crouch for their comments on drafts of this chapter. I acknowledge the injustices that are recorded in the jurisprudence that I analyse in this chapter and pay tribute to the women who are presented as victim-survivors, respondents or as petitioners and to their allies. Research for this paper was fully funded by the Australian Government through the Australian Research Council (ARC) Laureate Program 'Balancing Diversity and Social Cohesion in Democratic Constitutions'.

In making my claim, I study nine different emblematic cases involving gender justice heard by the Sri Lankan courts. Some of these cases were adjudicated by women judges while others were not. My reading of these judgments affirms Kumari Jayawardena's claims in the 1980s about feminist movements in the Third World. She illustrates how colonialism, the rise of nationalism and democratisation gave impetus to feminist movements in the Third World and at the same time constrained it. I read the selected jurisprudence through this lens to explain advances and retreats from gender justice in adjudication. Drawing from Jayawardena's work, I argue that unlike in the Global North, posing the 'woman question' of judges in the Global South offers misleading answers regarding women's inclusion and representation in adjudication. It draws attention away from structural problems that have plagued legal institutions and away from problematic values of the legal as well as political culture. I argue that in as much as it is necessary to ask the woman question of the judiciary, it is also necessary to ask it of the system of adjudication. My analysis suggests that any link between women judges and gender justice is tenuous. It suggests quite clearly that the ways in which the system of adjudication operates – that is the legal institutions, the law for resolving disputes and the legal and political culture within which disputes are resolved – better explains the dynamics of gender justice in adjudication.

This chapter is organised in four parts. In Part I, I clarify my focus and the specific questions that I raise. I then revisit Kumari Jayawardena's intervention in feminist discourse and explain how I use her work to frame my claim that in the Global South, the woman question that is asked of judging should be re-framed and posed to the system of adjudication. In Part II, I assess the positionality of women in law in Sri Lanka and in the judicial institution. In Part III, I use jurisprudence that impacts women's issues and jurisprudence by women judges in Sri Lanka to establish my claims regarding the woman question and judging. Here I examine nine cases (involving in total eleven different judgments issued by different courts). In Part IV, I draw from the assessment of jurisprudence in making my case for feminist imperatives for adjudication in the Global South.

Part I: Clarifying the Questions

Does a woman judge speak in a 'different voice'? For more than two decades this question has preoccupied feminist scholars concerned with gender justice in the Global North (Judicial Diversity Initiative; Feenan 2009, footnote 1). The Feminist Judgments projects in Canada, the United Kingdom, Ireland, Australia, New Zealand and the United States have now been extended to include India, the African continent and more recently international law (Hunter et al. 2010; Hodson and Lavers 2019). In this Part, I revisit and review this debate and consider the relevance of this question to understanding the challenges to gender justice in jurisdictions beyond the Global North. I suggest that the question ought to be framed differently, if this line of inquiry is to offer insights to contingencies of the Global South, such as the lack of guarantees for substantive equality for women and, in general, weak access to justice and delays.

Norms of Judicial Conduct

Feminist legal theory is committed to exposing the inconsistencies in impartiality and universality of procedural and substantive aspects of legal systems that in fact are based on privileged perspectives (Justice Lady Hale 2001, 497–498; Graycar and Morgan 2002; De Mel and Samararatne 2017). In the context of judging, however, to what extent can a commitment to feminism be maintained in light of the obligation of the judiciary to be independent and impartial? It has been argued by leading women judges of the world, such as Justice Ruth Bader Ginsburg and more recently by Justice Lady Hale, that it is possible to do so without compromising judicial norms (Justice Ginsburg 2016, 77; Justice Lady Hale 2005).

Moreover, the Bangalore Principles of Judicial Conduct, which serve as a guide to judicial conduct globally, recognise that a judge

> shall be aware of, and understand, diversity in society and differences arising from various sources, including but not limited to race, colour, sex, religion, national origin, caste, disability, age, marital status, sexual orientation, social and economic status and other like causes
>
> (Bangalore Principles of Judicial Conduct 2002, 5.1).

While the principles require that a judge may not 'manifest bias or prejudice' based on these grounds, the principles specifically recognise that these grounds may be 'legally relevant ... and may be the subject of legitimate advocacy' (Bangalore Principles of Judicial Conduct 2002, 5.5). The Commentary to the Bangalore Principles specifically provide that 'a judge should be familiar with the international and regional instruments that prohibit discrimination' including the Convention on the Elimination of All Forms of Discrimination against Women (CEDAW) (United Nations Office on Drugs and Crime 2007, para 183). The commentary notes that stereotyping undermines judicial impartiality and that judges 'should not be influenced by attitudes based on stereotype, myth or prejudice. A judge should, therefore, make every effort to recognise, demonstrate sensitivity to, and correct such attitudes' (United Nations Office on Drugs and Crime 2007, para 184).

Women Judges, Feminist Judging or Feminist Adjudication?

Globally, women's numerical and substantive representation in public life remains a practical challenge and is a matter of academic debate. In the field of law, a natural sequel to questions about women's entry, inclusion and participation in the legal profession was a similar process of questioning women's inclusion in the judiciary and their contribution to judging (Schultz and Shaw 2003). The inquiry into women's inclusion and/or taking into account women's perspectives, is described by Bartlett as 'asking the woman question' and as a feminist research method (Bartlett 1990; Delap 2011). The practice of asking the woman question predates feminisms of the twentieth century and has a much older history. A key feature of this question in nineteenth-century debates in the Western world, 'was to place under review how women might inhabit the spheres of formal politics, political argument or print culture, and what their qualifications were to do so' (Delap 2011, 320).

In law, broadly understood, Bartlett claims that asking the woman question involves 'identifying and challenging those elements of existing legal doctrine that leave out or disadvantage women and members of other excluded groups' (Bartlett 1990, 831). The inclusion of women in the judiciary since the 1980s in jurisdictions across the world gave feminist scholars the opportunity to reflect on these questions not only as a normative concern but also as a practical phenomenon. Scholarship reveals that it is difficult to establish plausible connections between the inclusion of women in the judiciary with the advancement of women's human rights or 'the feminist cause' as such.

Writing about the new Constitutional Court in South Africa, Ruth B Cowan notes that women justices do make a difference.

> They lent legitimacy to the judiciary, they have inspired other women to aim for judicial appointments, they have raised the comfort level of

women appearing in court and they have – through their extrajudicial
volunteer commitments – worked to increase access to justice

(Cowan 2013, 321).

However, it is logically difficult and theoretically problematic to uphold
a consequentialist approach to the inclusion of women in the judiciary.
It is difficult to argue for the inclusion of women in the judiciary
without falling prey to the stereotyping of such women. From a normative point of view, I agree with the argument that the inclusion of
women in the judiciary can only be defended on the grounds of the
intrinsic value of inclusion. As Rosemary Hunter points out, the
'assumptions about the difference that women in power would
make ... appear at best naïve and at worst essentialist' (Hunter 2008, 7).
Rackley notes 'Although "intuitively obvious" (at least to some), the search
for a distinctively female judicial voice has proved statistically elusive;
studies supporting gendered differences in judging are equivocal at best'
(Rackley 2009, 14).

More recently, Rosemary Hunter has argued that it is not necessarily
women judges who may make a difference but rather women judges who
are *feminist*. She chooses to focus on '*feminism* and power, rather than
women and power' (emphasis in the original) (Hunter 2008, 8).
Following Cotterrell, she describes feminism 'as a kind of voluntary
community of belief' (Hunter 2008, 8). For Rosemary, a *feminist* judge
is a woman judge who self-identifies as a feminist (Hunter 2008, 9). To
her 'the experience of being gendered female' is a 'crucial element of
feminism' (Hunter 2008, 8). She does recognise however that 'there is
much scope for disagreement on this point' (Hunter 2008, 8).
Furthermore, she concedes that while feminist judges may be expected
to be consistent in their feminist approach, other judges may engage in
'feminist judging' even if they are not necessarily self-identified feminists
(Hunter 2008, 9). Most importantly, she claims that her 'definition of
who counts as a feminist judge for normative purposes is ... necessarily,
temporally and culturally specific' (Hunter 2008, 10). Hunter takes the
view that answering the question on women and judging requires 'a more
detailed description of the practice of judging' (Hunter 2008, 17). She
suggests that the analysis should consider 'the court process, the outcome
of the case, the reasons given for the decision' and the extra-curricular
activities of the judge (Hunter 2008, 17). She uses the term 'feminist
judging' and describes this approach as including the following: (1)
Asking the woman question; (2) including women in legal discourse

and in the construction of legal rules; (3) challenging gender bias; (4) reasoning through contextualisation and particularity; (5) seeking remedies to injustices experienced by women; (6) promoting substantive equality; (7) openness and accountability in making difficult choices between competing interests; and (8) using feminist scholarship in decision-making (Hunter 2013, 401; Hunter 2008; Baines 2013, 382).

In contrast to focusing on *feminist judging*, Baines argues in favour of a focus on *feminist adjudication* which she describes as being a better way of approaching the question of women and judging. Baines points to the limits of self-identification by judges as 'feminist'. While she acknowledges that the reasons for reluctance on the part of judges to self-identify as feminists is unknown, she suggests that it is not unreasonable for a judge to hesitate from self-identification in her general attempt to adhere to the culture of judicial conduct (Baines 2013, 379). Baines argues that 'feminist legal scholars should study feminist judges on their own terms', and I would add that those terms should include the specific and high standards that apply to judicial conduct generally (Baines 2013, 387; Bangalore Principles of Judicial Conduct 2002). In any event, as Baines points out, feminist self-identification 'is a unilateral act which does not involve any scholarly analysis' (Baines 2013, 380).

I agree with Baines that 'feminist adjudication' is a more useful lens to adopt and 'an alternative to feminist self-identification' (Baines 2013, 380). Shifting the focus from feminist self-identification to feminist adjudication in judging demands more rigorous responses to the woman question. Baines describes the focus on feminist adjudication as an approach that is 'responsive to cultural, theoretical and political considerations'. This responsive approach has theoretical advantages. Firstly, it allows scholars and practitioners to identify the feminist impact of judging (whether in a single case or in the work of a court or a judge). Secondly, as Baines points out it places 'an onus on feminist legal scholars to make their own theoretical, cultural and political perspectives transparent when they study judicial feminism' (Baines 2013, 380). These advantages must be weighed against the limitations of 'feminist adjudication' that Baines identifies including the difficulties in interpretation of judicial silence about feminism, resolving judicial decision-making that may be inconsistent with feminism and assessing the feminist expectations cast on feminist judges by feminist scholars (Baines 2013, 393).

Reg Graycar's depiction of feminist adjudication as a process extends this debate further (Graycar 2013, 435). She asks, 'Has the feminist inquiry – often presented as "will women judges/decision-makers make a difference" – been misplaced?' She then asks:

> Should we instead focus on whether there is space for feminist insights to be introduced into the legal decision-making process, and if there is, at what stage? Can feminist insights assist in designing adjudication processes, rather than being introduced only at the decision-making stage?
>
> (Graycar 2013, 437).

Most importantly she asks 'What, if anything, distinguishes a "feminist" process from a "good" process? Are there particularly "feminist" ways of hearing evidence, of evaluating it and responding to it?' (Graycar 2013, 437). She notes that 'the call for increased participation by women and increasing diversity in judicial decision-making must be seen as an essential but nonetheless only a small part of a much bigger strategy, rather than as an end in itself' (Graycar 2013, 443).

In this chapter I read selected jurisprudence within this broader approach advocated by Graycar. A study of the dynamics of adjudication is more useful for understanding the contingencies of gender justice in jurisdictions like Sri Lanka in the Global South. It allows me to steer away from the debate on inclusion and/or representation of women in the judiciary, which as I have suggested, can limit or mislead the study of the dynamics of gender justice through adjudication. It opens up at least two lines of inquiry. First, this approach helps us to take account of the enduring challenges of nationalism and patriarchy as they play out in the law and its system of adjudication. Second, this approach takes the woman question to the heart of the challenge of gender justice in adjudication – can 'feminist insights' be incorporated into the redesigning of the adjudication process? In this chapter, I concern myself with the first line of inquiry.

Revisiting Feminism and Law in the 'Third World'

In arguing for the need to reframe the feminist imperatives in adjudication in the Global South, I need to clarify to some extent the following question. In what ways do the dynamics of feminism play out in law in jurisdictions beyond the Global North? I draw from Kumari Jayawardene's *Feminism and Nationalism in the Third World* in taking the view that histories of colonisation and democratisation, entangled with developments in international law since the establishment of the

United Nations, have impacted the evolution of law and systems of adjudication in the Global South in particular ways.

In 2017, *The Guardian* described Kumari Jayawardene's *Feminism and Nationalism in the Third World* as 'the best introduction to the history of women's movements in Turkey, Egypt, Iran, India, Sri Lanka, Indonesia, the Philippines, China, Vietnam, Korea and Japan' (*The Guardian* 9 August, 2017). Through an assessment of the women's movements in these countries, Jaywardena offers an account of the evolution of feminism that departs from its well-established and liberal counterpart. The result is a well-reasoned rejection of a linear account of the impact and evolution of the first and second waves of feminism on the women's movements of the Third World. Jayawardena claims that 'feminism was *not* imposed on the Third World by the West, but rather that historical circumstances produced important material and ideological changes that affected women, even though the impact of imperialism and Western thought was admittedly among the significant elements in these historical circumstances' (Jayawardena 2009, 2). In offering insights into the dynamics of feminism in these contexts, she pays attention to the following imperatives at play in the early twentieth century in the colonised world: (1) the attempts to 'shake off imperialist domination'; (2) to 'carry out internal reforms in order to modernize their societies'; and (3) 'the assertion of a national identity' (Jayawardena 2009, 3). She argues that these forces led to 'the paradoxical strategy of adopting Western models in order to combat Western aggression, reinforce cultural identity and strengthen the nation' (Jayawardena 2009, 3).

In her examination of the feminist movements in Sri Lanka, Jaywardena argues that, 'the emerging bourgeoisie successfully negotiated a transfer of political power which left the existing social structure unchanged' (Jayawardena 2009, 4). Consequently 'the pre-capitalist dogmas and religions have proved to be surprisingly enduring' and women and women's movements took a back seat with independence (Jayawardena 2009, 6). The rise of ethno-nationalism during this time constrained the ways in which the woman question could be approached. In their search for a national identity, the emergent bourgeoisies also harked back to a national culture: the new woman could not be a total negation of traditional culture. Although certain obviously unjust practices should be abolished, and women were involved in activities outside the home, they still had to act as the guardians of national culture, indigenous religion and family traditions – in other words, 'to be both "modern" and "traditional"' (Jayawardena 2009, 14).

The development of a feminist consciousness through the shaping of legal culture, the law and legal institutions was impacted by these developments. As Jayawardena notes:

> The women's movements ... achieved political and legal equality for women with men at the juridical level but failed to make any impression on women's subordination within the patriarchal structures of family and society. Feminist consciousness did not develop, except in rare exceptions, to the point of questioning traditional patriarchal structures
>
> (Jayawardena 2009, 24).

In her examination of Sri Lanka, she concludes that Sri Lanka is an example of:

> a society in which women were not subjected to harsh and overt forms of oppression, and therefore did not develop a movement for women's emancipation that went beyond the existing social parameters. It is precisely this background that has enabled Sri Lanka to produce a woman prime minister, as well as many women in the professions; but without disturbing the general patterns of subordination
>
> (Jayawardena 2009, 133).

Jayawardena points out how 'the impulse to assert a national identity' impacted society over and above the impulse to modernise and democratise. 'The net effect' she claims, 'was to keep women within the boundaries prescribed by the male reformers and leaders' (Jayawardena 2009, 256). Consequently, since independence when nationalism gained momentum, male politicians 'pushed' women 'back into their "accustomed place"' (Jayawardena 2009, 258). This history explains why we now have a paradoxical condition where women enjoy high levels of formal equality before the law in Sri Lanka but are still severely underrepresented in politics, the formal work force and positions of leadership in society, and do not enjoy substantive equality.

Feminism, Law and the Global South

Jayawardena's claims remain relevant despite the significant political, legal and economic changes that have come about since the publication of her work. Today the categories of the First and Third Worlds have been substituted with the categories of the Global North and South (Comaroff and Comaroff 2012). The Global South is described as a geographical location but also as a sensibility (Dann 2020). It has been argued that the Global South ought to be studied on its own terms but also that theoretical insights from the Global South could yield insights for the Global North as well (Dann 2020).

The global advancement of women's human rights through the evolution of international human rights law has led to significant gains, particularly in relation to violence against women at home, at work and in armed conflict. The commodification and recognition of women's labour has evolved in the context of the global entrenchment of the market economy. More recently, the re-emergence of illiberalism in many parts of the world is reinforcing patriarchy. Legal institutions, the law and legal culture have been implicated in many of these developments but have also been a site for resistance to them.

These developments, in some ways, gave women's movements in the Global South a fresh impetus but also highlight the different concerns that preoccupied them. For instance, in Sri Lanka, women had to 'take up the challenges posed by militant nationalism and state authoritarianism' (De Mel 2001, 236). De Mel observes that, 'It was a context in which it was difficult for women's groups to keep focusing on feminist/strategic issues as it had done up to the mid-1980s' (De Mel 2001, 235). Peace activism and labour activism are perhaps the areas in which Sri Lanka's contemporary women's movements have been most active. In certain instances, these feminist movements achieved gender justice through the law but in many other instances the law and legal institutions operating within the nationalist and patriarchal culture that Jayawardena describe have failed to uphold gender injustice.

The Questions

In this context, what does the study of judges and their exercise of judicial discretion reveal about the prospects for advancing gender justice through adjudication? Much of the debate on judging, women and difference has taken place in the Global North with a few exceptions (Dawuni and Kuenyehia 2019; Dawauni and Bauer 2015; Schultz and Shaw 2013). In what ways is this debate helpful in jurisdictions beyond those of the Global North? In this chapter I ask this question in relation to Sri Lanka. Sri Lanka's post-colonial and war-affected conditions resonate with similar jurisdictions in the Global South. Feminist scholarship and activism in Sri Lanka highlights that gender justice has been elusive in law reform as well as in litigation. However, women in the judiciary or the impact of judicial decision-making in ensuring respect for women's rights has not yet been the subject of detailed study. As I illustrate in Part III, asking the woman question of specific judges through a study of their judgments suggests that women judges do not make a difference. My contention is that asking this question produces misleading results. Given the paradoxical nature of feminist consciousness in Sri Lanka, it is more useful to reframe the woman question and apply it more broadly to the system of adjudication in Sri Lanka and other similar jurisdictions in the Global South.

With these interests in mind, I ask the following questions. In emblematic cases, what were the factors that posed challenges to the achievement of gender justice and which factors advanced gender justice? What do these factors reveal about judging, women and difference? In what ways should we revise (if at all) how we ask 'the woman question' in judging, in jurisdictions of the Global South?

I analyse decided cases where gender justice has been implicated in seeking answers to these questions. These are emblematic cases which have dealt with issues of gender justice and several of the benches that adjudicated them included women judges. These are public law cases involving the interpretation of the Constitution and the exercise of judicial discretion in the enforcement of criminal sanctions for violence against women. They involve the offences of rape, gang rape and statutory rape in criminal law, fundamental rights petitions and pre-enactment review of bills. Some of the case analysis includes judgments of the High Court, Court of Appeal and the Supreme Court. In total, I study eleven judgments – one trial-at-bar judgment of the High Court (*Attorney General* v. *Subasinghe* 2015); one judgment of the High Court (*Addararatchi* v. *the Republic* 1997);[1] two judgments on appeals against convictions before the Court of Appeal (*Addaraarachchi* v. *State* 2000; *Subasinghe* v. *Attorney General* 2019); three judgments on criminal appeals before the Supreme Court (*Gallage* v. *Addararachchi* 2002; *Somaratne Rajapakse* v. *Attorney General* 2010; *Attorney General* v. *Sampath* 2015); two judgments in fundamental rights of the Supreme Court (*Yogalingam Vijitha* v. *Wijesekera* 2001; *Manohari Pelaketiya* v. *Secy Min of Education* 2016); one judgment on references made to Supreme Court (SC Reference No. 03 of 2008); and one Special Determination on Bills by the Supreme Court (In Re Local Authorities (Special Provisions) Bill and Local Authorities Elections (Amendment)

---

[1] The name of the accused is spelt as *Addararatchi* by the High Court; as *Addaraarachchi* by the Court of Appeal; and as *Addararachchi* by the Supreme Court.

Bill 2010). Through a comparison of the context and jurisprudence in these cases, I suggest that the way we ask the woman question of judging in post-colonial and war-affected jurisdictions such as Sri Lanka, must be revisited.

Given my focus in this chapter on women and judging, the discussion would be incomplete without an engagement on the jurisprudence that emerged out of the appointment and purported impeachment of the first woman justice of Sri Lanka's Supreme Court who was also the first woman justice of the court.[2] However, except for certain instances during the inquiry by the Parliamentary Select Committee into allegations made against the justice, there is no evidence to suggest she was targeted on the basis of her gender in the challenge to her appointment or during her purported impeachment. Although constitutional issues arising from the purported impeachment of the first woman chief justice was adjudicated upon in a series of cases, I have not included those cases in the analyses I undertake here (*Silva* v. *Bandaranayake* 1997; SC Reference March 2012, 2013; *Bandaranayake* v. *Speaker of Parliament* 2013; *Attorney General* v. *Bandaranayake* SC 2014; *Thenuwara* v. *Speaker of Parliament* 2014). The jurisprudence in those judgments did not concern any issues related to gender justice specifically. In her recently published memoir, the chief justice does not suggest that the litigation involved matters of gender justice (Bandaranayake 2019).

Part II: Law and Women in Sri Lanka

What conditions and realities warrant a focus on women's issues in Sri Lanka's laws and system of adjudication? In this Part, I offer an overview of the explicit and implicit legal barriers faced by women in Sri Lanka. This illustration is followed by a more specific discussion of women and the Sri Lankan judiciary.

The Positionality of Women

Kumari Jayawardena's assessment that women in Sri Lanka enjoy formal equality but not substantive equality remains an accurate description of contemporary Sri Lanka. In principle, women have equal access to education, health care and employment. Population indications for

---

[2] In this chapter I use the term 'judge' in the generic sense and the term 'justice' to refer to a judge of the appellate courts of Sri Lanka.

women in Sri Lanka are on par with those of developed states.[3] More women are enrolled at universities in Sri Lanka, particularly in arts, law and management (Department of Census and Statistics 2014).[4] Despite these developments, substantive equality remains elusive for Sri Lankan women. Women's participation in representative government has remained under 10 per cent throughout Sri Lanka's history of constitutional governance (Department of Census and Statistics 2014).[5] Religious institutions deny women equal participation in leadership. Women's participation in the labour force is only at 35.5 per cent (Department of Census and Statistics 2014, 72). Women workers are the majority in sectors that earn the highest amounts of foreign exchange in Sri Lanka's economy – the plantation sector, the garment sector and migrant workers (Kottegoda 2006). However, relative to other sectors, these are the sectors with the weakest protection for workers. These sectors have no specific legal or policy initiatives to empower women workers. Rather, women work under exploitative conditions and are compelled to live in communities that pose serious risks to their physical integrity due to the risk of harassment or violence and the threat to their dignity due to the lack of respect for substantive equality.

Sri Lanka's post-independence history has been marred by intermittent communal violence, an internal armed conflict and two armed insurrections (Wickramasinghe 2006). In 1971 and 1989 respectively, youth, mainly Sinhalese, attempted to overthrow the state. State responses to these insurrections included extrajudicial killings and enforced disappearances (Rogers et al. 1998). Discrimination against Tamils was used by the Liberation Tigers of Tamil Ealam (LTTE) to justify an armed separatist movement, which resulted in horrific violence for almost three decades on the island (Rogers et al. 1998; Uyangoda 2005). In 2009, it ended with the military defeat of the LTTE. Women

---

[3] Women make up 51.6% of the population in Sri Lanka. Women's life expectancy at birth is 76.4 years (compared to 71.7 years for men); 94.6% of women are literate (compared to 96.9% of men); and the maternal mortality rate is 22.3 per 1,000 live births. (*The Sri Lankan Women: Partner in Progress* Department of Census and Statistics 2014).

[4] Women make up 59.9% of undergraduates. The highest percentages of women are found in arts (79.3%), law (82.9%) and indigenous medicine (71.4%). Even in the fields of medicine (59.9%) and science (47%) women are well represented. (*The Sri Lankan Women: Partner in Progress* Department of Census and Statistics 2014).

[5] In 2014 only thirteen Members of Parliament out of 225 were women (5.8%) and only eighteen members of the Provincial Councils out of 455 were women (3.9%) (*The Sri Lankan Women: Partner in Progress* Department of Census and Statistics 2014).

were involved in the two insurrections and were active in the LTTE as well (de Alwis 2002). Today, former LTTE women combatants face challenges in reintegration and war-affected women with disabilities face challenges in rebuilding their lives. Many victim-survivors of conflict–related sexual violence, including women, have not had access to justice or to reparations and experience stigma (Satkunanathan 2019; Hyndman and de Alwis 2004). As women heads of household or as active members of social movements seeking justice, women carry heavy burdens and responsibilities (FOKUS Women 2015; de Alwis 2009).

Women before the Law

The position of women before the law in Sri Lanka is a paradox. Sex is identified specifically as a prohibited ground of discrimination (Art. 12 (2) of the Constitution). Moreover, the Constitution declares that the right to equality shall not 'prevent' laws or policies for 'the advancement of women' (Art. 12(4) of the Constitution). However, the chapter on fundamental rights guarantees also provides that all written or unwritten laws existing at the time of adopting the Constitution shall remain in force notwithstanding inconsistencies with the fundamental rights guar-antees (Art. 16(1) of the Constitution). Despite the constitutional guarantee of equality and non-discrimination, Sri Lanka's legal system continues to enforce certain laws that expressly discriminate against women or reinforce gender stereotypes. These include provisions in *Tesawalamai* and Muslim law also known as personal laws (Matrimonial Rights and Inheritance (Jaffna) Ordinance of 1911; Muslim Marriage and Divorce Act 1951); laws that recognise primogeni-ture in the grant of state land (Land Development Ordinance 1935); paid leave from work that is available only for the mother (Maternity Benefits Ordinance 1939); and the criminalisation of abortion (ss 303 – 307 of the Penal Code of 1833). Proposals for reforming these laws have not been successful so far. In addition to these formal barriers to equality, women encounter practical barriers as well, which I have identified elsewhere (de Mel and Samararatne 2017). Studying barriers to access to justice is challenging due to difficulties in accessing court records, and tracking the progress of cases is practically challenging due to laws delays (de Silva 2018).

The Constitution only permits judicial review of pre-enactment legislation (Art. 124 of the Constitution). Sri Lanka has ratified CEDAW and the First Optional Protocol and has consistently fulfilled its reporting obligations.[6] Enabling legislation that would give effect to CEDAW in domestic law is yet to be enacted although proposals have been made for reform (Goonesekere and Samararatne 2015, 166). Recent progressive law reforms for the advancement of women's rights include the introduction of a 25 per cent quota of seats for women in local government institutions; the enactment of legislation against domestic violence; and the guarantee of equal rights to pass on Sri Lankan citizenship.[7]

The Judicial Institution

Sri Lanka's legal system is crippled by laws delays. A Parliamentary Sectoral Oversight Committee found that on average it takes seventeen years for the conclusion of a criminal case (Eighth Parliament of the Democratic Socialist Republic of Sri Lanka 2017). Civil litigation is known to take longer. The determination of a fundamental rights petition can take two years or more (Samararatne 2017, 58). Access to justice is weak in Sri Lanka. The state-funded legal aid programme cannot meet the demand for legal aid and community-led initiatives for legal aid are minimal (Jayasundere 2016). Women have access to and are included in legal institutions. However, women are not visible in positions of leadership in the Bar (Samararatne 2020).

The aforementioned context has to be borne in mind in understanding the Sri Lankan judiciary as an institution and also in its contribution to the advancement of gender justice. Since its establishment in 1801, there have been no formal barriers for the appointment of women to Sri Lanka's judiciary except in the appointment of *Quazis*. Only Muslim men can be appointed as *Quazis* in Sri Lanka (S 12, Muslim Marriage and Divorce Act 1951). The prohibition on appointment of women as *Quazis* remains in place in Sri Lanka despite proposals for reform (Report of the Committee Appointed to Consider Amendments to the Muslim Marriage and Divorce Act 2017). *Quazi* courts adjudicate disputes under Muslim law related to marriage and divorce. In addition to the prohibition on women appointments as *Quazis*, legal representation too is expressly prohibited before *Quazi* courts. The Muslim Law Reforms Action Group is at the forefront of seeking reforms to these

[6] Sri Lanka ratified CEDAW 11 June 1980 and the Optional Protocol 15 October 2002.
[7] Local Authorities Elections (Amendment) Act No. 16 of 2017; Prevention of Domestic Violence Act No. 34 of 2005; Citizenship (Amendment) Act No. 35 of 2003.

provisions of Muslim law in Sri Lanka (Marsoof 2011; Muslim Personal Law Reforms Action Group). There are two pathways to judicial office in Sri Lanka – as a career judge or as a judge appointed directly to the appellate courts. The pathway of a career judge is open to attorneys-at-law who qualify through the open selection process. Under the 1978 Constitution, this process is mandated under the Judicial Service Commission which is headed by the chief justice and two other judges of the Supreme Court. The pathway of direct appointments to the appellate courts has remained parallel to this process. In 2001, a Constitutional Council was introduced through the Seventeenth Amendment to the Constitution. The Constitutional Council was mandated, among other things, to approve the nominations by the president to the office of chief justice, president of the Court of Appeal, to the appellate courts and to the membership of the Judicial Service Commission (Art. 41(c)(4) of the Constitution). The Seventeenth Amendment was not implemented after 2005. In 2010, the Constitutional Council was replaced with a Parliamentary Council which could only make 'recommendations' to the president. In 2015, a modified Constitutional Council was reintroduced by the Nineteenth Amendment (Samararatne 2016).

In keeping with global trends, women's inclusion in the Sri Lankan judiciary has been recent. The first woman judge was appointed to a High Court in 1988, to the Court of Appeal in 1998 and to the Supreme Court in 1996.[8] In 2010, the first woman chief justice was appointed. Data reveals that although more women than men are entering the legal profession today, the higher judiciary remains dominated by men.[9] For instance, in 2013, the percentage of women entering the legal profession was 68.5% and in 2017 it was 65%. In comparison, in 2017, only two justices of the Supreme Court (18.2%) were women, and only two judges in the Court of Appeal (16.7%) were women. The lower courts had a higher number of women judges in 2017 with eleven from the High Courts of Civil Appeal/High Courts/Provincial High Courts (13.6%); seventy-four in the District/Magistrates Courts (33%); and fourteen in

---

[8] Justice Shirani Tilakawardene was the first woman judge to be appointed to the High Court and to the Court of Appeal respectively. Justice Shirani Bandaranayake was the first woman judge to be appointed to the Supreme Court.

[9] Gender Statistics made available by the Department of Statistics of Sri Lanka. (www .statistics.gov.lk/GenderStatistics/StaticalInformation/WomenEmpowerment)

Labour Tribunals (42.4%). In 2017, the overall number of women members of the judiciary was 105 out of 468 (28.9%).

Sri Lanka has thus far had nine women justices in total in the appellate courts.[10] In 2016, in her preliminary observations and recommendations during her visit to Sri Lanka, the Special Rapporteur on the independence of judges and lawyers noted that, 'Women in Sri Lanka have reached the highest positions in the justice system. However, their number decreases as the hierarchy of the court increases.' She noted that 'Sri Lanka can envisage a plan for parity in the justice system favouring women's engagement in the justice system' (Special Rapporteur on the Independence of Judges and Lawyers 2016).

Sri Lanka's judicial institution has faced threats to its independence at different points in its more recent history. Confidence in the judiciary has been undermined at times due to internal challenges to judicial independence as well. The International Bar Association has documented some of these developments (International Bar Association 2013; 2009; 2001). The introduction of the Constitutional Council in 2001, and its reintroduction in 2015, has increased transparency in judicial appointments and thereby addressed some of these concerns (de Silva 2011).

Previous studies on the judicial mind in Sri Lanka include studies on minority rights, right to liberty and devolution (de Almeida Guneratne et al. 2014; Law and Society Trust 2017). These studies suggest that judicial protection of constitutional and legal rights was strong during certain periods such as the 1990s but weak during other times. The study of the judicial mind in Sri Lanka has been cautious and tempered by the law on contempt of court. The Constitution vests the Supreme Court with the jurisdiction to determine matters relating to contempt of court (Art. 105 (3) of the Constitution). Common law principles have been used in the absence of legislation. The lack of specificity in the law of contempt of court has resulted in self-censorship and caution in public discussion of the judiciary. Consequently, democratic responses to the

---

[10] The following women justices have been appointed to Sri Lanka's Supreme Court: Justice Shirani Bandaranayake (1996–2013, ceased office due to impeachment and was reinstated, and retired in 2015); Justice Shiranee Tilakawardene (2003–2014); Justice Chandra Ekanayake (2008–2016); Justice Eva Wanasundera (2012–2018); Justice Rohini Marasinghe (2013–2015); Justice Murdu Fernando (2018 to date). The following women justices have been appointed to the Court of Appeal: Justice Shirani Tilakawardene (1998–2003, also served as the president of the Court of Appeal); Justice Deepali Wijesundera 2011–2019); Justice Kumudini Wickremasinghe (2015 to date); and Justice Deepika Abeyratne (2019 to date).

work of the court are affected in some ways. More recently however, the court has recognised the value of reasonable debate and discussion on the work of the court, as indicated in Chief Justice Nalin Perera's address at his ceremonial welcome. The chief justice remarked that 'To criticize a judgement fairly or even fiercely is no crime. When such criticism is fair, reasonable and objective and directed to a judgement which is a public document or to a public act of a judge in duty, it would not constitute contempt. Given that judges are not perfect, a fair and reasonable criticism must be encouraged and would be a necessary right to be availed when needed' (Chief Justice Nalin Perera 2018).

It is within this context that I claim that asking the woman question of women judges, feminist judges or of judging in general is misleading. I develop this claim in the next section.

Part III: Judging and the Woman Question

What can we learn about judicial attitudes towards gender justice through cases in which gender justice has in fact been advanced? What difference, if any, can we see where the bench included women judges? I analyse the judgments thematically – right to equality and non-discrimination, rape and consent, statutory rape and sentencing and conflict related sexual violence – in seeking answers to these questions.

The Right to Equality and Non-discrimination

Jurisprudence on women's right to equality and non-discrimination emerged in Sri Lanka only in the last decade and is under-developed. I have demonstrated elsewhere that the right to equality jurisprudence in general in Sri Lanka is primarily an enforcement of common law principles of administrative law rather than a contribution to the development of the right to equality or non-discrimination itself (Samararatne 2018). Beyond that, the court has limited itself to upholding formal equality.

In Re Local Authorities Election Bill is a Special Determination issued by the Supreme Court in the exercise of its pre-enactment judicial review (In Re Local Authorities (Special Provisions) Bill and Local Authorities Elections (Amendment) Bill 2010). This bill proposed, among other things, that 25 per cent of a nomination list for elections to local authorities 'may' include women and youth. Several petitioners, including women's groups, argued that this proposal violated the right to equality on three grounds. First, it was argued that women and youth were two unequal groups and that designating them to one category was unreasonable. Second, it was argued that the proposed clause violated obligations under CEDAW as well as the Women's Charter of 1991. The third argument was that the provision for affirmative action (for women, children and disabled persons) could be used to justify a mandatory quota exclusive to women.

The court held that the proposed quota was a violation of the constitutional guarantee of the right to equality. Justice Bandaranayake, the first woman justice of the Supreme Court who subsequently went on to be the first woman chief justice, wrote the determination on behalf of the court. She held that the recognition of affirmative action could only be used by the state as a 'shield' and not as a 'weapon' (In Re Local Authorities (Special Provisions) Bill and Local Authorities Elections (Amendment) Bill 2010, 1329). On this basis the court declared that,

> In order to ensure equal treatment in elections, especially for the voter to choose the most suitable candidate, it would be essential to remove any unnecessary restrictions in order to have a meaningful exercise of franchise. Introduction of restrictive quotas would not be a meaningful step in the light of ensuring such franchise and also would not be a step taken to guarantee the right to equal protection in terms of Article 12 of the Constitution
>
> (In Re Local Authorities (Special Provisions) Bill and Local Authorities Elections (Amendment) Bill 2010, 1330).

The court did not recognise the historically established marginalisation of women from representative politics in Sri Lanka since the introduction of universal franchise. Nor does the court consider the use of affirmative action in comparable jurisdictions, such as India, as a measure for correcting a historic injustice. The court narrows the applicability of Art. 12(4) to exceptional circumstances and does not respond to the argument made by the petitions about the unreasonableness of grouping together youth and women. In contrast, in 2016 when a mandatory quota was introduced for women in Local Government Authorities, the quota was not challenged before the Supreme Court nor did the court make any observations regarding its constitutionality (Decisions of the Supreme Court on Parliamentary Bills 2018, 13).[11] In 2018, in the first elections to

---

[11] Decisions of the Supreme Court on Parliamentary Bills, Vol XIII, 2016–2017 (July 2018) 13.

the local authorities since the introduction of the quota, the 25 per cent quota was in fact filled.

The case of *Manohari Pelaketiya* v. *Secy Min of Education* is the only case in which Sri Lanka's Supreme Court adopted an interpretation of the right to equality that promotes gender justice (*Manohari Pelaketiya* v. *Secy Min of Education* 2016). This case was also the first time the Supreme Court referred to the CEDAW. The judicial bench did not include any women justices. In this case, the court declared that sexual harassment was a violation of the right to equality for women. A schoolteacher at a state-funded school who had been subjected to sexual harassment by the school principal and another teacher made this petition to court. The court described the conduct complained of as 'oppressive and burdensome' (*Manohari Pelaketiya* v. *Secy Min of Education* 2016, 16). The teacher's complaints to the teacher in charge of discipline, to the Department of Education, the Teacher's Union and to the police were of no avail. The teacher eventually briefed the media about her harassment. The Department of Education argued that the teacher had violated the Establishment Code by speaking to the media and further noted that the department had presented a charge sheet against the respondent school teacher and principal and had recommended that they be sent on compulsory retirement. The court however held that the petitioner's exercise of her freedom of expression was reasonable and that 'the freedom of expression ... of sufferings and harm done to her by a few public servants is normal and natural even if she has made a mistake by acting contrary to the Establishments Code' (*Manohari Pelaketiya* v. *Secy Min of Education* 2016, 13). The principal and the teacher were ordered by the Court to pay the petitioner Rs 100,000 each as compensation.

In this case, the court recognised in clear and unequivocal language the physical, emotional and psychological harm caused to the teacher due to the sexual harassment that she experienced.

> I observe that continuous abuse and sexual harassment over a period of time would cause physical and mental damage to any human being. It is not possible for a female to resist such abuses unless she is a strong personality who could react and retort to such abuses and harassment and make the abuser to shamelessly withdraw, being exposed to the public at large of his indecency. Continuous threats and abuses could also make a person unwell both physically and mentally. My views expressed on the aspect of abuses would be endorsed by any law-abiding citizen, and it should be so
>
> (*Manohari Pelaketiya* v. *Secy Min of Education* 2016: 13).

These two cases lent themselves to adjudication on fundamental questions about constitutional interpretation and women's rights to equality. The bench which included the first woman justice of the Supreme Court took a narrow view, while a bench which did not include a woman justice adopted an interpretation that promoted women's rights in clear and definitive terms.[12] The contrasting approaches in these two cases highlight that it is not possible to draw a correlation between presence of a woman judge and the advancement of gender justice.

Rape and Consent

In a study of rape cases in Sri Lanka, it was noted that 'gender-based stereotypes and constructed social norms are invoked in judicial decisions as a discursive practice' (Abeywardena 2016, 41). The case that I assess here (which includes three judgments in total) affirms this finding. *Addararachchi* v. *the State* is a well-known case in which the judicial interpretation of consent by a sixteen-year-old girl to sexual intercourse became the subject of public debate (Pinto-Jayawardena and Anantarajah 2016, 61). The High Court accepted the complainant's account, and this contrasts with the approach of the Court of Appeal and of the Supreme Court, which rejected the complainant's account as unreliable. The incident took place in August 1993 and the final appeal was heard in May 2002. This case provides several insights into women in judging. The judge of the High Court was the first woman High Court judge in Sri Lanka. She had also been the first woman state counsel in Sri Lanka. The first woman judge of the High Court has, in her public engagements, been outspoken on women's rights and on the need to advance women's justice. In the Supreme Court, the first woman justice of the Supreme Court was a member of the bench that heard the final appeal in this case. The appellate courts disagreed with the High Court on three different aspects, providing us rich evidence for an assessment of questions about feminist adjudication.

First, the Supreme Court and the Court of Appeal disagreed with the approach taken in the High Court to the interpretation of evidence on the question of consent. The High Court noted

---

[12] The Supreme Court may include nine to eleven judges (Art. 120 of the Constitution). Cases are generally heard by a bench of three judges.

In order to give meaningful effect to women's right to control their own bodies, we must recognize that awareness of, or recklessness or wilful blindness to and absence of communicated consent is sufficient to [sic] found the mens rea of the offense of sexual assault

(Addararatchi v. the Republic 1997, 16).

In contrast, the Court of Appeal relied upon its perceptions of what was 'normal' and 'appropriate' behaviour for women in Sri Lankan society.

The fact that the prosecutrix went into the room of this unknown house with the accused-appellant in the dead of the night, without making any fuss, makes her version that she was an unwilling party to sexual intercourse highly improbable, having regard to the normal conduct and behaviour patterns of women and girls in Sri Lankan society. It is common sense that both of them went into this room for sensual enjoyment. Therefore when the prosecutrix says that accused-appellant had sexual intercourse with her against her will or without her consent, her story becomes unacceptable

(Addararachchi v. the State 2000, 406).

The Supreme Court noted that corroboration is not essential as a general rule and that 'In the Asian set-up refusal to act on the evidence of a victim of sexual assault in the absence of corroboration as a rule is adding insult to injury' (*Gallage v. Addarararchchi* 2002, 313). Nevertheless, in the present case, taking into account that two days passed before the complainant spoke about the incident, the court held that it could not 'disagree' with the finding of her unreliability by the Court of Appeal (*Gallage v. Addarararchchi* 2002, 314).

Second, the appellate courts also disagreed with the procedure adopted by the High Court in conducting the trial. The judge of the High Court postponed the trial by a day to allow a more senior state counsel to lead the evidence of the prosecutrix 'in spite of the patent discomfiture, embarrassment and shyness displayed by the prosecutrix' (*Addararatchi v. the Republic* 1997, 2). The appellate courts take issue with the manner in which evidence was led at trial. The Court of Appeal noted that,

holding the trial in camera was unnecessary for the reason that the prosecutrix had earlier given the same evidence in a crowded Court house before the Magistrate ... No Court should try to molly-coddle a witness as has happened in this case. The result could be very dangerous in that the prosecutrix would have got wrong signals to lie in Court

(Addararachchi v. the State 2000, 415).

The Supreme Court agreed with this observation (*Gallage v. Addararachchi* 2002, 315).

Third, the Court of Appeal rejected the interpretation of gender equality by the High Court. The Supreme Court made no mention of gender equality. The High Court made strong observations on the danger of stereotyping of women and upheld substantive gender equality.

> To say that a particular presence of a woman at a particular place, or attired in a particular manner provoked a man to lose control to act in a sexually violent manner, would be to give a license to the use of force and give rise to oppression of women and lead to a situation that was discriminatory and biased against women. This would lead to inequality and inequality leads to injustice ... The law precludes men from oppressing women, based on their physical strength alone
>
> (*Addararatchi v. the Republic* 1997, 16).

The Court further noted that,

> Especially as it has been perceived that this discrimination leads to oppressive behavioural patterns against women and this leads to violence against women both physically and sexually. That is why the law must veer away from stereotype thinking, and instead decide on the basis that all men and women have the fundamental right to be treated equally, as equal individuals, exercising equal rights
>
> (*Addararatchi v. the Republic* 1997, 22–23).

In contrast, the Court of Appeal, in holding that the High Court judge had overlooked material contradictions in the evidence before her, observed that 'Further on a reading of the judgement it would appear that the learned trial Judge had been misled and dazzled by some wrong notion of gender inequality' (*Addararachchi v. the State* 2000, 411).

In this case, in the High Court and in the Supreme Court respectively, two pioneering women justices of Sri Lanka applied their judicial minds to this case. The contrast in the approaches between the two courts to the evidence before them, suggest that a self-identified feminist woman judge can be a determining factor for gender justice. However, it illustrates how the overall outcome in the case was shaped by entrenched stereotypical norms that are enforced through the system of adjudication – in this case, judicial precedent. In such a context the presence of a woman justice alone (whether at High Court or the Supreme Court) does not necessarily advance gender justice in judicial decision-making.

Statutory Rape and Sentencing

The jurisprudence on rape reveals the challenges in advancing gender justice for women in terms of what constitutes consent to sexual intercourse. In contrast, jurisprudence on statutory rape reveals the challenges that arise when the need to establish consent to sexual intercourse is eliminated by law. In 1995, Sri Lanka revised the definition of statutory rape by increasing the age of consent up to sixteen years old and by introducing a mandatory minimum sentence of ten years (Section 364 (2)(e) of the Penal Code 1833). However, several issues have arisen in the implementation of this provision. Post-1995 it was perceived that this provision was misapplied to punish boys and men who were the partners of sexually active girls under the age of sixteen. To date, this remains an open question since the sexual activities of teenagers is understudied and socially is a matter of taboo.

In 2008, the High Court of the North Central Province referred a question to the Supreme Court on the mandatory minimum sentence to statutory rape (Art. 125(1) of the Constitution). The High Court queried whether the amendment of 1995 'had removed the judicial discretion when sentencing an accused' (SC HC Reference 2008). In making a determination on the reference, the Supreme Court held that the minimum mandatory sentence was unconstitutional as it violated the right to be free from torture and the right to equality. The court's reasoning was that the mandatory minimum sentence,

> resulted in legislative determination of punishment and a corresponding erosion of a judicial discretion and a general determination, in advance, of the appropriate punishment, without a consideration of relevant factors which proper sentencing policy should not ignore; such as the offender, and his age and antecedents, the offence and its circumstances (extenuating or otherwise), the need for deterrence, and the likelihood of reform and rehabilitation
>
> (SC HC Reference 03 of 2008, 7).

The court went on to observe that while a woman's consent is 'immaterial' in making a finding of guilt in statutory rape, it is relevant in the exercise of judicial discretion in sentencing. The High Court judge had identified the following reasons why judicial discretion ought to be exercised in sentencing in statutory rape: (1) Because it is common for girls under sixteen to be involved in love affairs; (2) because 'the imposition of a long custodial sentence would mean that the family life of the first accused would now be disrupted'; and (3) because such a sentence 'would not benefit the complainant'. The High Court judge further notes that 'the imposition of a minimum mandatory sentence for an offence committed consequent to a love affair between two persons in their youth is against her conscience' (SC HC Reference 03 of 2008, 4). The Supreme Court agreed with the High Court's observation that the lack of evidence in the medical report of 'the use of force' is evidence that sexual intercourse was 'consensual' (SC HC Reference 03 of 2008, 3).

In effect, the court engaged in judicial review of legislation, despite the fact it is expressly prohibited under the Constitution. Moreover, a study carried out in 2012 revealed that lower courts have since then relied on this judgment to issue suspended sentences to persons pleading guilty of statutory rape (Lawyers for Human Rights and Development 2012). Pinto-Jayawardena and Anantharajah note that 'These figures are tremendously problematic and reveal a significant judicial contribution to the climate of impunity for sexual violence' and that '[j]udicial leniency displayed towards the perpetrators is another aspect of the problem' (Pinto Jayawardena and Anantharajah 2016, 100–101). A case in point is *AG v. Sampath* (2015). A man (age not specified in the judgment) pleaded guilty to the charge of statutory rape. The victim was his wife's sister, fifteen years old at the time she became pregnant due to sexual intercourse with him. The High Court issued a suspended sentence which was reversed in the Court of Appeal. When the matter came up in appeal to the Supreme Court, the sentence was revised to a suspended sentence. Justice Eva Wanasundera, who was the first woman Attorney General in Sri Lanka and subsequently appointed to the Supreme Court, writing for the court, reasoned that the court must uphold the best interests of the child born to the victim. Court recalled that it was the upper guardian of the child and noted that,

> [t]he girl child of 10 years at present will not get the love and affection, care and support of the father to whom she looks up to at present and would not ever understand the concept of the State punishing him for 'statutory rape' committed on her mother, for which the girl is made to suffer for no wrong committed by her at any time her life, during her prime childhood which is included in the 10 years of rigorous imprisonment i.e. until she is 20 years of age. This fact is a matter of grave concern of this Court as 'the Court is the upper guardian of any child on earth'
>
> (*AG v. Sampath* 2015, 6).

However, the court does not explain why it does not exercise this same guardianship over the victim of statutory rape, who was a child herself at the time of the incident, and had to drop out of school due to the pregnancy. The court does not debate or even apply its mind to whether or not the victim had consented to sexual intercourse with the accused. The court remarks that the victim had not complained to the police. It was a neighbour who had been suspicious and made a complaint. In making this observation, the court does not seem to consider the related facts. The victim was the sister of the wife of the accused. Her parents had invited him to stay in their home as the sister had travelled overseas for employment. On the victim becoming pregnant, the parents had moved her to another village. These facts do not lead to the conclusion that the victim had consented to sexual intercourse. The facts do suggest however that she was under the control of her parents.

This jurisprudence on statutory rape suggests that legislative reform that was intended to advance gender justice has been subverted through the exercise of judicial discretion in sentencing. The jurisprudence reflects consensus across the different levels of judicial decision-making. The exercise of judicial discretion privileges perceptions about subsequent developments such as marriage (either between the victim and the perpetrator or to others), the welfare of the child born due to the incident and the absence of medical evidence of violence. Where the legislature has removed the burden of establishing the lack of consent, the exercise of judicial discretion in sentencing has reintroduced patriarchal norms to mitigate or suspend the enforcement of the law. These developments point to the ways in which a system of adjudication can produce outcomes that undermine gender justice to victims of sexual violence.

Conflict-Related Sexual Violence

The challenges in Sri Lanka in bridging the gap between the incidence of conflict-related sexual violence and investigation and prosecution of offenders is well documented (Jayawardena and Pinto-Jayawardena 2016: OHCHR 2015). I examine here two well-known examples of successful prosecution and a third example of a prosecution that was overturned in the Court of Appeal. The analysis highlights the ways in which courts have maintained silence regarding the impact of armed conflict, gender and ethnicity on victims of sexual violence, even where they have advanced gender justice.

In the case of *Yogalingam Vijitha* v. *Wijesekera* (2001), perhaps for the first time, the Supreme Court held that sexual violence constitutes torture, which is prohibited under the Constitution (Art. 11 of the

Constitution). A twenty-seven-year-old Tamil woman was arrested and detained arbitrarily and subjected to horrific forms of torture by the police. The Supreme Court upheld her petition and ordered the payment of compensation and ordered further that criminal proceedings be instituted against the police officers who were held responsible by court. The gruesome practices of torture recorded in this judgment are part of a consistent finding of the Sri Lankan Supreme Court of torture of men and women under police custody (Munasinghe and Celermajer 2017).

In this instance, the gender dynamics of the facts are striking. Yogalingam Vijitha was a volunteer teacher, twice displaced due to the war. Her aunt had arranged for her to be married to a Tamil man living in the south of the island. Subsequent to the registration of the marriage but before the customary ceremony, Yogalingam Vijitha had reason to believe that her legal husband was already married. She refused to go through with the customary ceremony and relocated to Trincomalee to avoid her husband. He threatened to have her arrested on trumped up charges through his 'connections' with the police. Subsequently she was arrested and held in remand custody during which period she was subjected to horrific forms of torture.[13] The court's findings in this case reveal the way in which gender, ethnicity and perhaps even poverty compound a woman's vulnerability before the law. The court noted that,

> The acts of torture meted out to her as set out above has affected her physically and psychologically and her matrimonial prospects had been shattered as a result of the mental and physical trauma that she had undergone at the hands of the police. She states that she is suffering from depression, loss of sleep, loss of appetite, loss of concentration, fear and nervousness
>
> (*Yogalingam Vijitha* v. *Wijesekera* 2001).

The court cites *Silva* v. *Kodithuwakku* and noted that 'Such methods can only be described as barbaric, savage and inhuman. They are most revolting and offend one's sense of human decency and dignity particularly at the present time when every endeavour is being made to promote and protect human rights' (*Yogalingam Vijitha* v. *Wijesekera* 2001). In its judicial reasoning however, the court chose to base its findings

---

[13] The forms of torture include covering her face with a plastic bag which had chilli powder mixed in petrol; forcing her to remove all her clothes except her underwear; being held down on a table by four policeman while four others pricked under her fingernails and toenails with paper pins; and being assaulted with a club while hung.

exclusively on the report of the Judicial Medical Officer. Such heavy reliance on the medical report can be problematic. Where the victim cannot support her claim with medical evidence, the court has been reluctant to recognise that the right to be free from torture has been violated (Samararatne 2014, 53). A similar issue arises in establishing rape where there is no medical evidence to establish physical violence as noted in the *Addararachchi* case.

The *Rajapakse v. Attorney General* case, more commonly known as the 'Krishanthy Kumaraswamy rape case' (named after the murdered rape victim), is one of the few cases in which criminal prosecution for conflict-related sexual violence was concluded successfully (*Somaratne Rajapakse v. Attorney General* 2010). An eighteen-year-old school girl returning home from school in Jaffna was arbitrarily detained at an Army check-point and subjected to gang rape and murdered in a bunker. Her mother, brother and neighbour who went looking for her were also murdered at the same checkpoint. Speaking at an interview, the female state counsel in the case noted that investigations were bolstered by the fact that it received strong support from the president at the time, who happened to be the first woman president in Sri Lanka (Kodikara 2016, 406).[14] Coincidentally, the final judgment on this case was issued by Justice Bandaranayake, the first woman justice of the Supreme Court who subsequently went on to be the first woman chief justice in Sri Lanka.

In discussing this case more recently, the former state counsel notes that the Tamil witnesses had been reluctant to participate in the trial as 'they felt it was a farce' (Kodikara 2016, 421). She recalls how they ran a story in the Tamil newspapers about the trial-at-bar held in Colombo, stating that 'The judges and the prosecutors were all Sinhalese, and they were ready for the trial but civilian witnesses who were Tamil were not cooperating' (Kodikara 2016, 421). The witnesses had then come forward to give evidence. The former counsel notes that 'victims were Tamil; accused were Sinhalese; prosecutors were Sinhalese' (Kodikara 2016, 421).

---

[14] President Chandrika Bandaranaike was the first (and only) woman president in Sri Lanka and the fourth woman president globally. Her mother, Sirimavo Bandaranaike, was the first woman prime minister of Sri Lanka and in the world. I would add that these achievements are not necessarily examples of women's advancement. Prime Minister Bandaranaike entered politics after the assassination of her husband Prime Minister SWRD Bandaranaike. In Sri Lanka and in South Asia, wives and daughters of prominent male politicians have been elected into power following the death or retirement of the male politician, thereby reflecting the patriarchal and feudal nature of representative politics in the region.

She reports how she was harassed during that time and she notes that 'Even though the climate was conducive for that kind of prosecution you did find a large number of such people who are racist' (Kodikara 2016, 422). The judgment on appeal, written by Justice Bandaranayake, upholds the conviction and rejects the grounds of appeal raised by the accused. The reference to the victims is minimal. There is no reference to the armed conflict and the serious implications of this crime in that context. For instance, the court observes that 'Krishanthi had been described as an intelligent student' (*Somaratne Rajapakse* v. *Attorney General* 2010, 121). The court maintains silence on the significance of this conviction.

Subhasinghe v. *Attorney General*, more commonly known as the Vishvamadu rape case (named after the location of the incident), is a case where in 2015 the Jaffna High Court convicted four army personnel of gang rape of a woman. An older woman, her daughter and the prosecutrix and her two children, had temporarily returned to Vishvamadu, to clear their land and prepare for resettlement. They had been displaced due to the war and were planning to return. During that time, at night, five army personnel came to their home and forced the two younger women to come out. The prosecutrix was subjected to gang rape. The other woman was asked to strip and was spared only because she was menstruating at the time. On the night of the incident itself, the older woman reported this matter to an army camp nearby. In convicting four of the five army personnel, the High Court of Jaffna noted the horrific nature of the crime. In imposing twenty-five years imprisonment and fines (for the default of which a further five years was imposed), the court took account of the gravity of the crime and referred to the reforms of the Penal Code in 1995 in line with Sri Lanka's obligations under CEDAW, and also noted that rape has been recognised as a war crime under the statute of the International Criminal Court and before the International Criminal Tribunal for the former Yugoslavia (ICTY) and the International Criminal Tribunal for Rwanda (ICTR). This case attracted national and international attention. A national newspaper reported that the conviction was 'due to the extraordinary bravery and persistence of the women at the centre of the trial who persisted in the face of direct threats and intimidation. This ranged from being asked to destroy evidence of the rape very early on to being offered bribes to "stay quiet" to being subjected to a second ordeal in court when they were asked the most searching questions in relation to their trauma' (Pinto Jayawardena 2017).

In 2019, the accused were acquitted by the Court of Appeal. Justice KK Wickremesinghe, a woman judge, writing on behalf of the Court of Appeal noted that the lower court 'has not considered the infirmities of the identification and not given his mind in considering the evidence and therefore it will not be safe to act on the evidence available' (*Subasinghe* v. *Attorney General* 2019, 4). Therefore, the court concluded that it is 'an [sic] unsafe to sustain the conviction based on the evidence available' (*Subasinghe* v. *Attorney General* 2019, 4). The acquittal is brief and provides no other reasons and fails to refer to specific legislative provisions. It does not recall the incident in any form or recognise its broader context.

The successful outcomes in the *Yogalingam Vijitha* case and in the *Krishanthy Kumaraswamy* case point to contingencies that advance gender justice. In the *Yogalingam Vijitha* case, her medical record was strong, and she had access to legal aid. In the *Krishanthy Kumaraswamy* case, investigation and prosecution was supported through political will. Even then, in both cases, the harm to the victims, and how their vulnerability to sexual violence is compounded due to their ethnicity and gender, was not recognised by court. The presence or the absence of a woman justice did not make a difference in this regard. Some of this harm was recognised in the High Court judgment of the *Vishvamadu* case but in the acquittal by the Court of Appeal there is no mention of it.

Part IV: Adjudication and Gender Justice

In light of the jurisprudence analysed in Part III, what are the implications of asking the woman question of judicial decision-making? My assessment leads me to the following findings: (1) it affirms that the gender of judges is not necessarily a determining factor in the advancement of gender justice; (2) that the exercise of judicial discretion often reflects stereotypical perceptions about gender and therefore affirms patriarchy; (3) that in general Sri Lankan jurisprudence provides minimal recognition to the impact of discrimination and violence experienced by women; and (4) that laws delays have the effect of denying gender justice.

Women Justices and Judging

In the cases analysed in Part II, it was evident that women justices in Sri Lanka have not necessarily made a 'feminist' contribution to jurisprudence. With the exception of the judgment of the High Court in the *Kamal Addararachchi* case and to some extent in the *Vishwamadu* case, courts confine themselves to formal and gender-neutral reasoning. Even the gender-sensitivity demonstrated by the High Court in the *Kamal Addararachchi* case was rejected by the appellate courts and the High Court judge was reprimanded by both the Court of Appeal and the Supreme Court. These cases therefore affirm the view that the presence of women justices does not necessarily further gender justice. The *Kamal Addararachchi* case suggests that even where a woman justice attempts to advance a gender-sensitive approach its impact can be limited by the other courts which do not share that view.

The cases also show that medical evidence is essential in establishing the lack of consent in cases of rape and in sentencing for statutory rape. The standard of proof beyond reasonable doubt, including the credibility of a woman witness can be difficult to establish in a wider social context in which women do not enjoy substantive equality. In contrast, in the exercise of pre-enactment judicial review of bills, the court did not apply its mind to statistics or research studies in forming its opinion on the constitutional validity of a quota for women. Rather, the court adopted a narrow and formal interpretation of the right to equality, denying affirmative action that is mandated by the Constitution.

In the *Manohari Pelaketiya* case the court did advance gender justice. In the determination of fundamental rights, the standard of proof is one of a balance of probability. The credibility of the victim was not questioned by the court. Notably, this case was decided by a bench that did not include a woman justice.

Feminist Consciousness and Judicial Discretion

Manohari Pelaketiya v. Secy Min of Education is perhaps the only example of jurisprudence that upholds women's right to equality and non-discrimination in Sri Lanka. The case is an example of the feminist approach to adjudication that I explained in Part I. Regardless of whether women justices were involved, the judicial determination advanced gender justice. The jurisprudence included women in the construction of legal rules (in this case the right to equality), challenged gender bias, contextualised its reasoning, provided a remedy and upheld substantive equality. By rejecting the argument by the respondents that the complainant violated the Establishment Code by speaking to the media, the court demonstrated responsiveness to cultural and political considerations.

The court affirmed 'the constitutional imperative of giving due recognition to womenfolk resulting in equality and non-discrimination among sexes' (*Manohari Pelaketiya* v. *Secy Min of Education* 2016, 15–16). Justice Gooneratne, writing on behalf of the court, further noted that 'Sri Lanka boasts of both constitutional as well as international obligations to ensure equity and gender-neutral equality which this Court cannot simply ignore' (*Manohari Pelaketiya* v. *Secy Min of Education* 2016, 15). The feminist consciousness demonstrated in this judgment is a sharp contrast to the judicial approach in the Special Determination on the Local Government (Elections) Bill, *Sampath* v. *Attorney General* and the *Kamal Addararachchi* case.

In contrast, the other cases that I discuss reflect stereotypical gender norms and patriarchal values. This finding affirms previous findings about 'structural inequity' that women encounter before the law and in seeking remedies through the courts. Pinto-Jayawardena and Anantharajah for instance note that 'The experience of victims of sexual violence has largely been one of disappointment, where the law has served to consolidate the privileged, patriarchal position of men. This broader structural inequity leaves women without means of legitimate redress' (Pinto-Jayawardena and Kirsty Anantharajah 2016, 96). They argue that this structural inequity is evident in jurisprudence as well. Pinto-Jayawardena and Anantharajah point out how 'anti-feminist mythology' is promoted not only by lawyers in certain instances but also in jurisprudence (Pinto-Jayawardena and Kirsty Anantharajah 2016, 96). They note that 'Sri Lankan jurisprudence has exhibited this insidious message from a more elevated and socially influential platform: the judicial bench. This rhetoric and judicial attitude can be linked to the strengthening of harmful societal notions, promoting a culture of inequality and marginalizing victims of sexual violence and Sri Lankan women more generally' (Pinto-Jayawardena and Kirsty Anantarajah 2016, 96). These normative gaps, or 'effects of this mythology' as Pinto-Jaywardena and Anantharajah describe them also emanate 'from the respected forum of the courtroom' and have the effect of entrenchment of 'harmful societal attitudes towards rape victims, and women, more generally' (Pinto-Jayawardena and Kirsty Anantharajah 2016, 99).

A Legacy of Silence and Delay?

Harm to women and to the cause of gender justice is caused by silence and non-recognition of gender justice in the jurisprudence as well as by laws delays. In *Search for Justice: The Sri Lanka Papers* Pinto-Jaywardena and Anantharajah discuss the idea of the 'weight of silence' in relation to the subject of sex in Sri Lanka. I would extend this 'weight of silence' to Sri Lanka's jurisprudence on issues of gender justice. Pinto-Jayawardena and Anantharajah note that,

> A culture of silence exists with regard to sex in Sri Lanka - violent or otherwise. It mirrors and compounds another culture of silence - that [sic] exercised by communities when human rights are violated . . . It is the result of years of violence, abuse of power by those in control, and impunity that has often left Sri Lankan citizens feeling unprotected and subject to reprisals if they dare to speak about abuse
>
> (Pinto-Jayawardena and Kirsty Anantarajah 2016, xxiii).

In this context, they ask the question 'Can a truth and justice process be socially transformative, reducing the need or desire for silence?' (Pinto-Jayawardena and Kirsty Anantharajah 2016, xxiv).

The cases discussed in this chapter are examples of the silence and non-recognition of the gendered nature of discrimination and of violence in the human experiences that were adjudicated upon in court. In the *Krishanthy Kumaraswamy* case, the Supreme Court maintained silence over the fact that the crimes were committed against civilians in the context of an internal armed conflict, that it had serious implications for discrimination and violence based on ethnicity and the gruesome nature of the gang rape. In the Special Determination on Local Government (Elections) Bill, the court did not even acknowledge the historic lack of representation of women in representative politics in Sri Lanka. Similarly, in *Sampath* v. *Attorney General* the court is silent and even indifferent to the victim of statutory rape and the way in which the incident interrupted the victim's life. In the *Kamal Addararachchi* case, the three courts approached the question of the recognition of the mental and psychological harm differently. The High Court noted the difficulties that the complainant would have in leading evidence in open court 'specially when such testimony had to be unfolded in the presence of several members of the opposite sex, more importantly in the presence of the alleged perpetrator of the offence' (*Addararatchi* v. *the Republic* 1997, 3). The court takes cognisance of the complainant's age and her social circumstances and the how the trauma of her experience affects her ability to recall specific details during the trial (*Addararatchi* v. *the Republic* 1997, 11). The Court of Appeal however notes that the point about 'post-traumatic experience' was referred to by the senior state counsel in his written submissions but that such evidence had not been led by a medical witness during the trial. On that basis the Court of Appeal held that the High Court had used 'inadmissible evidence in coming to an adverse finding' (*Addararachchi* v. *the State* 2000, 419). The complainant's first recall of the incident was to a matron at a police station, on her second night at the police station. The High Court relied on this recall as corroboration of the incidence, while the Court of Appeal rejected the witness as inadmissible and hearsay (*Addararachchi* v. *the State* 2000, 414).

The silence and non-recognition in Sri Lanka's jurisprudence is compounded by the inordinate laws delays experienced. On the question of delays, *Search for Justice: The Sri Lanka Papers* notes that delay can 'ultimately thwart justice altogether as witnesses forget details, succumb to intimidation, age, ill health or simply give up. As those injustices pile up, faith in the system inevitably diminishes' (Jayawardena and Kishali Pinto-Jayawardena 2016, xliv). In *Manohari Pelaketiya* v. *Secy Min of Education* the schoolteacher experienced sexual harassment from 2007 and filed a fundamental rights petition in 2012. The judgment in her favour was issued in 2016. It took her nine years to vindicate herself since her first experience of sexual harassment. Similarly, in the *Kamal Addararachchi* case, the incident took place in 1993, the judgment of the High Court was issued in December 1997. The Court of Appeal judgment was issued December 2000 and the final judgment on appeal was issued by the Supreme Court in May 2002. The litigation took nine years. The statutory rape in *Sampath* v. *Attorney General* took place in August 2003, the High Court trial commenced October 2008 and the Court of Appeal judgment was issued July 2012. The final judgment was issued March 2015, thirteen years after the incident. As noted by court, the baby born to the victim is more than ten years of age by this time. In the *Vishwamadu* case, the gang rape was in 2010, the conviction by the High Court was in 2015 and the acquittal by the Court of Appeal was in 2019, a total of nine years.

The timeframe of these cases reveals that women victims of discrimination and/or violence experience drawn-out litigation in which the court is silent, denies or fails to recognise gender injustice. These experiences require that an inquiry into women and judging in contexts such as that of Sri Lanka adopt a broader frame of analysis that goes beyond the individual judges adjudicating upon cases.

Remedies and Beyond

The outcomes in these cases including the remedies that were provided raises several further questions which I do not engage with in this chapter. In Sri Lanka, torture and sexual harassment are penal offences (S 345 Penal Code 1833: Convention against Torture Act 1994). Did the Attorney General's Department prosecute the respondents in the *Yogalingam Vijitha* case and in the *Pelaketiya* case? In the *Yogalingam Vijitha* case, the Supreme Court made a specific directive to that effect. As a High Court is not a court of record, information on subsequent prosecution, if any, is not easy to retrieve. Equally importantly, what institutional changes followed the successful outcomes in these cases? What steps, if any, did the Department of Police or the Department of Education take to prevent recurrence?

Writing about the SC verdict in the *Addararachchi* case, a newspaper column ends with the observation that 'none of the courts that heard the case appear to have commented on the evidence that emerged of the serious neglect of a young girl by the adults who ought to have been responsible for her – her divorced parents and the aunt with whom she was residing' (*The Island* 2002). As the High Court noted, the prosecutrix was seventeen years old at the time of the incident with no immediate family that would support or care for her. How did the long drawn-out court proceedings, in which her account of the incident was rejected, impact her and her life in society? In the *Pelaketiya* case, how was the teacher's professional and personal life impacted by the litigation and her success in court? In the *Vishvamadu* case, only the identity of the accused was disputed and not the actual incident itself. What does gender justice look like for the women in that case in light of the recent acquittal by the Court of Appeal?

A significant point to note here is that judgments issued by the Court of Appeal and the Supreme Court are issued in English and proceedings are also in English. How many of these litigants had these judgments read and/or explained to them? How did they feel about the judicial adjudication of their constitutional rights and legal rights being carried out in a language other than their first language (which would be Sinhala or Tamil)? These questions about remedies and the impact of litigation beyond the adjudication process affirm my claim and concern about judging and gender justice in the context of the Global South. It requires a study of the system of adjudication that goes beyond the assessment of the role of individual judges, and ought to include legal institutions, the law and the legal culture within which adjudication takes place.

What Makes a Difference? Reframing Feminist Imperatives

We will not have feminist judges or feminist adjudication until we have
the opportunity to redesign the forums in which we want those people to
participate as well

(Graycar 2013, 455)

The jurisprudence that I have discussed in this chapter reflects Kumari
Jaywardena's claims about the absence of a feminist consciousness in Sri
Lanka. Her arguments regarding the entrenchment of nationalism and
cultural notions in Sri Lankan life offers, at least in part, one explanation.
The cases that I have examined establish that Sri Lanka's jurisprudence
on women's right to equality, and in relation to the rape, statutory rape
and conflict-related violence, fails to adequately recognise issues of
gender justice. Even where the litigation advances gender justice, the
impact that criminal conduct has on women often goes unrecognised.
Stereotypical understandings of a woman used in evaluating the evidence
of the complainant in the *Kamal Addararachchi* case, the priority given
in *Sampath* v. *Attorney General* to a notion of 'fatherhood' of the child
born in the case of statutory rape where the mother herself was a child
when she was raped, illustrates the way in which Kumari Jaywardena's
arguments can be extended to judging and jurisprudence.

Sri Lanka's experience is a reminder that judging ought to be interpreted in context. The Sri Lankan context is one of patriarchy, ethnic
overdetermination, executive overreach and politicisation of public institutions and of concerns of corruption. Progressive law reform and the
strengthening of the rule of law has been the exception rather than the
norm. The system of adjudication lacks witness protection even though
relevant legislation has been adopted (Pinto-Jayawardena and
Anantarajah 2016, 71ff). The mandate and office of the Attorney
General is in question due to questions regarding the impartiality of
the Department (Pinto-Jayawardena and Anantarajah 2016, 90ff).
Allegations of politicisation, corruption and militarisation have undermined law enforcement by the police (Pinto-Jayawardena and
Anantarajah 2016, 102 onwards). Consequently, victims of gender injustice face serious challenges in seeking justice and remedies in bringing
their grievances to court.

Therefore, the woman question *in judging* ought to be framed as a
question of *feminist adjudication*. Legal institutions and the law reflect
structural issues that constrain gender justice and operate with a legal
and political culture that is shaped and informed by ethno-nationalism

and patriarchy. These issues must be acknowledged and addressed in explaining the challenges experienced in seeking gender justice in the Global South. This broader perspective would include an appreciation for institutional reform, policy interventions, law reform and constitutional reform as elements of an approach that seeks to develop a feminist approach to adjudication. It allows us to pay attention to the woman question in procedural and substantive aspects of the law, in relation to legal institutions, and to use feminist scholarship in developing that approach. It would draw attention to the need to include women in legal discourse and in the construction of legal rules. It ought to provide the legal basis and institutional support for challenging gender bias. A feminist approach to adjudication would encourage reasoning through contextualisation and particularity. Consequently, it would be possible to grant remedies to injustices experienced by women and to promote their substantive equality within an open and accountable process. However, this is not only a question of reforming the process, substance and culture of adjudication but it is also a question of political will and political culture. For instance, the marginalisation of women from political discourse in Sri Lanka and the related issue of disregard for gender justice in political debate is also a barrier to the development of feminist adjudication. These insights are relevant to jurisdictions that are similar to Sri Lanka, but are also relevant in accounting for judging and for gender justice in the Global North.

I return to the question of whether the inclusion of women judges advances gender justice. In terms of diversifying the judiciary and increasing its legitimacy through inclusivity, the inclusion of women judges does advance gender justice. Beyond that, whether women justices do in fact make a difference in jurisdictions such as Sri Lanka is hard to establish. The jurisprudence available thus far suggests that they do not. The analysis I have undertaken however does establish that the jurisprudence displays a lack of consciousness or sensitivity to how law impacts women – whether in terms of equality or in violence against women. A transformation of such a system cannot be limited to ensuring the inclusivity of women in the judiciary or in other institutions involved in the administration of justice. The development of a feminist consciousness requires law reform to revise legislation that discriminates against women, and the development of a legal culture in which there is recognition and sensitivity to the discrimination and exclusion experienced by women. Until these transformations take place, the advancement of gender justice, including advancements by judges, is most likely to remain ad hoc.

References

Abeywardena, Sandani NY. 2016. 'Images, Myths and Stereotypes: A Critical Discourse Analysis of the Construction of the "Female" in Judicial Pronouncements on Rape in Sri Lanka'. *Law and Society Review*, 27(341) (December): 37–44.

Alwis, M. de. 2009. 'Interrogating the "Political": Feminist Peace Activism in Sri Lanka'. *Feminist Review*, 91(1): 81–93.

Baines, Beverly. 2013. 'Must Feminist Judges Self-identify as Feminists?' in *Gender and Judging*, edited by U. Schultz and G. Shaw, 379–398, Oxford: Hart.

Bandaranayake, Shirani. 2019. *Hold Me in Contempt*. Colombo: Sarasavi.

Bartlett, KT 1990. 'Feminist Legal Method'. *Harvard Law Review*, 103(4): 829–888.

Comaroff, Jean and Comaroff, John L. 2012. *Theory from the South or How Euro-America Is Evolving toward Africa*. Boulder, CO: Paradigm.

Cowan, Ruth B 2013. 'Do South Africa's Women Judges Make a Difference?' in *Gender and Judging*, edited by U. Schultz and G. Shaw, 317–333, Oxford: Hart.

Dann, Philipp. 2020. 'The Southern Turn in Comparative Constitutional Law: An Introduction' in *The Global South and Comparative Constitutional Law*, edited by Philipp Dann et al., Oxford: Oxford University Press.

Davies, Sara E. 2017. 'Where There Is No Justice: Gendered Violence and Harm in Post-Conflict Sri Lanka'. *The International Journal of Human Rights* 21(9): 1320–1336.

Dawuni, J. and Bauer, G. (eds). 2015. *Gender and the Judiciary in Africa: Moving from Obscurity to Parity?* New York: Routledge.

Dawuni, J. and Kuenyehia, A. (eds). 2019. *International Courts and the African Women Judge: Unveiled Narratives*. New York: Routledge.

de Almeida Guneratne, Jayantha et al., 2014. *The Judicial Mind in Sri Lanka: Responding to the Protection of Minority Rights*. Colombo: Law & Society Trust.

de Alwis, Malathi. 2002. 'The Changing Role of Women in Sri Lankan Society'. *Social Research* 69(3): 675–691.

2009. 'Interrogating the "Political": Feminist Peace Activism in Sri Lanka'. *Feminist Review* 91: 81–93.

de Mel, Neloufer. 2001. *Women and the Nation's Narrative*. Lanham, MD: Rowman and Littlefield.

de Mel, Neloufer and Samararatne, Dinesha. 2017. 'The Law's Gender: Entanglements and Recursions – Three Stories from Sri Lanka'. *On_Culture: The Open Journal for the Study of Culture* 3.

de Silva, CR 2011. 'A Recent Challenge to Judicial Independence in Sri Lanka: The Issue of the Constitutional Council' in *The Culture of Judicial Independence: Conceptual Foundations and Practical Challenges*, edited by S. Shetreet and C. Forsyth, 373–385, The Hague: Martinus Nijhoff.

de Silva, Shenali. 2018. 'A Snapshot of the Criminal Justice System: Building A Picture through Sexual Violence Cases in the Court of Appeal'. Colombo: Law & Society Trust.

Delap, L. 2011. 'The "Woman Question" and the Origins of Feminism' in *The Cambridge History of Nineteenth-Century Political Thought*, edited by G. S. Jones and G. Claeys, 319–348, Cambridge: Cambridge University Press.

Department of Census and Statistics. 2014. *The Sri Lankan Women: Partner in Progress.*

Eight Parliament of the Democratic Socialist Republic of Sri Lanka, Sectoral Oversight Committee on Legal Affairs (Anti Corruption) & Media, 2017. *Recommendations Pertaining to the Expeditious and Efficient Administration of Criminal Justice.* 20 September.

Feenan, Dermot. 2009. 'Editorial Introduction: Women and Judging'. *Feminist Legal Studies* 17: 1–9.

FOKUS (Sri Lanka). 2015. *A Report on the Status of Female Heads of Households and Their Access to Economic, Social and Cultural Rights.*

Goonesekere, Savitri and Samararatne, Dinesha. 2015. 'Human Rights of Women' in *Review of the Implementation of Beijing Platform for Action – Sri Lanka 1995–2014*, 161–202, Colombo: CENWOR.

Graycar, R. and Morgan, J. (end ed). 2002. *The Hidden Gender of Law.* Alexandria, VA: The Federation Press.

Graycar, Reg. 2013. 'A Feminist Adjudication Process: Is There Such a Thing?' in *Gender and Judging*, edited by U. Schultz and G. Shaw, 435–457, Oxford: Hart.

Hodson, Loveday and Lavers, Troy (eds). 2019. *Feminist Judgments in International Law.* Oxford: Hart.

Hunter, Rosemary. 2008. 'Can *Feminist* Judges Make a Difference?' *International Journal of the Legal Profession* 15(1–2) (March–July): 7–36.

2013. 'Justice Marcia Neave: Case Study of a Feminist Judge' in *Gender and Judging*, edited by U. Schultz and G. Shaw, 399–418, Oxford: Hart.

Hunter, Rosemary et al. (eds). 2010. *Feminist Judgments: From Theory to Practice.* Oxford: Hart.

Hyndman, Jennifer and de Alwis, Malathi. 2004. 'Bodies, Shrines and Roads: Violence, (Im)mobility and Displacement in Sri Lanka'. *A Journal of Feminist Geography* 11(4): 535–557.

International Bar Association. May 2009. *Justice in Retreat: A Report on the Independence of the Legal Profession and the Rule of Law in Sri Lanka.*

November 2011. *Sri Lanka: Failing to Protect the Rule of Law and the Independence of the Judiciary.*

April 2013. *A Crisis of Legitimacy: The Impeachment of Chief Justice Bandaranayake and the Erosion of the Rule of Law in Sri Lanka.* London.

Jayasundere, Ramani. 2016. 'Legal Aid in Sri Lanka: The Past and the Present, Challenges and Possibilities' paper presented at the National Forum on Access to Justice, 16 June 2016, Colombo, Sri Lanka.

Jayawardena, Kumari. 2009. *Feminism and Nationalism in the Third World*. Colombo: Social Scientists Association.

Jayawardena, Kumari and Pinto-Jayawardena, Kishali. 2016. *The Search For Justice: The Sri Lanka Papers*. New Delhi: Zubaan.

Ginsburg, Justice RB. 2016. *My Own Words*. New York: Simon & Schuster.

Hale, Justice Lady B. 2005. 'Making a Difference – Why We Need a More Diverse Judiciary'. *Northern Ireland Legal Quarterly* 56: 281.

Kodikara, Chulani. 2016. 'An Interview with Prashanthi Mahindaratne: The Krishanthi Kumaraswamy Case' in *The Search for Justice: The Sri Lanka Papers*, edited by Kumari Jayawardena and Kishali Pinto-Jayawardena, 405–424, New Delhi: Zubaan.

Kottegoda, Sepali. 2006. 'Bringing Home the Money: Migration and Poverty in Gender Politics in Sri Lanka' in *Poverty, Gender and Migration*, edited by Sadhna Arya and Anupama Roy, 49–71, New Delhi: SAGE.

Law & Society Trust. 2017. 'The Law and Society at a Crossroads: An Introduction to the Evolution of the Judiciary in Sri Lanka' in *South Asia Judicial Barometer*, 45–118, Colombo: Law & Society Trust.

Lawyers for Human Rights and Development. 2012. *Justice – Suspended? A Study on Suspended Sentences for Sexual Offenders*.

Marsoof, Justice S. 2011. *The Quazi Court System in Sri Lanka and Its Impact on Women*. Colombo: Muslim Women's Research and Action Forum/Women Living under Muslim Laws.

Munasinghe, Vidura and Celermajer, Danielle. 2017. 'Acute and Everyday Violence in Sri Lanka'. *Journal of Contemporary Asia* 47(4): 615–640.

Office of the High Commissioner for Human Rights (OHCHR) 2015. *Report of the OHCHR Investigation on Sri Lanka*. (A/HRC/30/CRP.2 16 September 2015). United Nations.

Pinto-Jayawardena, Kishali and Anantarajah, Kirsty. 2016. 'A Crisis of 'Legal Indeterminacy' and State Impunity' in *The Search For Justice: The Sri Lanka Papers*, edited by Kumari Jayawardena and Kishali Pinto-Jayawardena, 36–169, New Delhi: Zubaan.

Rackley, Erika. 2009. 'Detailing Judicial Difference'. *Fem Leg Studies* 17: 11–26.

Report of the Committee Appointed to Consider Amendments to the Muslim Marriage and Divorce Act. 2017.

Rogers, John D. et al. 1998. 'Sri Lanka: Political Violence and Ethnic Conflict'. *American Psychologist* 53(7) (July): 771–777.

Samararatne, Dinesha. 2014. 'Judicial Protection of Human Rights' in *Sri Lanka: State of Human Rights: 2014*, edited by Dinesha Samararatne, 25–67, Colombo: Law & Society Trust.

——— 2016. 'The Constitutional Council and the Independent Commissions: The New Framework for Depoliticising Governance' in *The Nineteenth*

Amendment to the Constitution: Content and Context, 148–174, Colombo: Centre for Policy Analysis.

2017. 'Judicial Interpretation of Fundamental Rights' in *Sri Lanka: State of Human Rights: 2017*, edited by Dinesha Samararatne, 35–68, Colombo: Law & Society Trust.

2018. 'Judicial Borrowing and Creeping Influences: Indian Jurisprudence in Sri Lankan Public Law'. *Indian Law Review* 2(3): 205–223.

2020. 'Gendering the "Legal Complex": Women in Sri Lanka's Legal Profession'. *Journal of Law and Society* 47(4): 666–693.

Satkunanathan, A. 2019. 'The Treatment of Former Combatants in Post-War Sri Lanka: A Form of Arbitrary Detention or Rehabilitation?' in *Routledge Handbook of Human Rights in Asia*, edited by F. de Varennes and CM Gardiner, 184–196, Abingdon: Routledge.

Schultz, U. and Shaw, G. (eds). 2003. *Women in the World's Legal Professions*. Oxford: Hart.

United Nations Office on Drugs and Crime. 2007. *Commentary on the Bangalore Principles of Judicial Conduct*. United Nations.

Uyangoda, Jayadeva. 2005. 'Ethnic Conflict, Ethnic Imagination and Democratic Alternatives for Sri Lanka'. *Futures* 37(9) (November): 959–988.

Wickramasinghe, N. 2006. *Sri Lanka in the Modern Age: A History of Contested Identities*. Colombo: Vijitha Yapa.

Cases

Addaraarachchi *v.* State [2000] 3 Sri LR 393

Addararachchi *v.* the State [2000] 3 Sri LR 393

Addararatchi *v.* the Republic HC 7710/96, HC Minutes 22 December 1997

Anthony Fernando *v.* Sri Lanka, Communication No. 1189/2003, United Nations Human Rights Committee, U.N. Doc. CCPR/C/83/D/1189/2003 (2005)

Attorney General *v.* Bandaranayake SC Appeal 67/2013, SC Minutes 21 February 2014

Attorney General *v.* Subasinghe HCJ1569/12, HC Minutes 7 October 2015

Attorney General *v.* Sampath SC Appeal No. 17/2013, SC Minutes 12 March 2015

Bandaranayake *v.* Speaker of Parliament CA (Writ) 411/2012, CA Minutes 7 January 2013

Decisions of the Supreme Court on Parliamentary Bills 2018

Gallage *v.* Addararachchi [2002] 1 Sri LR 313

In Re Local Authorities (Special Provisions) Bill and Local Authorities Elections (Amendment) Bill as reported in Parliamentary Debates (Hansard) 194(11) 16 November 2010, 1316

Manohari Pelaketiya *v.* Secy Min of Education SC/FR 76/2012, SC Minutes 28 Sept 2016

SC Reference 3/2012, SC Minutes 1 January 2013
SC Reference No. 03/08 SC Minutes 15 October 2008
Silva *v.* Bandaranayake [1997] 1 Sri LR 92
Somaratne Rajapakse *v.* Attorney General [2010] 2 Sri LR 113
Subasinghe *v.* Attorney General CA 250-252/2015, SC Minutes 10 October 2019
Thenuwara *v.* Speaker of Parliament SC(FR) 665 – 667 and 672/2012, SC Minutes 24 March 2014
Yogalingam Vijitha *v.* Wijesekera SC (FR) 186/2001, SC Minutes 23 August 2001

Treaties and International Standards

Bangalore Principles of Judicial Conduct 2002
Convention for the Elimination of All Forms of Discrimination against Women 1981

Legislation

Constitution of Sri Lanka 1978
Convention Against Torture Act No. 22 of 1994
Land Development Ordinance No. 19 of 1935
Maternity Benefits Ordinance 1939
Matrimonial Rights and Inheritance (Jaffna) Ordinance of 1911
Muslim Marriage and Divorce Act No. 13 of 1951
Muslim Marriage and Divorce Act, No. 13 of 1951
Penal Code of Sri Lanka 1833

Websites

Judicial Diversity Initiative, Research Repository (England and Wales) https://judicialdiversityinitiative.org/research (accessed 15 May 2020)
Muslim Personal Law Reforms Action Group https://mplreforms.com (accessed 27 June 2020)

Newspaper Articles and Press Releases

'Feminism and Nationalism in the Third World by Kumari Jayawardena – Review' *The Guardian,* 9 Aug 2017
'Final Verdict on the Kamal Addararachchi Case' *The Island,* 2 June 2002

'Urgent Structural Reforms Needed to Eliminate Discrimination against Women and Ensure Gender Justice', Kishali Pinto-Jayawardena *The Sunday Times*, 13 March 2017

Preliminary Observations and Recommendations of the Special Rapporteur on the Independence of Judges and Lawyers – Ms. Mónica Pinto Colombo, 7 May 2016

Speech of the Chief Justice Perera at the Ceremonial Sitting of the Supreme Court, 22 October 2018, reproduced at http://dbsjeyaraj.com/dbsj/archives/61197

4

Women in the Thai Judiciary

Obstacles and Challenges[*]

SARAH BISHOP

On 1 October 2020, women assumed the two most senior positions in Thailand's largest court system, the Courts of Justice. As well as this being the first time women had concurrently held these positions, this was also the first time a woman was president of the Supreme Court and only the second time a woman was president of the Appeal Courts. Other milestones have also been achieved in recent decades. In 2002, the first woman became a Constitutional Court judge; in 2010 the first woman became a Supreme Administrative Court judge; in 2017 the first woman became the head of a division in the Supreme Administrative Court; and in 2018 the first woman became the president of the Appeal Courts. Both the number of women who are judges and the number of women who hold higher level judicial positions have also increased.

With these developments, it may seem that the opportunities for women in the Thai judiciaries are, or are rapidly progressing towards being, equal to those of men. This impression is reinforced by existing English-language studies that comment on women in the Thai legal professions and judiciaries (Supin 2008; Usamard 2010; Munger 2019, 13–14, 19, 24–26; McCargo 2020, 33). These studies create an impression that women faced few obstacles in gaining access to the legal professions and that their representation in them has increased rapidly. By doing this, they also create an impression that any inequalities that do exist will be easily displaced.

These English-language studies, however, capture only a very small part of women's efforts to enter the legal professions (Supin 2008, 214; Usamard 2010, 129–130; Munger 2019, 25); misdate or overlook key milestones (Supin 2008, 214, 216; Usamard 2010, 134–135; McCargo 2020, 198, n18); and do not test suggestions that the unequal representation of women is due only to historical biases (Usamard 2010, 140;

---

[*] This chapter was not edited by the volume editor, at the request of the author, and all errors in the chapter are the authors own.

Munger 2019, 19). These limitations contribute to the impressions that they create.

As sustaining an impression that there is equality can hinder efforts to reduce it, this chapter undertakes a new appraisal of the experiences of women in the Thai judiciaries. This appraisal draws heavily on Thai sources and on data not considered in previous studies. It also interprets the data using methods not previously applied in the Thai context.

The new appraisal indicates that women have faced significant obstacles and challenges in gaining access to the Thai legal professions and that their access to and representation in those professions has increased slowly and only after persistent and often collective effort from women. It also indicates that, despite the recent developments, women still face greater obstacles and challenges in entering into and progressing in the Thai judiciaries than men. As such, contrary to what may otherwise be assumed, it is desirable that there be ongoing efforts to improve opportunities for women in the Thai judiciaries.

This chapter also contributes to broader literatures on women in the Thai workforce and women in judiciaries. With respect to the former, one of the most significant contributions is confirming the presence of dynamics similar to those identified in studies of women in other sectors of that workforce (see especially Iwanaga 2008; Natenapha 2009) in a new domain. The study also brings increased attention to the importance of domestic advocacy in increasing the opportunities for women in the Thai public sector workforce (c.f. Supin 2008), and provides new examples of challenges that women have faced in the Thai workforce.

As to the literature on women in judiciaries, this chapter contributes to this literature by using the method of drawing comparisons across court systems, a method previously used to explore opportunities for women in recognition judiciaries (see e.g. Kenney 2013), to study career judiciaries. The chapter also brings increased attention to aspects of women's experiences less emphasised in previous studies, such as the influence that opportunity for career progression may have on women's decisions to enter judiciaries, and challenges that women may face where the survival of court systems is uncertain; courts are seen to be politicised; judges face physical risks; and the prestige of the judiciary is founded predominantly in non-legal sources.

This chapter proceeds in four parts: Part I introduces the Thai legal system; Part II explores women's entry to the Thai legal professions; and Parts III and IV explore obstacles and challenges for women in the Thai civilian judiciaries in recent times. Part III does so focusing on data on the number of women and men judges; court rules and procedures; and differences across the court systems. Part IV does so drawing on statements of judges.

Part I: The Thai Legal System

The Thai legal system is a lesser studied and less widely known legal system. As such, before considering the experiences of women in the Thai legal professions, it is useful first to introduce this system. The current Thai legal system has its origins in reforms that began around 1888. These reforms were aimed primarily at showing Thailand to be a civilised nation and, by doing this, avoiding colonisation and having foreign powers lift claims to extraterritorial jurisdiction. The resulting legal system was a hybrid with elements adopted from civil and common law traditions, and, to a lesser extent, the former Siamese tradition (Rungsaeng 1990).

At most times from the reforms until 1997, Thailand had two court systems: Courts of Justice and Military Courts. At most times, in four southern Muslim-majority provinces, judges with expertise in Islamic law, Datoh Yutitham, also sat with regular judges in the Courts of Justice to decide cases on family law and succession involving Islamic parties. Adoption of this system in the South was influenced by observations of British systems in Malaya (Loos 2006, 73–99).

Courts of Justice judges were initially appointed ad hoc by the minister of justice. Since 1935, however, as is common in civil law traditions, judges have been recruited through competitive exam. For most of the period, judges enjoyed exceptionally high prestige, which derived not primarily from their legal power, but from a claim to act 'in the name of the King' and from a cultivated image of judges as being exceptionally virtuous, noble, wise and loyal (Kitpatchara 2018, 98).

Starting in 1997, the system was again reformed. The Courts of Justice were separated from the Ministry of Justice and new court systems were created. The structure of the court systems as of 2020 is shown in Figure 4.1. The court systems are largely independent of each other. Each has its own administrative body and its own rules for the recruitment, promotion and dismissal of judges. Until 2017, there was also no scope for decisions to be appealed across court systems.

The Courts of Justice has remained the largest court system. It is a court system of general jurisdiction. As of 2020, there were 272 courts in this system. These included 260 first-tier courts (161 courts of general

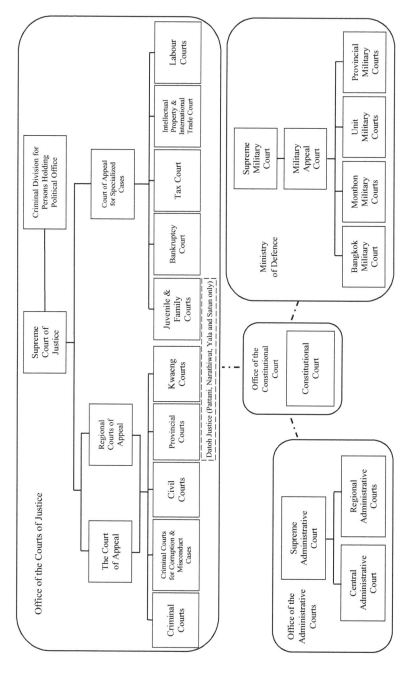

Figure 4.1 Thai court structure

jurisdiction and 99 specialist courts); eleven appeal courts (one central appeal court, nine regional appeal courts, and one specialist appeal court); and one Supreme Court. The system of having Datoh Yutitham sit in some courts has also been retained.

The other court system that existed prior to 1997 is the Military Court system, but this is not considered in this chapter. Data on this court system are difficult to access and the structure of the judiciary is different because in all courts (except for the Supreme Court) the majority of the bench consists of commissioned military officers who rotate through postings to the court.

The first of the new court systems created was a Constitutional Court. In 1997, judges were first appointed and in 1998 this court decided its first cases. It was a fifteen-member court and was a court of specialist jurisdiction with the authority to decide cases when power was delegated to it by the Constitution, and, due its interpretation, legislation. Following a coup in 2006, this court was abolished. It was succeeded by a nine-member Constitutional Tribunal and then by two nine-member Constitutional Courts. All have had similar jurisdiction.

The other new court system was the Administrative Court system. This system has jurisdiction over most administrative law cases. In 2000, judges were first appointed to this system, and in 2001 courts in this system decided their first cases. As of 2020, there were sixteen courts in this system: fifteen lower courts (fourteen regional courts and a central court) and a Supreme Court.

The post-1997 reforms were controversial. Since 1997, Thai courts, and especially the Constitutional Courts and Tribunal, have also increasingly been seen as politicised. As a result, the Constitutional and Administrative Courts have frequently faced the threat of abolishment. Judges, especially in the Constitutional and Administrative Courts but also to some extent the Courts of Justice, have also faced increased scrutiny and have suffered some loss of prestige.

Part II: Women's Entry to the Thai Legal Professions

Having introduced the Thai legal system, this chapter now focuses on the experiences of women in the Thai legal professions. This part explores the past resistance to allowing women opportunity in those professions; how this resistance has been overcome; and the rates at which women have historically entered those professions. This discussion enhances appreciation of the likelihood that women today still face greater obstacles and challenges in gaining opportunity in those professions than men; assists in identifying what might reduce those obstacles and challenges; and provides context for assessing women's contemporary levels of representation in those professions.

Accounts of women's entry to the Thai legal professions often begin in March 1928 with Raem Phromobon (Khunying Raem Phromobon Bunyaprasop) gaining permission to study law. It is often suggested that her modesty, her father having been the chief of police and her father having known the minister of justice, contributed to her gaining this permission (Jittima 1995, 35–36; Cremation Volume 2008, 29). Raem has also stated that her interest in law came from her father having 'employed' her as a child to summarise legal texts (Jittima 1995, 35; Suksun 1995, 23). Accounts like this can make it seem that all that was required for women to be able to study law was for a woman with the right interests, attitude and connections to seek permission to do so.

Beginning the account earlier reveals that for women to be able to study law was not so easy. While Raem was the first Thai woman to be permitted to study law, she was not the first to seek permission to do so. It is generally agreed that the first Thai woman to seek permssion to study law was Phongsri Wephara and that she did so while the minister for justice was Chao Phraya Abhairaja Maha Yuttithammathorn (Lop Suthat) (Cremation Volume 2008, 29), which places her attempt between 1911 and 1926. In 1926, there was also an article in a women's periodical which stated that 'about 8 or 9 years ago' the author had met three 'high class women' who had sought to study law (Jittima 1995, 32–33). It is possible that other women had made similar attempts.

Like Raem, these women were likely well connected. Phongsri, like Raem, came from a legal family. Her father, Khunluang Phraya Kraisi (Pleng Wephara), whilst born a commoner, was the first Thai called to the English Bar and held senior bureaucratic posts (Rungsaeng 1990, 280–290). Phongsri's name was also conferred on her by the Queen, pointing to even higher connections (Rungsaeng 1990, 290). As for the other women, while their identity is unknown, that they are described as 'high class' indicates that they were likely relatively well connected to those who held power at the time.

Women had also made collective efforts to overcome obstacles to studying law. In 1926 and 1927, a women's periodical published articles that made their case. The arguments advanced in the articles included arguments about the benefits of allowing women to practice law, such as that it would aid in spreading legal knowledge, would show the civilised status of the nation and would improve the prosperity of the nation. They also included arguments founded in equality, such as that other publicly funded schools (like schools for teachers and doctors) were open to women, and that allowing women to practice law would help them earn a living. The articles also issued a call for women to jointly apply to study law (Jittima 1995, 32–34).

By acknowledging this earlier history, it can be seen that women faced obstacles even in gaining permission to study law. These obstacles were great enough that well-connected women were unable to gain permission, and that women were moved to work together to seek to overcome the obstacles. As to what enabled the obstacles to be overcome in 1928, it seems probable that the minister would have been aware of the collective demands made in 1926 and 1927 and that the pressure that these demands created would have influenced his decision.

While formal barriers to women studying law began to be lifted in 1928, the numbers of women who graduated were initially low. Raem was the first to do so in 1931 and she was followed by one more in 1933 and four more in 1935. By 1942, only twenty-seven women had graduated and by 1947 only seventy-eight had done so (Boonyen 1964, 105, 109, 111). This was the case even though in two months in 1928 'around' ten women enrolled (Cremation Volume 2008, 30), and even though from 1934 legal education was provided by an open university that freely admitted women (Suksun 1995, 26).

Part of the reason why so few women graduated law was likely that many did not yet see opportunity in law. Like Raem, many women who graduated law in earlier periods came from legal families and stated that it was their family situation that led them to see opportunity in, or be pushed into, law (see e.g. Cremation Volume 2008, 135; Special Interview 2003, 50). Others, meanwhile, have reported that law was a fallback option for them (Oraphan 2017), or that their family and friends tried to persuade them not to study law (Suprani 1993).

Part of the reason was likely also that women still faced extra challenges. These likely included extra pressures faced as members of a minority and extra difficulties experienced in finding support. Both are indicated in a reflection written by Raem in which she states that her experience was tumultuous due to her entry to the law school generating widespread interest; that she considered withdrawing after failing an exam; and that her success was facilitated by being able to seek help from one teacher as she knew his wife (Raem 1984, 285–286). It is likely other women had similar experiences and faced greater challenges finding support.

In 1947, there was a development that partly altered this situation. This was the formation of a women law graduates' organisation. This organisation was active in advocating for women's rights. This resulted in women lawyers regularly speaking at universities, schools and on radio and appearing in other news media. This increased the visibility of opportunities for women in law. The organisation also arranged training and networking events and facilitated access to scholarships for women (Suppatra 1992a, 1992b), thus increasing the support available to them.

Following formation of this organisation, the number of women law graduates increased greatly. Between 1948 and 1952, 101 women graduated. In the five previous years, only fifty-one did so (Boonyen 1964, 111). The visibility and support provided by the women law graduates' organisation likely contributed to this increase. Opportunity for women in law was, however, still limited and women continued to graduate from law at lower rates than they graduated from courses where their degrees gave them access to jobs that was more equal to that of men (Jittima 1995, 76–83).

In the 1940s and early 1950s, one way in which women's opportunities were still limited was that they could not become judges. In 1939, soon after the first women law graduates reached the age where they could apply to be judges, a law was enacted that stated that judges must be male.[1] Women did not immediately challenge this restriction. In the 1926 and 1927 campaign, women's demands for rights to study law were on several occasions conditioned on it 'not yet' being necessary to allow them to be judges (Jittima 1995, 33–34). This wording indicates that women were already interested in being judges, but that they did not yet expect to be able to achieve that outcome. The lack of immediate challenge to the restriction introduced in 1939 was likely a product of similar sentiment.

By 1952, women challenged the restriction. The Women's Cultural Society (a state-connected organisation that shared much of its membership with the women law graduates' organisation) asked the government to amend laws that limited women's rights to work in the public service, including laws that prevented them from being judges (Jittima 1995, 89–91).

---

[1] *Act on the Judicial Service B.E. 2482* (1939) s 23(2).

By this stage there had already been change. In 1951, laws were enacted that created juvenile courts and required that they have lay judges, at least one of whom must be a woman, to assist in deciding cases.[2] This likely emboldened women to challenge the restriction further.

Even with the earlier changes and the support of the state-connected organisation, the proposal was resisted. When it came before parliament in 1954, a former judge spoke against it suggesting that, whilst it might be appropriate for 'housewives and women' to decide cases involving children, it was inappropriate for them to work in regular courts as this could require them to live outside Bangkok, be away from home for 'two to three' days at a time and decide murder cases.[3] While the law was amended, a provision was added allowing regulations to be issued to prohibit 'men or women' being appointed to judicial positions if due to the 'characteristics, quantity or quality of the work' it was deemed inappropriate to appoint them.[4]

Resistance also continued after the law was amended. In 1959, a regulation was issued that restricted women to being judges in juvenile courts only. The reasons given were that under custom and previous laws there had not been a woman judge and, taking into account family relations and the nature of the work, it was 'not yet appropriate' to appoint women to other courts.[5] In the courts, meanwhile, Chalorjit Jittarutta, who became the first woman judge in 1965, had to sit the recruitment exam three times to be recruited (Praphaphan 1998, 31). On one occasion, she even placed second but only one person was recruited (OCJ 2004, 48). It was rumoured this happened because the courts were not yet ready to accept a woman (OCJ 2004, 179).

Despite the limited success of the 1952 challenge, women did not immediately push for greater change. A large part of the reason for this was likely that from the late 1950s to 1973 Thailand was under authoritarian rule. This reduced space for civil society action (Jittima 1995, 118–151). While the women law graduates' organisation continued to champion law reform in some domains (Suppatra 1992a, 269–271), women's rights to be judges were not among them.

In 1973, following student-led uprisings that displaced the government, space for civil society action opened up. A constitution drafting

---

[2] *Act on Establishment of Juvenile Courts B.E. 2494* (1951) s 18.
[3] Report of House of Representatives Meeting 10/2497 (1954) (Ordinary Meeting), 107–109.
[4] *Act on the Judicial Service B.E. 2497* (1954) ss 20, 22.
[5] Ibid.

process that was underway also changed course. A new drafting body was appointed and its 299 members included sixteen women of whom two were members of the women law graduates' organisation. During drafting, the women law graduates' organisation led efforts to push in and outside the drafting body for the constitution to state that men and women were equal (Suppatra 1992a, 271; Jittima 1995, 157–162, 213–145). While this proposal was resisted (Jittima 1995, 228–234), the statement was added.[6]

After enactment of the Constitution, the women law graduates' organisation drew on this added statement and the momentum provided by 1975 being International Women's Year, to campaign for revocation of the regulation that restricted women to being judges in juvenile courts only (Jittima 1995, 166–167). In 1975, the regulation was revoked. The reason given was its inconsistency with the Constitution.[7] The change, however, came nine months after the constitution was enacted. It was also only in 1992 that the courts abandoned practices that prevented women being appointed to some more powerful positions (Praphaphan 1998, 31–32).

Following the changes in 1975 and 1992, the number of women judges increased greatly. While Somlak Jadkrabuanpol has noted that in 1971 when she became a judge she was only the sixth women to do so (1989, 170); by 1987, there were sixty-two women judges and women constituted 5.92 per cent of the judiciary (Usamard 2010, 135) and by 1998 there were 396 women judges and women constituted 17.41 per cent of the judiciary (Praphaphan 1998, 17). As with increases in the number of women studying law, these increases followed increases in the opportunities for women to have careers that were varied and could include taking on roles at higher levels.

From this analysis it can be seen that it was only after sustained and often collective effort that women gained entry to the Thai legal professions; and that, even after women gained formal rights of entry, there was often obdurate resistance to allowing them opportunity. It can also be seen that the lack of opportunity, including of career progression opportunity, likely effected not only the rate at which women were able to enter the professions but also the rate at which they sought to do so. These insights influence the approach taken in subsequent parts of this chapter.

---

[6] 1974 Constitution s 28.
[7] *Ministerial Regulation Number 7 B.E. 2518* (1975).

Part III: Women in the Thai Judiciaries since 1997

Remaining parts of this chapter focus on the contemporary situation for women in the Thai judiciaries. The focus in this part is on data on the numbers of women and men judges, court rules and procedures and differences across the court systems. For each civilian court system, it first introduces the data. It then explores trends presented by the data, including by how it compares to data for the other court systems, and likely causes for the trends. The analysis starts at 1997 because, as noted in Part I, this is when major court reforms began. It is also close to the end date of the last detailed study of a Thai judiciary (Praphaphan 1998). The analysis is approached on the basis that women likely still face greater obstacles and challenges in entering into and progressing in the judiciaries than men and that lower rates of entry into, or progression of women in, the judiciaries should not be readily attributed to women being less interested in doing so than men.

The approach taken is supported by insights from Part II of this chapter. This is because the presence of past obdurate resistance to allowing women opportunity in the legal professions increases the likelihood that there will still be such resistance. It is also because the persistent effort invested by women in securing rights to enter the legal professions, and the fact that their rate of entry to the legal professions has increased after opportunity for them to assume higher roles has increased, indicates that they have had an interest in being judges and in assuming higher roles.

As well as considering new Thai data and bringing new methods to the study of the Thai data, this part also uses a method previously less used in studying career judiciaries. This is the drawing of comparisons across court systems. In this part, this method is used to provide an additional way to identify where women have likely been under-represented and how court rules and procedures likely contributed to this. Use of this method also helps establish that women likely face obstacles and challenges not just in one Thai judiciary but in all of them.

The analysis in this part indicates that, while women likely still face obstacles and challenges in all Thai judiciaries, the extent and manner in which the obstacles and challenges manifest across the court systems likely differs. It also identifies ways that court rules and procedures may contribute to this. As the analysis is across only a few court systems, the indications of how court rules and procedures may contribute cannot be absolutely relied on. They do, however, provide some guidance on issues on which efforts to improve opportunity for women in the Thai judiciaries may focus. They could also provide a starting point for analyses across a larger range of career judiciaries.

Courts of Justice

As noted in Part 1, the Courts of Justice is the oldest and largest Thai court system. It is also the court system discussed in Part II of this chapter. It thus makes sense to begin consideration of the contemporary situation for women in the Thai judiciaries with this court system. Data on women judges in the Courts of Justice are presented in Figure 4.2 and Tables 4.1–4.3. Figure 4.2 charts the percentage of women judges in the Courts of Justice since 1965. It includes the overall percentage of woman judges and, for 2010 to 2018, the percentage of women judges in the highest standard pay category. Tables 4.1–4.3 record the number and percentage of women judges by pay category in 1998 and from 2010 to 2018.

In 2000, the pay categories changed. Levels 2 to 4 used before 2000 were roughly equivalent to levels 1, 2 and early level 3 used after 2000.[8] After 2000, judges will have spent one to two years as trainees; one to three years at level 1 and up to five years at level 2. Periods at other levels have been less regulated. At levels 1 and 2, judges will have been in courts of first instance and not had leadership roles. At level 3, judges will have been in courts of first instance or appeal courts and might have had leadership roles. At level 4, judges will have been in Appeal or Supreme Courts and/or had leadership roles. Only the Supreme Court president has been level 5.[9]

The other categories are special categories. Senior judges are judges who have reached retirement age and continued working. As of 2020, judges could enter this category from age sixty and had to do so at age sixty-five. They cannot hold some leadership roles.[10] Datoh Yutitham, as noted in Part I, are judges who are appointed for their expertise in Islamic law and sit with regular judges to decide cases on family law and succession involving Islamic parties in four southern provinces.

There are three key observations to make on the situation of women judges in the Courts of Justice. These are that, of the Thai civilian court systems, it is the court system in which women judges have the highest

---

[8] *Act on the Judicial Service B.E. 2521* (1978) ss 15, 18.
[9] *Act on the Courts of Justice Judicial Service B.E. 2543* (2000) ss 13, 15, 17, 20(2).
[10] *Act on Principles for Appointment ... B.E. 2542* (1999) ss 6, 6/1, 10.

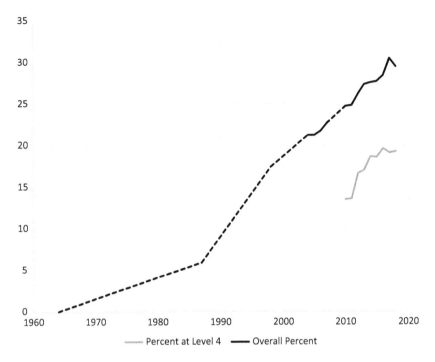

Figure 4.2   Percentage of Courts of Justice judges who are female (not including trainees) (1965–2018).
Source: Praphaphan 1998; OCJ 2004; Usamard 2010; OCSC 2011–2019

representation; that in this court system, women judges' representation has in all cases declined as positions increase in seniority; and that there is a specialist role, that of Datoh Yutitham, which does not appear to have ever been held by a woman.

In some ways it is surprising that women judges have the highest representation in the Courts of Justice. This is because in this court system, unlike the other Thai civilian court systems, some judges serving after 1997 will have been recruited before 1997. As careers in this judiciary can last up to forty years, this could have been as far back as the 1960s, 1970s and 1980s when few women entered the judiciary. Although the number of judges in the Courts of Justice has more than quadrupled from 1987 to 2018, this legacy could still be expected to have reduced women's overall representation.

The Courts of Justice is, however, the Thai civilian court system with the most open and most gender-blind recruitment processes. Judges can

Table 4.1 *Men and women in the Courts of Justice by pay category (2010–2018)*

	Trainee		Level 1		Level 2		Level 3		Level 4		Level 5		Senior Judges		Datoh Judges		Total (not including trainees)	
	M	W	M	W	M	W	M	W	M	W	M	W	M	W	M	W	M	W
2010	51	67	75	26	514	308	1707	586	603	94	1	0	224	13	8	0	3132	1027
2011	51	68	75	26	516	311	1712	591	605	95	1	0	225	13	8	0	3142	1036
2012	55	82	13	12	533	355	1687	589	663	132	1	0	213	16	8	0	3118	1104
2013	12	3	55	82	508	344	1717	609	660	135	1	0	210	16	9	0	3160	1186
2014	27	17	11	4	297	287	1901	720	673	154	1	0	237	23	9	0	3129	1188
2015	67	70	11	4	269	275	1928	731	672	153	1	0	212	23	9	0	3102	1186
2016	147	100	67	70	130	165	2046	820	666	162	1	0	227	29	9	0	3146	1246
2017	40	105	100	146	147	169	1914	854	738	174	1	0	270	48	9	0	3179	1391
2018	59	119	97	65	189	197	1924	860	731	174	1	0	269	48	9	0	3220	1344

Source: OCSC 2011–2019

Table 4.2 *Percentage of women in the Courts of Justice by pay category (2010–2018)*

	Trainee	Level 1	Level 2	Level 3	Level 4	Level 5	Senior Judges	Datoh Judges	Total (not including trainees)
2010	56.78	25.74	37.47	25.56	13.49	0	5.49	0	24.69
2011	57.14	25.74	37.61	25.66	13.57	0	5.46	0	24.80
2012	59.85	48.00	39.98	25.88	16.60	0	6.99	0	26.15
2013	20.00	59.85	40.38	26.18	16.98	0	7.08	0	27.29
2014	38.64	26.67	49.14	27.47	18.62	0	8.85	0	27.52
2015	51.09	26.67	50.55	27.49	18.55	0	9.79	0	27.66
2016	40.49	51.09	55.93	28.61	19.57	0	11.33	0	28.37
2017	72.41	59.35	53.48	30.85	19.08	0	15.09	0	30.44
2018	66.85	40.12	51.04	30.89	19.23	0	15.14	0	29.45

Source: OCSC 2011–2019

Table 4.3 *Men and women in the Courts of Justice by pay category (1998)*

	Level 2–4			Level 5			Level 6			Level 7			Level 8			Level 9			Total		
	M	W	%W	M	W	%W	M	W	%W	M	W	%W	M	W	%W	M	W	%W	M	W	%W
1998	1180	340	22.37	435	48	9.94	196	7	3.45	52	1	1.89	14	0	0	1	0	0	1878	396	17.41

Source: Praphaphan 1998

be recruited from age twenty-five and, while there are alternate entry pathways for those who have studied abroad or have certain experience, it is possible to enter with minimal experience. Recruitment is also by competitive exam and, while the exams have an oral component, this is intended to test only knowledge.[11]

This makes it less surprising that it is in the Courts of Justice that women judges have the highest representation. This is because the young age of recruitment and requirement for only minimal experience should mean that to the extent that women have historically studied law in lower numbers than they do now, or that women have faced obstructions in progressing other careers, this should not have significantly impacted the number recently eligible to enter this judiciary. It is also because the use of exams and a focus on knowledge of the law should limit scope for gender biases to impact recruitment decisions.

Whether these rules and processes are providing women and men equal opportunity is difficult to assess. A better assessment would be possible with additional data, such as data on the number of women and men to sit recruitment exams and their performance in different parts of the exams (cf. Boigeol 2013, 126, 128). However, whilst it was in 2015 that women first constituted a majority of Thai law graduates (Munger 2019, 34), in most years from 2010 to 2018 a majority of those in this court system's judicial trainee program have been women. In some years, a majority of judges at levels 1 and 2 have also been women (Table 4.1). This indicates that women likely do not face considerably greater obstacles than men in entering this judiciary.

While women and men may have relatively equal opportunity to enter this judiciary, however, their opportunities after entry are likely not equal. This is indicated, in part, by the second trend observed: the decline in women judges' representation as positions increase in seniority. Similar trends have been observed in other career judiciaries (see e.g. Boigeol 2013, 129–130; Schultz 2013, 152–153). It has been suggested that in the Thai Courts of Justice this decline can be accounted for by the fact that women only recently started to enter this judiciary in large numbers (Usamard 2010, 136, 140). Promotions in the Thai Courts of Justice are based largely on 'seniority', with seniority based partly on year of recruitment. There is also no lateral entry into higher levels of this judiciary, careers in this judiciary typically last thirty to forty years, and

---

[11] Ibid. ss 26–31.

women only began to enter this judiciary in large numbers in the 1990s. It is thus probable that the decline is partly due to women's more recent entry.

Attributing the decline entirely to women's more recent entry, however, may conceal inequalities that still exist. It is thus important to query the extent to which it can do so. For German courts, the suggestion that women's more recent entry accounted entirely for a decline has been refuted by showing that women's representation at higher levels had plateaued and had not reached the level that it should have if men and women had had similar career trajectories (Schultz 2013, 152–153).

For the Thai Courts of Justice, this cannot be as definitively done. From 2014 to 2018 there was a slowing down of the rate at which women's representation in the highest standard pay category (level 4) increased. In 2015 and 2017 there were also dips in their representation at that level (Figure 4.2, Table 4.2), which could indicate the beginning of a plateauing. As these trends are only present over a few years, however, the dips could still be mere temporary anomalies.

As to women judges' representation reaching levels that it should have if men and women had had similar career trajectories, in 2018 19.23 per cent of judges in the highest standard pay category (level 4) were women (Table 4.2). In contrast, in 1998, 22.37 per cent of judges in lower pay categories (levels 2–4) were women (Table 4.3). This 3.14 per cent difference indicates women might not have progressed at the same rate as men. As a judicial career can last forty years, however, there is still some chance that the difference may be due to judges who were at higher levels in 1998 still holding positions.

While the data is inconclusive, however, there is reason to expect that there have also been other causes for the decline. One of these is that women and men may have had different experiences of career progression. This has previously been suggested to have occurred in the Thai Courts of Justice (Praphaphan 1998, 20–33) and in other career judiciaries (see e.g. Boigeol 2013, 129–132; Schultz 2013, 152–163). The differences, it has been suggested, result from women's choices and obligations and from the attitudes that they encounter from others (see e.g. Praphaphan 1998, 20–33; Kay and Gorman 2008, 305–311, 315–320; Schultz 2013, 152–163).

Accounts of promotion in the Thai Courts of Justice often suggest that promotion is based almost entirely on seniority and that seniority is determined based almost entirely on when a judge was recruited and on their performance in recruitment exams (see e.g. Somlak 2017;

McCargo 2020, 36–37). The reality of promotion is, however, more complex. While seniority is influential, other criteria must also be considered. These include experience and assessments of performance and appropriateness, and also, more exceptionally, social etiquette and societal attitudes.[12] Seniority is also assessed based not only on time of recruitment and performance on recruitment exams, but also recent positions held and recent pay levels (Praphaphan 1998, 26). These can be affected by the fact that some positions must be applied for; that judges can trade postings; and that taking leave which exceeds allowed periods, which for maternity leave is only ninety days, can affect pay rises.[13]

Once this is recognised, it is apparent that women's career progression may be affected by the attitudes of others and by their own choices and obligations. It could, for instance, be affected by how the attitudes of others impact the work that they delegate to women and how they assess women's performance and women's appropriateness to positions. With social etiquette and societal attitudes as criteria, these could additionally be affected not only by others own biases but also their assessments of society's biases. As to women's choices and obligations, these may affect what work they seek, what positions they apply for, and what trades of positions they propose and accept.

The data considered in this chapter do not enable assessment of the extent to which women and men have had different experiences of career progression. The milestone appointments highlighted in Part I do show that some women have been able to progress in their careers. This, however, should not be taken as evidence of equality of opportunity. It is still possible, as appears to have been the case in the Administrative Courts, that the number of women allowed to hold higher positions may have been capped. As indicated by the evidence in Part IV, it is also possible that to get the same opportunities as men, women may have had to be more exceptional than, or make more sacrifices than, men.

Another possible cause for the decline is that women may have left judicial careers early at higher rates than men. This trend has been observed in legal professions in other countries. It has been attributed to several factors including women having faced greater obstacles in combining legal careers and family responsibilities than men; women

---

[12] *Courts of Justice Judicial Commission Regulations on Principles ... B.E. 2554* (2011) regs 9–11, 13.
[13] Ibid. reg 34/1.

having felt excluded from opportunity to take on rewarding work; and women experiencing sexual harassment (Kay and Gorman 2008, 319–320).

In the Courts of Justice, judges move postings every two to five years and postings may be in locations with little infrastructure to support regular commutes or the management of complex needs. As postings are largely determined by seniority, early career judges are also likely to have little control over their postings. To the extent that women have had greater caring responsibilities or have been more expected to fit their careers around a partner's priorities than men, these conditions could be expected to have been especially difficult for them to manage and so to have led more women to have left judicial careers early.

As to the other factors, as has been explored and will be explored further in Part IV, women may have had less opportunity for rewarding careers than men or may have encountered sexual harassment. This too could have led more women to leave early.

Finally, it must not be overlooked that there is a specialist judicial role in this court system, that of Datoh Yutitham, which appears not to have been held by a woman. Thai laws do not prevent women being Datoh Yutitham.[14] This makes the absence of women in this role even more notable, especially given the historical, social and cultural ties between the Thai provinces where Datoh Yuthitham serve, and neighbouring Malaysia, where considerable effort has recently been invested in securing rights for women to serve as Syariah judges (Chapter 7).

Administrative Courts

The second largest Thai civilian court system is the Administrative Court system. This court system is also the system that structurally has the most in common with the Courts of Justice. It thus makes sense to consider it next. Data on women judges in the Administrative Courts are presented in Figure 4.3 and Tables 4.4 and 4.5. Figure 4.3 charts the percentage of women judges in the Administrative Courts from 2001 to 2018. Tables 4.4 and 4.5 record the number and percentage of women judges by category from 2001 to 2018. The executive categories used capture the chief justices and deputy chief justices of the lower courts and the president and vice presidents of the Supreme Court.

---

[14] *Act on the Courts of Justice Judicial Service B.E. 2543* (2000) ss 52–54.

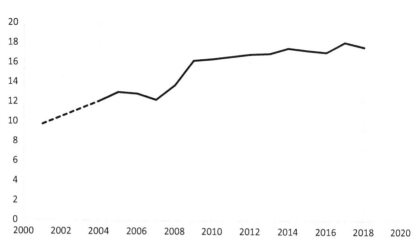

Figure 4.3 Percentage of Administrative Court judges who are female (2001–2018). *Source*: Declaration of the Office of the Prime Minister on Appointment of Supreme Administrative Court Judges 2000; Declaration of the Office of the Prime Minister on Appointment of Judges of Administrative Courts of First Instance 2001; OAC 2005–2019.

There are three key observations to make on the situation of women judges in the Administrative Courts. First, that representation of women judges in the Administrative Courts has been lower than in the Courts of Justice; second, that in the Administrative Courts, unlike in the Courts of Justice, women judges' representation has not declined in all cases as positions increase in seniority; and third, that while lateral entry to the Supreme Administrative Court is possible, no women have been appointed to the court that way.

The differences in representation of women judges in the Administrative Courts and Courts of Justice have been considerable. As of 2018, there had been only three years where representation of women judges in the Administrative Courts had reached even the 1998 Courts of Justice levels. Since 2014, the representation of women judges in the Administrative Courts has also been lower than the representation of women judges in the highest standard Courts of Justice pay category (level 4) (Tables 4.2 and 4.5).

In the Administrative Courts, unlike in the Courts of Justice, women judges' low representation cannot be attributed even partly to historically distant hiring patterns. This is because, as noted in Part I, the first Administrative Court judges were recruited in 2000. Women judges' low representation must, therefore, be attributed to more recent causes.

Table 4.4 *Men and women in the Administrative Courts by court and role (2001–2018)*

	Courts of First Instance (All)		Courts of First Instance (Exec)		Supreme Court (All)		Supreme Court (Exec)		Total Number of Judges	
	M	W	M	W	M	W	M	W	M	W
2001	77	10	Unknown	unknown	15	0	unknown	unknown	92	10
2002	unknown	unknown	9	3	unknown	0	unknown	0	unknown	Unknown
2003	unknown	unknown	14	4	unknown	0	unknown	0	unknown	Unknown
2004	103	16	14	4	13	0	3	0	116	16
2005	127	21	14	4	13	0	3	0	140	21
2006	126	21	14	4	16	0	3	0	142	21
2007	126	20	14	4	17	0	3	0	143	20
2008	140	25	14	4	17	0	3	0	157	25
2009	150	33	12	4	20	0	3	0	170	33
2010	160	34	16	3	18	1	3	0	178	35
2011	163	35	18	4	17	1	3	0	180	36
2012	156	35	17	5	21	1	3	0	177	36
2013	155	35	16	5	21	1	3	0	176	36
2014	154	36	17	5	20	1	3	0	174	37
2015	154	35	21	5	18	1	2	0	172	36
2016	146	33	27	5	28	3	3	0	174	36
2017	166	40	27	5	28	3	5	0	194	43
2018	153	36	28	4	38	5	5	0	191	41

Source: Declaration of the Office of the Prime Minister on Appointment of Supreme Administrative Court Judges 2000; Declaration of the Office of the Prime Minister on Appointment of Judges of Administrative Courts of First Instance 2001; OAC 2005–2019.

Table 4.5 *Percentage of women in the Administrative Courts by court and role (2001–2018)*

	Courts of First Instance (All)	Courts of First Instance (Exec)	Supreme Court (All)	Supreme Court (Exec)	Total Number of Judges
2001	11.49	Unknown	0	0	9.80
2002	unknown	25	0	0	Unknown
2003	unknown	22.22	0	0	Unknown
2004	13.45	22.22	0	0	12.12
2005	14.19	22.22	0	0	13.04
2006	14.29	22.22	0	0	12.88
2007	13.70	22.22	0	0	12.27
2008	15.15	22.22	0	0	13.74
2009	18.03	25	0	0	16.26
2010	17.53	15.79	5.26	0	16.43
2011	17.68	18.18	5.56	0	16.67
2012	18.32	22.73	4.55	0	16.90
2013	18.42	23.81	4.55	0	16.98
2014	18.95	22.73	4.76	0	17.54
2015	18.52	19.23	5.26	0	17.31
2016	18.44	15.63	9.68	0	17.14
2017	19.42	15.63	9.68	0	18.14
2018	19.05	12.5	11.63	0	17.67

Source: Declaration of the Office of the Prime Minister on Appointment of Supreme Administrative Court Judges 2000; Declaration of the Office of the Prime Minister on Appointment of Judges of Administrative Courts of First Instance 2001; OAC 2005–2019.

There are two that seem possible: the low recruitment of women and the high attrition of women who are recruited. Of these causes, that most supported by the data is the low recruitment of women. This is because the data indicate a high year-on-year stability in the numbers of women judges (Table 4.4). There is also no record of regular recruitment to create this stability. There is, however, a record of appointments of judges in which the number of men appointed has consistently been much higher than that of women. This is partly reflected in Table 4.4 in the differences evident in years when there have been large increases in the number of judges. Actual differences, however, have been greater. This contrasts to the Courts of Justice where since 2010 the intake of women appears to have mostly been higher than the intake of men (Table 4.2).

There are several reasons why the recruitment of women judges in the Administrative Courts might have been lower than that in the Courts of Justice. One is that there were likely fewer women eligible. Candidates to be Administrative Court judges must be at least thirty-five years old; be qualified in law, political science, public administration or social science; and have considerable experience.[15] This age and experience requirement are higher than those in the Courts of Justice and mean that, to the extent that women have historically studied in lower numbers than they do now or have faced obstructions in progressing other careers, this is more likely to have limited the number of women eligible to be Administrative Court judges than Courts of Justice judges.

Representation of women in Administrative Court judicial intakes has, however, also been lower than that in the likely pool of eligible candidates. By way of example, one attribute which has qualified persons to be lower court judges is having been a civil servant at level 8 or above for three years. Three years before the first lower court judges were appointed, 17.81 per cent of civil servants at level 9, a much more exclusive level, were women (OCSC 2017, 52). In contrast, only 11.49 per cent of the first lower court judges appointed were women (Table 4.5). In subsequent years, the only year that the percentage of women lower court judges appointed has exceeded that of women civil servants at level 9 has been 2009. In other years the difference has been similar to that for the first group of judges.

This contrasts to the situation in the Courts of Justice where, as explored, women appear to have often been in the majority in intakes even though they have been in the minority in the likely pool of eligible candidates (there, recent law graduates). Also, while the difference in age of eligibility across the court systems is ten years, as of 2018 levels of representation of women in the Administrative Courts were close to those in the Courts of Justice not ten but twenty years earlier (Tables 4.3 and 4.5). These comparisons indicate that differences in the number of women eligible to be recruited cannot fully account for the differences across the systems.

Another reason why the recruitment of women judges might have been lower in the Administrative Courts than in the Courts of Justice is

---

[15] *Act on Establishment of Administrative Courts and Administrative Court Procedure B.E. 2542* (1999) ss 13, 18.

that eligible women may have been less likely to apply. There are at least three reasons this might have been the case. The first reason is that recruitment to the Administrative Courts occurs at a later life stage. This means that the difficulty of combining a judicial career and family responsibilities, suggested to possibly lead to high attrition of women judges in the Courts of Justice, may instead lead women to not apply. The second is that recruitment to the Administrative Courts occurs at a later career stage. By this later stage, women are likely to have had to overcome gender biases to advance one career. This might reduce their willingness to move institutions, and hence their willingness to apply. The third is that judges in the Administrative Courts have less job security and face a greater risk of reputational damage than Courts of Justice judges. This is because the Administrative Courts have frequently faced the threat of abolishment and have been more involved in politically controversial cases than the Courts of Justice. As gender biases may mean that women face particularly strong challenges in establishing a reputation and finding jobs, this might have reduced women's willingness to apply more than it reduced that of men.

A final reason why the recruitment of women judges in the Administrative Courts might have been lower than that in the Courts of Justice is that the success rate of women applicants may have been lower. Recruitment to the Administrative Courts, unlike to the Courts of Justice, is based not only on assessments of knowledge, but also of appropriateness and of ability made based on written materials, interviews and opinions of people in relevant spheres.[16] There is thus considerable potential for applicants' success to be impacted by differences in their ability to network and by the gender biases of decision makers.

As the data relied on in this chapter do not include data on applicants for Administrative Court positions, it is not possible to assess the extent to which each of these causes has contributed to the low recruitment of women judges. Consideration of the second and third observations for the Administrative Courts, however, indicates that gender biases of decision makers likely played some role.

The second observation for the Administrative Courts is that, unlike in the Courts of Justice, the representation of women judges has not in all

---

[16] *Administrative Court Judicial Commission Regulations on Methods for Selection of Judges of Administrative Courts of First Instance ... B.E. 2544* (2001) regs 3, 4; *Administrative Court Judicial Commission Regulations on Methods for Selection of Judges of the Supreme Administrative Court ... B.E. 2544* (2001) regs 3–5.

cases declined as positions have increased in seniority. Until 2016, the percentage of women lower court executives was almost always higher than that of women lower court judges. Women's representation on the Supreme Administrative Court has, however, always been lower than that in the lower courts (Table 4.5). The likely cause of these trends is the effect of gendered biases on women's career progression opportunities, and, in particular, of tokenism. That is to say, of a desire to appear inclusive, but also a failure to genuinely address factors that limit women's opportunities. This is important to highlight as tokenism obstructs recognition of inequality and thus can hinder efforts to reduce it. It also impacts women's experiences (Jefferson and Johnson 2020, 129–141).

Rules for promotion in the Administrative Courts historically allowed the broad discretionary decision-making that enables tokenism. In the lower courts, until 2011, while rules indicated that judges considered for executive roles should have been in the Administrative Courts for a number of years, there was flexibility.[17] And, while in 2011, seniority was added to criteria to be considered in promotions, until 2015, it was only one of several criteria to be used to assess knowledge, appropriateness and ability.[18] As for the Supreme Administrative Court, until 2017, persons from in and outside the Administrative Courts applied for positions and the process was then similar to the lower court recruitment process discussed previously.[19]

That tokenism was influential, meanwhile, is indicated by the number of women in higher roles having been low and stable, the timing of women's promotions and the limited appointment of women to powerful roles. While from 2002 to 2018 the number of lower court executives almost tripled, the number of women executives remained between three and five. Until 2017, there were also never more than three women in any type of lower court executive role or on the Supreme Court (Table 4.4). This stability, especially against a background of expansion, indicates a desire to have women visible but also a capping of their numbers.

---

[17] *Administrative Court Judicial Commission Regulations on Methods for Selection of Judges of Administrative Courts of First Instance … B.E. 2544 (2001) regs 5–8.*

[18] *Administrative Court Judicial Commission Regulations on Moving and Promoting Judges of Administrative Courts of First Instance B.E. 2554 (2011) reg 21.*

[19] *Administrative Court Judicial Commission Regulations on Methods for Selection of Judges of the Supreme Administrative Court … B.E. 2544 (2001) regs 3–5.*

As to the timing of women's promotions, of the seven women promoted to lower court executive roles between 2004 and 2018, six were promoted around the same time as other women left such roles. As in that period only seven women left such roles and they did so in only four years, and as men left such roles in another six years, this timing is unlikely to have been coincidental (OAC 2005–2019). This trend again indicates a desire to have women visible but also a capping of their numbers.

The limited appointment of women to more powerful roles, meanwhile, is evident in both the lower and Supreme Courts. Of the lower courts, the Central Administrative Court was by far the largest. If each year in an executive role in that court is treated as one unit, from 2002 to 2018 women held only 6.15 per cent of those units (OAC 2003–2019). This is lower than could be expected given in that period women held between 12.5 and 25 per cent of lower court executive roles (Table 4.5). Again, it seems, there was a desire for visibility, but, in this case, a reluctance to give power.

As to the Supreme Administrative Court, women's movement to this court was especially slow. By the time Maneewan Phromnoi became the first woman appointed, three of the other seven judges who had become lower court chief justices by the same time had already been appointed. Of the other four, meanwhile, only two were men and one of those had left the courts. Of that cohort, therefore, only one man and three women remained eligible. Seven men who had attained lower court executive positions later than Maneewan or had held positions lower than hers had also already been appointed (OAC 2005–2011; C.12 2009). Notably, this occurred even though women applied in earlier years (Usamard 2010, 136).

The final observation for the Administrative Courts is that, while lateral entry to the Supreme Administrative Court has been possible, no woman has been appointed to that court that way. Notably, this has been the case even though twelve of the forty men appointed since 2001 have been appointed in such a way (OAC 2003–2019; C.12 2009, 2015). That no women have been laterally appointed indicates that women who had not had an opportunity to prove themselves individually to decision makers have struggled to be appointed.

In 2017, the rules for recruitment and promotion in the Administrative Courts were changed. The changes bring Administrative Court rules and procedures closer to those in the Courts of Justice. It is too early to tell, but will be interesting to observe, what impact this will have on women judges' representation.

Constitutional Courts and Constitutional Tribunal

The remaining civilian courts are the Constitutional Courts and Tribunal. As noted in Part I, due to military coups, there have been several such courts. Unlike the other civilian court systems, they have been single tier court systems. Of the fifty-two judges appointed to these court systems between 1997 and October 2020, only one has been a woman. That woman, Saowanee Asawaroj, was appointed to the first Thai Constitutional Court in April 2003 and served on that court until it was abolished after a coup in September 2006. That court was a fifteen-member court and Saowanee was the twenty-second judge appointed to it. She was a law professor and was appointed to one of the five positions for 'experts in law'.

Part of the reason why there has been only one woman appointed to these courts may be that, similar to the situation in the Administrative Courts, there may have been relatively few women eligible and willing to be appointed. Regarding eligibility, while there has been variation, the types of experience that have qualified persons to be judges on these courts have included having been a judge of the Supreme Court of another court system; a member of a constitutional organisation; a government minister; a senior prosecutor or bureaucrat; a professor of law, political science or a related field; or a lawyer with thirty years' experience.[20]

Especially in earlier years, few women will have met these criteria and in some appointment categories none will have done so. It was, for instance, only in 2000 that Saowanee became the first Thai woman to be a law professor (Special Interview 2003, 51) and in 2010 that Maneewan became the first woman judge on the Thai Supreme Administrative Court. By 1997, however, there were women who were Courts of Justice Supreme Court judges (Oraphan 2017), government ministers and bureaucrats of sufficient seniority (Praphaphan 1998, 33–35). Lack of eligible women thus cannot fully account either for the single appointment, or for it not coming earlier.

As for willingness to be appointed, to an even greater extent than in the Administrative Courts, judges on these courts have had to accept low job security and the risk of reputational damage. Even without the threat

---

[20] 1997 Constitution ss 255–6; 2006 Constitution s 35, 2007 Constitution ss 204–5; 2017 Constitution s 200.

of the courts being abolished, roles on these courts have been for limited terms.[21] After abolishment of the first court, it has also been clear that even that term is uncertain and that being reinstated to former roles may be difficult (see Udomsak 2007, 18–21). These courts have also been widely seen to be politicised and their judges, including Saowanee, have been subjected to individual criticism (Special Interview 2003, 52).

As with the Administrative Courts, these conditions could have affected women's willingness to be appointed. Indeed, there are reports that by 2006 it was difficult to find anyone willing to be appointed (Udomsak 2007, 17; Wasan 2014, 27–28). During selection of the first Constitutional Court judges, however, women's networks urged selectors to choose a woman (Sunee 2004, 263), and as that was a moment of optimism for the court, it would be surprising if no women were then willing. Saowanee, also, was appointed on only her second nomination (Special Interview 2003, 52). It seems, therefore, that there could at least have been an earlier appointment of a woman, and possibly could have been appointments of more women.

A final possible contributing factor is that decisions on appointments may have been influenced by gender biases. For these courts, recruitment processes, while varying, have relied on combinations of nomination, election by peers, selection by a committee and senate approval.[22] There was thus scope for gender biases to have impact.

Part IV: Obstacles and Challenges Faced

This chapter has shown, through considering data on the numbers of women and men judges and court rules and procedures, that women likely still face greater obstacles and challenges in gaining opportunity in the Thai judiciaries than men. It has also identified possible sources for those obstacles and challenges, including family responsibilities, gender biases and exposure to sexual harassment. This part now draws on published statements of judges and others to explore some of the forms that these obstacles and challenges have taken.

The statements drawn on in this part come from several sources. Two are studies of obstacles and challenges faced by women judges (Praphaphan 1998; Usamard 2010). One of these is by a woman judge

---

[21] 1997 Constitution s 259; 2007 Constitution s 208; 2017 Constitution s 207.
[22] 1997 Constitution ss 255, 257; 2006 Constitution s 35; 2007 Constitution ss 204, 206; 2017 Constitution ss 200, 203–4.

(Praphaphan 1998). The others are an interview with a woman judge (Special Interview 2003); an article by a woman judge targeted at younger women judges (Somlak 1989, 165); and a publication from a Courts of Justice seminar stated to be intended to 'encourage Thai women to realise their role, importance and ability in establishing justice in Thai society' (OCJ 2004, 2). These origins bear on the weight that can be attached to the statements. This is especially so for statements from the Courts of Justice seminar publication as they were made by speakers in their professional capacity. The stated purpose of the publications also influences what statements could be expected to be included in them, and for those where that purpose was not to explore obstacles and challenges faced, makes inclusion of statements on this more remarkable.

Historically in Thailand, as noted in Part II, 'family relations' were cited as a reason to restrict women's rights to be judges.[23] While the restriction has been lifted, women are still expected to prioritise caring for their husbands, children and parents. These expectations are so strong that, even in the publication from the Courts of Justice seminar which was stated to be intended to encourage women to see a role for themselves in law (OCJ 2004, 2), a senior woman lawyer emphasised that women's primary duties were as wives, mothers and daughters and stated that in working in law they must not forget these duties (171–172). A senior women prosecutor also stated that if taking on leadership roles may impact family warmth, women should not take them on (161).

The likelihood that women judges' careers were affected by these expectations was mentioned many times in the Courts of Justice seminar publication (OCJ 2004, 27, 69, 98, 161, 171–172, 174, 180, 190, 200). This included the president of the Supreme Court commenting that, when it was considered that women judges also have duties to take care of their families, their commitment to both their families and work was praiseworthy (27). Notably, this statement did not suggest that there should be any change to the burdens carried.

In contrast, the burdens were rarely mentioned in women's narratives of their own careers. When these burdens were mentioned in such narratives, half the mentions were to husbands providing support. One judge noted that her husband gave up his job to avoid conflicts of interest (Special Interview 2003, 51); and another that when her children were young and she had to work away her husband 'understood' and took care

---

[23] *Ministerial Regulation Number 4 B.E. 2502 (1959).*

of them (OCJ 2004, 77). The only other references were a judge stating that she took three postings to the same region because her husband was there (OCJ 2004, 89–90), and another that she traded postings to a region with insurgency so she could care for her mother (OCJ 2004, 116). The impact of family burdens was also minimised in the study by the women judge (Praphaphan 1998, 31).

This mix of mentions could be interpreted in several ways. One could be that family responsibilities were shared and not a significant obstacle or challenge for women. A better interpretation, however, is likely that women are cautious of reinforcing stereotypes of prioritising families over careers and at the same time are reluctant to invite social censure for prioritising careers over families, and so choose not to mention the compromises made.

This links to a second set of obstacles and challenges: those that result from gender stereotypes. This type of obstacle was strongly emphasised in the study by the woman judge (Praphaphan 1998, 29–33). That study and comments in the Courts of Justice seminar publication suggest that in Thailand women are perceived to be trustworthy, hardworking, com-passionate and good with detail and children; but to lack vision and decisiveness, and to be family- rather than work-oriented, physically and emotionally fragile and unwilling to take risks (Praphaphan, 1998, 29–30, 32; OCJ, 2004, 27, 48, 49, 87, 97–98, 180).

Women may also confront challenges that arise from their general social status. In Thai Theravada Buddhism, being born female indicates that one has less karmic merit than being born male. In some regions, women are also seen to be 'polluted' by menstruation and so are denied access to some areas and roles in some ceremonies (Juree 2008, 33–34; Hamburg 2008, 97–98, 103). The potential for this status to impact women judges is increased by the fact that, as noted in Part I, the prestige of the Thai judiciary is founded in part in a cultivated image of being especially virtuous, noble, wise and loyal (see Kitpatchara 2018).

Statements from judges suggest that the stereotypes affect how others treat women judges. This includes suggestions that the stereotypes result in women judges being more likely to be allocated research work (Praphaphan 1998, 30) and less likely to be posted to the provinces (Usamard 2010, 137) or to be allocated murder or rape cases (OCJ 2004, 33), or work that requires travel, decisiveness, resolution of imme-diate problems or delegation of work to or supervision of others (Praphaphan 1998, 30, 32). It also includes suggestion that the stereo-types may affect how women are interviewed for promotion (Usamard 2010, 136).

As to women's general social status, no suggestion was found that this affects how women are treated in judging contexts. Somlak's account, however, indicates it may affect how they are treated when performing roles expected of them at religious, royal and state functions. Somlak recounts having had to endure uncomfortable stares after taking the seat she was entitled to by her rank at a state function (184), and having had the order in which garlands were presented at a state function changed so they passed male to female, female to male, rather than following seniority (1989, 178–179). Men performing the same roles are less likely to face such challenges.

The stereotypes and women's social status may also influence how women conduct themselves. This influence may result not only from women's desire to fit in or succeed, but also from fear that their actions may impact opportunities for other women. This potential for their actions to impact opportunities for other women was referenced by two Thai women judges (Somlak 1989, 185; OCJ 2004, 108), and is recognised to be likely where women are in institutions in smaller numbers as in such situations they tend to face additional scrutiny and be perceived not as individuals but as representative of all women (Jefferson and Johnson 2020, 129–134).

Women's accounts suggest that there has been some variation in how they have responded to the stereotypes. Several women judges have suggested that to fit in or succeed they have had to act like men (Praphaphan 1998, 33; OCJ 2004, 76; Usamard 2010, 137). This suggests an effort to counter all stereotypes. One woman judge, however, has suggested a need to be humble but have a hidden decisiveness (OCJ 2004, 93); and a woman lawyer has suggested a need for women to express their views but not be aggressive, to be decisive but not obstinate and to use their attention to detail but not be overly fastidious (OCJ 2004 93, 171). This suggests a more complex balancing act that involves partially accepting and attempting to positively use the stereotypes.

While there has been some variation, there are areas in which women judges' accounts suggest consistent efforts to counter the stereotypes. One such area is physical frailty. In their accounts, many women judges emphasise having resolved not to be deterred by physical risks, and urge other women to do likewise (Somlak 1989, 171–173; OCJ 2004, 85, 93, 115–118; Usamard 2010, 137). They also recount having done things like confronting a yard intruder or choosing to stay in a region with insurgency after another judge was killed despite male judges asking for a transfer out of the region (OCJ 2004, 117–118). The way women recount these experiences, and especially the comparisons they draw to men, indicate they have felt less freedom to make certain self-interested choices than men.

As to women's social status, this status means that some actions available to men to show the qualities that support judicial prestige may not be available to women. A clear example is that, as woman cannot be ordained as monks, they cannot participate in a regular program whereby judges are ordained for a short period and dedicate the merit attained to the King, thus showing both virtue and loyalty (Kitpatchara 2008, 103). As they cannot participate in such actions, women may have to invest greater effort in showing the same qualities in other ways.

Finally, being in the minority may increase women's exposure to sexual harassment (Jefferson and Johnson 2020, 136–140). Indications that this occurs are found in the fact that Somlak warns young women judges that they are likely to experience an inappropriate level of interest in their appearance (185) and recounts having had an official address her in a sexualising way by suggesting her court's football team won because they had her as a focus for their hearts (1989, 178).

All of this suggests that while women have sometimes been able to succeed in the Thai judiciaries, to do so they have likely had to be more exceptional than, and make more sacrifices than, men. This should lead not only to increased respect for the women who succeed, but also to increased attention to ways to change this situation.

Conclusion

This chapter has drawn on several methods to explore opportunities, obstacles and challenges for women in the Thai judiciaries. These have included methods commonly used in the study of women in judiciaries, such as exploration of women's entry to the legal professions and analysis of data on the numbers of women and men judges; court rules and procedures; and statements of judges. They have also included a method — comparison across court systems — seemingly not previously used to study career judiciaries.

Through use of these methods, this chapter has shown that, with persistent and often collective effort, women have improved their access to the Thai legal professions. It has, however, also shown that improving access was not easy; and that, even with the improvements, women likely still face greater obstacles and challenges in entering into and progressing in the Thai judiciaries than men. It has also identified what some of those obstacles and challenges likely are, and some ways that court rules and procedures likely contribute to them.

Significantly, many of the insights on obstacles and challenges faced would not have been possible without drawing comparisons across court systems. This method was useful both in identifying where women were likely under-represented and identifying how court rules and procedures likely contributed to this. The usefulness of this method in this analysis indicates it has potential for wider use in the study of career judiciaries. The findings made may also provide a starting point for analyses across a broader range of such judiciaries.

This chapter also drew attention to some aspects of women's experiences in judiciaries that have been less emphasised in previous studies and could warrant further consideration. These included the connection between career progression opportunity for women and their inclination to enter the legal professions, explored in Part II; ways courts having an uncertain future and being seen as politicised may influence women's decisions to become judges, explored in Part III; and pressures women judges may face to make non-self-interested choices, and challenges they may confront due to judicial prestige having a cultural base, explored in Part IV.

For Thailand itself, meanwhile, this chapter has clearly indicated that it is desirable for there to be ongoing effort to improve opportunities for women in the Thai judiciaries. This is important because recent appointments of women to high positions in the judiciaries and flaws in the prior literature may cloud recognition both of the fact that opportunity for women is not equal to that of men, and of how difficult it may be to change this. This chapter has also identified issues on which future efforts to improve opportunities for women may focus, and has indicated that if there is to be improvement, active effort will likely be required.

References

Articles/Books/Reports

Boigeol, Anne. 2013. 'Feminisation of the French "Magistrature": Gender and Judging in a Feminized Context'. In *Gender and Judging*, edited by Ulrike Schultz and Gisela Shaw, 125–143. Oxford: Hart.

Boonyen Wotong. 1964. 'Establishment of Administrative Educational Institutions in Thailand: Case Study of Establishment of the University of Moral and Political Sciences as a Tool for Administration in the Early Democratic Era in Thailand' [kan chattang sathaban kansueksa nai thang pokkhrong khong prathet thai : bot sueksa chapho korani kan chattang mahawitthayalai wicha thammasat lae kanmueang nai laksana thi pen upakon to kan pokkhrong rabop prachathippatai samai roemton nai prathet thai]. Masters Thesis. Thammasat University.

C.12. 2009. 'This Is the Administrative Courts (2)' [thi ni sanpokkhrong (2)], December 11, *Thai Rath*, www.thairath.co.th/content/52128.

2015. 'The New Group of Supreme Administrative Court Judges' [tulakan san po.kho. sungsut chut mai]. *Thai Rath*, November 24, 2015. www.thairath.co .th/content/541332.

Cremation Volume from the Royal Funeral of Khunying Raem Phromobon Bunyaprasop, Mo.Por.Cho., Mo. Wo.Mo., Tor.Jo., at the Crematorium in Front of Isariyaphorn Pavilion Thepsirintharawas Temple, Bangkok, Monday 29 September 2008 [anuson ngan phraratchathan phloeng sop khunying raem phrommobon bunyaprasop mopocho, mowomo, tocho na meru luang na phlapphla itisriyaphon wat thepsirinthrawat krungthepmahanakhon, wan chan thi 29 kanyayon phoso 2551]. 2008. Bangkok: Family of Khunying Raem Phromobon Bunyaprasop.

Hamburg, Cambria G. 2008. 'Prohibited Spaces: Barriers and Strategies in Women's NGO Work in Isaan, North-Eastern Thailand'. In *Women and Politics in Thailand: Continuity and Change*, edited by Kazuki Iwanaga, 95–124. Copenhagen: NIAS Press.

Iwanaga, Kazuki, ed. 2008. *Women and Politics in Thailand: Continuity and Change*. NIAS Press.

Jefferson, Renee Knake and Hannah Brenner Johnson. 2020. *Shortlisted: Women in the Shadows of the Supreme Court*. New York: New York University Press.

Jittima Pornarun. 1995. 'Women's Rights Movement in Thai Society 1946–1976' [kan riakrong sitthi satri nai sangkhom thai phoso 2489–2519]. Masters Thesis. Chulalongkorn University.

Juree Vichit-Vadakan. 2008. 'Women in Politics and Women and Politics: A Socio-Cultural Analysis of the Thai Context'. In *Women and Politics in Thailand: Continuity and Change*, edited by Kazuki Iwanaga, 27–53. NIAS Press.

Kay, Fiona and Elizabeth Gorman. 2008. 'Women in the Legal Profession'. *Annual Review of Law and Social Science* 4(1): 299–332.

Kenney, Sally J. 2013. 'Which Judicial Selection Systems Generate the Most Women Judges? Lessons from the United States'. In *Gender and Judging*, edited by Ulrike Schultz and Gisela Shaw, 461–480. Oxford: Hart.

Kitpatchara Somanawat. 2018. 'Constructing the Identity of the Thai Judge: Virtue, Status and Power'. *Asian Journal of Law and Society* 5(1): 91–110.

Loos, Tamara. 2006. *Subject Siam: Family, Law, and Colonial Modernity in Thailand*. Ithaca, NY: Cornell University Press.

McCargo, Duncan. 2020. *Fighting for Virtue: Justice and Politics in Thailand*. Ithaca, NY: Cornell University Press.

Munger, Frank. 2019. 'The Evolution of Law, the Legal Profession and Political Authority'. *NYLS Legal Studies Research Paper No. 3347143.* http://dx.doi .org/10.2139/ssrn.3347143.

Natenapha Wailerdsak. 2009. 'Corporate Women Managers'. In *The Changing Face of Management in Thailand*, edited by Tim Andrews and Sununta Siengthai, 248–268. New York: Routledge.

Office of the Administrative Courts (OAC). 2003. 'The Administrative Court Annual Report 2002' [rai-ngan kan patibatngan khong san pokkhrong lae samnakngan sanpokkhrong pracham pi 2545].

   2004. 'The Administrative Court Annual Report 2003' [rai-ngan kan patibatn-gan khong san pokkhrong lae samnakngan sanpokkhrong pracham pi 2546].

   2005. 'The Administrative Court Annual Report 2004' [rai-ngan kan patibatn-gan khong san pokkhrong lae samnakngan sanpokkhrong pracham pi 2547].

   2006. 'The Administrative Court Annual Report 2005' [rai-ngan kan patibatn-gan khong san pokkhrong lae samnakngan sanpokkhrong pracham pi 2548].

   2007. 'The Administrative Court Annual Report 2006' [rai-ngan kan patibatn-gan khong san pokkhrong lae samnakngan sanpokkhrong pracham pi 2549].

   2008. 'The Administrative Court Annual Report 2007' [rai-ngan kan patibatn-gan khong san pokkhrong lae samnakngan sanpokkhrong pracham pi 2550].

   2009. 'The Administrative Court Annual Report 2008' [rai-ngan kan patibatn-gan khong san pokkhrong lae samnakngan sanpokkhrong pracham pi 2551].

   2010. 'The Administrative Court Annual Report 2009' [rai-ngan kan patibatn-gan khong san pokkhrong lae samnakngan sanpokkhrong pracham pi 2552].

   2011. 'The Administrative Court Annual Report 2010' [rai-ngan kan patibatn-gan khong san pokkhrong lae samnakngan sanpokkhrong pracham pi 2553].

   2012. 'The Administrative Court Annual Report 2011' [rai-ngan kan patibatn-gan khong san pokkhrong lae samnakngan sanpokkhrong pracham pi 2554].

   2013. 'The Administrative Court Annual Report 2012' [rai-ngan kan patibatn-gan khong san pokkhrong lae samnakngan sanpokkhrong pracham pi 2555].

   2014. 'The Administrative Court Annual Report 2013' [rai-ngan kan patibatn-gan khong san pokkhrong lae samnakngan sanpokkhrong pracham pi 2556].

2015. 'The Administrative Court Annual Report 2014' [rai-ngan kan patibatn-gan khong san pokkhrong lae samnakngan sanpokkhrong pracham pi 2557].

2016. 'The Administrative Court Annual Report 2015' [rai-ngan kan patibatn-gan khong san pokkhrong lae samnakngan sanpokkhrong pracham pi 2558].

2017. 'The Administrative Court Annual Report 2016' [rai-ngan kan patibatn-gan khong san pokkhrong lae samnakngan sanpokkhrong pracham pi 2559].

2018. 'The Administrative Court Annual Report 2017' [rai-ngan kan patibatn-gan khong san pokkhrong lae samnakngan sanpokkhrong pracham pi 2560].

2019. 'The Administrative Court Annual Report 2018' [rai-ngan kan patibatn-gan khong san pokkhrong lae samnakngan sanpokkhrong pracham pi 2561].

Office of the Civil Service Commission (OCSC). 2011. *Government Civilian Workforce 2010* [kamlang khon phak rat nai fai phonlaruean 2553]. Office of the Civil Service Commission.

2012. *Government Civilian Workforce 2011* [kamlang khon phak rat nai fai phonlaruean 2554]. Office of the Civil Service Commission.

2013. *Government Civilian Workforce 2012* [kamlang khon phak rat nai fai phonlaruean 2555]. Office of the Civil Service Commission.

2014. *Government Civilian Workforce 2013* [kamlang khon phak rat nai fai phonlaruean 2556]. Office of the Civil Service Commission.

2015. *Government Civilian Workforce 2014* [kamlang khon phak rat nai fai phonlaruean 2557]. Office of the Civil Service Commission.

2016. *Government Civilian Workforce 2015* [kamlang khon phak rat nai fai phonlaruean 2558]. Office of the Civil Service Commission.

2017. *Government Civilian Workforce 2016* [kamlang khon phak rat nai fai phonlaruean 2559]. Office of the Civil Service Commission.

2018. *Government Civilian Workforce 2017* [kamlang khon phak rat nai fai phonlaruean 2560]. Office of the Civil Service Commission.

2019. *Government Civilian Workforce 2018* [kamlang khon phak rat nai fai phonlaruean 2561]. Office of the Civil Service Commission.

Office of the Courts of Justice (OCJ), ed. 2004. *The Role of Women in the Justice Process: Academic Seminar in Honour of Her Majesty Queen Sirikit on the Auspicious Occassion of the Celebration of Her Sixth Cycle on 12 August 2004* [botbat satri nai krabuankan yutitham : kan sammana wichakan chaloem-phrakiat somdet phranangchao siri ki phraboromrachininat nueang nai okat phraratchaphithi maha mongkhon chaloemphrachonphansa 6 rop 12 sin-ghakhom 2547]. Bangkok: Office of the Courts of Justice.

Oraphan Chantharawongphaisan. 2017. 'Interview Revealing the Life of "Female Judge" Somlak Jadkrabuanpol from "Daughter of Cavalryman" to "Female Referee"' [samphat poet chiwit 'phuphiphaksa ying' somlak chatkrabuanphon chak 'luksao thahan ma' su 'than pao ying']. online. *Matichon.* 13 August. www.matichon.co.th/prachachuen/interview/news_627676.

Praphaphan Udomjanya. 1998. *Women on the Executive Path in the Thai Public Service: Judicial Work* [phuying bon senthang nakborihan nai rabop ratchakan thai: ngan dan tulakan]. Bangkok: Gender and Development Research Institute.

Raem Phromobon Bunyaprasop. 1984. 'A Slice of Memory' [siao nueng haeng khwam song cham]. In *Thammasat 50 Years* [thammasat 50 pi], edited by Charnvit Kasetsiri, 285–298. Bangkok: Thammasat University.

Rungsaeng Kittayapong. 1990. 'The Origins of Thailand's Modern Ministry of Justice and Its Early Development'. PhD. University of Bristol.

Schultz, Ulrike. 2013. '"I Was Noticed and I Was Asked . . ." Women's Careers in the Judiciary: Results of an Empirical Study for the Ministry of Justice in Northrine-Westfalia, Germany'. In *Gender and Judging*, edited by Ulrike Schultz and Gisela Shaw, 145–166. Oxford: Hart.

Somlak Jadkrabuanpol. 1989. '"Women Judge"' ['balang ying']. *Dulpaha* 36 (2): 165–185.

———. 2017. 'The Position of Supreme Court President from My Perspective' [tamnaeng prathan sandika nai mum mong khong khaphachao] *Matichon.* 4 August. www.matichon.co.th/columnists/news_616455.

———. 2003. 'Special Interview Prof. Dr. Saowanee Asawaroj Thailand's First Female Constitutional Court Judge' [samphat phiset so doro saowani atsawawarot tulakan san ratthathammanun ying khon raek khong prathet thai]. *New Law Magazine* 1(1): 49–52.

Suksun Dangpakdee. 1995. 'Society's Expectations of Thai Women in the "Nation Building" Period, 1938–1944' [khwam khatwang khong sangkhom to satri thai nai samai sang chat phoso 2481–2487]. Masters Thesis. Chulalongkorn University.

Sunee Chaiyarose. 2004. 'Synthesizing Feminism, Democracy and Human Rights: Sunee Chaiyarose's Self-Portrait' [kan lom ruam udomkan feminit prachathippatai lae sitthi manutsayachon : sueksa phan prasopkan suni chairot]. Masters Thesis. Thammasat University.

Supin Kachacupt. 2008. 'Women's Equal Rights and Participation in the Thai Bureaucracy'. In *Women and Politics in Thailand: Continuity and Change*, edited by Kazuki Iwanaga, 198–236. NIAS Press.

Suppatra Singkhaloka. 1992a. 'History of Demanding Women's Rights from Beginnings to Success'. [prawatti kan roemton khong kan riakrong sitthi satri chonkrathang samret]. In *The Sign of Progress Is the Status of Women*

[khrueangmai haeng khwam rungrueang khue saphap haeng satri], edited
by Suppatra Singkhaloka, 265–272. Bangkok: Ruenkaew Printing.

1992b. 'History and Work of the Women's Lawyers Association of Thailand
under the Royal Patronage of Her Majesty the Queen' [prawat lae phonngan
khong samakhom bandit satri thang kotmai haeng prathet thai nai phra-
borom rachinupatham]. In *The Sign of Progress Is the Status of Women*
[khrueangmai haeng khwam rungrueang khue saphap haeng satri], edited
by Suppatra Singkhaloka, 327–343. Bangkok: Ruenkaew Printing.

Suprani Khongnirandonsuk. 1993. 'Khunying Suppatra Singkhaloka Godmother
of the Chao Phraya River Basin'. *Manager Magazine*, March. http://info
.gotomanager.com/news/details.aspx?id=9550.

Udomsak Nitimontree. 2007. 'Experiences of a Judge of 3 Courts' [prasopkan
khong tulakan 3 san]. *Administrative Courts Journal* 7(1): 15–22.

Usamard Siampukdee. 2010. 'Status of Women Profession: Gender Equality of
Judicial Occupation in Thailand'. *Journal of Ritsumeikan Social Sciences and
Humanities* 2010(3): 123–144.

Wasan Soiphisut. 2014. *(Un)fun Tales in the Constitutional Court* [rueang (mai)
sanuk nai san ratthathammanun]. Bangkok: Ton Tham.

Constitutions (Thailand)

'Constitution of the Kingdom of Thailand B.E. 2517 (1974)' [ratthathammanun
haeng ratcha-anachak thai phoso 2517].

'Constitution of the Kingdom of Thailand B.E. 2540 (1997)' [ratthathammanun
haeng ratcha-anachak thai phoso 2540].

'Constitution of the Kingdom of Thailand (Interim) B.E. 2549 (2006)' [ratthatham-
manun haeng ratcha-anachak thai (chabap chuakhrao) phoso 2549].

'Constitution of the Kingdom of Thailand B.E. 2550 (2007)' [ratthathammanun
haeng ratcha-anachak thai phoso 2550].

'Constitution of the Kingdom of Thailand B.E. 2560 (2017)' [ratthathammanun
haeng ratcha-anachak thai phoso 2560].

Laws (Thailand)

'Act on Establishment of Administrative Courts and Administrative Court
Procedure B.E. 2542 (1999)' [phraratchabanyat chattang sanpokkhrong lae
withi phicharana khadi pokkhrong phoso 2542].

'Act on Establishment of Juvenile Courts B.E. 2494 (1951)' [phraratchabanyat
chattang sankhadideklaeyaowachon phoso 2494].

'Act on Principles for Appointment to and Holding of Positions of Senior Judges
B.E. 2542 (1999)' [phraratchabanyat lakken kan taengtang lae kan damrong
tamnaeng phu phiphaksa awuso phoso 2542].

'*Act on the Courts of Justice Judicial Service B.E. 2543* (2000)' [phraratchabanyat rabiap kharatchakan fai tulakan san yutitham 2543].

'*Act on the Judicial Service B.E. 2482* (1939)' [phraratchabanyat rabiap kharatchakan fai tulakan phoso 2482].

'*Act on the Judicial Service B.E. 2497* (1954)' [phraratchabanyat rabiap kharatchakan fai tulakan phoso 2497].

'*Act on the Judicial Service B.E. 2521* (1978)' [phraratchabanyat rabiap kharatchakan fai tulakan phoso 2521].

'*Administrative Court Judicial Commission Regulations on Methods for Selection of Judges of Administrative Courts of First Instance, Heads of Division of Administrative Courts of First Instance, Deputy Chief Justices of Administrative Courts of First Instance and Chief Justices of Administrative Courts of First Instance B.E. 2544* (2001)' [rabiap ko. sopo. wa duai withikan khatlueak tulakan sanpokkhrong chan ton tulakan huana khana sanpokkhrong chan ton rong athibodi sanpokkhrong chan ton lae athibodi sanpokkhrong chan ton phoso 2544].

'*Administrative Court Judicial Commission Regulations on Methods for Selection of Supreme Administrative Court Judges, Heads of Division of the Supreme Administrative Court, Vice Presidents of the Supreme Administrative Court and President of the Supreme Administrative Court B.E. 2544* (2001)' [rabiap ko. sopo. wa duai withikan khatlueak tulakan sanpokkhrong sungsut tulakan huana khana sanpokkhrong sungsut rong prathan sanpokkhrong sungsut lae prathan sanpokkhrong sungsut phoso 2544].

'*Administrative Court Judicial Commission Regulations on Moving and Promoting Judges of Administrative Courts of First Instance B.E. 2554* (2011)' [rabiap ko. sopo. wa duai kan yai lae kan luean tamnaeng khong tulakan nai sanpokkhrong chan ton phoso 2554].

'*Courts of Justice Judicial Commission Regulations on Principles for the Appointment, Promotion, Transfer and Raising of Salary and Position Payments for Judicial Officials B.E. 2554* (2011)' [rabiap khanakammakan tulakan san yutitham wa duai lakken kan taengtang kan luean tamnaeng kan yokyai taengtang lae kan luean ngoen duean lae ngoen pracham tamnaeng kharatchakan tulakan phoso 2554].

'*Declaration of the Office of the Prime Minister on Appointment of Judges of Administrative Courts of First Instance*' [prakat samnak nayokratthamontri rueang taengtang tulakan nai sanpokkhrong chan ton]. 12 February 2001.

'*Declaration of the Office of the Prime Minister on Appointment of Supreme Administrative Court Judges*' [prakat samnak nayokratthamontri rueang taengtang tulakan nai sanpokkhrong sungsut]. 27 March 2000.

'*Ministerial Regulation Number 4 B.E. 2502* (1959) *Issued under the Act on the Judicial Service B.E. 2497* (1954)' [kotkrasuang chabap thi 4 phoso 2502 ok tam khwam nai phraratchabanyat rabiap kharatchakan fai tulakan 2497].

'Ministerial Regulation Number 7 B.E. 2518 (1975) *Issued under the Act on the Judicial Service B.E. 2497* (1954)' [kotkrasuang chabap thi 7 phoso 2518 ok tam khwam nai phraratchabanyat rabiap kharatchakan fai tulakan 2497].

Other

'Report of House of Representatives Meeting, Meeting 10/2497 (1954) (Ordinary Meeting)' [rai-ngan kan prachum saphaphuthaenratsadon khrang thi 10/2497 (saman)]. 9 September 1954. Ananda Samakhom Throne Hall.

5

The Promise and Paradox of Women Judges in the Judiciary in Indonesia

MELISSA CROUCH[*]

Over the past two decades, studies of Indonesian law have broadly been animated by one theme, law reform, and one question, how law reform is used as a tool for social change. In 1998, the fall of Suharto and the demands for democracy and the rule of law led to major efforts at constitutional and political reform, including significant court reform (Crouch 2019a). Established as part of the process of democratic reform and constitutional amendment, the Constitutional Court remains the most popular judicial institution in Indonesia and is essential to the maintenance of democratic gains and constitutional rights protection.

However, in terms of gender on the bench, there has only ever been one female judge out of nine on the bench at any one time. Symbolically, the Constitutional Court does not begin to meet global demands for women's equal representation in the judiciary for the world's third largest democracy. Yet Indonesia's Constitutional Court is important because it is a forum for the ongoing struggle for democracy. Judicial appointments to the Constitutional Court draw public scrutiny and controversy. In 2018, the only female judge of the Constitutional Court, Justice Maria Farida Indrati, retired from her position after serving for the maximum of two terms, or ten years in total (2008–2018). Public debate over her replacement concerned whether the appointed judge should be a woman or not, a rerun of the merit versus gender representation argument (Thornton 2007). Her replacement shows the politics of intersectionality in Indonesia in terms of gender and religion: another female judge was

[*] I would like to thank the Sir Louis Matheson Library of Monash University and Dr Rheny Pulungan (subject librarian, Indonesian Studies) for ensuring I had access to a book paying tribute to Justice Maria Farid Indrati (Faiz 2018), despite the extended library shutdown due to the Covid-19 crisis. The Asia Studies collection at libraries like Monash University, the National Library of Australia, the Australian National University and the University of Melbourne are essential to further knowledge on Asia in Australia.

appointed, but this time they are Muslim (the religion of the majority), in contrast to Justice Indrati's affiliation with the minority Christian community.

The legacy of Justice Indrati's two terms on the court also generated public debate on her role as a female judge, her dissenting judgments and her views on women, interreligious marriage, child protection, pornography and religion. This occurred at a time when Indonesia experienced its #MeToo moment. There was national social outcry – particularly from women's rights groups – over the legal conviction of a female victim of sexual harassment for allegedly defaming her male harasser.[1]

To begin to address the relative absence of women from studies of Indonesian law, in this chapter I focus on the role of women in the legal profession and judiciary in the *reformasi* era in Indonesia. To what extent can we speak of the feminisation of the judiciary in Indonesia, both in a thin sense of entrance to the profession and in a thick substantive sense of gender equality? I consider the wider social and legal context of steps forward and backwards in gender equality in Indonesia, and then review existing legal scholarship to identify where and how women appear.

I then develop the idea of a model minority judge as one who is perceived to be part of a minority community (whether religious, ethnic, cultural or otherwise) and whose conduct while in judicial office is considered to be exemplary in terms of ethics, integrity, intellect and professionalism. That is, to prove their worth, women from minority groups may be held to higher standards on ethics, intellect and professionalism, in contrast to male judges who do not necessarily need to work to meet these same standards. I explore the role and influence of Justice Indrati as an example of a model minority judge. I then briefly review the entrance of women into the Supreme Court and lower courts, focusing on Justice Albertina Ho as another example of a model minority judge. These women judges are clearly trailblazers and role models promoting gender equality and anti-corruption. The paradox is that some women who have entered the judiciary perpetuate gender inequality. I conclude by suggesting that any agenda for research on the feminisation of the legal profession in Indonesia needs to hold in tension both the promise and paradox of women judges in terms of the potential to promote or stall gender equality.

---

[1] See Crouch, cited in Massoula 2019; Crouch 2019b; Cahaya 2018.

Steps Forward and Backwards in Gender Equality in Indonesia

Discussions concerning legal equality for women in Indonesia are dominated by the key issues of democratic participation and religion. In the *reformasi* era post-1998, studies of women in Indonesia focus on the role and agency of Muslim women activists (Rinaldo 2013); the challenges for women under Islamic law in Aceh (Afrianty 2016; Feener 2016); debates over state regulation of sexuality and pornography (Crouch 2009; Pausacker 2012); the intersection between gender and custom, particularly among the matrilineal Minangkabau (von Benda-Beckman and von Benda-Beckman 2013); and the impact of local religious regulations such as dress codes for women (Crouch 2009). There is a growing literature on the role of women in politics, and emerging studies of how female incumbency improves female candidate placement and electability in national and local politics in Indonesia (Rosenfield 2012).

Yet the literature is unusually silent on women in the legal profession and has not yet considered their role and contribution to legal and judicial reform in Indonesia post-1998. The relative absence of studies on women in the law in Indonesia is evident from major comparative studies of women in the legal profession that do not include women in Indonesia (for example, Abel and Lewis 1989; Michelson 2013; Schultz and Shaw 2013, 2003; Dieterhlermann, and Atanasiu 2006; Kay and Gorman 2008; but see Bedner and Kouwagam 2020).

The history of the struggle for gender equality in Indonesia is often traced back to Kartini (1879–1904) who is remembered for her advocacy on education for women, as well as for her opposition to polygamy (Jayawardena 2009, 141–146). Among her achievements is the establishment of a school for daughters of Javanese officials, although her life and advocacy was cut short at the young age of twenty-five years old when she tragically died in childbirth.

In the early 1910s, the first women's movement known as Putri Mardika (Independent Women) was formed and it was affiliated with the Budi Utomo movement against Dutch colonial rule. There were several institutional milestones for the women's movement in the 1920s and 1930s, including the First Indonesian Women's Congress; the establishment of the Federation for Indonesian Women's Association; participation in the Congress of Asian Women; and the formation of the Indonesian Women's Congress (KOWANI) during Japanese occupation. During World War II, women were finally granted the franchise in Indonesia.

There are several key issues for women's rights that feature in both past and present struggles, and these include the issue of polygamy, child marriage (see UNICEF and BPS 2020), the rights of Muslim women to divorce and interreligious marriage. In 1937, debate over many of these issues arose when a draft Marriage Ordinance proposed to grant women the right to divorce their husband and banned the practice of polygamy. But opposition from Islamic groups at the time meant that the government backed down from the proposal.

Suharto's New Order, from 1965 to 1998, was a period characterised by a particular state view of women that Julia Suryakusuma has termed 'State Ibuism' (1988). State Ibuism as a concept and practice of the state was a means to define and confine women to roles as wives and subordinates to men. The state characterised women in a position of submission to men and as located within the family, and this image of Indonesian women was propagated by state institutions and shaped their policies (Robinson 2000, 141; Blackburn 2004, 141).

Within this context, in the 1970s, the same issues of polygamy, child marriage, divorce rights and interreligious marriage arose, and this time culminated in the Marriage Law 1974 (see Cammack et al. 2008). However, the law still permitted polygamy, although it added certain conditions on the practise of polygamy. The law allows girls of sixteen years old to marry and identifies the man as the head of the household. The law is ambiguous as to the issue of interreligious marriage. Despite these issues, in 1984, the government did sign on to the international agenda for women's equality by ratifying the United Nations Convention on Discrimination against Women (CEDAW).[2]

Today, Indonesia's population is almost 90 per cent Muslim, yet it is not a country based on Islamic law. Instead, the state has endorsed a compromise known as Pancasila, that affirms belief in God but does not mandate Syariah law. The transition from authoritarian rule in 1997–1998 saw horrific crimes and violence committed, particularly against women. In response, in 1998, the National Commission on Violence against Women (Komnas Perempuan) was established. In 1999, the government passed a new law on human rights and chapter 9 of the law affirms that women's rights are human rights.[3] The political landscape was also fundamentally changed as the law guaranteed women's representation in political parties and in elections, as well as

---

[2] Law 7/1984 on CEDAW.
[3] Law 39/1999 on Basic Human Rights.

in the legislature, executive and judiciary. In 2000, the president advanced this agenda further by issuing a decree on a National Gender Mainstreaming Policy.

In addition to new legislation and policy, at the constitutional level the state affirmed its commitment to individual rights. In 1999–2002, the amendments to the Constitution added some political and civil rights such as the right to life, as well as social and economic rights such as the right to be married, a right to health services and to social security. In 2002, a law on child protection was passed.

Women's advocacy groups have continued to push for greater representation in the legislature for women. In 2003, the law for the first time recommended that all political parties ensure that women make up at least 30 per cent of their candidates in a constituency and by 2008 this became mandatory (Butt 2015, 158). In 2004, the government made a significant show of support for women's equality by passing a law on the elimination of domestic violence.[4] In 2005, Indonesia became a signatory to the International Covenant on Civil and Political Rights ('ICCPR') and the International Covenant on Economic, Social and Cultural Rights ('ICESCR'), both of which protect women's rights (Article 26 and Article 3, respectively).[5]

Yet there have been wider ideological challenges to the women's movement. For example, in 2005, the Indonesian Ulama Council, the peak quasi-governmental Islamic body, issued a fatwa against liberalism, secularism and pluralism. While only persuasive and without legal status, this fatwa had a dampening effect on advocacy for these ideas. As a strategic move, the idea of liberalism is often not expressly stated by its supporters, but instead there is talk of progressive Muslims or the idea of progressive Islam as an attempt to manoeuver around the stigma associated with liberalism. This fatwa and wider ideological debate has also affected the women's movement, and many women's groups in Indonesia do not necessarily hold liberalism as a core value.

More recently, in 2019, the Marriage Law was reformed to address the issue of child marriages by increasing the legal age of marriage for girls from sixteen to nineteen years old (with parental permission, or twenty-one years without permission), which is now consistent with the

---

[4] Law 23/2004 on the Elimination of Domestic Violence.
[5] See Law 11/2005 and 12/2005, respectively. These Covenants became Indonesian Law according to Law 24/2000 on International Treaties.

age for boys.[6] Despite these legal steps forward, the gap in gender inequality in Indonesia remains wide. For example, Indonesia ranks 88th in the World Economic Forum's Gender Gap index. While there have been some legislative gains, there have also been legal steps backwards, and the social and economic position of women is not one of equality with men. In the workforce, there is a particular concentration of women in low-paying jobs, in the informal sector, or in non-remunerated roles. Women remain at greater risk of poverty and disadvantage.[7]

Since 1998, one of the major changes in governance that has affected women is the shift to decentralisation. Despite the national government retaining power over matters of religion, one consequence of decentralisation is that local governors and mayors have issued local regulations (*peraturan daerah*, perda) that restriction and regulate what women can wear and do – such as rules mandating the wearing of the headscarf, placing curfews on women unless they are accompanied by a male companion,[8] prohibiting women from travelling with a man by motorbike, permitting polygamy, banning men and women from swimming together,[9] prohibiting prostitution or requiring women to wear long skirts rather than tight jeans in Aceh (Crouch 2009).

For example, more than twenty religious regulations across several provinces specifically attempt to impose Muslim dress codes for men and women. These religious regulations apply to both men and women, but are often directed to specific groups, such as students, civil servants, employees of educational institutions and people attending official ceremonies. For women, the dress requirements stipulate that they must wear long-sleeved tops that are loose-fitting and not see-through, a long skirt or pants that are also loose, and a headscarf that covers the hair, ears and neck.[10] Some of these religious regulations apply all the time; others stipulate that Muslim clothing must only be worn on Fridays.

In addition, another national issue has been the banning of pornography. In 1999, there was a proposed bill on Anti-pornography and Pornographic Acts. The bill sought to regulate public expressions of sexuality, claiming that it would protect the community and promote

---

[6] Law 16/2009 amending Law 1/1974 on Marriage.

[7] Oxfam, '*Towards a More Equal Indonesia*' (Briefing Paper, February 2017), p. 14.

[8] See for example Art. 6(1) of the Perda of Gorontalo 10/2003 on Solving Social Problems.

[9] For example, see Appeal of the Bupati Tasikmalaya No. 556.3/BN/03/908/2001.

[10] For example, see Perda of Sawahlunto/Sijunjung (West Sumatra) 2/2003 on Muslim Clothing, Art. 7.

good religious morals. Although the national bill was unsuccessful at this time, some local leaders sought to regulate morality by prohibiting prostitution.[11] By 2005, the bill was again on the legislative agenda and was passed by the legislature in October 2008. The law has a wide definition of what constitutes illegal pornographic acts and contains harsh penalties for breaches of the law.[12] Both the content of this law and its implementation have been a cause of concern for women's rights groups.

There has therefore been a mixture of steps forward and backwards in the legal struggle for gender equality. Two wider social considerations are important to keep in mind: the salience of Islam to national politics, and the impact of Covid-19 on women, although it is too early to offer an assessment of the latter. In the more than two decades of reform since 1998, Islam and religion has featured prominently in public discourse and has often been an issue confronting women judges in Indonesia, as I will later show.

Women, Law and the State in Independent Indonesia: An Agenda

Both the progress and remaining challenges for gender equality set the context for an agenda on the study of women in the legal profession in Indonesia. An examination of the entrance of women in the legal profession in Indonesia, or a thin account of feminisation of the judiciary, upends assumptions made in the comparative literature on women in the legal profession. For example, scholarship often implicitly assumes that the legal profession in countries in the Global North are at a certain stage in terms of women's entrance to the profession, and that the Global South is behind in terms of the numbers of women in the profession. Indonesia's history of first female judicial appointments show this assumption to be false. An example is in 1966 when Sri Widojati Notoprojo was appointed as the first female judge of the Indonesian Supreme Court, which was some fifteen years before the appointment of the first female judge on the United States Supreme Court (Lev 1996, 191).[13]

---

[11] See for example Perda of Garut (West Java) 6/2000 on Morality; Perda of Indramayu (West Java) 7/1999 on Prostitution.

[12] Law 44/2008 on Pornography.

[13] In 1981, Sandra Day O'Connor was appointed to the US Supreme Court.

A thicker concept of feminisation in the judiciary requires careful consideration. What difference, if any, do women judges make in Indonesia? How do they act as judges – do they conform to certain stereotypes or do they change the nature of judging? By studying the role of the Constitutional Court, I show that it is often precisely because women judges are conservative and formalist in their approach to constitutional interpretation, and openly reject the label feminist, that they are appointed to the judiciary and generally maintain public trust while in office. In particular, the first women judge of the Constitutional Court was successful because she was considered to be a model minority judge.

In this chapter, I focus on women judges in the Supreme Court and Constitutional Court. I acknowledge that there are inevitably problems of representation and scale when studies only focus on elite lawyers (see Munger 2012), or for that matter, elite judges or judges in the Constitutional Court in Jakarta as opposed to judges in rural courts. Yet the Constitutional Court is also the only court that can hear rights claims and has been called upon to decide on constitutional matters that affect women.

An agenda for the study of women in the legal profession needs to take stock of what has been written and to what extent women and gender have featured. The history of women in the legal profession and the judiciary in any part of the world is inevitably tied up with the history of the state. My purpose here is to identify where women appear in accounts of modern legal history.

English-language research on Indonesian law during the immediate post-independence period and during the New Order (1965–1998) was primarily undertaken by Dan S Lev (1933–2006), as the lone and pre-eminent foreign scholar of Indonesian law of his generation. In many ways, a reading of Dan S Lev's seminal work on the politics of courts and legal practice in Indonesia might suggest a lack of attention to women and issues of gender in the judiciary. He does not focus in detail on the specific backgrounds of individual judges, but instead on the life and careers of specific lawyers. His work on cause lawyers focuses on prominent male advocates such as Yap Thian Hien (1913–1989; Lev 2011) and Adnan Buyung Nasution (1934–2015; Lev 1978).

Women appear briefly in Lev's work in two ways. First, women feature as the wives of prominent lawyers. Lev mentions the wife of Yap Thian Hien, Khing, and the wife of Adnan Buyung Nasution, Ria, and how they advocated for their husbands when they were under arrest because of their activism against the state (Lev 2011, 332). Second, and more importantly, women feature as parties – some as victims, other as applicants – in court cases, at the mercy of a judge. Lev was the first to chronicle the way that the Religious (Islamic) Courts became a crucial form for women seeking divorce (Lev 1972). This was a significant achievement because, prior to his book, there had never been a study of Indonesia's Islamic Courts in English and it is unusual for scholars of Islamic studies to focus on Islamic Courts outside of the Middle East. Lev suggests that the courts facilitate women's agency to gain a divorce, making Indonesia's Islamic Courts among the most progressive in the Muslim world (Lev 1996; see also 1972). Indonesia now has one of the largest Islamic judiciaries in the world in terms of the number of judges (that is, judges of the Religious Courts).

Lev later turned his attention briefly to feminist activism in Indonesia in a volume on *Fantasizing the Feminine in Indonesia* (1996). Lev notes that it has often been middle-class women who have driven the political fight for feminism (1996, 192), which is a reminder of the ways in which gender intersects with issues of class and economic status.

At the elite level, the rise of women to prominent political positions is well-known. This includes Megawati Sukarnoputri as the country's first female president (2001–2004) and Sri Mulyani Indrawati as the minister for finance (2005–2010; 2016–ongoing). There are other women famous in the domestic context such as Susi Pudjiastuti, the former Minister of Maritime Affairs and Fisheries (2014–2019). While in office, she cultivated a strong social media profile and is well known for her tough stance on vessels found to be fishing illegally in Indonesian waters. She was responsible for prioritising a policy of literally destroying foreign fishing vessels, sometimes even before a case had been heard in court (see Saptaningrum 2019).

Aside from politics, there are no exact figures on the number of women in the legal profession, in part because there are no exact figures on the profession more broadly (Bedner and Kouwagam 2020). While cause lawyers and the role of the Indonesian Legal Aid Institute both during and after the New Order have been the subject of several studies (Lev 1972; Crouch 2011; Lindsey and Crouch 2013), none focus on women. The study of towering male legal figures of both the Suharto and post-1998 era focus on men such as the late Adnan Buyung Nasution (Dezalay and Garth 2013).

If we take a cursory glance at high-profile legal actors in contemporary Indonesia, the prominent figures who come to mind are often male lawyers such as Todong Mulya Lubis, the protégé of Nasution (Lubis

2014); Munarman who is a former leading human rights lawyer turned Islamist (Crouch and Lindsey 2013), or Hotman Paris Hutapea, a lawyer who is controversial and has gained popularity on social media such as Instagram both for the flaunting of his wealth, his lack of ethics and his behaviour towards women.

The role of the chief justices of the Constitutional Court has been described as one of 'judicial heroes' (Hendrianto 2018), but all of the chief justices have been men. There has also been debate about the intersection between judging and religion, and what it means to be both a judge and a Muslim on the Constitutional Court (Hosen 2016). Like many studies of judicial profiles, Hosen finds that a judge's religion and education may be relevant but is not the only factor that influences their approach to constitutional interpretation. The only female judge on the Constitutional Court at the time of Hosen's study was a Christian and so she does not feature in his study because of his focus on Muslim judges.

Overall, there is much work to be done in the study of women judges' in Indonesia. An agenda for the study of women in the legal profession needs to begin with consideration of the profiles of women judges on the bench and the contributions of trailblazing women in Indonesian legal history. I take steps in this direction by next considering Justice Indrati as one of those trailblazing women judges.

Women and the Constitutional Court

The Model Minority Judge

The Constitutional Court has been central to democratisation in Indonesia. The establishment of the court was the culmination of long-standing demands for the power of judicial review to be given to the courts. In its first term from 2003 to 2008, the Constitutional Court did not have any women judges on the bench. In 2008, well-known reformer Adnan Buyung Nasution led the selection team for appointments to the Constitutional Court, while Mahfud MD (former Constitutional Court Chief Justice) was the legal advisor to the president at the time. The selection team appointed Maria Farida Indrati to the bench, which was the first appointment of a woman to the Constitutional Court. She served two terms on the Constitutional Court and retired in 2018.

In this section I begin to explore the feminisation of the Constitutional Court through the ten-year term of Justice Indrati. Why was she appointed and how did her education and academic background contribute to her credibility? What, if anything, did her status as the only female judge on the court mean for the decisions that she made? What kind of a legacy does she leave regarding court decisions on issues of gender? I respond to these questions by first painting a picture of her educational and academic background as a formalist constitutional lawyer and as a model minority judge. I then explain how she used the power of dissenting or concurring judgments to make her mark on court decisions on issues of gender equality.

I define a model minority judge as a judge who is perceived to be part of a minority community (whether religious, ethnic, cultural or otherwise) and whose conduct while in judicial office is considered to be exemplary in terms of ethics, integrity, intellect and professionalism. That is, people from minority groups may become a judge or gain a strong reputation because of their high standards on ethics, sharp intellect and strong sense of professionalism. Their standards and capacity often contrast with that of some judges from majority groups, who are not necessarily held to the same standards.

Appointments to the Constitutional Court are achieved by one of several career pathways. Many judges first built a successful career as an academic, while others had a career as a lawyer or as a member of the legislature. Prior to her appointment in 2008, Maria Farida Indrati was a professor of law at the University of Indonesia. Justice Indrati's educational background was formative to her approach to law and ultimately to her appointment as a judge. She studied at the University of Indonesia Law Faculty, graduating in 1975 from the country's most prestigious law school. While a student, Maria studied under Professor Hamid S Attamimi, who in the 1970s–1980s was the most influential constitutional lawyer and advisor to the Suharto government. She was influenced both by Attamimi and the thought of his predecessor, Soepomo (1903–1958).

In brief, Attamimi (1928–1995) was a PhD graduate from the prestigious Faculty of Law of the University of Indonesia and went on to become a deputy cabinet secretary in Suharto's government (1983–1993). He developed the idea that Indonesia was a 'village republic' in which customary law principles could be the basis of constitutional rule (though this idea drew on the work of others such as Gandhi). He supported a strong presidency. Attamimi was a proponent of Soepomo's integralist theory of law, in which the state knew what was best for the people and the state was said to work in harmony with the people. Rather than a focus on individual rights, integralism emphasises the interconnectedness of state and society, and the duties of the individual to their community. As a result of Soepomo's role as one of the key drafters of the original 1945 Constitution, the Constitution reflects this idea of integralism.

Attamimi developed an approach to lawmaking derived partly from Austrian jurist Hans Kelsen's pure theory of law, which has gained wide acceptance in Indonesia. Up until now, Attamimi's formalist approach to lawmaking is still considered to be the core conceptual foundation of Indonesia's legal system. Evidence of the influence of his approach can be found in Law No. 12/2011 on the establishment of laws and regulations, which sets out a hierarchy of laws in Indonesia. Justice Indrati adopts this well-accepted formalist approach to her work on lawmaking, her role as a scholar and then her role as a judge. She is among a handful of constitutional law scholars who specifically studied and wrote about the application of Hamid Attamimi's conceptual framework to Indonesia's approach to lawmaking. She also developed expertise in administration and lawmaking.

During her time in office, Justice Indrati was considered to be a model minority judge in terms of both her ethics, integrity and professionalism, and her legal principles and formalism. Concerning her personal integrity and ethics, former Chief Justice Mahfud MD notes that she was regarded with respect by her colleagues for fasting every Monday and Thursday. The research staff of the Constitutional Court comment on her work ethic and her reputation as a defender of the rights of women and children. Implicitly, her credibility contrasts with the reputation of two Constitutional Court judges who in the 2010s were convicted for corruption.

In addition, Justice Indrati is one of the most frequent dissenting judges on the Constitutional Court. During her tenure on the court, Justice Indrati wrote at least twenty dissenting and concurring opinions (Faiz 2018). In Indonesia, Constitutional Court judges are able to write dissenting judgments (Butt 2018) despite there being no tradition of this in the civil law system. Justice Indrati has been affectionately been referred to as 'The Great Dissenter', although male judges have also issued dissenting decisions at times. This raises interesting questions about a gendered perspective on dissenting judgments. What is more remarkable is not just that Justice Indrati wrote dissenting judgments, but that she did not request that they be excluded from the decision. Under regulations of the Constitutional Court, a dissenting judge can in fact ask for their dissenting judgment to be omitted from the decision in that case.

Justice Indrati provided reasons for her concurrent or dissenting opinions and made those reasons publicly available.

Notable Judgments of Justice Maria Farida Indrati

In her time on the Constitutional Court (2008–2018), Justice Indrati was an advocate of women's and children's rights, as reflected in both her concurring and dissenting opinions in constitutional challenges against laws which discriminate against women and children (Faiz 2018). Her standing as a model minority judge is reflected in her principled approach to some rights cases. I focus on three types of cases that exemplify this approach: her decisions on matters concerning women and children, religious freedom and legislative quotas for women. While I acknowledge that she also played an important role in issuing decisions on matters to do with elections, the administration and lawmaking, I do not cover these decisions here.

In the first set of cases, Justice Indrati built a reputation as a defender of the rights of women and children, even though she declined to identify herself as a feminist and instead emphasised her commitment to the law rather than to specific values. There are three relevant decisions concerning pornography, the age of marriage and children born out of wedlock.

In the pornography case, the petitioners argued that several provisions of the pornography law were unconstitutional and opposed to numerous rights in the Constitution as well as the principle of legal certainty. Justice Indrati issued a dissenting judgment.[14] Ultimately she held that Article 1 (1) of the pornography law lacked legal certainty and therefore contradicted Article 28D(1) of the Constitution. She acknowledged the intense public debate caused by the law and the rejection of this law by minority groups from the provinces of Bali, North Sulawesi and Papua because it was perceived that the law may limit the practice of certain traditional customs. Regarding the provisions of the law that emphasised a role for the community, she expressed fears that this may lead to people acting as judge against others, implicitly acknowledging the violent actions and intimidation of groups such as the Islamic Defenders Front. She noted concern about the potential negative impact that the implementation of this law would have on women and children. She also identified other laws where pornography was already regulated and criminalised, and

---

[14] Constitutional Court Decision Number 10-17-23/PUU-VII/2009, 393–407.

questioned the need for another law on pornography. She was clear that her judgment in finding that the definition of pornography lacked legal certainty should not be taken as her support for pornography. Yet the most controversial aspect of her dissent was her opening lines where she emphasises her positionality by stating: 'As a woman, a mother of three, and a teacher of students . . .' She was criticised for framing her dissent in this way and since then has not expressed her judgments in such personal terms.

In 2012, the Constitutional Court heard a case concerning the issue of the rights of a child born out of marriage, or the wedlock case (Butt 2012). The petitioners successfully challenged the provision of the Marriage Law that held a child only has a legal relationship with its mother, paving the way for a child born out of wedlock to also inherit from their father. Justice Indrati issued a separate opinion in this case.[15] She agreed that a child born out of marriage is the responsibility of both parents, although was careful to note that she thought all marriages should be registered with the state. She suggested that the essence of registration was to protect women and children. Her concurring opinion is important for the characteristic concern she showed for any negative effects due to the implementation of the law. She affirmed the constitutional rights of the child in Articles 28B(2) and 28D(1) but the Constitution also showed concern for the social and psychological welfare of children born out of wedlock. She won support from minority groups because she recognised legal pluralism by acknowledging that marriages may be conducted according to religion or adat (local traditions). She emphasised that both biological parents have a responsibility to care for a child born out of wedlock.

Finally, in the age of marriage case, Justice Indrati issued a dissenting opinion after the court rejected a petition arguing that the minimum legal age of sixteen for girls to marry was unconstitutional.[16] In her dissent, she recognised the potential negative impacts upon a girl who is married at sixteen years old, who may stop attending school and who may be more vulnerable to abuse or violence in marriage. She noted that child marriages often arise because of social and economic circumstances. She stressed the risks and dangers girls face in pregnancy and childbirth, and the various medical complications that may arise such as anemia, depression or a higher risk of cervical cancer. She was concerned

---

[15] Constitutional Court Decision Number 46/PUU-VII/2010, 38–44.
[16] Constitutional Court Decision Number 30-74/PUU-XII/2014, 234–240.

for the physical, intellectual and psychological well-being of girls. She emphasised the progress that has been made in the forty years since the introduction of the Marriage Law, with the inclusion of Articles 28A to 28J in the Constitution that are there 'to protect, fulfil and respect the rights of a child' and the importance of the ratification of CEDAW. She identified that, from 1999 to 2008, several laws such as the Child Protection Law define a child as someone younger than eighteen years old. She noted that this suggests that the Marriage Law is no longer appropriate and should be amended to eighteen years old. She held that the phrase 'sixteen years old' created legal uncertainty and conflicted with several constitutional provisions (Article 1(1), 28B(2) and 28C(1). She was explicit about the positive role that judges could play in social change and noted that court decisions could be a broader part of the role of 'law as a tool of social engineering'. Her dissenting judgment was ahead of its time. As mentioned earlier, in 2019, the Marriage Law was in fact amended and the legal age of marriage for girls was increased to nineteen years old (with parental permission, or twenty-one years without permission), which is now consistent with the age for boys.[17]

In a second set of cases, Justice Indrati upheld the right to religious freedom and this was again a reason that minority groups approved of some of her decisions. I discuss the main case concerning the Blasphemy Law. In brief, in 2010, the court heard a case challenging the constitutionality of the Blasphemy Law. Although the petitioners were unsuccessful, Justice Indrati issued a dissenting judgment in support of the petitioners case.[18] Indonesia has many minority religions and beliefs, and there had been an increase since 1998 in criminal charges being laid against individuals from minority groups for allegedly blaspheming Islam (see Crouch 2012).

In this landmark case, Justice Indrati again expressed concern for the implementation of the law, in this instance noting that the Blasphemy Law had resulted in the violation of the right to religious freedom in some cases. She found that the mention of only six recognised religions discriminated against *aliran* (mystical beliefs).

Similar to the Age of Marriage case, Justice Indrati emphasised the inclusion of Articles 28E, 28I and 29 in the Constitution and the further

---

[17] Law 16/2019 amending Law 1/1974 on Marriage.
[18] For extended discussion on this and subsequent cases for judicial review of the Blasphemy Law, see Crouch 2012, 2013 and 2016. Constitutional Court Decision Number 140/PUU-VII/2009, 312–322.

recognition of the right to religious freedom in the law on human rights and the ratification of the ICCPR. Going beyond this, she also relied on the classic distinction in international law between forum internum and forum externum, and that there are no limits on the internal aspect of religious freedom. Her judgment however was limited in that it failed to discuss the application and scope of the constitutional grounds for limitations on the right to religious freedom, which was the basis on which the majority decided the case. Her decision in the 2010 case was overshadowed by a subsequent case in 2013. In the second constitutional challenge to the Blasphemy Law, Justice Indrati joined with the majority in rejecting the application and upholding the constitutionality of the law. As she did not issue a separate decision, her reasons for doing so are unknown.

The third and final issue that Justice Indrati became known for, aside from the rights of women and children and religious freedom, is the issue of legislative quotas for women. In the legislative quota case,[19] the issue was whether the provision in the law to require political parties to have at least 30 per cent women candidates was constitutional. In a dissenting judgment, Justice Indrati held that the provision was constitutional. In this decision she first discussed some of the well-established reasons for quotas for women in parliament, as set out by Hanna Pitkin in her book *The Concept of Representation* (1967).

Justice Indrati explained at length the various responsibilities Indonesia has as a signatory to CEDAW, which includes a requirement of at least 30 per cent women's representation and that at least one in three candidates are women (Article 53, 55). She emphasised that affirmative action in the form of a 30 per cent quota for women candidates at all levels of legislative elections was a way of ensuring that this commitment was more than mere rhetoric. She based her dissent on the provision in the Constitution that confers a right on every person to assistance in order to ensure equal opportunity (Article 28H(2)). In effect, she argued that quotas for legislative candidates were necessary as a special measure to ensure that women's right to equal opportunity to be elected as a member of the legislature is realised.

While I have only provided a brief overview of her contribution as a judge in this chapter, it is relevant to end with a brief note on her judicial replacement. As Justice Indrati's retirement neared, there was a core

---

[19] Constitutional Court Decision Number 22-24/PUU-VI/2008, 109–115.

question at the heart of the public debate over her judicial replacement: should her replacement be a woman? In many respects, the debate trod well-worn lines of merit versus women's representation. In the end, she was replaced by another female judge, Professor Enny Nurbaningsih. The only difference was that while Justice Indrati is a Catholic, a minority religion in Indonesia, Justice Nurabaningsih is a Muslim. The replacement of one female judge with another seems to have cemented the idea that the Constitutional Court should have at least one, or perhaps only one, female judge among its nine members. Yet intersectionality is clearly an issue, with her judicial replacement this time being a woman, which reflects the influence of religion in law and politics in recent decades.

Before being appointed to the court, Justice Enny Nurabaningsih was a professor of Constitutional Law at the School of Law, Gadjah Mada University, Yogyakarta. Born in 1962, Nurbaningsih is a Muslim who comes from the Bangka Belitung Islands, off Sumatra. In many respects, her expertise is similarly doctrinal and primarily focused on administrative law. Her doctorate dissertation was on the implementation of the authority of local governments to regulate regional affairs through local government regulation (*perda*).

From 2014 to 2017, Justice Nurabaningsih was appointed by the government to lead the National Law Development Body,[20] which sits under the Ministry of Law and Human Rights. In this role, she led the preparations for the amendment of the Penal Code. Under her leadership, the preparation of the draft of the amended penal code was finalised and submitted to the national legislature (DPR) for discussion. Human rights activists have raised several concerns over the draft Penal Code and students across Indonesia also took to the streets in late 2019 to protest the bill, among other issues. The bill includes a proposal to resurrect the offence of defaming the president, which in 2007 was in fact declared unconstitutional by the Constitutional Court.[21] It includes provisions that would ban extramarital sex, restrict the ability of women to obtain an abortion, restrict the promotion of contraception and potentially target the LGBTI community. Some observers have speculated that Justice Nurabaningsih's appointment to the court is a safe pick for the president, who can be assured that she would reject any constitutional challenge to provisions of the draft Penal Code, particularly to the provisions regarding defamation of the president. This remains to be

---

[20] Badan Pembinaan Hukum Nasional, BPHN.
[21] Constitutional Court Decision No. 013-022/PUU-IV/2006.

seen. Justice Nurabaningsih remains the only woman among the nine Constitutional Court judges.

Women Judges in the Supreme Court and Lower Courts

Separate from the Constitutional Court, the nature and impact of the feminisation of the judiciary in the general court system has a different trajectory. I offer a preliminary analysis of the entrance of women into the general court system, however the question of whether more sub-stantive gender equality is evident in judicial decision-making requires further research. For many years, the number of women judges was low in the Supreme Court and in the general courts. Under the New Order era, the Supreme Court was the highest court in the judicial system, but it did not have the power of judicial review. There were no women on the bench of the Supreme Court until the late 1960s. In 1968, this all changed when Sri Widojati Notoprojo was appointed as the first woman judge. She was a leader in many respects, and held positions as chairperson of the Law Professionals Association (Pengabdi Hukum) and chairperson of the Jakarta branch of the main professional association for judges, known as the Indonesian Judges Association (IKAHI).

While the entrance of women to the Supreme Court did not gather momentum until the 1980s, by the late 1990s the Supreme Court had eight female judges out of fifty-one. The entrance of women judges from independence until the latter years of the Suharto era is illustrated in Table 5.1.

Table 5.1 *Women judges in the Supreme Court 1950s–1990s*

Year	Women Judges	Male Judges	Total Number of Judges	% of Women Judges on the Bench
1950	–	6	6	–
1954	–	5	5	–
1965	–	3	3	–
1968	1	6	7	14
1974	1	15	16	6.25
1982	9	42	51	17.65
1992	8	43	51	15.69
1994	8	43	51	15.69

Source: Pompe 2005

Table 5.2 *Women judges on the Supreme Court 2011–2018*

Year	Women Judges	Male Judges	Total Number of Judges	Percentage of Women Judges on the Bench
2011	6	46	52	11.5%
2012	5	38	43	11.6%
2013	4	44	48	8.3%
2014	3	46	49	6.1%
2015	4	46	50	8%
2016	4	45	49	8.2%
2017	4	44	48	8.3%
2018	4	48	52	7.7%

Source: Annual Reports of the Supreme Court 2011–2018

In 2018, more than twenty years later, there were 1,900 women judges across all courts supervised by the Supreme Court in Indonesia, which constitutes around 27 per cent of the total number of judges supervised by the Supreme Court.[22]

One reason the number of women entering the Supreme Court remains low is because the number of applications from women candidates remains low. In 2018, a selection round for appointments to the Supreme Court was held by the Judicial Commission. Out of twenty-five candidates who passed the first selection test, only two were women. But both failed in the interview, and so the four candidates who were selected for the fit and proper test were men (The Jakarta Post 2017). This appointment round was significant because in recent years there have been political barriers to appointments to the Supreme Court generally. Overall, there has been a decline in the number of women judges. Women judges are now just 7 per cent of the Supreme Court bench, down from 17 per cent in the 1980s. This decline is both because of the decrease in the number of women in the bench combined with the increase in the total number of judges on the bench over time.

There has been very little movement in the total number of women on the bench, ranging from three to six women in the past ten years. The glass ceiling remains, as no woman has held the position of chief justice.

---

[22] Cited from the speech of the Chief Judge of the Supreme Court to open the women judges meeting in 2018: Hasimsyah (2018); further on the history of women judges in the Supreme Court: see (Mys 2010).

Beyond the Supreme Court, most women judges serve in the courts of first instance, known as the District Courts.[23] The largest number of women judges serve the second-class district court (295 judges), with a further 198 women judges in first class (1B) courts and seventy-one women judges in first class (1A) courts. In addition, there are 2,949 female public prosecutors, or women make up approximately 30 per cent of public prosecutors in Indonesia (Afandi 2019).

Two women judges hold the position of the chief justice of the Appellate Court. Overall, although the number of women judges continues to be low compared to the number of male judges, the recognition for women judges and gender issues within the judiciary has slowly increased. For example, in 2003, the Indonesian Judges Association (IKAHI) initiated a women judges meeting for the first time. Women judges have become active in different judicial forums and networks at the regional level in Southeast Asia and across Asia more broadly. In 2008, the IKAHI's women judges met for the fourth time with a gathering of almost 500 women judges. This event was symbolic because it was also the first such event that was opened by the chief justice of the Supreme Court.

On one hand, there are female judges within the general court system who also fit the profile of a model minority judge. For example, Justice Albertina Ho is a female judge who was born in 1960 in the remote eastern region of North Maluku. A Christian, Justice Albertina Ho is a graduate of the Law Faculty of Gadjah Mada University, Yogyakarta. In 1990, she became a judge in Slawi District Court, Central Java. In 1996, she was appointed as a judge to the busier Yogyakarta District Court. In 2005, she was assigned as the secretary to the vice chief justice of the Supreme Court, Marianna Sutadi, and served in that position until 2008 (Hukumonline 2010).

In late 2008, Justice Albertina Ho was transferred to the South Jakarta District Court, a court that handles many cases concerning corruption. In this position, she aided the Anti-corruption Court that operated from the District Court. She developed a strong reputation as a clean judge and this was built from her role in high-profile cases such as the major case of Gayus Tambunan, a state tax official who was found guilty of corruption. The case made her a hero among civil society organisations and anti-

---

[23] There are two classifications of courts under the Supreme Court, the classification is based on the size of the court and the quality of facilities. Each class comprises of two subclasses, namely A and B.

corruption advocates. Justice Ho's profile as a clean judge of integrity has come with consequences for her career, as she was later transferred to a post in the Sungai Liat District Court, Bangka Belitung, a remote island court. Her rotation was controversial because it was suspected to be a form of retaliation against her decision to convict the accused in corruption cases. She has since served in numerous other locations in high judicial roles, including as a judge in Medan, as vice chief judge of the Palembang District Court and as the chief judge of the Bekasi District Court.

Justice Ho has cultivated a reputation of strong leadership on issues concerning women and children through her role as a member of the Supreme Court Working Group on Women and Children. This working group made major progress in reform within the judicial system with a focus on mainstreaming a gender perspective in the courts. In 2016, at a meeting of ASEAN women judges in Bangkok, a commitment was made that the judiciary of member countries' would work to produce policies to respect and protect women's rights. In 2017, the efforts of the Indonesian Working Group culminated in the introduction of a Supreme Court Regulation that specifically addresses the protection of women in court and is intended to offer guidance to judges in the treatment of women as defendants, witnesses or victims in cases.[24] The Supreme Court subsequently developed and organised a series of training for judges to realise the goals of gender equality and justice in this regulation (Arijaya 2017).[25] The introduction of this regulation has not been without opposition, with some opponents suggesting that this guidance contradicts the obligation of a judge to act impartially, according to the law on judges.

Yet, the role of women judges on the Supreme Court is not necessarily an advance for gender issues. Thin feminisation in terms of entrance to the judiciary does not necessarily lead to thick feminisation in terms of substantive changes for gender equality. There are also women judges whose decisions do not support gender equality. One example is Justice Sri Murwahyuni, a judge of the Supreme Court. In 2018, she was one of the judges on the bench of the Supreme Court that heard a case concerning a female victim of sexual harassment, a case that can be understood as

---

[24] Supreme Court Regulation No. 3/2017 on the guidelines in court cases related to women in conflict with the law.

[25] For one landmark decision perceived to be gender sensitive, see Supreme Court 2018, 68–75.

Indonesia's #MeToo moment. The respondent in the case, Baiq Nuril Maknun, was an administrator at a high school in Mataram. She was sexually harassed by the principal of the school (Cahaya 2018). She recorded one of his telephone calls about his sex life as evidence of sexual harassment. While the defamation case against her was not successful at first instance,[26] in 2018 the Supreme Court agreed with the appeal by the principal and convicted the woman for defamation, sentencing her to six months jail.[27] In June 2019, her application for review (*peninjauan kembali*) was denied by the court. This caused significant social outcry, particularly from women's rights groups in Indonesia and later led to a presidential pardon.

Aside from the Supreme Court, it is important to acknowledge the entrance of women judges in the Islamic Courts. The Islamic Courts have long been a focus of scholarship, beginning with Lev's seminal text (1972) and extending to Stijn van Huis' contemporary study considering the relevance of Lev's analysis for the present (van Huis 2015, 2019). In the 1960s, the Indonesian Ministry of Religion and Directorate of Religious Justice sought to address the issue of female representation on the bench. These efforts at reform had to overcome classical Islamic jurisprudence that requires a judge to be male (Nurlaelawati and Salim 2017, 101). In 1989, the numbers of women on the bench increased further after reforms to the court. The Religious Courts have slightly higher numbers of women judges compared to the general courts. In one study of whether women judges make a difference in the Religious Courts, Nurlaelawati and Salim (2017) find that some female judges display a lack of gender sensitivity or understanding of the best interests of female litigants. They suggest that this lack of attention to gender issues is exacerbated by the judicial panel system, although this requires further research.

This overview of women judges in the Supreme Court and the lower courts demonstrates that there has been a gradual increase in the number of women judges over time and that there have been more recent structural efforts to ensure substantive equality. There are women judges who also fit the model minority judge profile, such as Justice Ho, although much more work needs to be done examining women judicial

[26] The case was brought under the Law 11/2008 on Information and Electronic Transactions, Art. 27(1).
[27] District Court of Mataram No. 265/Pid.Sus/2017/PN Mtr, 26 July 2017; Supreme Court Decision No. 574/Pid.Sus/2018.

profiles, identifying how they entered the profession and progressed in their career. As Indonesia does not have a strong tradition of judges writing separate opinions, it is often not possible to identify the particular position of any one judge in a case and so analysing whether the presence of women judges makes a difference to the outcome of cases on gender equality is difficult.

Conclusion

Since 1998, women have played an important role in Indonesia's process of political and legal reform. The courts, particularly the Supreme Court, have grown in status and prominence. The establishment of the Constitutional Court was a crucial moment in law reform and this institution remains a central actor in law reform and the prospects for social change. The courts remain an important forum for the determination of issues concerning women's rights and gender equality – from interreligious marriage to polygamy, child marriage, domestic violence, sexual harassment, inheritance, divorce and child custody.

To explain the influence and public profile that some women judges have in Indonesia, I have suggested the concept of the model minority judge. A model minority judge is a judge who affiliates with a disadvantaged or minority community. Given that women do not yet make up half of the judiciary, women judges are often a minority on the bench. A minority judge is a model judge if they display exemplary levels of professionalism, superior intellect and are free from corruption. Given that issues of integrity and corruption have plagued the courts, judges from the majority group (Muslim men) are not necessarily held to this standard.

In this chapter I have begun to chart an agenda for studies of Indonesian women in the legal profession and the judiciary. The lack of scholarship on women in the legal profession is not because women have been absent from the bench, from legal practice and from advocacy, but rather due to lack of scholarly attention. An agenda for the study of women in the legal profession should analyse the entry of women into the profession and their rise to prominent positions but should also go beyond this to focus on thicker conceptions of feminisation of the judiciary in terms of whether and how women judges make a difference.

In acknowledging women's roles in legal reform and the judiciary since 1998 in Indonesia, I do not suggest that women judges' always play a positive role nor that reform on issues of women's rights, gender equality and non-discrimination has gone far enough. While there have been steps towards reform in support of women's equality, at times women judges themselves may be part of the issue and work against such reforms.

In this chapter, I have identified the paradox at the heart of the feminisation of the judiciary. Women judges such as Justice Maria Farida Indrati on the Constitutional Court attained her position and level of influence precisely because of her status as a model minority judge, a Catholic woman who is respected for her strong work ethic and integrity and her highly formalist approach to constitutional interpretation. In her dissenting judgments, Justice Indrati has offered cautious support on issues related to gender equality and religious freedom, which has bolstered her model minority status, particularly among minority communities and progressive activists. Similarly, Justice Albertina Ho in the general courts is known as a leader on women's rights and is also known for her strong stance against corruption. In contrast, we cannot ignore the way that some women judges' like Justice Sri Widojati Notoprojo on the Supreme Court work against this agenda. The case of Indonesia reminds us that the idea of the feminisation of the judiciary is complex and contested. This cuts to the heart of the relationship between gender and legal change in Indonesia. The paradox is that women judges offer both promise in advancing gender equality through legal formalism and remain a potential barrier to gender equality in Indonesia.

References

Afandi, Fachrizal (2019) 'The Justice System Postman: The Indonesian Prosecution Service at Work' in Melissa Crouch (ed.) *The Politics of Court Reform: Judicial Change and Legal Culture in Indonesia*. Cambridge: Cambridge University Press.

Affrianty, Dina (2015) *Women and Sharia in Northern Indonesia*. London: Routledge.

Amanda, Putri K, Shaila Tieken, Sharyn G Davies and Santi Kusumaningrum (2019) 'The Juvenile Courts and Children's Rights: Good Intentions, Flawed Execution', in Melissa Crouch (ed) *The Politics of Court Reform: Judicial Change and Legal Culture in Indonesia*. Cambridge University Press.

Arijaya, Rahmat (2017) 'Inilah Materi Pelatinhan PERMA Nomor 3 Tahun 2017' *Direktorat Jenderal Badan Peradilan Agama* (22 September) https://badilag .mahkamahagung.go.id/seputar-ditjen-badilag/seputar-ditjen-badilag/ini lah-materi-pelatihan-perma-nomor-3-tahun-2017

Bedner, Adriaan and Santy Kouwagam (2020) 'Indonesia: Professionals, Brokers and Fixers', in Richard Abel, Olev Hammerslav, Ulrike Schultz and Hilary Sommerland (eds.) *Lawyers in 21st Century Societies*, Volume 1. London: Hart Publishing.

Benda-Beckman, Franz and Keebet von (2013) *Political and Legal Transformations of an Indonesian Polity: The Nagari from Colonisation to Decentralisation.* New York: Cambridge University Press.

Blackburn, Susan (2004) *Women and the State in Modern Indonesia.* New York: Cambridge University Press.

Bourchier, David and Vedi Hadiz (eds.) (2003) *Indonesian Politics and Society: A Reader.* London: Routledge.

Butt, Simon (2018) 'The Function of Judicial Dissent in Indonesia's Constitutional Court' 4(1) *Constitutional Review* 1–26.

(2015) *The Constitutional Court and Democracy in Indonesia.* Leiden: Brill Nijhoff.

(2012) 'Illegitimate Children and Inheritance in Indonesia' 37(3) *Alternative Law Journal* 1.

Cahaya, Gemma Holliani (2018) 'Defamation Convict Allegedly Harassed Multiple Times by Superior', 15 November, *The Jakarta Post*, www.thejakartapost .com/news/2018/11/15/defamation-convict-allegedly-harassed-multiple-times-by-superior.html

Cammack, Mark, Lawrence Young and Tim Heaton (2008) 'Legislating Social Change in an Islamic Society: Indonesia's Marriage Law', in T Lindsey (ed.) *Indonesia: Law and Society*, 2nd ed. Sydney: Federation Press.

Crouch, Melissa (2019a) 'The Judicial Reform Landscape in Indonesia: Innovation, Specialisation and the Legacy of Dan S Lev', in Melissa Crouch (ed.) *The Politics of Court Reform: Judicial Reform and Legal Culture in Indonesia.* Cambridge: Cambridge University Press, pp. 1–28.

(2019b) 'Women in an Era of Anti-Elitism in Asia', 8 July, *Asian Currents*, http://asaa.asn.au/women-in-an-era-anti-elitism-in-asia

(2018) 'Religion, Constitutionalism and Inequality: Perspectives from Asia' 13 (2) *Asian Journal of Comparative Law* 223–243.

(2016) 'Constitutionalism, Islam and the Practise of Religious Deference: The Case of the Indonesian Constitutional Court' 16(2) *Australian Journal of Asian Law* 1.

(2014) *Law and Religion in Indonesia: Conflict and the Courts in West Java.* London: Routledge.

(2012) 'Law and Religion in Indonesia: The Constitutional Court and the Blasphemy Law' 7(1) *(May) Asian Journal of Comparative Law* 1– 46.

(2011) 'Cause Lawyering, the Legal Profession and the Courts in Indonesia: *The Bar Association Controversy*' Law. ASIA Journal 63–86.

(2009) 'Religious Regulations in Indonesia: Failing Vulnerable Groups?' 43(2) *Review of Indonesian and Malaysian Affairs* 53–103.

Crouch, Melissa and Lindsey, Tim (2013) 'Cause Lawyers in Indonesia: A House Divided' 31(3) *Wisconsin International Law Journal* 620–645.

Dezalay, Yves and Bryant G Garth (2013) *Asian Legal Revivals: Lawyers in the Shadow of Empire*. Chicago: University of Chicago Press.

Dieterhlermann, Claus and Isabela Atanasiu (eds.) (2006) *The First Women Lawyers: A Comparative Study of Gender, Law and the Legal Professions*. London: Bloomsbury Publishing.

Faiz, Pan Mohammad (ed.) (2018) *Serviam: Pengabdian dan Pemikiran Hakim Konstitusi*. Jakarta: Aura Publishing.

Feeley, Malcolm M (2012) 'Judge and Company: Courts, Constitutionalism and the Legal Complex', in Terence C Halliday, Lucien Karpik and Malcolm M Feeley (eds.) *Fates of Political Liberalism in the British Post-Colony: The Politics of the Legal Complex*. Cambridge: Cambridge University Press, 493–521.

Feener, Michael (2014) *Sharia and Social Engineering: The Implementation of Islamic Law in Contemporary Aceh, Indonesia*. Oxford: Oxford University Press.

Hasimsyah (2018) 'Ketua MA: Hakim Perempuan Mampu Bersaing dengan Hakim Laki-Laki', 22 January, *Varia Peradilan*, https://variaperadilan.com/2018/01/22/ketua-ma-hakim-perempuan-mampu-bersaing-dengan-hakim-laki-laki

Hendrianto, Stefanus (2018) *Law and Politics of Constitutional Courts: Indonesia and the Search for Judicial Heroes*. London: Routledge.

Hidayat, Rofiq (2018) 'Prof Enny Nurbaningsih: Terobsesi Pembaharuan Sistem Hukum Sejak SMA', 22 April, *Hukum Online*, www.hukumonline.com/berita/baca/lt5adb32bd41112/prof-enny-nurbaningsih–terobsesi-pembaharuan-sistem-hukum-sejak-sma

Hosen, Nadirsyah (2016) 'The Constitutional Court and Islamic Judges in Indonesia' 16(2) *Australian Journal of Asian Law* 1–11.

Huis, S C V (2015) *Islamic Courts and Women's Divorce Rights in Indonesia: The Cases of Cianjur and Bulukumba*. PhD Thesis, the University of Leiden https://openaccess.leidenuniv.nl/handle/1887/35081

Hukumonline (2010) 'Albertina Ho', *Merdeka*, www.merdeka.com/albertina-ho/profil; RFQ, 'Albertina Ho: Sosok Pengadil Berfilosofi Air', 27 December, *Hukum Online*, www.hukumonline.com/berita/baca/lt4d1845f37175d/albertina-ho-sosok-pengadil-berfilosofi-air

Indrati, Maria Farida (2007) *Ilmu Perundang-Undangan,* Volume 1. Jakarta: Kanisius.

The Jakarta Globe (2010) 'Judging by Her Record, Maria Farida Is Not Afraid to Stand Out', 21 April, www.thejakartaglobe.com/home/judging-by-her-record-maria-farida-is-not-afraid-to-stand-out/370619

The Jakarta Post (2017) 'Supreme Court Recruits 1500 Judges after 7 Year Break', 6 November, www.thejakartapost.com/news/2017/11/06/supreme-court-recruits-1500-judges-after-7-year-break.html

Jayawardena, Kumari (2009) *Feminism and Nationalism in the Third World*. Social Scientists Association.

Kay, Fiona and Elizabeth Gorman (2008) 'Women in the Legal Profession' 4 *Annual Review of Law and Social Science* 299–332.

Kolibonso, Rita Serena (1999) 'The Gender Perspective: A Key to Democracy in Indonesia', in Arief Budiman, Barbara Hartley and Damien Kingsbury (eds.) *Reformasi: Crisis and Change in Indonesia*. Monash: Monash Asia Institute.

Lev, Daniel S (2011) *No Concessions: The Life of Yap Thiam Hien, Indonesian Human Rights Lawyer*. Seattle: University of Washington Press.

(2000) *Legal Evolution and Political Authority in Indonesia: Selected Essays*. The Hauge: Kluwer Law International.

(1996a) 'On the Other Hand', in Laurie J Sears (eds.) *Fantasizing the Feminine in Indonesia*. Durham, NC: Duke University Press.

(1996b) 'Between State and Society: Professional Lawyers and Reform in Indonesia', in D S Lev and R McVey (eds.), *Making Indonesia*. Ithaca, NY: Southeast Asia Publications, Cornell University Press.

(1992) *Lawyers as Outsiders: Advocacy versus the State in Indonesia*, Working Paper No. 2 (November). School of Oriental and African Studies, University of London.

(1987) *Legal Aid in Indonesia*. Working Paper No. 44. Monash University, *Southeast Asian Studies*.

(1978) 'Judicial Authority and the Struggle for an Indonesian Rechtsstaat' 13(1) *Law and Society Review* 37–71.

(1976) 'Origins of the Indonesian Advocacy' 21 (April) *Indonesia* 147.

(1973a) 'Judicial Unification in Post-Colonial Indonesia' 16 (October) *Indonesia* 1–37.

(1973b) *Bush Lawyers in Indonesia: Stratification, Representation and Brokerage*. Working Paper No. 1. Berkeley: UC Law and Society Program.

(1972a) 'Judicial Institutions and Legal Culture', in Claire Holt (ed.) *Culture and Politics in Indonesia*. Ithaca, NY: Cornell University Press.

(1972b) *Islamic Courts in Indonesia: A Study in the Political Bases of Legal Institutions*. Berkley: University of California Press.

(1965a) 'The Lady and the Banyan Tree: Civil Law Change in Indonesia' 14(2) *American Journal of Comparative Law* 282–307.

(1965b) 'The Politics of Judicial Development in Indonesia' *Comparative Studies in Society and History* (January).

Lubis, Todong Mulya (2014) *Recrowning Negara Hukum: A New Challenge, A New Era*. Policy Paper No. 6. University of Melbourne Law School.

Merdeka, 'Albertina Ho' (n.d.) www.merdeka.com/albertina-ho/profil

Munger, Frank (2012) 'Globalization through the Lens of Palace Wars: What Elite Lawyers' Careers Can and Cannot Tell Us about Globalization of Law (Book Review)' 37(2) *Law & Social Inquiry* 476–499.

Mys (2010) 'Srikandi-Srikandi di Kursi Agung', 24 December, *Hukum Online*, www.hukumonline.com/berita/baca/lt4d145b5284d4d/srikandisrikandi-di-kursi-agung

Nurlaelawati, Euis and Arskal Salim (2017) 'Female Judges at Indonesian Religious Courtrooms: Opportunities and Challenges to Gender Equality', in N. Sonneveld and M. Lindbekk (eds.) *Women Judges in the Muslim World: A Comparative Study of Discourse and Practice.* Leiden: Brill.

(2013) 'Gendering the Islamic Judiciary: Female Judges in the Religious Courts of Indonesia' 51 *Al-Jami'ah* 248.

Nurmila, Nina (2018) *Women, Islam and Everyday Life Renegotiating Polygamy in Indonesia.* London: Routledge.

Pausacker, Helen (2012) 'Playboy, the Islamic Defenders' Front and the Law: Enforcing Islamic Norms in Post-Soeharto Indonesia?' 13(1) *Australian Journal of Asian Law* 1–20.

Pompe, Sebastian (2005) *The Indonesian Supreme Court: A Study of Institutional Collapse.* Ithaca, NY: Cornell University Press.

Rachman, Dylan Aprialdo (2018) 'Jadi Hakim MK, Ini Profil Enny Nurbaningsih', 13 August, *Kompas*, https://nasional.kompas.com/read/2018/08/13/13231361/jadi-hakim-mk-ini-profil-enny-nurbaningsih

Rinaldo, Rachel (2013) *Mobilizing Piety: Islam and Feminism in Indonesia.* New York: Oxford University Press.

Robinson, Kathryn (2000) 'Indonesian Women: from Orde Baru to Reformasi', in Edwards and Roces (eds.) *Women in Asia: Tradition, Modernity and Globalisation.* Sydney: Allen & Unwin.

RFQ (2010) 'Albertina Ho: Sosok Pengadil Berfilosofi Air' 27 December, *Hukum Online*, www.hukumonline.com/berita/baca/lt4d1845f37175d/albertina-ho-sosok-pengadil-berfilosofi-air

Rosenfield, Sarah Shair (2012) 'The Alternative Incumbency Effect: Electing Women Legislators in Indonesia' 31(3) *Electoral Studies* 576–587.

Saptaningrum, Indri (2019) 'The Fisheries Court: Government-Led Judicial Development' in Melissa Crouch (eds) The Politics of Court Reform: Judicial Change and Legal Culture in Indonesia. Cambridge, Cambridge University Press. pp218–244.

Schultz, Ulrike and Gisela Shaw (eds.) (2013) *Gender and Judging.* London: Hart Publishing.

Supreme Court (2018) *Pedoman Mengadiki Perkara Perempuan Berhadapan Dengan Hukum,* Mahkamah Agung Republik Indonesia, http://mappifhui.org/wp-content/uploads/2018/01/Pedoman-Mengadili-Perkara-Perempuan-Berhadapan-dangan-Hukum-MaPPI-FHUI-2018.pdf.

(2017) *Laporan Tahunan*. Jakarta: Mahkamah Agung Republik Indonesia.

Suryakusuma, Julia (1988) *State Ibuism: The Social Construction of Womanhood in the Indonesian New Order*. Depok: Komunitas Bambu.

Thornton, Margaret (2007) 'Otherness on the Bench: How Merit Is Gendered' 29 (3) *Sydney Law Review* 391.

UNICEF and BPS (2020) *Prevention of Child Marriage*. Jakarta: BPS, Statistics Indonesia.

University of Indonesia (n.d.) 'Prof Dr Maria Farida Indrati SH, MH', http://staff .ui.ac.id/user/744/publications

Van Huis, Stijn Cornelius (2019) 'The Religious Courts: **Does Lev's analysis still hold?**', in Melissa Crouch (ed.) *The Politics of Court Reform: Judicial Change and Legal Culture in Indonesia*. New York: Cambridge University Press.

Ziegenhain, Patrick (2008) *The Indonesian Parliament and Democratisation*. Singapore: ISEAS.

Laws

Law 1/1974 on Marriage
Law 7/1984 on CEDAW
Law 39/1999 on Basic Human Rights
Law 24/2000 on International Treaties
Law 23/2004 on the Elimination of Domestic Violence
Law 11/2005 on the ICESCR
Law 12/2005 on the ICCPR
Law 44/2008 on Pornography
Law 11/2008 on Information and Electronic Transactions
Law 16/2009 amending Law 1/1974 on Marriage

Constitutional Court Cases

Constitutional Court Decision Number 22-24/PUU-VI/2008
Constitutional Court Decision Number 140/PUU-VII/2009
Constitutional Court Decision Number 10-17-23/PUU-VII/2009
Constitutional Court Decision Number 46/PUU-VII/2010
Constitutional Court Decision Number 30-74/PUU-XII/2014
Constitutional Court Decision Number 68/PUU-XII/2014

6

Filipino Women Judges and Their Role in Advancing Judicial Independence in the Philippines

IMELDA DEINLA*

The advancement of women in the legal profession is testament to how far gender equality has broken barriers for women in the Philippines. Filipino women have attained considerable progress in social, economic and political fields. Since 2006, the Global Gender Gap Report has consistently placed the Philippines among the top countries in the world with the highest gender parity – and the highest in Asia (World Economic Forum 2020). This gender report measures gender-based gaps in access to resources and opportunities, demonstrating improvement in reducing disparities between men and women. With greater opportunities and rights, Filipino women have become active participants in building democratic institutions and the administration of justice in the country.

This chapter is an opportunity to interrogate whether gender makes a difference in promoting judicial independence. Specifically, I consider whether having women judges on the court enhances judicial independence, and whether women judges decide cases differently to men. These questions are explored against the background of a legal profession and judiciary that is regarded historically as a masculine institution where rules and laws are mostly drawn up and interpreted by men.

Considering that the surge of women lawyers and judges in the Philippine judiciary in the past thirty years coincides with the march towards democratisation, this chapter examines the role that women members of the legal profession, including women judges, play in shaping judicial independence and more broadly, the administration of justice in the Philippines. What have been the factors that allow women to enter the legal profession, and increase their membership in the judiciary? Do women judges decide differently compared to male judges?

* My deep gratitude to Ronnel Deinla, fourth–year law student at the Dela Salle University in Manila, for providing valuable research assistance.

178

How do women judges uphold or compromise judicial independence? How do they handle or manage external political pressures as well as influences from their peers?

To answer these questions, this chapter relies upon court decisions, publicly available information on the composition of law firms and the judiciary, and the public profiles of leading women judges. I chose to study the period 2001–2019, which includes the current administration and two governments preceding it. The period 2001–2010 under the presidency of the first elected woman president (Macapagal-Arroyo) set a new record in appointing more women judges in the Supreme Court. The next government under President Benigno Aquino III (2010–2016) was the first to appoint a woman chief justice. This eighteen-year period represents the two past Philippine administrations of President Gloria Macapagal-Arroyo (2001–2010) and Benigno Aquino III (2010–2016), as well as the government of Rodrigo Duterte (2016 to present). These three governments differ in governance styles and the relationship between the government and the judiciary, as well as the difference in the role that women judges play in political controversies. Macapagal-Arroyo was brought to power at first through the second people power revolution in January 2001, toppling a highly corrupt administration of President Joseph Estrada. On her later years in office, she attempted to impose emergency powers and regulate fundamental freedoms but was thwarted by the court. Aquino was ushered to the presidency campaigning good governance and accountable government, and led a relatively stable liberal regime. Aquino had an uneasy relationship with the Supreme Court, and was perceived to mostly involve the appointees of Macapagal-Arroyo. It was in his term that the first successful impeachment proceeding against a sitting chief justice, Renato Corona, occurred. Aquino appointed the first woman chief justice, Lourdes Sereno. The Duterte government has been seen as facilitating an illiberal regime. In his first few years in office, removal proceedings were launched against independent accountability mechanisms including the ouster of Sereno. Cases were selected based on the importance of constitutional issues adjudicated and the perceived policy preferences of the executive from the decisions. These cases involve executive privileges, constitutional amendment initiatives, restrictions or regulations on fundamental freedoms, contentious social issues and private cases with strong public interest. All of the cases also involve constitutional questions, and made headlines because of the personalities involved. I interviewed four women trial court judges on their contemporary experience, which adds to these case data. These judges prefer to remain anonymous, so they are not named.

This chapter offers an initial basis for future scholarly inquiry into the understudied link between gender and judicial independence in the Philippines. I argue that despite their low number in the upper echelons of the judiciary, the Supreme Court, Filipino women judges have been a strong voice in articulating and advancing judicial independence through various episodes of the country's journey through constitutional democracy. As women judges also increase their numbers in the lower courts, they have become a force in strengthening the administration of justice. This suggests that the appointment of more well-trained women judges through a merits-based process could be a strategy to uphold judicial independence.

Judicial Independence, Women and the Courts

An independent and effective judiciary has become an important pillar of constitutional democracy and the rule of law in the Philippines. The judiciary, specifically the Philippine Supreme Court, is a pioneering institution in the region. The Philippines Supreme Court was regarded as one of the most powerful and politically respected appellate courts in existence (Haynie 1998, 460). In the pre-authoritarian period, the court was known for its independence and integrity and for playing an activist role in safeguarding democracy, particularly during the post-EDSA revolution[1] that toppled the authoritarian regime of Ferdinand Marcos. It was during this period of democratisation when an increasing number of women judges were appointed to the bench. From 1986 to 2020, when the democratic government of President Corazon Aquino was inaugurated, there have been thirteen women justices appointed to the Supreme Court, the highest and penultimate appeals court in the Philippines. By comparison, only two women justices were appointed during the twenty-one-year reign of Marcos (1971–1986): in 1973, Cecilia Munoz-Palma was the first woman justice appointed to the court and in 1976, Ameurfina Melencio Herrera was appointed.

In recent years and with the rise of populist leaders, democratic institutions such as the judiciary and other accountability mechanisms have increasingly been besieged. This is also true in the Philippines (Deinla

---

[1] The people power revolution that happened in 1986 took place in the Epifanio delos Santos Avenue or EDSA, hence the popular reference to this event as EDSA revolution.

and Dressel 2019). Heads of independent accountability mechanisms have been subjected to vilification and harassment, such as the Commission on Human Rights, and some officials have been evicted from office such as the removal of the first female chief justice, Maria Lourdes Sereno. The use of legal mechanisms intended as tools for accountability have instead been turned into instruments of political vendetta. The process of impeachment designed to check the abuse of authority by high officials has been turned into a political weapon (Deinla and Reyes 2021).

The courts – whether in times of autocracy or stable democracies – are inherently vulnerable to political, institutional and social pressures that affect their capacity to render impartial decisions, guard against abuse of power and ensure constitutional boundaries. As the third pillar of government, the judiciary is also considered to have the least power, dependent as it is on the moral suasion of its decisions and cooperation of enforcement bodies. The judiciary is known as the guardian of constitutional democracy because of its capacity to render judgments free from 'fear or favour', and to make authoritative decisions based on reasoned judgment according to law.

Since the 1980s and with the advent of democratisation, the world has seen the emergence of powerful courts that have authority to decide on 'mega political cases', or those cases that involve adjudicating political contests, the balance of power among different parts of government and the legitimacy of government actions (see Ginsburg 2003; Dressel 2012; Ciencia 2012). The Philippine Supreme Court and the Philippine judiciary in general was a beneficiary of that movement, as evident in the 1987 Philippine Constitution (Pangalangan 2014). The court's judicial review powers and provisions for financial independence, security of tenure and administrative supervision of the courts have turned it from a 'kangaroo court' to the 'gods of Padre Faura'. The latter is a popular phraseology among lawyers indicating the perceived omnipotence of justices, both in their legal and political influence but particularly with reference to their power to declare their interpretation of the law as final.

Yet judicial power and constitutional guarantees are no longer enough – or are *sine qua non*, to exercising judicial independence. In fact, judicial power if exercised without accountability also contributes to injustice and abuse of authority. If exercised without restraint and judiciousness, judicial power becomes the adversary of judicial independence. Apart from external politics and institutional capacity and cohesion, public support and judicial leadership (Hendrianto 2016) are important factors that allow the courts to be independent and insulate it from both internal and external political pressures.

There are few studies on the relationship between gender and judicial independence. One study in the High Court of Australia did not find a direct relationship between gender and judicial independence but rather a pattern of collegiality – and conformity – particularly by new members of the bench (McLoughlin 2015). In that study, women judges tend to suppress their feminist voice and show a tendency to conform to majority opinion. This finding suggests that having more women judges does not necessarily result in gender-responsive decisions.

In some studies, a common theme that emerges is that of a 'different voice perspective' which means that while women judges arrive at the same legal conclusion as male judges, they do so from different gender perspectives (Gilligan 1982; Miller and Maier 2007). This has been demonstrated, to a certain extent, in an article on the way female justices of the Philippine Supreme Court, under a female chief justice, Maria Lourdes Sereno, fared in terms of how they evaluate and decide cases with a gender dimension (Salcedo 2019). In this study, it was shown that these women judges bring their own experiences and perspectives to the bench. They are also embedded in a broader political setting that affects their relationships in the courts and therefore their appreciation and decisions in taking a particular position. Justice Sereno was subjected to the threat of impeachment and then a *quo warranto* proceeding triggered by her opposition to President Rodrigo Duterte's controversial drug policies. In August 2017, Sereno was first subjected to impeachment, a constitutional process requiring a higher standard of removal of constitutional officers from office. On 5 March 2018 she was subject to *quo warranto* proceedings (a general process for removing public officials) initiated by the Solicitor General. The latter proceeding was initiated when those who supported her impeachment in the lower house failed to transmit the articles of impeachment to the Senate, which has the power to conduct a trial in a constituted tribunal. Her removal via *quo warranto* proceedings was seen as resulting from gender bias, as she was subjected to much higher scrutiny of her management style compared to her male predecessors. The ouster initiative was visibly supported, and cheered on, by eight of her colleagues, one of whom was a woman. Justice Teresita De Castro was the lone woman justice who testified against Sereno during the impeachment proceeding and concurred with the majority in the *quo warranto* proceeding (see Deinla, Taylor and Rood 2018). De Castro was later appointed as the replacement chief justice for two months from

August to October 2018. These contemporary developments and chal-lenges for women in the judiciary have been proceeded by a longer struggle to gain entry to the profession itself.

Women Judges in the Philippine Judiciary: From Suffragists to Judges, Bar Topnotchers and Constitutionalists

The historical narrative of how women gained their place in the judiciary is important. The participation of women in the legal profession and in the judiciary has come through a long and difficult path. The Philippine administration of justice has a long provenance dating back to the Spanish colonisation. Prior to that, the judicial function was fused with the executive (Johnson 1916). In 1885, the first lower courts, the 'justice of the peace', were established in each judicial district. These appoint-ments have come 'from lawyers, from persons with some academic title, or from those whose position and circumstances gave sufficient warrant. When no such person could be found, the lot fell upon the *gobernador-cillo* (or governor of a province)' (Diamonon 1919, 131). That was a long 300 years. These positions were all held by men. At the local level, the administration of justice was performed by local rulers or administrators who are usually the elites and *encomenderos*, or those who were given lands by the crown. This resulted in untold sufferings and injustices to the people. It was during the American colonisation that a modern judicial system was created for the purpose of establishing a civilian government after a period of military occupation by United States forces. In 1901, the Philippine Commission mandated the establishment of the judiciary consisting of the Supreme Court, appellate court and trial courts across the country.

The progressive participation of women judges in the Philippine judiciary coincided with the global trend towards recognising women's rights. Many of the early prominent women lawyers have made signifi-cant contributions to recognising women's rights, the administration of justice and judicial independence. There were only two known women lawyers towards the end of the American colonial period. On 30 March 1911, Maria del Pilar Francisco de Villacerna was the first female lawyer admitted to the Philippine bar (Supreme Court of the Philippines n.d.) but nothing is known of her and whether she practised her profession. It was Natividad Almeda Lopez, admitted to the bar in 1914, who is known as the first female practising lawyer in the early twentieth century, defying Spanish Catholicism's injunction against women assuming a public and administrative role (Alcantara 1994). Unlike the pre-colonial status of women, when women had active 'extra-domestic' roles, Filipino women during Spanish times were relegated to the home.

The introduction of universal education paved the way for women to enter the legal profession. The American colonial period saw the opportunity for women to obtain college education and thus to pursue a career or profession. Almeda Lopez broke from the tradition, supported by her husband who was a governor of a province in the Luzon area. In 1961, she became the first woman judge appointed as presiding judge at the municipal trial court in Manila and later the first female justice appointed to the Court of Appeals, the intermediate appeals court. She was also a pioneering figure in the suffragist movement that was the site of early feminism in the Philippines (Kalaw 1952). Almeda Lopez would join various campaigns in public squares in the Southern Luzon area, as well as participate in radio programs to mobilise women to go out and vote for a plebiscite granting women the right to vote in 1937 (Casambre and Rood 2012). Almeda Lopez has been remembered by her descendants as 'a strong-willed, energetic, piano-playing eccentric lady' and being 'pro-poor' (Lolarga 2012). In one case, Judge Almeda Lopez overruled the defence of double jeopardy in a sexual violence case, although that decision was subsequently overturned by the Supreme Court (*Mendoza v. Almeda-Lopez* 1937).

Another pioneering woman lawyer was Tecla San Andres-Ziga who graduated from the University of the Philippines, the law school established by Americans and considered to be one of the most prestigious in the country. In 1930, she became the first woman to top the Philippine bar examinations. The Philippine bar examinations, patterned after the American bar, is regarded as one of the most difficult professional licensure examinations. Every November, it is administered on four consecutive Saturdays by the Supreme Court Bar Examination Committee. The examination and results usually attract wide media coverage. After practising at a private DeWitt law office in Manila, Ziga went on to have a distinguished career in the public service, first by serving at the Department of Justice and later as an elected member of Congress and the Senate in 1955 and 1963, respectively.

At the apex of the court hierarchy is the Supreme Court, which is the ultimate appeals court invested with powers to review laws and regulations, as well as acts of state officials. Below the Supreme Court are two appellate courts, the Court of Appeals and the Court of Tax Appeals. Two of the earliest women justices – Cecilia Munoz Palma and

Ameurfina Melencio-Herrera – have been known to uphold the rule of law and independence of the court. They have been lauded as 'judicial heroes' during the authoritarian regime of Ferdinand Marcos (Panganiban 2018). On 11 June 1901, the Supreme Court was established but it was not until 1973 that the first woman justice was appointed to the Supreme Court, when former President Ferdinand Marcos appointed Cecilia Munoz Palma to the bench. Justice Palma was a graduate of the University of the Philippines and in 1937 topped the bar examinations. She was among the minority justices who dissented in martial law cases where the applicants were attempting to challenge the constitutionality of martial law and cases involving the derogation of fundamental rights. She was one of few minority justices who penned or supported decisions adverse to the government and her appointing authority, the president of the Philippines. It is said that the 1987 Constitution is based upon these dissenting judicial voices (such as the dissent in ratification cases like *Javellana* v. *Executive Secretary*) and cases upholding the right to due process (*People* v. *Purisima*). This foundation ensured that the democratic 1987 Constitution cast aside the 'political question' doctrine in favour of the power of constitutional review as a means to ensure judicial accountability over the political process.

On her retirement from the judiciary, Justice Munoz Palma became part of the opposition party campaigning against martial law and atrocities during that period. In 1984, she campaigned for and won a seat in Congress and chaired the Constitutional Committee that drafted the 1987 Constitution. In 1979, she was succeeded in the Supreme Court by Ameurfina Melencio-Herrera. Melencio Herrera also graduated from the University of the Philippines and in 1947 topped the bar examinations. In 1982, she became well known for disclosing the manipulation of the bar examinations that had enabled the son of of a Marcos-appointed justice to pass the examinations (*The New York Times* 1982). After the people power revolution in 1986, she was one of only four justices who were reappointed to the court by President Corazon Aquino.

In sum, from the Spanish colonial times and until the 1970s, there were a few pioneering women lawyers and judges. They were products of a more liberal period that started to open the public space for women to vote, to gain education and participate in government affairs. Their professional successes and exemplary contributions to the judiciary can be traced back to their academic achievements and high degree of professional commitment. Although all four of them came from well-connected political families – Almeda Lopez and Ziga were married to governor-husbands; Munoz-Palma being a daughter of a member of Congress; and Herrera being a granddaughter of the first president of the Philippines, Emilio Aguinaldo – all of them were judicial and public officers of high integrity. Two of them, Palma and Herrera, were part of the post-EDSA process that re-established constitutional democracy and the rule of law. I now turn to elaborate on the factors contributing to the opening of space for Filipino women in the legal profession and judiciary.

The Entry of Filipino Women Lawyers in a Predominantly Masculine Legal Profession

The Philippine courts, and the broader legal profession, are known as masculine and male-dominated. The judiciary is also considered to be one of the most powerful professions. Since the Spanish colonial times, it was noted that 'the "abogado" (lawyer) has held high prestige in Filipino society' and legal training was seen from the early twentieth century as a way to 'advancement' for the able and ambitious Filipino (Abueva 1965, 271). The legal–client relationship appears to be 'analogous to the roles of representative, intermediary and broker often expected of a politician' while legal knowledge is advantageous for the politician because of 'the baffling intricacies of Philippine law and the art and expertise of living with it that has evolved' (Turner 1987). As observed by the first Attorney General for the Philippines in the early days of American colonial rule, 'Lawyers formed a larger part of the cultured class in the Philippines than the members of any other profession' (Wilfley 1904). The legal profession has produced many presidents, members of the house of representatives, members of the senate, heads of government bodies and leaders of private entities. Nine out of fifteen presidents of the Philippines were lawyers. Prior to 1986, there was only one non-lawyer president, Ramon Magsaysay. President Corazon Aquino, was the first female president and a non-lawyer. The current president (Duterte) and vice president (Maria Leonor Gerona Robredo) are members of the Philippine bar.

Until the present times, lawyers are still regarded by the elites and the public as the most prestigious professional group. The fanfare surrounding the yearly bar examinations and the public announcement of those who topped the bar examinations on primetime media demonstrates the high status of lawyers in Philippine society. Some law firms have even attained the status of 'The Firm' in reference to its capacity to facilitate, disrupt or promote power arrangements in politics and society. These firms are the wheels behind the corridors of power as they are entrusted with the most important or sensitive cases and transactions of the most powerful people. Anecdotal accounts point to the role of these firms, or powerful lawyers, to ensure a person is chosen for important positions in the government, whether lawyer or non-lawyers. These firms, through their connections with politicians and big business, also play a role in the appointment of judges and justices. Many lawyers in the well-connected firms are successful in themselves being appointed to senior government positions. Under the current administration of Rodrigo Duterte, the presidential spokesperson, justice secretary and chief government counsel have all come from private law firms.

The post-Marcos era has seen a rise in the entry of women in the legal profession, and the judiciary. The 1987 Philippine Constitution sought to strengthen the judiciary in response to unchecked abuse of power and massive human rights violations during that period and more broadly, to improve the administration of justice. The Supreme Court was provided with expanded powers of judicial review to enhance the function of constitutional checks and balance (see Gatmaytan 2011). The democratisation period also brought with it the creation of more courts across the country including the strengthening of special courts (Sandiganbayan, the anti-graft court); creation of quasi-judicial bodies (Commission on Elections, Commission on Human Rights, Civil Service Commission); and other legal support institutions (Ombudsman, in charge of investigation of graft and corruption). Special institutions were established like the Presidential Commission on Good Government (PCGG) that was tasked to go after ill-gotten wealth of the Marcos family.

Other existing bodies were given expanded powers, jurisdiction and resources. For example, the Court of Tax Appeals (CTA) had been expanded and enlarged with the passage of legislation[2] resulting in the creation of more positions as well as elevating the status of judges to the level of a Court of Appeals justice. The public defender's office, previously known as the Citizen's Legal Assistance Office during the Marcos regime, was reorganised as the Public Attorney's Office (PAO). The PAO is reconstituted to serve as the country's frontline agency in delivering free legal aid to indigents in judicial, quasi-judicial and civil proceedings, and the provision of non-judicial services such as counselling, mediation and conciliation. Over the years, PAO has been established in all parts of the country and public lawyer's salaries were also raised to attract

---

[2] Republic Act No. 8292, 23 April 2004 and Republic Act No. 9503, 5 July 2008.

high-quality lawyers. Government departments such as the Department of Agrarian Reform was vested with quasi-adjudication functions owing to the passage of the new land reform legislation that aims to address and resolve centuries-old agrarian conflict.[3]

All these reforms in the post-Marcos era have provided opportunities for women to join the legal profession and be employed in the private, public and non-government sectors. Although there is no comprehensive data available on women representation in the private sector, women lawyers are employed in corporate legal and management positions. In 2020, a tabulation of fifteen law firms in the Philippines (Asian Business Law Journal 2019) including both small firms and the largest law offices, reveals that 36 per cent of partner and senior positions are women. Eight of these firms or 53 per cent, however, register 40 per cent and above of women in senior positions, which suggests that women's representation is concentrated in certain law firms.

The increasing number of women in law firms is an important development considering that these more established large firms have primarily had male lawyers as founders. One explanation as to why the number of women has traditionally been low is that junior women partners prefer to leave the firm and take up positions in private corporations or join the government and the judiciary. Long hours and intense work in law offices are also disincentives to many women lawyers, especially those wanting to have families and children. Hence, women lawyers also prefer to put up small or brick and mortar law offices to allow them work flexibility, although there are also many unmarried women lawyers who run their own offices. The position of women lawyers in law offices is consistent with the overall trend in the corporate management positions, where women account for between 37 and 43 per cent of senior positions, mostly as human resource director, chief finance officer and chief operating officer. In 2019, the Philippines topped the 'Women in Business' global ranking conducted among thirty-two countries in developed and developing countries by Grant Thornton International, demonstrating that Filipino women have advanced considerably in senior management roles in the private sector (Lucas 2020).

Whilst there has been a revitalisation in the legal profession after authoritarian rule, there was also a parallel blossoming of the Philippines' feminist and women's rights movement (see Roces 2012).

---

[3] Republic Act No. 6657, Comprehensive Agrarian Reform Law (CARL), 10 June 1988.

Together with judicial reform, the rise of the women's movement was the impetus towards more women joining the legal profession. The 1987 Constitution itself provided the legal and policy framework towards recognition of the role of women in nation building, specifically the fundamental equality before the law of women and men (Article 11, Section 14); recognition of women's maternal and economic role (Article XIII, Section 14); and women's special health needs (Article XIII, Section 11).

After the revolution in 1986, more women's non-government organisations were established after being inspired by the successes of women's organisations fighting the dictatorship. The outpouring of funding support from international development organisations following the assumption to the presidency of the first Filipina president, Corazon Aquino, allowed for many women's NGOs to flourish (see Clarke 1995). During this period, NGOs and organisations with women's rights and empowerment as their core agenda have been established in many parts of the country. Many women lawyers headed or were employed in the NGO sector. For example, the Women's Legal Bureau Inc. (now the Women's Legal and Human Rights Bureau or WLB) was the first feminist legal NGO in the Philippines pioneering legal service and advocacies on pressing women's human rights issues. In 1990, WLB was founded by two feminist women lawyers who graduated from the University of the Philippines. A coalition of women's NGOs have been formed or existing ones strengthened since that period to advocate on various women's rights issues resulting to the passage of important legislation advancing women's rights and welfare. Some of these laws are the New Family Code (6 July 1987) that dismantled many discriminatory provisions against women; the Republic Act No. 6725 (1989) that strengthened the prohibition on discrimination against women on the terms and conditions of employment; the Local Government Code (Republic Act No. 7160, 1990) providing for women's participation in local governance; the Anti-rape Law (Republic Act No. 8353, 1997); the Anti-violence against Women and Children Law (Republic Act No. 9262, 2004); and the Reproductive Health Law (Republic Act No. 10354, 2012). These law reform initiatives are critical to women's rights and equality in the Philippines.

Filipino Women in the Administration of Justice

The trend towards the demonopolisation of the legal profession by men has been part of the broader pattern of Filipino women improving their social, economic and political positions. The Integrated Bar Association

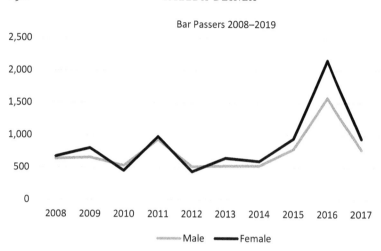

Figure 6.1   Number of students who passed the bar exam by gender (2008–2017).
Source: Data provided by the Integrated Bar of the Philippines (IBP)

of the Philippines (IBP), the compulsory bar membership body, puts the number of living lawyers at 40,000. The major advances in women's gender equality in the Philippines shadows the development of many women entering the legal profession. The period from 2010 to 2020 demonstrates this. Figure 6.1 shows an almost equal, if not higher proportion, of women passing the bar examinations in this ten-year span. Throughout this period, women who passed the bar comprise 54 per cent of all persons who sat the bar exam, with a 3:10 ratio compared to a 2:10 ratio for men. Women are also high achievers in terms of their performance in the bar examinations, with 53 per cent comprising the bar topnotchers or those passers who achieved the top ten highest rating (Figure 6.2).

There is no available data on the number and proportion of women entering law schools. Anecdotal accounts however point to an almost equal number of men and women entering the law school. There are around 90 law schools in the Philippines. In general, however, Paqueo and Orbeta (2019) show that Filipino women have a higher completion rate than men in terms of basic and college education, a trend that started in the 1970s and intensified in the 1990s. In their study, it was noted that Filipino men lag behind women in education. At present, the pattern continues with women outperforming men in high school enrolment (71.3 per cent versus 60.2 per cent) and parity in college enrolment (40.4 per cent) according to the 2020 WEF Global Gender Gap Report.

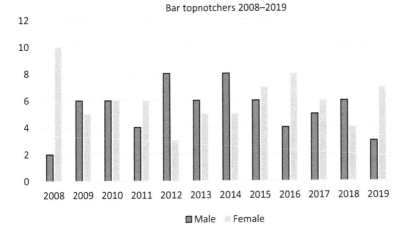

Figure 6.2   Top ten bar passers by gender.
Source: Data provided by the Integrated Bar of the Philippines (IBP)

It is only logical to expect that more women would take up legal studies and engage in the practice of law from the late 1980s onwards. The rate of enrolment and completion rate of Filipino women law students is reflected in their numbers in the judiciary. The almost equal number of men and women in the judiciary has been a trend in many other countries (OECD 2017).

The number of women in the judiciary in the Philippines mirrors the trend in more developed jurisdictions: women make up more than 50 per cent of judges but are under-represented in senior judicial positions. This is the case for the secular courts of the Philippines but not in the Shari'ah court system, a special court created by virtue of Presidential Decree 1083 in recognition of Filipino Muslims' culture and religious practices (see Ali 2010). Women judges in the secular courts serve in different levels of the court system, from the lowest courts to the upper courts. Table 6.1 shows that the number of women judges is almost equal to men judges in the trial courts – the Municipal Circuit Trial Courts (MCTC), the Municipal Trial Courts (MTC) and the Metropolitan Trial Courts (MeTC). Except for the Court of Tax Appeals (CTA) which has an overwhelming number of women justices, a majority of judges of the appellate and higher level courts (the Supreme Court, the Court of Appeals (CA) and Sandiganbayan) are men. The CA however has seen an increasing number of women joining the ranks; most Supreme Court justices are nominated from the appellate court.

Table 6.1 *Number of women judges in the judiciary (as of 13 July 2019)*

Courts	Male Judges	Women Judges	% of Women Judges	Vacancies
Supreme Court	15	3	20	0
Court of Appeals	34	25	42	10
Sandiganbayan	13	8	38	0
Court of Tax Appeals	2	5	71	0
Regional Trial Court	556	271	33	548
Metropolitan Trial Court	160	121	43	120
Municipal Trial Court	117	134	53	103
Municipal Circuit Trial Court	192	163	46	120
Shari'ah District Court	1	0	0	4
Shari'ah Circuit Court	24	1	4	26

The Shari'ah courts exhibit the lowest level of women's representation among judges. Since its establishment in 1983, there have been only three women judges appointed in the circuit court level and none in the district court level. In 2020, there was just one female judge out of thirty positions filled. Some conservative thinkers in Mindanao believe that women are not appropriate for the position based on Islamic jurisprudence (Deinla and Taylor 2014). This is in contrast to other parts of Southeast Asia such as Indonesia and Malaysia, where women have been recruited in the Shari'ah courts as judges (see Chapters 5 and 7).

Despite the small proportion of women in the higher court level, as reflected in Table 6.1, women lawyers have created a strong presence and have elevated their position in the judiciary. The appointment process to judgeship is complex and requires an application for the position, being shortlisted by the Judicial and Bar Council (JBC) and finally being selected and appointed by the president. That women are succeeding in this process despite the difficulties demonstrates their capacity as well as their ability to network and socialise, skills important in securing an appointment. Appointment to judgeship remains highly political, despite the institutionalisation of the Judicial and Bar Council. After all, the appointment stops with the president who alone ultimately determines who will get the post. Most crises that have divided the Philippine Supreme Court such as the impeachment proceedings of three chief justices – Hilario Davide, Renato Corona and Lourdes Sereno – can be traced back to the controversy surrounding the appointments of these justices (Deinla and Reyes 2021) Most of the four women judges who participated in the study for this chapter point to the efforts at reaching out and establishing support for their application and selection. Women – as well as male applicants – need extensive professional and social networks to secure appointments. They need to reach the 'corridors of power' (influence) to support their bids to become judges. Justice Sereno proved that with excellent academic credentials from prestigious schools, a woman could reach the top ladder of the judiciary. Top universities mostly based in Manila are said to be the 'breeding ground for future leaders' and networks formed within are also deeply connected with social, political and economic networks outside. Coming from a modest family background, Sereno earned a scholarship for her undergraduate degree in economics at the Ateneo and graduated at the top of her class at the UP College of Law. She is a member of a well-connected all-women sorority at the University of the Philippines (UP), the Portia Sorority, which also counts many women justices such as Palma and Hererra as members. She thereafter worked in one of the largest law firms as well as taught at UP.

Filipino Women Judges and Judicial Independence

The Philippine Supreme Court, as the penultimate court, has been vested with expansive judicial powers under the 1987 Philippine Constitution to settle actual controversies and to determine the validity of government actions. It is composed of a chief justice and fourteen associate justices who sit *en banc* or on divisions in deciding cases. Members are appointed by the president but undergo a vetting process in the JBC. Prior to the 1987 Constitution, the president alone made the assessment and appointment of the justices using their discretionary powers. Indeed, the politicisation of the Supreme Court was heightened during the Marcos regime; he appointed many justices who were likely to uphold his wishes (see Tate and Haynie 1993). As such, the Philippine judiciary has been referred to as the 'Marcos judiciary' or even a 'kangaroo court' when judges were perceived to be compliant to the wishes of the executive (Chanco 2018). There was also wide public perception of incompetency and inefficiency, as well as reports of corruption of judges (see Vitug 2010). Initiatives to reform the appointment process to the judiciary was in response to the politicisation and inefficiency of the judiciary.

The 1987 Constitution specifically prescribed the establishment of the Judicial and Bar Council[4] to act as a vetting mechanism in the appointment of judges. This was designed to enhance accountability and transparency in the judicial appointment process. As a key institutional innovation prescribed by the Constitution, the Judicial and Bar Council is composed of seven members from academia, the bar council, Congress, the private sector, the Secretary of Justice, a retired justice and the chief justice of the Supreme Court who is designated as *ex officio* chair. The JBC is tasked with receiving applications, screening candidates and preparing a list of three qualified nominees that will be sent to the president for selection.[5] The rationale for the creation of the council as clearly stated by its proponent, former Chief Justice Roberto Concepcion: 'it is an innovation made in response to the public clamour in favour of eliminating politics from the appointment of judges' (JBC website).

There has also been an unwritten practice in the appointment of the chief justice based on seniority or from among the more senior associate justices. This has been observed even after the Marcos regime and into the democratisation period. This tradition of seniority had been observed during the Macapagal-Arroyo presidency but was broken with the appointment of Sereno by President Benigno Aquino in 2012. Sereno's appointment has suffered from two 'anomalies': being the youngest and being the first woman appointed to the position. During the presidencies of Arroyo and Aquino, the court exercised its independence in many highly contentious constitutional cases. For example, the Supreme Court made decisions that affirmed the constitutional balance of power (Arroyo's attempt to proclaim emergency powers); overturned attempts to limit fundamental rights of citizens (executive order limiting the right to assembly); and upheld progressive legislation (reproductive health law).

The practice of impeaching a chief justice, however, has become common in the Philippines. In 2003, over fifteen years ago, Hilario Davide was served – unsuccessfully – with two impeachment proceedings. In 2011, Renato Corona, the chief justice appointed during the last few months of Arroyo's term, was successfully ousted through impeachment. Impeachment, as a function of fractious elite political competition, has become either an instrument of accountability or a political weapon. The spectre of removing a justice has become a 'sword of Damocles' to the justices and to the independence of the Supreme Court.

---

[4] Sec. 8, Art. VIII, 1987 Philippine Constitution.
[5] Ibid.

The court under the Duterte administration has suffered the lowest public trust rating during the impeachment and consequent removal from office of Chief Justice Sereno (Deinla and Reyes 2021). Decisions on controversial political cases have been widely seen as bowing to the wishes of the president and all of his appointees have voted in favour of the executive position on the matter (Buan 2019). In fact, the Philippines continues to fall in the World Rule of Law Index and is among those countries with the most significant drop in ranking over the last five years (World Justice Project 2020).

It is unclear and difficult to measure whether gender balance or more women in the judiciary promotes judicial independence. The answer is not straight forward, and like male judges, women judges work within the same political or economic constraints. They are also subject to the same appointment process that, despite the reforms, has remained contentious and politicised. The presence of a small number of women justices in the Supreme Court, as the court that decides on major political controversies among elites and between government and the people, does not necessarily represent the broader trend of how women judges behave and decide on cases, particularly those that check on executive powers. The Supreme Court in the last fifteen years has suffered from legitimacy issues and decline in public trust of the court, particularly during the Macapagal Arroyo administration and during impeachment proceedings of the two former chief justices.

In evaluating the performance of women judges in the Supreme Court, I tabulated five important cases in each of the last three administrations – Macapagal-Arroyo, Benigno Aquino III and Duterte – and show how women judges voted (Table 6.2). The cases listed here have been selected on the basis that the executive, particularly the president, has a strong interest for or against the outcomes.

During the Duterte administration, all the cases I examined have been decided in favour of legal and policy outcomes desired by the president. During the Macapagal-Arroyo and Aquino administrations, only two cases were ruled in favour of the administration – protecting executive privilege against disclosure (*Senate* v. *Ermita*) and validating the midnight appointment of a new chief justice, Renato Corona, within two months of the next presidential elections (*De Castro* v. *Judicial and Bar Council*). Two cases were also decided in favour of the Aquino administration – dismissing a petition to seek compensation from the United States in the destruction of Tubattaha reef (*Adigo* v. *Swift*) and the passage of the highly controversial but progressive legislation on reproductive health rights (*Imbong* v. *Ochoa*). This independent streak in the

Supreme Court has been observed in the post-Marcos era as it plays a role in consolidating democracy. The Supreme Court in these two administrations has a more varied composition that also prevents the executive from exerting strong political pressure. This is unlike in the Duterte regime where an overwhelming majority of justices were appointed under his term. By the end of Duterte's term in 2022, thirteen out of fifteen justices will have been appointed by him.

A caveat is made that the purpose of this tabulation is not to discuss extensively how judges voted in terms of their rationale for their votes but merely to show the voting patterns, particularly in cases where the executive has a strong preference. Among the three governments, it was during the term of the woman president Macapal-Arroyo that the highest number of women justices was appointed to the Supreme Court – five, compared to three each for Aquino and Duterte. There was however a period under Macapagal-Arroyo where there were two women justices due to retirement from service.

I now turn to briefly explain the issue in five selected cases under each of the relevant political regimes, as the background to the case. I then turn to how women judges' voted in these cases.

Selected Cases under Duterte (2016–2020)

In *Ocampo* v. *Enriquez*, the legal question concerned the discretion of the executive to determine who can be given a heroes' burial at the *Libingan ng mga Bayani* (cemetery for heroes). The case pertains to the decision of President Duterte to finally allow a heroes' burial for Marcos after a request by his family was denied by previous administrations.

The issue in *Lagman* v. *Medialdea* was whether an armed siege by Islamists could be classified as rebellion or insurrection to justify the declaration of martial law not only in Marawi City but in the whole of the Mindanao area. The filing of criminal information against and subsequent arrest of Senator Leila De Lima (*De Lima* v. *Guerrero*), former secretary of justice in the Aquino administration who investigated the alleged death squad in Davao City and critic of Duterte's drug war, is being assailed for being invalid and issued with grave abuse of discretion. Senator De Lima was investigated by Duterte's allies in Congress for her alleged involvement in the proliferation of drugs in the national penitentiary and on this basis the Department of Justice panel conducted an investigation and filed a criminal information against her.

At issue in *Flight Attendants and Stewards Association of the Philippines* v. *Philippine Airlines (FASAP v. PAL)* was the validity of retrenchment of airline employees by the Philippines' largest airline, PAL. Running for twenty years, the case was already decided in favour of the employees by a division in the Supreme Court. Through a letter sent by PAL's attorney, the very influential Estelito Mendoza, the case was revived and decided by the court sitting *en banc* in favour of the airlines.

Finally, the *Republic* v. *Sereno* case pertains to the dismissal of Chief Justice Sereno through *quo warranto*.

Selected Cases under Aquino (2010–2016)

In *Biraogo* v. *Philippine Truth Commission*, the question of whether the establishment of an ad hoc Philippine Truth Commission (PTC) violates the equal protection clause was at issue. The PTC was established by President Aquino to collate data, investigate and recommend prosecutions for graft and corruption of officials in the past administration of Arroyo.

In *Biraogo* v. *Ochoa* the issue was whether the pork barrel system transgresses the separation of powers and the non-delegable nature of legislative powers, diluted congressional oversight and flouted public accountability. This practice has been used to gain congressional control by allocating 'priority development' funds to legislators for decades. Massive corruption has been exposed prior to the filing of the case by concerned citizens.

In *Arigo* v. *Swift*, the issue involved a petition for a writ of *kalikasan* (environmental suit) to restore and gain damage over the destruction of the Tubbataha reefs caused by a United States navy ship running aground.. At issue was whether the doctrine of state immunity could be invoked against exercise of jurisdiction by Philippine courts.

Imbong v. *Ochoa* is a legal challenge to the government's reproductive health law on the ground of being contrary to religious freedom and violating the right to life of unborn children.

The question in *Enrile* v. *Sandiganbayan* was whether bail could be granted to Senator Juan Ponce Enrile, who was accused of plunder for diversion or misappropriation of his pork barrel allocation. Senator Enrile was one of the legislators investigated during the Aquino government for corruption. After helping topple the Marcos regime, he became a member of the Senate and is alleged to have supported coup plots against Corazon Aquino, the mother of President Benigno Aquino.

Selected Cases under Arroyo (2001–2010)

In *Senate* v. *Ermita*, President Arroyo issued an executive order requiring members of the executive and armed forces to secure approval from the president before they can testify in congressional inquiries. It involved the question of whether the said government order frustrates the power of inquiry by the legislature. The investigation arose from hearings conducted involving a massive corruption scandal hounding the Arroyo government.

Bayan v. *Ermita* challenges a law and the Arroyo government's 'calibrated pre-emptive response' that allows police to violently disperse protesters and rallyists under the 'no permit, no rally' rule. The petitioners argue that this government policy curtails the right to peaceful assembly and for redress of grievances protected under the 1987 Constitution.

David v. *Arroyo* is a landmark case involving President Arroyo's proclamation of a state of national emergency. The emergency decree was justified to thwart an alleged conspiracy to unseat or assassinate the president. This led to security personnel conducting warrantless arrests and the raiding of newspaper offices deemed critical of the government.

Lambino v. *COMELEC* sought to compel the Commission on Elections (COMELEC) to hold a plebiscite for the purpose of amending the 1987 Constitution. Among the questions in the plebiscite is whether to extend the term limits of the president. The Lambino group, seen as connected with the president, presented a list of over six million qualified voters in support of the petition.

Finally, in *De Castro* v. *JBC*, the issue is whether Arroyo is prohibited from appointing a new chief justice after the presidential elections were held and before her term ends. Called a 'midnight appointment', Arroyo had appointed ousted Chief Justice Corona through this process.

Below I set out how women judges on the Supreme Court voted under these three political eras (Tables 6.2–6.4). The numbers following the case titles represent the number of all justices who voted for, dissented or abstained from the case. The numbers in the columns represent the number of votes of women justices. For example, in the 2016 case of *Ocampao* v. *Enriquez*, a total of nine judges voted for and four judges voted against; of the three women on the bench, two voted for and one voted against (Table 6.2). In another example, in the 2018 case of *Republic* v. *Sereno*, eight judges voted for, six voted against and one abstained; of the three women on the bench, one voted for, one dissented and one abstained.

Table 6.2 *Votes of women judges of the Supreme Court under Duterte (2016–2020)*

	Ocampo v. Enriquez, 8 November 2016 (9–4)	Lagman v. Medialdea, 4 July 2017 (11–4)	De Lima v. Guerero, 10 October 2017 (9–6)	FASAP v. PAL 13 March 2018 (7–2–5)	Republic v. Sereno 11 May 2018 (8–6–1)
Decision					
Concur	2	2	1	1	1
Dissent	1	1	2	0	1
No part	0	0	0	1	1
On leave			1	1	

Table 6.3 *Votes of women judges of the Supreme Court under Aquino (2010–2016)*

	Biraogo v. Truth Commission 7 December 2010 (15–0)	Belgica v. Ochoa 19 November 2013 (14–0–1)	Arigo v. Swift 16 September 2014 (13–0–2)	Imbong v. Ochoa 8 April 2014 (15–0)	Enrile v. Sandiganbayan 18 August 2015 (8–4–3)
Decision					
Concur	3	2	3	3	1
Dissent	0	0	0	0	2
No part	0	0	0	0	0
On leave	0	0	0	0	0

Table 6.4 *Votes of women judges of the Supreme Court under Arroyo (2001–2010)*

	Senate v. Ermita 20 April 2006 (14–0–1)	Bayan v. Ermita 25 April 2006 (14–0–1)	David v. Arroyo, 3 May 2006 (8–6–1)	Lambino v. COMELEC, 25 October 2006 (15–0)	De Castro v. JBC, 20 April 2010 (9–3–3)
Decision					
Concur	4	5	5	5	1
Dissent	1	0	0	0	1
No part	0	0	0	0	0
On leave	0	0	0	0	0

In the tables, women judges concur or agree with the majority decision most of the time. In at least nine of these fifteen cases, the majority of the women justices voted with the prevailing decisions. This could be consistent with the theory that women judges ignore or downplay their feminist voice and, in McLoughlin's study, the proclivity to follow the majority decision particularly in their early years. A closer look at their voting pattern, however, shows that seven of the cases where women concurred with majority decisions are decisions against the government or affirming a progressive legislation (*Imbong* v. *Ochoa*). These cases were decided during the Aquino and Macapagal-Arroyo administrations. Women justices also voted as one in these cases, with one case (*Senate* v. *Ermita*) having only one dissent and a split in the other two. In Duterte, where all five cases were decided to favour government preferences, the women judges did not vote as one but cast varied votes or did not take part in the decision. These cases demonstrate that a more liberal government has engendered an independent court and independent judges, including women judges. It also shows that women judges are not shy to cast their votes against government preferences even when there is extreme political pressure, as in the Duterte cases.

Women justices voted for cases where the executive has a strong interest. For example, the Duterte era cases such as the implementation of martial law in Mindanao (*Lagman* v. *Medialdea 2017*); allowing a hero's burial for former dictator Ferdinand Marcos (*Ocampo* v. *Enriquez 2016*); in denying bail and affirming the criminal charge against Senator Leila De Lima, a fierce critic of Duterte's drug war and extrajudicial killings (*De Lima* v. *Guerero 2017*); and in removing Sereno from office (*Republic* v. *Sereno 2018*). In *De Lima*, the assailed lower court decision was decided by a woman trial judge. The lone woman justice who voted for Sereno's removal, Justice De Castro, also testified against Sereno during the impeachment trial. In the executive privilege case, women justices voted to bar scrutiny of congressional enquiry into corruption scandals involving government officials.

Many of the women judges have also clearly made their mark in safeguarding constitutional democracy, justice and the rule of law. Their voting pattern, though a small percentage in the court's composition, demonstrates their capacity for independence and to give impartial decisions. There is clearly a diversity of voices of women judges across these governments. They voted for cases that limit the powers of the executive in the past two administrations such as invalidating the congressional pork barrel system under Aquino (*Belgica* v. *Ochoa*); the emergency powers (*David* v. *Arroyo*); limiting freedom of assembly (*Bayan* v. *Ermita*); and preventing an initiative to unconstitutionally amend the constitution (*Lambino* v. *Commission on Elections*) under Macapagal-Arroyo.

It was clearly women power on display in *David* v. *Arroyo* when a bench of all women judges voted unanimously to declare unconstitutional the state of emergency declared by Arroyo. Had they not voted as one, then President Macapagal-Arroyo would have succeeded in declaring a state of emergency that would have given her more powers and eroding fundamental rights protected in the 1987 Constitution.

In the Arroyo period, women justices also took on a leadership role in writing three of the most significant cases in this period – Justice Angelina Sandoval-Gutierrez in *David*; Justice Conchita Carpio-Morales in *Ermita*; and Justice Estela Perlas-Bernabe in *Belgica*. Later, during President Aquino's time, Justice Carpio-Morales would lead on accountability reforms and the drive to hold powerful politicians to account through the office of the Ombudsman. Up until her retirement in 2018, after completing a seven-year term as Ombudsman, Justice Carpio-Morales was targeted for vilification and ouster proceedings because of her role as the head of the Ombudsman (as were the heads of other independent institutions). Impeachment against Ombudsman Carpio-Morales did not progress, however.

Under the Duterte administration, women judges have also shown their fortitude to go against the grain in highly contentious cases. In the *De Lima* case, two out of three women justices rendered dissenting opinions against Senator Delima's arrest, amidst the high popularity of the president and the declaration of violent war on drugs. One of these dissenters, Chief Justice Sereno, would later be removed from the bench through a highly politicised – and to many, an unjust, case (Deinla, Taylor and Rood 2018).

The Experiences of Women Judges

Aside from these court decisions, I conclude my analysis with reflections on the interviews conducted with women judges. Women judges and clerks of courts in the trial courts have displayed exemplary performance in the discharge of their functions. One way that judicial performance is rewarded is through annual judicial excellence awards conferred by the Society for Judicial Excellence in collaboration with the Supreme Court. For many years, women judges have dominated the Judicial Excellence

Awards.[6] The award recognises the outstanding performance of judges and legal support staff in the judiciary. Two of the lower court judges who participated in the scoping interview were recipients of the awards. One of the judges also teaches in a law school and has been involved in advocacy and initiatives for judicial reform and in raising the quality of the administration of justice. One respondent used to work in an NGO advocating for women's rights and providing legal protection for victims of violence.

All four judges when asked about the process of appointment to the bench pointed to two challenges: the length of time needed to secure their appointment and the imperative for 'connections' to support their application up to the appointing authority. These issues confront both men and women aspiring judges. One respondent, however, intimated that women stereotyping exists such as when women judges are expected to wear feminine dresses or don 'ballgowns' during ceremonies. The 'padrino' system is an all-too common feature of appointment to public office in the Philippines which is often equated with the prevalence of personalistic rather than purely merit-based appointments, especially in high-level positions in government such as in the judiciary. This creates an expectation that judges will be beholden to the appointing power or to those who helped them secure their positions. Does being a woman affect the way they decide cases? All four responded that they abide by the law and jurisprudence in weighing cases brought before them.

While political pressure and corruption have always been blamed for judicial partiality, women judges' also point to other factors that affect their judging. Lacking adequate resources to effectively run their operations adds pressure to their task. This also makes them rely more on local government units (LGUs) for resources which could in turn potentially undermine how they are perceived by the public. Politicians who hold local elected offices could also put pressure on judges by asking back for favours in cases they have interest in. Indeed, one of the judges interviewed stated how a mayor requested to meet with her in relation to a case pending before her court. When asked how they manage these types of pressure, the women judges said that they only need to be firm in saying 'No'. They said that they have to display an appearance of distance

---

[6] There are only four years on record: 2012, 2014, 2018 and 2019. Women made a sweep in these years – four out of five in 2012, all four awards in 2014, seven out of nine in 2018 and four out of eight in 2019.

even outside the courtroom and minimise socialising outside of the bench. All four of the women judges have a life-long passion for serving justice and correcting the public perception that the Philippine justice system is corrupt. One respondent also expressed disdain over a practice of some judges asking for sponsorships from local governments, politicians or the private sector for attending conferences and conventions.

Filipino women judges, despite their many achievements in overcoming institutional and political barriers, still face tremendous challenges in performing their duties to serve justice. All four women judges expressed apprehension over their personal security and the need to look out for their own safety under a climate of violence and impunity in the country. This anxiety is shared by all members of the legal profession. Since 2001, over 200 lawyers have been killed, according to the Integrated Bar of the Philippines. Of this number, forty-eight deaths have occurred since Duterte assumed office in 2016, which includes nine public prosecutors and seven judges (Gavilan 2018). Seven of these deaths were of women lawyers or prosecutors.

Conclusion

Studies on gender and decision-making have produced mixed results but more often affirm a diversity of voices among women judges. Women still occupy a small percentage of senior judicial posts. In the case of the Philippine judicial system, I have shown that in resolving significant constitutional issues and contentious political cases there is a diversity of voices among women judges in the highest court, the Supreme Court. Sometimes women judges concur with the majority while at other times they have joined the dissent of the minority. The cases discussed show that Philippine women judges voted as one in most of the cases decided against government preferences under liberal political regime. Under an illiberal government, they have split their votes. Overall, women judges have shown their capacity and fortitude for judicial independence in both liberal and illiberal times.

Since the period when women qualified and joined the legal profession and the judiciary, women lawyers and judges have made their mark, individually and collectively. By topping the bar examinations, they have proven their capacity in performing any job that requires legal knowledge and skills. They have progressively demonopolised a historically male-dominated legal profession in the public and private spheres, which is a significant achievement. They have increasingly climbed the steep ladder of influential private law firms that were the traditional bastion of male lawyers.

Many women are making waves as lawyers in government offices and private corporations, or as solo legal practitioners doing all-rounder jobs. Women judges and lawyers show exemplary dedication and service in administering justice in their constituencies and defying public perception that courts are corrupt or ineffective. Filipino women lawyers have also been part of the broader civil society movement that has been vital in reclaiming democracy and fundamental freedoms. They have been active in sustaining an imperfect democracy, advocating human rights and crafting progressive legislation on gender equality.

There is a compelling case to support the view that Filipino women judges are a force in advancing judicial independence and constitutional democracy. Based on data focused on the last three administrations – 2001 up to the present – many women judges continue to strive to promote judicial independence and serve justice and the rule of law. There is a strong imperative to continue to support the appointment of women in the judiciary, especially so in the upper courts responsible for constitutional decision-making. For example, women justices made decisions that were independent of the executive under the Macapagal-Arroyo when there were five women (comprising 33 per cent of the members). Although it is often referred to as the 'Arroyo Court' for having sided with the executive on some accountability cases, this court did in fact resist attempts by the executive to impose a state of emergency and attempts to limit fundamental rights in some cases. The united stance of women justices in the case of *David* thwarted the president's attempts to exercise extraordinary powers.

In most of the cases in the Aquino era, there is also a pattern of consensus decision-making among women justices, except for the case in *Enrile*. These cases demonstrate that women judges hold their ground even against the political pressure of their appointing authority, by finding common ground and supporting each other's legal opinions. Although all of the cases I considered under the Duterte government were decided by the Supreme Court in favour of the government, at least some of the women judges have shown courage by dissenting and going against the powerful voices in the court.

Many Filipino women judges and lawyers have not only made their individual mark on law and politics but have been part of a collective movement to provide equal rights for women, from suffrage to universal education, and to bring a democratic way of life after decades of authoritarian rule. This shows the power of deep structural and institutional reforms at work to provide women with opportunities and a voice in decision-making. Justice Teresita De Castro, one of the proactive justices in the initiative to remove Justice Sereno, was chair of the Committee on Women in the court and was one of the government peace negotiators during the administration of Presidents Corazon Aquino and Fidel Ramos.

Since the 1970s, Filipino women lawyers and judges, especially in the more senior levels, fought for their rights and for their place under a new political order. They are as much constrained by politics within and outside the courts as they are by their backgrounds and experiences. In the next generation of Filipino women judges, many appointed at a relatively young age (below forty years old), we can observe whether this 'tradition' of advocacy and activism continues. This chapter has shown that the pendulum of judicial independence has swayed back and forth through various political episodes but overall, women judges have strived for judicial independence even in times of political pressure. The appointment of more women judges in the upper court level of the judiciary should therefore be part of the broader strategy for judicial independence.

References

Abueva, Jose V. 1965. Social Backgrounds and Recruitment of Legislators and Administrators in the Philippines. *Philippine Journal of Public Administration,* 9,10–29.

Asia Business Law Journal, 6 August 2020, www.vantageasia.com/the-philippines-law-firm-awards-2019

Alcantara, Adelamar. 1994. Gender Roles, Fertility and the Status of Married Filipino Men and Women. *Philippine Sociological Review,* 42, 1/4, 94–109.

Ali, Anshari P. 2007. The Legal Impediments to the Application of Islamic Family Law in the Philippines. *Journal of Muslim Minority Affairs,* 27, 1, 93–115.

Buan, Lian. 2019. 'Who Voted for Duterte in the Supreme Court?', Rappler, 18 August, www.rappler.com/newsbreak/iq/237983-supreme-court-who-voted-for-duterte

Casambre, Athena Lydia and Rood, Steven. 2012. *Early Feminism in the Philippines,* 7 March, https://asiafoundation.org/2012/03/07/early-feminism-in-the-philippines

Ciencia, Alejandro. 2012. *From Judicialization to Politicization of the Judiciary: The Philippine Case* in Dressel, Bjoern, ed. *The Judicialization of Politics in Asia* (New York: Routledge).

Chanco, Boo. 2018. 'Kangaroo Court', *Philippine Star*, 16 April, www.philstar.com/business/2018/04/16/1806220/kangaroo-court

Clarke, Gerard. 1995. Non-governmental Organisations (NGOs) and the Philippine State: 1986–1993. *South East Asia Research*, 3, 1, 67–91.

Diamonon, Victoriano. 1919. A Study of the Philippine Government during the Spanish Regime. A Master's thesis at the University of Iowa Research Online, https://ir.uiowa.edu/cgi/viewcontent.cgi?article=4112&context=etd

Deinla, Imelda. 2018. 'A Wave of Violence against Lawyers Is Crippling the Philippines' Justice System', *World Politics Review*, 20 November, www.worldpoliticsreview.com/trend-lines/26817/a-wave-of-violence-against-lawyers-is-crippling-the-philippines-justice-system

Deinla, Imelda and Dressel, Bjoern. 2019. *From Aquino II to Duterte: Change, Continuity – or Rupture* (Singapore: Institute of Southeast Asian Studies), 1–36

Deinla, Imelda and Reyes, Ma. Lulu. 2021. 'Tipping the Balance? Politics, Personalities and Institutions in the Philippines Supreme Court', in Taylor, Veronica and Rood, Steve, eds. *Contesting the Philippines* (Singapore: ISEAS).

Deinla, Imelda and Taylor, Veronica. 2015. *Towards Peace: Rethinking Justice and Legal Pluralism in the Bangsamoro*. RegNet Research Paper No. 2015/63, 23 January, https://papers.ssrn.com/sol3/papers.cfm?abstract_id=2553541

Deinla, Imelda, Taylor, Veronica and Rood, Steven. 2018. 'Philippines: Justice Removed, Justice Denied', *The Lowy Interpreter*, 17 May, www.lowyinstitute.org/the-interpreter/philippines-justice-removed-justice-denied

Freedom House. 2019. 'Philippines: Attacks against Lawyers Escalating', 19 September, https://freedomhouse.org/article/philippines-attacks-against-lawyers-escalating

Freudenheim, Milt and Slavin, Barbara. 1982. 'The World in Summary, Bolt from the Bench', *New York Times*, 9 May, www.nytimes.com/1982/05/09/weekinreview/the-world-in-summary-bolt-from-the-bench.html

Gavilan, Jodesz. 2018. 'Judges, Prosecutors, Lawyers Killed under Duterte Gov't' (updated 1 March 2020), Rappler, www.rappler.com/newsbreak/iq/216239-list-judges-prosecutors-lawyers-killed-under-duterte-government

Gatmaytan, Dante. 2011. The Judicial Review of Constitutional Amendments: The Insurance Theory in Post-Marcos Philippines. *Philippine Law and Society Review*, 1, 1, 74–89.

Gilligan, Carol. 1982. *In a Different Voice: Psychological Theory and Women's Development* (Cambridge, MA: Harvard University Press).

Ginsburg, Tom. 2003. *Judicial Review in New Democracies: Constitutional Courts in Asia* (Cambridge: Cambridge University Press)

Haynie, Stacia. 1998. Paradise Lost: Politicisation of the Philippine Supreme Court in the Post-Marcos Era. *Asian Studies Review*, 22, 2, 459–473.

Hendrianto, Stefanus. 2016. The Rise and Fall of Heroic Chief Justice: Constitutional Politics and Judicial Leadership in Indonesia. *Washington International Law Journal*, 25, 3, 489.

Johnson, D. C. 1916. Courts in the Philippines, Old: New, *Michigan Law Review*, 14, 4, 300–319.

Judicial and Bar Council. 2020. http://jbc.judiciary.gov.ph/index.php/about-us/judicial-and-bar-council/3-about-jbc

Lolarga, Elizabeth. 2012. 'Natividad Almeda Lopez–Suffragist, Lawyer, a Woman Ahead of Her Time', *Philippine Daily Inquirer*, 16 December, https://lifestyle.inquirer.net/81351/natividad-almeda-lopez-suffragist-lawyer-a-woman-ahead-of-her-time

Lucas, Daxim L. 2020. 'PH Tops "Women in Business" Global Ranking', *Philippine Daily Inquirer,* 23 February, https://business.inquirer.net/291145/ph-tops-women-in-business-global-ranking

McLoughlin, Kcasey. 2015. The Politics of Gender Diversity on the High Court of Australia. *Alternative Law Journal*, 40, 3, 166–170.

Miller, Susan and Maier, Shana. 2008. Moving Beyond Numbers: What Female Judges Say about Different Judicial Voices. *Journal of Women, Politics and Policy*, 29, 4, 527–559.

Organisation for Economic Cooperation and Development. 2017. 'Women in the Judiciary: Working towards a Legal System Reflective of Society', March , www.oecd.org/gender/data/women-in-the-judiciary-working-towards-a-legal-system-reflective-of-society.htm

Pangalangan, Raul. 2014. 'The Philippines' Post-Marcos Judiciary: The Institutional Turn and the Populist Backlash', in Jiunn-rong Yeh and Wen-Chen Chang, eds. *Asian Courts in Context* (Cambridge: Cambridge University Press, 356–374).

Panganiban, Artemio. 2018. 'Judicial Brinkmanship', *Philippine Daily Inquirer*, 19 August, https://opinion.inquirer.net/115477/judicial-brinkmanship

Paqueo, Vicente B. and Orbeta, Aniceto C. Jr., 2019. 'Gender Equity in Education: Helping the Boys Catch Up', Discussion Papers DP 2019-01, Philippine Institute for Development Studies, https://ideas.repec.org/p/phd/dpaper/dp_2019-01.html

Roces, Mina. 2012. *Women's Movements and 'the Filipina': 1986–2008* (Honolulu: University of Hawai'i Press).

Tate, C. Neal and Haynie, Stacia L. 1993. Authoritarianism and the Functions of Courts: A Time Series Analysis of the Philippine Supreme Court, 1961–1987. *Law and Society Review*, 27, 4, 707–740.

Salcedo, Emily Sanchez. 2019. A Five-Year Gender Equality Score Card for the Philippine Supreme Court under Its First Woman Chief Justice: Opportunities Seized and Missed. *International Journal of the Legal Profession*, 27, 2, 145–159.

Supreme Court of the Philippines (n.d). 'Maria V. Francisco Is the First Woman Admitted to the Bar in 1911', http://sc.judiciary.gov.ph/3237

Turner, Mark. 1987. 'The Quest for Political Legitimacy in the Philippines: The Constitutional Plebiscite of 1987', in Turner, Mark, ed. Regime Change in the Philippines, https://openresearch-repository.anu.edu.au/bitstream/1885/133697/1/Regime_Change_in_the_Philippines.pdf

Villanueva, Pura Kalaw. 1952. *How the Filipina Got the Vote* (Manila, publisher unidentified).

World Justice Project Rule of Law Index. 2020. https://worldjusticeproject.org/our-work/research-and-data/wjp-rule-law-index-2020

List of Cases

Arturo De Castro *v.* Judicial and Bar Council (GR No. 191002, 17 March 2010)

Bayan et al. *v.* Eduardo Ermita (GR No. 169838), 18 July 2006)

Candido Mendoza *v.* Natividad Almeda Lopez et al. (GR No. 45663, 29 September 1937), www.chanrobles.com/scdecisions/jurisprudence1937/sep1937/gr_45663_1937.php

Edcel Lagman et al. *v.* Salvador Medialdea (GR No. 231658, 4 July 2017)

Flight Attendants and Stewards Association of the Philippines (FASAP) *v.* Philippine Airlines (PAL) (GR No. 178083, 13 March 2018)

Greco Belgica *v.* Executive Secretary Paquito Ochoa (GR No. 208566, 19 November 2013) 710 SCRA 1

James M Imbong *v.* Executive Secretary Paquito Ochoa (GR No. 204819, 8 April 2014)

Juan Ponce Enrile *v.* Sandiganbayan (GR No. 213847, 18 August 2015)

Josue Javellana *v.* Executive Secretary GR No. 36142, March 31, 1973) 50 SCRA 30

Leila De Lima *v.* Judge Juanita Guerero (GR No. 229781, 10 October 2017)

Louis Biraogo *v.* Philippine Truth Commission (PTC) (GR Nos. 192935 and 193036, 7 December 2010)

Pedro Arigo *v.* Scott Swift (GR No. 206510, 16 September 2014)

People of the Philippines *v.* Judge Amante Purisima (GR No. L-40902, 20 November 1978), https://lawphil.net/judjuris/juri1978/nov1978/gr_42050_66_1978.html

Randolf David et al. *v.* Gloria Macapagal-Arroyo et al. (GR No. 171396, 3 May 2006)

Raul Lambino et al. *v.* Commission on Elections (GR Nos. 174153 and 174299, 25 October 2006)

Saturnino Ocampo et al. *v.* Rear Admiral Ernesto Enriquez (GR No. 225973, 8 November 2016)

Senate of the Philippines *v.* Eduardo Ermita (GR No. 169777, 20 April 2006)

7

One Decade of Female Judges in the Malaysian Shariah Judiciary

Promises to Keep and Miles to Go

KERSTIN STEINER*

I'm optimistic that one day society will see no difference between males and females when it comes to being a judge in Syariah Court.

Nenney Shuhaidah Shamsuddin as cited in Jayatilaka (2019)

In 2016, Nenney Shuhaidah Shamsuddin, with her colleague Noor Huda Roslan, was one of the first two female judges to be appointed to a Syariah High Court in Malaysia. Her appointment and her focus on women's rights in the Syariah court quickly brought her to international attention.[1] Indeed, her appointment signified a milestone in Malaysia's road to accepting women as judges in the Syariah[2] legal system. In general, Malaysia has a chequered past regarding appointing women in decision-making in the judicial system. This history is marked by women being initially confined to supporting roles, gaining positions in the lower courts and then slowly making their way into the higher courts. While the pace of women's entry was arguably slow in the civil non-religious system,[3] it is even slower in the Syariah legal system. According to the

* I would like to thank the participants of the Women in Asia Conference 2019 for the comments on an earlier draft of this paper. Special thanks also to my friends and colleagues in Malaysia, especially Zainah Anwar, executive director of Musawah, and the team from Sisters in Islam as well as associate professor Ramizah wan Muhammed, for their kind assistance in sourcing some of the local material for me.
[1] In 2018, she was included in the BBC's '100 Women in 2018' (BBC 2018).
[2] Please note that there are numerous local variations of spelling syariah, including shari'a, syrie, syaria etc. The most common variant syariah is used throughout the chapter.
[3] There are different ways in which the perceived dichotomy between religious and non-religious legal systems in Malaysia is labelled. In the context of this contribution, I will use the label civil non-religious legal system to describe the non-religious legal system sometimes called only civil or secular legal system.

Global Gender Gap Report 2020, 233),[4] Malaysia dropped from rank 90 in 2006 when the index was initiated down to 117 in 2020 in the political empowerment category,[5] illustrating that Malaysia still has a long way to go to achieve gender equality compared to other countries. This is even though women were appointed to the two highest positions in the Malaysian non-religious judiciary in 2019. For the specific index measure concerning the right to equal justice, which measures whether women have the same rights to give testimony and sue in court as well as hold public or political office, Malaysia received a score of 0.75 out of 1 in the right to equal justice, with 1 being the worst score (Global Gender Index 2020, 52, 233). The reasons for these poor scores are of course based on the characteristics of the Syariah legal system: women do not have the same rights in terms of the weight of their testimony, nor do they have equal rights in commencing proceedings; moreover, there are limited appointment of women to the Syariah judiciary.

Indeed, while women were able to hold supporting roles in the Syariah legal system, 2020 marks the ten-year anniversary of the first appointment of women to the Syariah court bench. Several issues hindered the appointment of women as Syariah court judges, including (1) the question of interpreting Islam and especially the Islamic rules prohibiting the appointment of women to hold public offices; (2) the clash between a particular interpretation of Islam and the international human rights of women; and (3) issues of a plural legal system, which is further complicated by the federal nature of Malaysia.

In this chapter, the first section flags some key issues regarding the appointment of women to the bench in general and in Malaysia in particular, with reference to Islam, plural legal systems and human rights. This is followed by a short overview of the Islamic judiciary introducing the impediments that the federal system poses for the appointment of female judges. The third section examines the discourse surrounding the

---

[4] The Global Gender Gap Report has been published by the World Economic Forum since 2006. It indexes countries in order to measure gender equality allowing a cross-country perspective but also evaluating the global trajectory towards gender equality.

[5] The political empowerment index in the Global Gender Gap report consists of several indicators including women in parliament, ministerial positions, number of heads of states and women as judges.

appointment of female judges to the Syariah courts. It reflects on the arguments in favour and against the appointment of female judges from an Islamic legal perspective and places them in the Malaysian context. It provides an overview of how the attitude towards female Syariah court judges has changed over the last three decades before concluding with an update of the current status quo and the challenges ahead.

Women and the Judiciary: Issues of   Pluralism, Islam and Human Rights

Malaysia's society is multiracial and multireligious in nature. In terms of population, the different religions comprise 61.3 per cent Muslims, 19.8 per cent Buddhists, 9.2 per cent Christians and 6.3 per cent Hindus.[6] As such Islam plays an important role in Malaysia's social, cultural, political and legal framework. Article 3 of the Constitution states that 'Islam is the religion of the Federation, but other religions may be practiced in peace and harmony in any other part of the Federation.' Owing to the special status of Islam, Malaysia has a plural legal system that facilitates the co-existence of civil non-religious law and Syariah law.

This plural system has consequences for the appointment of women in the judiciary. Under a certain strict interpretation of Islamic law, women have limited opportunities in respect to holding public offices. Some readings of Islamic law do not allow women to be appointed to the bench (Moghadam 2017, XII). This conservative understanding of Islamic law is traced back to some founding jurists of Sunni Islam, such as Shafi'i,[7] Maliki and Ibn Hanbali. This view is based on an interpretation of Qur'anic *sura* an-Nisa 4:34 which states that men are protectors over women. As such, women are not able to fulfil the role of judges as it would place them in a position of power over men (Sisters in Islam 2009). The Sunni Hanafi school of thought, on the other hand, allows for

---

[6] See the 2010 Census (Government of Malaysia (2010).

[7] In Malaysia, the law refers to the Shafi'i school of legal thought as the main *maddhab* (school of thought) although it allows the Mufti to use any of the other Sunni *maddhab* where 'public interest' so requires. This is slightly different for the Syariah courts; here the Shafi'i *maddhab* is not exclusively mentioned as a source. Instead, *hukum syarak* (Islamic law) is defined as Islamic law according to any recognised *maddhab*. See respectively section 39(1) and (2) of the Administration of Islamic Law Act (No. 505) of 1991 (Federal Territories); section 2 of the Administration of Islamic Law Act (No. 505) of 1991 (Federal Territories).

women judges except for cases involving certain offences such as *hudud*[8] and *qisas*[9] (Zin 2017, 153).[10]

Nevertheless, there are some Muslim countries that allow women to be appointed as judges early on. These include Indonesia where, despite following the same Shafi'i school of thought like Malaysia, women have been hearing cases on Islamic family since the 1960s (Nurlaelawati and Salim 2017, 101); or Middle Eastern countries like Iraq since the late 1950s, or Lebanon since the last 1960s, where women were appointed to the Syariah bench (Sonneveld and Lindbekk 2017, 10). Despite developments in these regions, a significant number of Muslim countries held and practised a conservative view until the new millennium. As Sonneveld and Lindbekk (2017, 12) summarised, the start of the new millennium saw a number of Muslim-majority countries appointing their first female judge to the civil courts (Egypt in 2003; Bahrain in 2006; UAE in 2008); the appointment of women as judges in an Islamic court (West Bank in 2009); or significantly increasing the number of female judges to the bench (see developments in Algeria, Jordan or Pakistan).

These judicial appointments come in the wake of a broader global movement to recognise the rights of women (Sonneveld and Lindbekk (2017, 13). Women's human rights are prescribed in numerous international human rights covenants including the International Covenant on Civil and Political Rights (ICPPR); International Covenant on Economic, Social and Cultural Rights (ICESCR); Convention on the Elimination of Discrimination against Women (CEDAW); the Beijing Platform of Action 1995; and the Security Council Resolution 1325 on Women, Peace and Security, adopted in October 2000, to name a few of the most important ones. These human rights documents prohibit a discrimination based on gender and moreover request for women to be allowed to hold public offices. The Beijing Platform of Action 1995 (para. 190a) for instance requests that governments

---

[8] *Hudud* literally means 'limit' or 'restriction' and is used to refer to harsh physical punishments, such as stoning or amputation, which are fixed punishments for serious crimes, in particular for crimes considered to be 'claims of God' such as theft, fornication, drinking and apostasy. While hudud enactments have been made for Kelantan and Terengganu they are deemed unconstitutional and are not implemented or applied in any Malaysian state.

[9] *Qisas*, literally 'retaliation', used to refer to crimes for which a punishment of retaliation is seen as appropriate; for example, murder or intentionally causing injury.

[10] This restriction is based on the limitations for women in providing witness testimony in these criminal cases.

[c]ommit themselves to establishing the goal of gender balance in governmental bodies and committees, as well as in public administrative entities, and in the judiciary, including, inter alia, setting specific targets and implementing measures to substantially increase the number of women with a view to achieving equal representation of women and men, if necessary through positive action, in all governmental and public administration positions.

Consequentially, there is a potential incompatibility between human rights and certain interpretations of Islamic law in respect to women's rights. This is indeed a well-documented, long-standing debate on cultural–religious reservations or even rejection of the relevance of international human rights to Islam.[11]

This perceived clash of international human rights and certain interpretations of Islamic law is of direct relevance to Malaysia. In 1995, when Malaysia ratified CEDAW, it stipulated several reservations – like several other Muslim-majority countries where Islamic law is applicable – declaring that

> Malaysia's accession is subject to the understanding that the provisions of the Convention do not conflict with the provisions of the Islamic Shariah law and the Federal Constitution of Malaysia . . . further, the Government of Malaysia does not consider itself bound by the provisions of articles 2 (f), 5 (a), 7 (b), 9 and 16 [of CEDAW] . . .
>
> In relation to article 11, Malaysia interprets the provisions of this article as a reference to the prohibition of discrimination on the basis of equality between men and women only.[12]

Article 7(b) gives women equal rights 'to participate in the formulation of government policy and the implementation thereof and to hold public office and perform all public functions at all levels of government'. This reservation basically ensured that the status quo practice of not allowing women to be appointed to the Syariah court bench continued and did not constitute a breach Malaysia's international human rights obligations. In 1998, the government of Malaysia further clarified its initial reservations to article 7(b) stating that 'the application of said article 7(b) shall not

---

[11] There is a significant scholarship on the conflicts of claims of international human rights and Islam in general and women's rights. See for example Shaheen Sardar Ali (2000); Abdullah A. An-Na'im (1990); Abdullah An-Na'im (2001); Ann Black, Hossein Esmaeili and Nadirsyah Hosen (2013, 20–22); Ann Elizabeth Mayer (2013); Ahmad S. Moussalli (2001); Jaclyn Ling-Chien Neo (2003); Omid Safi (2003); Arvind Sharma (1987).

[12] See UN Database, www.un.org/womenwatch/daw/cedaw/reservations-country.htm, accessed 30 March 2020.

affect the appointment to certain public offices like the Mufti, Syariah Court Judges, and the Imam which is in accordance with the provisions of the Islamic Syariah law' (UN Women n.d., note 41). In 2005, almost a decade later, an NGO Shadow Report Group[13] (p. 6) observed that there was 'a resistance by the government to fully submit to the spirit of the CEDAW Convention'.

The issue is therefore how the Malaysian government resolves the perceived clash between commitments to international human rights obligations and safeguarding the special position that Islam holds based on Article 3 of the Constitution. In 2014, Najib Razak, then prime minister, was quoted as saying that

> 'Humanrightism', a liberal way of thinking that places secular law above religion, has to be addressed swiftly as it is against Islamic teaching.
>
> He said such way of thinking, which had been accepted as a new 'religion' and was being spread rapidly in the country and abroad, was a threat to Muslims, as it rejected Islamic values.
>
> [Those who describe to such liberal thinking] do everything, claiming to be championing human rights.
>
> This is a deviant [way of] thinking and a threat, which is dangerous to Islam.
>
> We will never accept and give in to the demands for the right to reject Islam or deny the implementation of Islamic teachings, which have been done through syariah law
>
> (Najib Razak as cited in Alagesh 2014).[14]

Such reference to international human rights obligations has been of limited use in public discourse in Malaysia, as it has been rebuffed by the government and by certain political parties. Notwithstanding, civil society organisations[15] and even the judiciary[16] have made use of Malaysia's obligations under international human rights.

---

[13] Hereafter called 2005 NGO Shadow Report.

[14] Please note that only the printed version of the newspaper has this quote. The article is not available in the online version.

[15] For a discussion on women's human rights and Islam in general, see Steiner (2019a). Neo (2013, 537) observed that there is 'strong women's rights activism in Malaysia' with some of the 'best-organized' and 'most effective civil society groups in the country.

[16] For a discussion of how international human rights obligations were used by the judiciary in overturning decisions on unilateral conversion of children by one parent, see Steiner (2013).

Further, Muslim-majority countries quite often have a plural legal system where non-religious civil and Islamic legal system co-exist.[17] This means that the appointment of women has had different trajectories depending on the bench they are appointed to. In some countries it is difficult or prohibited for women to be appointed to the bench in both systems, while other countries allow women to be appointed to the bench in both civil and Islamic court systems (Indonesia). In some countries, women were first appointed to the bench in the civil legal system and then later to the bench in the Islamic legal system, as is the case in Malaysia. In the Malaysian civil non-religious judicial system, women have a long history of being appointed to the bench. There are three superior courts in Malaysia: the Federal Court, the highest court; the Court of Appeal; and the two High Courts, the High Court of Malaya as well as the High Court of Sabah and Sarawak. Since the 1960s, female judges have been sitting in both the subordinate courts and in the superior courts since the 1980s – albeit with restrictions on the type of cases they can hear. Former Chief Justice Tun Zaki Tun Azmi commented that

> it is desirable that a variety and disparate level of voices be heard in the halls of Justice, Judges are trained in articulating comprehensive notions of objectivity. Having Judges with different views (whether men or women) ensures that the Malaysian Judiciary is open and sensitive to other points of view
>
> (Tun Zaki Tun Azmi as cited in Federal Court of Malaysia 2012, 99).

Several women have broken the glass ceiling by entering the Malaysian civil non-religious judiciary. For example, Tan Sri Dato' Seri Siti Norma binti Yaakob was the first female judge to be appointed to the High Court in 1983, the Court of Appeal (1994–2000), the Federal Court (2001–2004) and ultimately chief judge of Malaya (the third highest ranking judge in the country) in 2005. Following her retirement in 2007, Tan Sri Dato' Seri Siti Norma binti Yaakob was appointed as the first female judge of the Dubai International Financial Centre (DIFC) Courts in 2008. She paved the way for other women to be appointed to the superior courts. Yet for a few years, she was the only female judge in the Federal Court:[18]

---

[17] This is for instance especially the case in Asian Muslim–majority countries such as Indonesia, Brunei and Pakistan. Even Muslim-minority countries like Singapore have a plural legal system in which civil law and Islamic law co-exist.

[18] See the Malaysian Judiciary Yearbook, which is the annual report published by the Federal Court of Malaysia.

it is lonely at the top. Her Ladyship remained the one and only female Judge in the Federal Court until August 2003, when Justice Rahmah Hussain joined her.

Although the female Judicial presence in the Federal Court was taken up by Justice Rahmah Hussain in August 2003 and subsequently Justice Heliliah Yusoff in October 2009, the Federal Court remained very much an all-male preserve for the next few years

(Federal Court of Malaysia 2012, 99).

While women were able to be appointed as civil judges, the number of female judges was 'dismal'. Only five out of sixteen judicial commissioners are women, while three out of thirty-six High Court judges and two out of six Federal Court judges are women (NGO Shadow Report 2005, Article 7.1, para. 4.1). Over the past decade, the number of female judges in the civil non-religious courts, and especially the superior courts, slowly and steadily increased, as shown in Table 7.1.

Table 7.1 *The percentage of women in the civil non-religious judiciary of the superior courts*[19]

	2012	2013	2014	2015	2016	2017	2018
Federal Court	22.2%	25%	20%	18.2%	27.3%	33.3%	31.8%
Court of Appeal	18.2%	25%	31.8%	30.8%	41.4%	46.7%	51.9%
High Court (Judge)	46.2%	48.4%	50%	50%	50%	36.5%	32.1%
High Court (Judicial Commissioner)	33.3%	34.8%	21.2%	19.4%	25.6%	31.6%	31.3%

In general, there has been a very slow increase of women on the bench in the higher courts of Malaysia. However, the majority of women are appointed in the High Court, which is the lowest of the superior courts of Malaysia.[20] Moreover, they are mostly selected as judicial commissioner with the full power of a judge but a limited two-year appointment.

[19] Data from 2012–2016: KPWMK (Ministry of Women, Family and Community Development) 'Statistics on Women, Family and Society', www.kpwkm.gov.my, accessed 19 April 2019. Data from 2017–2018: Malaysian Yearbook 2017 and 2018 with list of judges/ judicial commissioner.
[20] The civil non-religious courts in Malaysia are divided into two categories, the subordinate courts including the Magistrate's Courts and Sessions Courts. The superior courts consist of the High Court, the Court of Appeal and the Federal Court which is the highest court of the land.

During this time, they must prove themselves and might then be appointed to the court on a more permanent basis. Commenting on the overall increase of female judges, Datuk Hasnah Dato' Mohammed Hashim, a female judge at the Court of Appeal, noted that

> [t]he ratio of female as opposed to male judges is still impressive and the Malaysian Judiciary stands tall amongst the ranks of other Judiciaries around the world, since women judges make up more than half of the judges in the Superior Courts where there are now 45 women as opposed to 81 male
>
> (Datuk Hasnah Dato' Mohammed Hashim as cited in Federal Court of Malaysia, Malaysian Judiciary Yearbook 2014, 44).

In 2019, two women were appointed to the highest positions in the Malaysian judiciary, as chief justice and as president of the Court of Appeal. Tan Sri Tengku Maimun binti Tuan Mat[21] was appointed as the first female chief justice,[22] building upon a distinguished career as a judicial commissioner (2006–2007) and as a judge at several High Courts (2007–2013), the Court of Appeal (2013–2018) and the Federal Court (2018–2019). Dato' Rohana binti Yusuf was selected as the president of the Court of Appeal, the second highest court in Malaysia and the second highest position in the Malaysian judiciary. Her appointment was the first time a woman has held this office. Again, her appointment came after a distinguished career, she served eighteen years in the Judicial and Legal Services before joining the private sector. Returning to the judiciary in 2005, she was appointed as judicial commissioner to the High Court in Kuala Lumpur. In 2013, she was appointed to the Court of Appeal and subsequently appointed as a judge to the Federal Court in 2018.[23] Their careers are examples of trailblazing women in Malaysia's judiciary.

In contrast, in the Syariah legal system, the appointment of women to the bench started only recently. In the early 2000s, Malaysia's long road

---

[21] See Office of the Chief Registrar Federal Court of Malaysia, www.kehakiman.gov.my/en/about-us/court/federal-court/chief-justice and Judicial Appointments Commission, www.jac.gov.my/spk/en/commission/members-of-jac/25-about2/68-the-right-honourable-tan-sri-tengku-maimun-binti-tuan-mat.html, accessed 30 June 2020.

[22] The chief justice is the head of the judiciary and thus the highest-ranking judge in Malaysia.

[23] See Office of the Chief Registrar Federal Court of Malaysia, www.kehakiman.gov.my/en/about-us/court/appeal-court/president-court-appeal and Judicial Appointments Commission, www.jac.gov.my/spk/en/25-about2/261-the-right-honourable-dato-rohana-binti-yusuf.html, accessed 30 June 2020.

to overturn the restrictions on women entering the bench began. This agenda was initiated by the Malaysian federal government and very slowly was taken up by the different religious political authorities, for example, the various rulers, religious councils, etc. This uptake has been further complicated by the fact that Malaysia has a federal system of government with Islamic matters being in the prerogative of the individual states where the power over Islamic matters is left to each individual state. The following two sections will take a closer look at these issues.

The Islamic Judiciary: Issues of Federalism and Islam

The Syariah legal system during pre-colonial and colonial times was under the purview of the individual states. The Federal Constitution of 1957, the predecessor of the Constitution of Malaysia of 1963, divided powers between the federal and state governments. Malaysia is based on a federal system with thirteen states and three federal territories. Islamic matters have long been closely linked to the individual states and their respective rulers, so it was not surprising that this principle of dividing power was enshrined in the Constitution of independent Malaysia. Legislative and executive powers over most aspects of Islamic legal tradition other than Islamic banking and finance were given to the individual States.[24] This means that there is no single system of Islamic law in Malaysia and moreover there are significant differences in the interpretation of Islamic law, procedure and so forth.[25]

The individual states also retain power over the Syariah courts, while the federal government has executive and legislative power over criminal and civil law and the courts that dealt with these matters.[26] The Syariah courts have limited jurisdiction in civil and criminal matters. In the civil area, the courts are restricted to Islamic family law disputes including betrothal, marriage and divorce. In regards to its criminal jurisdiction, the Syariah courts are limited to offences prescribed by law perpetrated by persons professing the Islamic faith, including matrimonial offences such as wife abuse and infidelity; sexual offences, such as illicit

---

[24] According to Item 1 of the State List (List II) of the Ninth Schedule of the Constitution.
[25] Discussing this in different specific contexts, see for instance Steiner (2011) for zakat and Steiner (2019a) in the context of Islamic family law.
[26] According to Item 4 of the Federal List (List I) of the Ninth Schedule of the Federal Constitution.

intercourse outside marriage (*zina*), close proximity between sexes in private (*khaluat*), incest and prostitution; offences relating to intoxicating drinks, drinking, selling and buying alcohol; offences relating to the 'five pillars' of Islam such as failure to attend the Friday sermon, non-payment of zakat fitrah, failure to fast during the month of Ramadan and renouncing Islam or failure to report and register a conversion; and miscellaneous offences not listed. The punishment is limited by the so-called '3–5–6 formula', that is, three years or a fine not exceeding MYR 5,000 and includes a provision that any whipping punishment ordered should not exceed six strokes.[27]

In the 1980s, the Syariah court system underwent major changes. At the federal level, a 'Committee at Officer Level' was established to study the Syariah courts. The report proposed to restructure the Syariah courts, including a separation of the courts from the religious councils; changes to the jurisdiction of the Syariah courts; and improvements to the status and position of Syariah court judges (Lindsey and Steiner 2012, 195, 96).

More important is the states' legislative power regarding appointment and promotion of judges for the Syariah court. The individual states have different appointment and qualification requirements. In the Federal Territories, the Yang di-Pertuan Agong on the advice of the minister of Islamic affairs after consultation with the Majlis Agama Islam Wilayah Persekutuan (Council of Islamic Religion in the Federal Territories) appoints the chief Syariah judge, Syariah Appeal Court judges and Syariah High Court judges.[28] In Malacca, the Yang di-Pertuan Agong on the advice of the Majlis Agama Islam Melaka appoints the chief Syariah judge.[29] The other judges – that is, the Syariah Appeal Court judges, the Syariah High Court judges and Syariah Subordinate Court judges – are then appointed by the Yang di-Pertuan Agong on the advice of the Majlis Agama Islam Melaka and the chief Syariah judge.[30] In Johor, the ruler on the advice of the Majlis Agama Islam Negeri Johor

---

[27] Section 2 of the Syariah Courts (Criminal Jurisdiction) Act (No. 355) of 1965. These limitations have regularly been an issue when it comes to aspirations to implement *hudud* crimes, for which the punishment would exceed these limitations, see Lindsey and Steiner (2012, 289, 290) and Steiner (2019b).

[28] Sections 41(1) and 44(1) of the Administration of Islamic Law Act (No. 505) of 1993 (Federal Territories)

[29] Section 44(1) of the Administration of the Religion of Islam Enactment (No. 7) of 2002 (Malacca).

[30] Sections 45(1), 46(1) and 47(1) of the Administration of the Religion of Islam Enactment (No. 7) of 2002 (Malacca).

appoints the chief Syariah judge,[31] who then with the Majlis advise on the appointment of the Syariah Appeal Court judges and the Syariah High Court judges.[32] However Syariah Subordinate Court judges can be appointed on the advice of the chief Syariah judge alone.[33]

The different state enactments provide the required qualification for judges. In general, to be appointed to the higher Syariah courts as a chief Syariah judge or a Syariah High Court judge, a person must be a citizen of Malaysia and have experience in the Syariah court system. This requirement for experience can be met can be either if a person is a judge of a Syariah High Court, a *kadi*, a registrar of a Syariah court or a prosecutor,[34] or in special circumstances a person considered learned in Islamic law.[35] In this context, it is noteworthy that the state of Pahang, for instance, still has some gender restrictions in place – only a male Muslim can be appointed as a chief Syariah judge or Syariah High Court judge.[36]

For appointments to the lower Syariah courts, the requirements to qualify for the bench are different in the various states due to the federal structure of Malaysia. In the Federal Territories, the only statutory requirement is to profess the religion of Islam.[37] The same is true also for judges appointed to a Syariah Subordinate Court, here judges can be appointed from the public service or joint services[38] or be members of the general public service of the Federation.[39]

---

[31] Section 56 of the Administration of the Religion of Islam Enactment (No. 16) of 2003 (Johor).
[32] Sections 57(1) and 58(1) of the Administration of the Religion of Islam Enactment (No. 16) of 2003 (Johor).
[33] Section 59(1) of the Administration of the Religion of Islam Enactment (No. 16) of 2003 (Johor).
[34] See, for example, Section 41(2) of the Administration of Islamic Law Act (No. 505) of 1993 (Federal Territories); Section 44(2) of the Administration of the Religion of Islam Enactment (No. 7) of 2002 (Melacca); and Section 56(2) of the Administration of the Religion of Islam Enactment (No. 1) of 2003 (Selangor).
[35] See, for example, Section 41(2)(b)(ii) of the Administration of Islamic Law Act (No. 505) of 1993 (Federal Territories).
[36] According to Section 43(3)(a) of Administration of Islamic Law Enactment (No. 3) of 1991 (Pahang).
[37] Section 42(1) of the Administration of Islamic Law Act (No. 505) of 1993 (Federal Territories).
[38] Section 59(1) of the Administration of the Religion of Islam Enactment (No. 1) of 2003 (Selangor)
[39] Section 44(1) of the Administration of Islamic Law Act (No. 505) of 1993 (Federal Territories).

In summary, the individual states can set the rules as to who is qualified to be appointed as a judge in the Syariah courts. As discussed in the following section, this has significant implications for the appointment of women as Syariah judges, because the states can differ in their interpretation of Islamic rules regarding whether women can be appointed to the bench.

Appointing Women in the Islamic Judiciary: The Long and Windy Road

As early as the 1960s, in neighbouring Indonesia women were appointed to the Syariah court bench. By the late 1980s, Indonesia 'fully accommodated female judges in the religious courtrooms' (Nurlaelawati and Salim 2017, 102). This is interesting as Indonesia, like Malaysia, predominantly follows the Shafi'i school of thought which generally advocates a conservative position and does not allow the appointment of women as judges in the religious courts. In Malaysia in the early 1980s, the debate as to whether women can be appointed to the Syariah court bench finally gained traction.

In 1982, the National Fatwa Committee issued a *fatwa*[40] that women should not be appointed as judges in the Syariah legal system, reflecting a conservative interpretation of Islamic law. The National Fatwa Committee was established in the 1970s to create greater uniformity in Islamic matters. Opinions of the National Fatwa Committee are sought by the Conference of Rulers. The fatwa can then be adapted by the individual ruler and only if published in the respective state Government Gazette, it will become binding in the state (Lindsey and Steiner 2012, 87).

The committee claimed that its decision in the 1982 *fatwa* was derived from a *hadith*[41] that stated that 'people who appoint women as rulers will never be successful' (Zin 2017, 156). This interpretation was reflected in various state enactments, for instance, the aforementioned rules regarding the appointment of the chief Syariah judge and a Syariah Hight Court judge in Pahang[42] explicitly stating that the appointee has

---

[40] *Fatwa* is the legal opinion of a qualified religious scholar to a specific question that is not directly dealt with on the Quran or hadith.
[41] *Hadith* are traditions, the recorded words and deeds, of the Prophet Muhammad, one of the main sources of Islamic law.
[42] Section 43(3)(a) Administration of Islamic Law Enactment (No. 3) of 1991 (Pahang).

to be male.[43] This is a reflection of a conservative interpretation of certain classical Islamic texts, as mentioned. Indeed, it appeared as if it was non-controversial that women cannot be appointed as Syariah judges. For instance, a 1986 *fatwa* issued in Terengganu illustrates this by simply stating that there is no need to answer the question because to be a Syariah court judge the appointee must be male.[44]

It has been a long road to slowly accept that women are indeed qualified to be judges and to commence the process of appointing women to the Syariah court bench. For the first decade after the 1982 national *fatwa* was issued, there was hardly any public discourse on this debate. This started to change in the 1990s with several events contributing to this change in opinion. In August 1995, in conjunction with the Fourth World Conference on Women, Malaysia ratified the Convention on the Elimination of All Forms of Discrimination against Women (CEDAW) albeit with reservations, as discussed. While those reservations were lifted, the implementation of gender equality and allowing women to hold certain positions initially lacked political will and support. As such, since the late 1990s, civil society started to lobby for the appointment of women to the Syariah court bench. In 1997, several women's groups issued a memorandum requesting the reform of Islamic law, including the request to allow the appointment of female Syariah court judges (Othman 1997). This campaign coincided with general dissatisfaction of the Syariah legal system, especially the perceived low level of qualification and lack of competence among junior male judges with regard to family law matters (Zin 2017,157). In 2002, Sisters in Islam (SIS), a women's human rights NGO, published a pamphlet 'Women as Judges'. In 2009, a revised edition argues that women are qualified to hold the position of a judge and shows that 'interpretations that discriminate against women were influenced mostly by cultural practices and values which regarded women as inferior and subordinate to men' and (Sisters in Islam 2009).

In 1999, Abdul Hamid, then minister in the prime minister's department, raised the possibility of appointing women to the Syariah court

---

[43] Most other enactments might refer to the appointee as 'he' but that does not necessitate a gender restriction. Section 4(2) of the Interpretation and Words Act (No. 388) of 1948 and 1967 states that '[w]ords and expressions importing the masculine gender include females'.

[44] The original text reads 'Pelantikan orang perempuan sebagai hakim: Jawapan: Tidaklah harus dan tidak sahbagi orang-orang perempuan menjadi hakim syarie kerana salah satu syarat hakim syarie itu mestilah terdiri dari kaum lelaki' as cited in Abdullah (2016).

bench at the UMNO[45] General Assembly (Ali 1999). It took another five years for the government to act upon this. Finally in August 2004, the government's stance officially changed when Abdul Hamid Othman, then religious advisor to then prime minister Abdullah Ahmad Badawi, announced that women could be appointed to the Syariah court bench (Ahmad 2004, 20). In 2005, the NGO Shadow Report 2005 (Article 5, para. 1.2) commented on the implementation of CEDAW that '[t]hrough practice and convention, the environment is hostile towards any women holding formal positions as judges, *muftis* (State chief authority on Hukum Syarak), or *ulamaks* (Islamic intellectual scholars)'. In fact, the 2005 NGO Shadow Report (Article 7, para. 4.2) criticised the low number of female judges in general and singled out that so far, no women had been appointed to the Syariah court bench specifically.

While the political will to address this issue was slowly developing, two major obstacles needed to be addressed: the 1982 national *fatwa* and the fact that Islam was a matter of the individual states. To overcome these issues, in April 2006, the National Fatwa Committee issued a *fatwa* allowing women to be appointed as Syariah court judges, thus overruling its own pervious 1982 *fatwa*. The 2006 *fatwa* is extremely short, simply declaring that women should be appointed as judges in cases other than *hudud* and *qisas* – certain criminal cases. It was stipulated that the decision to select and appoint the women should be made with care and following the general rules of appointment.[46] The then chairperson of the National Fatwa Committee summarised the proceedings as follows: '[s]ome of those (muftis and appointed specialists who attended the meeting) disagreed, some agreed but with conditions and some agreed without any conditions' (Council chairman Prof Datuk Shukor Husin as cited in *New Straits Times* 28 July 2006). In the end, it was agreed that women could be appointed based on merit, integrity, qualifications as well as experience (*New Straits Times* 28 July 2006).

---

[45] Until recently UMNO (United Malays National Organisation, Pertubuhan Kebangsaan Melayu Bersatu) has been the dominant party in the ruling coalition that had been in power from independence until the 2018 election. It has been instrumental in shaping national and international politics. For more details on the relationship between Islam and politics, see Steiner (2018).

[46] The original text reads 'Ugama Islam Malaysia Kali Ke–73 yang bersidang pada 4–6 April 2006 telah membincangkan Hukum Melantik Wanita Sebagai Hakim Syar'ie. Muzakarah telah memutuskan bahawa wanita harus dilantik menjadi Hakim Syar'ie dalam kes-kes selain kes hudud dan qisas. Pemilihan dan pelantikan hendaklah dibuat dengan penuh teliti dan teratur' (JAKIM 2015, 212).

However, for the *fatwa* to take effect in the individual states, it has to be passed by the respective states. Yet not all individual states followed suit, only the Federal Territories passed it. Initially the states of Kelantan, Sarawak and Kedah declared that they would not pass the *fatwa*.[47] Going a step further, a few days after the national *fatwa* was decided, Selangor for instance passed its own *fatwa* declaring that a women should not be able to be appointed as a Syariah judge referring to a Qur'anic verse and specific *hadith*.[48] Indeed Surah an-Nisa 4:34[49] and this particular *hadith*[50] have been cited numerous times in order to legitimise the decision to prohibit women from being appointed as judges.

Those states initially opposed to the implementation of the 2006 *fatwa* had the support of Chief Syariah Judge Datuk Sheikh Ghazali Abdul Rahman. In a 2007 article, he based his claim that women could not be judges on classical jurisprudence, especially the Shafi'i school of thought, discussed previously. According to this opinion, women are not sufficiently competent or qualified for the appointment as a judge. Instead, they could serve in roles such as registrars, research officers for higher Syariah court judges, even as *sulh*[51] (mediation) officers and other

---

[47] Department of Islamic Affairs within the prime minister's department as referred to in Najibah Mohd Zin (2017, 158, 159).

[48] The original text reads 'Mesyuarat Jawatankuasa Fatwa Negeri Selangor yang bersidang pada 26–27 Jun 2006 telah memutuskan seperti berikut:

> i. Wanita tidak harus memegang jawatan sebagai hakim syar'ie. Ini berdasarkan dalil-dalil seperti berikut maksudnya: "Kaum lelaki adalah pemimpin dan pengawal bertanggungjawab terhadap kaum wanita oleh kerana Allah melebihkan orang-orang lelaki (dengan beberapa keistimewaannya) atas orang-orang perempuan. Dan juga kerana orang-orang lelaki telah membelanjakan (memberi nafkah) sebahagian daripada harta mereka. Manakala sabda Rasulullah Shollallahu 'Alaihi Wassalam: bermaksud" sesuatu bangsa yang dipimpin oleh wanita tidak akan Berjaya'.

*Nota: Fatwa ini berkaitan dengan Pindaan Terhadap Sighah Hukum Pelantikan Hakim Syar'ie Wanita, rujuk MJKFNS Kali Ke–2/2016 (12/4/2016)

[49] Surah an-Nisa 4:34 states that 'Men are qawwamuna over women, (on the basis) that Allah has (faddala) preferred some of them over others and (on the basis) of what they spend of their property (for the support of women).' The issue here is the translation of *qawammuna* and *faddala* which have been constructed to say that men have power over women and are superior to women (Aishath Muneeza 2014, 319, 320).

[50] This *hadith* has been translated as 'When the news reached the Prophet (s.a.w.) that the Persians had made the daughter of Chosroe their ruler he observed: That a nation can never prosper which has assigned its reign to a woman' by Sisters in Islam (2009: 8).

[51] *Sulh*, mediation process in the Syariah courts which must be attempted before for instance, a marriage can be dissolved.

functions within the judiciary (Abdul Rahman 2007). Since the mid-1990s, women had been working in these supportive roles. One arguably more or less immediate positive development from that fatwa was the increased number of women in supportive roles. For example, in Kelantan, women could be mediators (*suhl* officers) from 2007 onwards.

The 2006 national *fatwa* was also greeted by women's organisations with less enthusiasm than one might have expected. Nora Murat, then legal advisor in SiS, commented on the issue of qualifications and whether women would indeed be considered as qualifying for this position:

> There are many capable women who can be judges and I hope that the system used to appoint the female judges will be the same as the one used for male judges. We look forward to the appointment of the first woman Syariah judge
>
> (Nora Murat as cited in *New Straits Times* 28 July 2006).

The Women's Section of Jemaah Islah Malaysia (JIM) pointed to the slow take up of this issue and to the perception of the capabilities of female judges. Jemaah Islah Malaysia (Islamic Reform Congregation of Malaysia) is a Muslim NGO in Malaysia with links to the global Muslim network. Its women's wing has been strongly advocating for women to have the freedom to pursue professional careers albeit within the limits of what is seen as permissible in Islam (Mohamed 2004, 142). JIM's head of the Women Section Dr Harlina Halizah Siraj stated,

> There has been a misunderstanding over the capabilities of women judges who have been blamed for being emotional, less critical and less objective when making decisions
>
> (Dr Harlina Halizah Siraj as cited in *New Straits Times* 28 July 2006).

In 1999, Ali (1999) asked whether it would take another decade before women would be appointed to the Syariah court bench. This timeline was more or less correct, it would take more than half a decade for the *fatwa* to be overturned and more than another half decade for the first women to be appointed to the bench.

In 1994, Norhadina Ahmad Zabidi was among the first women accepted into a supporting role in the Syariah judicial system. In 2006, she held the position of Selangor Syariah Court chief registrar and was the only woman to generally qualify for an appointment to the Syariah bench when the national *fatwa* was passed (Dermawan 2006, 126, 127). Yet she would not be appointed to this position – not unsurprisingly as Selangor had passed a state *fatwa* contradicting the national *fatwa* and prohibiting women from being appointed to the bench in 2006 – and it would take another several years before a woman would hold that role. Instead the first appointments of women to the Syariah bench were only made in May 2010. Suraya Ramli and Rafidah Abdul Razak, both officials at Malaysia's Islamic judiciary department, were appointed as Syariah court judge in the Federal Territories, specifically in Kuala Lumpur and the administrative capital of Putrajaya respectively (Zin 2012). In 2013, two more women were appointed to the lower Syariah courts; Sarah Fawzia Ahmad Fuzi, who had been a *sulh* officer for three years and practising lawyer for two years, and Norhidayah Mat Darus, a practising lawyer and a research officer to the chief Syariah judge of Pahang (Zin 2017, 167).

The appointment of female judges saw a re-emergence of the discourse over what type of cases those female judges could hear. Unlike as stipulated in the 2006 fatwa, which set limitations within the criminal jurisdiction, the debate did concern the civil jurisdiction of the Syariah courts. Malaysia's then chief Syariah judge Tan Sri Ibrahim Lembut opinioned that there would be 'minor' limitations on the cases that women judges could hear:

> Whatever a male judge can hear, a female judge can also hear, except on marriage via judicial guardianship, because that would require a male judge to carry out the rites,[52]
>
> (Chief Syariah Judge Tan Sri Ibrahim Lembut as cited in Razak Ahmad 2010).

Later it was confirmed that female judges could indeed hear all types of cases – civil and criminal alike (Salbiah Ahmad 2010).

As of 2011, there were 24.1 per cent women in Syariah judiciary,[53] with women having been appointed to the *supportive roles* (in italics in Table 7.2) of Syariah and *sulh* officers or registrars. The data from 2012 to 2016 (see Table 7.2) illustrates the gradual change that has been taking place in the Syariah courts. Appointments of women to the bench have been very slow, there has not been a floodgate of appointments but a

---

[52] As mentioned, there has usually been a discussion whether female judges can hear certain criminal cases, that is *hudud* and *quisas* cases. Then chief Syariah judge Ibrahim Lembut raised the question whether they could indeed hear cases where they are required to act as legal guardians in family matters, etc. This guardianship role is usually restricted to males only.

[53] Positions include the chief registrar of the State Syariah Court, Syariah judges, *Sulh* officers and Syariah officers (Suhakam 2017, 18).

Table 7.2 *The gender of judges and judicial officers in the Syariah legal system[a]*

	2012		2013		2014		2015		2016	
	Male	Female	Male	Female	Male	Female	Male	Female	Male	Female
Director General/Syariah Chief Judge	1	0	1	0	1	0	1	0	1	0
Judges of the Court of Appeal	5	0	6	0	5	0	5	0	5	0
State Syariah Chief Judge	14	0	14	0	14	0	14	0	14	0
Chief Registrar of the State Syariah Court	13	1	14	0	11	3	12	2	12	2
Syariah Judge	103	4	143	5	131	5	66	8	66	8
Sulh Officer	40	44	44	22	28	20	24	20	26	20
Syariah Officers	44	26	33	11	58	32	52	32	52	32

[a] The data from 2012–2016 is based on the statistics provided by the Ministry of Women, Family and Development, www.kpwkm.gov.my, accessed 10 November 2017.

minor trickle, and this includes to the positions in the lower Syariah courts.

By early 2016, the states of Malacca, the Federal Territories, Kelantan, Perlis and Sabah lifted their restrictions and allowed Muslim women to become Syariah court judges (Mayuri Mei Lin 2016), which accounts for the overall increase in Muslim women being appointed to the bench.

The data also illustrate the very slow progress being made in providing career advancement for women judges. In the Federal Territories, the aforementioned first two female appointees were eventually transferred to different posts, instead of being promoted to the Syariah High Court. After their departure in 2013, two other female judges were appointed to take their positions on the bench (Zin 2017, 167).

In mid-2016, history was made when Selangor appointed two women, Noor Huda Roslan and Nenney Shuhaidah Shamsuddin, to a Syariah High Court for the first time in Malaysia (*Malay Mail Online* 27 June 2016). Indeed, one commentary on social media considered the end of a male–only Syariah court system as '[o]ne of the signs of the end of the world'.[54] These appointments are noteworthy for two reasons. Foremost, Selangor as mentioned had explicitly contradicted the 2006 national *fatwa* with its own state *fatwa*. It now had to pass a new *fatwa* allowing women to be appointed to the bench. In April 2016, it did so with an extremely short *fatwa* stating that women are allowed to be appointed as Syariah court judges in civil cases but not in criminal cases.[55] Moreover, Selangor also made up for lost time and appointed women to the Syariah High Court, but not the lower Syariah court. The Malaysian Human Rights Commission acknowledged those appointments in Selangor as milestones that 'overcomes gender stereotyping issues often associated with Shari'a administrations and the courts' (Suhakam 2017, 18).

---

[54] Professor Raihanah Abdullah shared this message that she received at a seminar on 'Women as Judges and Leaders' organised by IAIS and Jakess on 19 July 2016. It is cited in Koshy (2016).

[55] The original text reads:

Mesyuarat Jawatankuasa Fatwa Negeri Selangor kali ke-2/2016 yang bersidang pada 12 April 2016 bersamaan 4 Rajab 1437H memutuskan bahawa:

Harus bagi mana-mana wanita muslim memegang jawatan sebagai Hakim Syar'ie dalam kes Mal tetapi tidak harus dalam kes jenayah berat (ad-dima').

*Nota; Fatwa ini berkaitan dengan keputusan Hukum Pelantikan Hakim Syarie' Wanita dalam Mesyuarat Jawatankuasa Fatwa Negeri Selangor kali ke-3/2006 pada 18/6/2006.

The challenge for the appointment of any women to a higher court and the reason for the slow progress is of course the requirement that an appointment to the higher Syariah courts requires significant experience as a Syariah court judge, and some states' enactments require up to ten years' experience.[56]

According to Datuk Dr Mohd Na'im Mokhtar, then Selangor Syariah chief judge, the appointment of women as judges was possible due to changes in the legislation as well as the 'good relationship between the Syariah Court, Jakess and the support of the Sultan and Selangor Religious Council' and of course the support by the Sultan of Selangor (Koshy 2016). In general, Selangor has been more recently a trailblazer in the advancement of women to the Syariah bench, albeit a slow burning one. In 2016, seven female judges were appointed to the lower Syariah courts – meaning half of all female Syariah judges at that point in time where from Selangor alone. In the area of supportive roles, four women were appointed as registrar of the Syariah High Court and another four women were appointed as assistant registrar (Suhakam 2017, 18).

In 2017, Terengganu appointed the first female, Professor Dato' Seri Zaleha Kamarudin, as Syariah Court of Appeal judge. She was previously appointed as rector of the International Islamic University in 2011, the first time in the world that a woman was appointed to lead an Islamic university. Her appointment to the Syariah Court of Appeal was made for a term of three years. Also, in 2017, Terengganu appointed the first three female judges to the lower Syariah Courts (David 2017). Despite this progress for women judicial appointments to the Syariah bench, as of 2017, overall only twenty-seven of the country's 160 Islamic court judges are women (*Al Jazeera America* 2017).

Conclusion: The Way Ahead

Indeed, since 2016–2017, not much progress has been made since those groundbreaking appointments in Malaysia. In 2019, commenting on the progress made in the civil-non-religious system especially with the appointment of two women to the two highest positions in the civil non-religious system, Majjidah Hashim, the communications officer of SIS stated

---

[56] Section 58 (2) of the Administration of the Religion of Islam Enactment (No. 1) of 2003 (Selangor) originally required that a person must have served a minimum of ten years.

SIS welcomes the appointment of more women judges at the judicial administration level in Malaysia. These appointments demonstrate that women are willing and capable of rising to leadership positions at the administration level.

However, syariah courts have not seen much progress in this area with many states lacking women judges. In the interest of providing and expanding access to justice for women, this gap needs to be urgently narrowed as well

(Majjidah Hashim as cited in Vijaindren 2019).

The promise of the Beijing Platform of Action 1995 to have a minimum of 30 per cent of women in positions of decision-making is still far from being achieved twenty-five years later. Progress has been made to over-come the 'legal' obstacles of being appointed to the bench in the Syariah court system in Malaysia. The Shafi'i *maddhab* interpretation of Islamic law which was originally adhered to and applied in this context was a major obstacle to overcome. It took over two decades for the National Fatwa Committee to overrule its previous decision allowing women to be appointed as Syariah court judges if they met the qualification require-ments. For the *fatwa* to take effect in the individual states, it had to be passed by the respective states with some states declaring they would not pass it while other states remaining silent on this issue.

Progress was initially very slow and by early 2016, only the five out of thirteen states allowed Muslim women to become Syariah court judges. By mid-2016 history was made when more states came around and allowed women to be appointed to the bench and with more states allowing them to be appointed to the higher Syariah courts. Since then the number of women appointed as judges in the Syariah court has been slowly increasing and women are also making their way into the higher Syariah courts.

Malaysia has clearly commenced its journey on the rocky road to appointing women to the Syariah bench and providing women with career progression opportunities in the Syariah legal system. Yet it still has miles to go to catch up with its fellow Muslim-majority countries who commenced this journey much earlier. As the example of Selangor shows, with the will of all involved stakeholders, especially bureaucracy and politics, progress can be made in a short time. The initial steps have been made and the 'legal' obstacles have been removed, it is now a matter for states to be implementing those changes and to ensure that the promises are being kept.

References

Abdul Rahman, Ghazali (2007), 'Kriteria Perlantikan Hakim Syarie Wanita (Criteria for the Appointment of Women Judges)', 23(1) *Jurnal Hukum*, 1–23.

Abdullah, Raihanah (2016), 'Muslim Women in Charge: Contemporary Trends & Challenges', *Seminar on Women as Judges and Leaders*, 19 July. Seminar organised by IAIS and Jakess. Kuala Lumpur.

Ahmad, Salbiah (2010), 'First Women Syariah Judge a Major Step Forward', *Malaysiakini*, 10 August, www.malaysiakini.com/news/139646, accessed 6 October 2020.

(2004), 'The Polemics of Muslim Women to Public Office', *Malaysiakini*, 24 August, https://m.malaysiakini.com/news/29425, accessed 6 October 2020.

Al Jazeera America (2017), 'The Female Face of Islamic Law in Malaysia', 16 August, www.aljazeera.com/features/2017/08/16/the-female-face-of-islamic-law-in-malaysia/?gb=true, accessed 6 October 2020.

Alagesh, T. N. (2014), 'Nation Must Combat Liberalism', *New Straits Times*, 14 May.

Ali, Aishah (1999), 'A Long Wait for Women to Be Syariah Court Judges', *New Straits Times*, 27 June.

Ali, Shaheen Sardar (2000), *Gender and Human Rights in Islam and International Law: Equal Before Allah, Unequal before Man?* The Hague: Kluwer Law International.

An-Na'im, Abdullah (2001), *Toward an Islamic Reformation: Civil Liberties, Human Rights and International Law*. Syracuse, NY: Syracuse University Press.

An-Na'im, Abdullah A. (1990), 'Islam, Islamic Law and the Dilemma of Cultural Legitimacy for Universal Human Rights' in Claude E. Jr. Welch and Virginia A. Leary (eds.) *Asian Perspectives on Human Rights*. Boulder, CO: Westview Press, 31–54.

BBC (2018), '100 Women in 2018', www.bbc.com/news/world-46225037, accessed 20 June 2020.

Black, Ann, Hossein Esmaeili and Nadirsyah Hosen (2013), *Modern Perspectives on Islamic Law: The Nature of Law, and Its Relationship with Religion, in Islam*. Cheltenham: Edward Elgar Publishing.

David, Adrian (2017), 'First Female Judge of Terengganu Syariah Court of Appeal Vows to Tackle High Number of Divorces', *New Straits Times*, 16 October, www.nst.com.my/news/crime-courts/2017/10/291762/first-female-judge-terengganu-syariah-court-appeal-vows-tackle-high, accessed 6 October 2020.

Dermawan, Audrey (2006), 'One Woman Eligible as Syariah Judge', New Straits *Times*, 28 April.

Federal Court of Malaysia (2014), 'The Malaysian Judiciary: Yearbook 2014', www
.kehakiman.gov.my/en/annual-report-judiciary, accessed 20 June 2020.
   (2012), 'The Malaysian Judiciary: Yearbook 2012', www.kehakiman.gov.my/en/
   annual-report-judiciary, accessed 20 June 2020.
Government of Malaysia (2010) '2010 Census, Population Distribution and Basic
   Demographic Characteristics', www.mycensus.gov.my/banci/www/index
   .php?&id=3&page_id=35, accessed 23 January 2020.
Jabatan Kemajuan Islam Malaysia (JAKIM) (2015), 'Kompilasi Pandangan
   Hukum: Muzakarah Jawatankuasa Fatwa Majlis Kebangsaan Bagi Hal
   Ehwal Ugama Islam Malaysia'.
Jayatilaka, Tania (2019), 'Malaysia's First Female Syariah High Court Judge on
   Tough Decisions & Gender Equality', *Malaysia Tatler*, 28 June, https://my
   .asiatatler.com/society/first-female-syariah-high-court-judge-in-malaysia-
   nenney-shuhaidah-shamsuddin, accessed 6 October 2020.
Koshy, Shaila (2016), 'Judicial Appointments Mark a Positive Step', *The Star
   Online*, 20 July, www.thestar.com.my/news/nation/2016/07/20/judicial-
   appointments-mark-a-positive-step, accessed 6 October 2020.
Lindsey, Tim and Kerstin Steiner (2012), *Islam, Law and the State: Malaysia and
   Brunei: Islam, Law and the State in Southeast Asia*. 3 vols. London: I.
   B. Tauris.
The Malay Mail Online (2016), 'Shariah High Court Appoints First Women Judges
   in Malaysia', 27 June, www.malaymail.com/news/malaysia/2016/06/27/the-
   first-two-women-shariah-high-court-judges-in-malaysia/1150203, accessed
   6 October 2020.
Mayer, Ann Elizabeth (2013), *Islam and Human Rights Tradition and Politics*,
   5th ed. Boulder, CO: Westview Press.
Mayuri Mei Lin (2016), 'Women's Groups Want all Female Judges Allowed into
   Shariah System', *The Malay Mail Online*, 20 February, www.malaymail.com/
   news/malaysia/2016/02/20/womens-groups-want-all-female-judges-
   allowed-into-shariah-system/1064521, accessed 6 October 2020.
Maznah Mohamad (2004), 'Women's Engagement with Political Islam in
   Malaysia', 16(2) *Global Change, Peace & Security*, 133–149.
Moghadam, Valentine M. (2017), 'Making the Case for Women Judges in the
   Miuslim World' in Nadia Sonneveld and Monika Lindbekk (eds.) *Women
   Judges in the Muslim World*. Leiden: Brill, XI–XIIX.
Moussalli, Ahmad S. (2001), *The Islamic Quest for Democracy, Pluralism and
   Human Rights*. Gainesville: University Press of Florida.
Muneeza, Aishath (2014), 'Appointment of Female Judges in Muslim Countries',
   16(2) *European Journal of Law Reform*, 317–328.
Neo, Jaclyn Ling-Chien (2003), 'Anti-God, Anti-Islam and Anti-Quran:
   Expanding the Range of Participants and Parameters in Discourse over

Women's Rights and Islam in Malaysia', 21 *UCLA Pacific Basin Law Journal*, 29–74.

New Straits Times (2006), 'Yes to Women Syariah Judges', 28 July.

NGO Shadow Report (2005), 'NGO Shadow Report on the Initial and Second Periodic Report of the Government of Malaysia: Reviewing the Government's Implementation of the Convention on the Elimination of All Forms of Discrimination against Women (CEDAW)'.

Nurlaelawati, Euis and Arskal Salim (2017), 'Female Judges at Indonesian Religious Courtrooms: Opportunities and Challenges to Gender Equality' in Nadia Sonneveld and Monika Lindbekk (eds.) *Women Judges in the Muslim World*. Leiden: Brill, 101–121.

Othman, Muharyani (1997), 'Women Want Reform and Justice', *New Straits Times*, 23 Juanuary.

Razak Ahmad (2010), 'Malaysia's First Women Islamic Judges Draw Debate', *World News*, 4 August, https://article.wn.com/view/2010/08/04/Malaysias_first_women_Islamic_judges_draw_debate, accessed 6 October 2020.

Safi, Omid, ed. (2003), *Progressive Muslims: On Justice, Gender and Pluralism*. Oxford: Oneworld.

Sharma, Arvind, ed. (1987), *Women in World Religions*. Albany: State University of New York Press.

Sisters in Islam (2009), '*Women as Judges*'. Malaysia: Sisters in Islam.

Sonneveld, Nadia and Monika Lindbekk (2017), 'Introduction: A Historical Overview of Gender and Judicial Authority in the Muslim World' in Nadia Sonneveld and Monika Lindbekk (eds.) *Women Judges in the Muslim World*. Leiden: Brill, 1–22.

The Star (2006), 'Women Syariah Judge Only Awaiting Royal Assent', 19 August.

Steiner, Kerstin (2011), 'Variations of "Unpacking" a Global Norm in a Local Context: An Historical Overview of the Epistemic Communities That Are Shaping Zakat Practice in Malaysia' in John Gillespie and Pip Nicholson (eds.) *Law and Development and the Global Discourses of Legal Transfers*. Cambridge: Cambridge University Press, 356–378.

(2013), 'The Case Continues? The High Courts in Malaysia and Unilateral Conversion of a Child to Islam by One Parent', 14(2) *Australian Journal of Asian Law*, 1–15.

(2018), 'Malaysia at the Crossroads? The Never-Ending Discourse between Islam, Law, and Politics', 4 Journal of Religious and Political Practice, 256–277.

(2019a), 'Islam, Law and Human Rights of Women in Malaysia' in Niamh Reilly (ed.) *International Human Rights: Human Rights of Women*. Singapore: Springer.

(2019b), 'To Harmonize or Not to Harmonize? Syariah Criminal Law in Malaysia', Summer *Berita*.

Suhakam (Human Rights Commission of Malaysia) (2017), 'An Independent Report to the Committee on the Convention on the Elimination of All Forms of Discrimination against Women (CEDAW)'. Malaysia: SUHAKAM.

Vijaindran, Audrey (2019), 'Do More to Barrow Gender Gap', *New Straits Times*, 7 December.

World Economic Forum (2020), Global Gender Gap Report 2020, www3.weforum .org/docs/WEF_GGGR_2020.pdf

Zin, Najibah Mohd (2017), 'Female Judges in Malaysian Shariʿa Courts: A Problem of Gender or Legal Interpretation?' in Nadia Sonneveld and Monika Lindbekk (eds.) *Women Judges in the Muslim World*. Leiden: Brill.

8

Gender on the Bench Matters for Sustainable Development

Examining Women in the Judiciary of Nepal through the Lens of Motility

SUBAS P. DHAKAL,[1] SHARADA SHRESTHA
AND GAURI DHAKAL

In the twenty-first century, the nexus between women's empowerment and sustainable development has become a worldwide priority. For instance, the 2030 United Nations Agenda for Sustainable Development (UN 2015) and two of the Sustainable Development Goals (SDG) – SDG5 and SDG16 – emphasise the global responsibility towards gender equality and women's representation in public institutions such as the judiciary (see UNSRIJAL n.d.). This increased attention to gender parity is because of the growing recognition that the opportunity gap between men and women remains significant, particularly in developing countries. While the #MeToo movement in North America brought the issue of violence against women and other long-overlooked social realities to global attention (Ozkazanc-Pan 2019), some have pointed out that it might take an entire millennium to accomplish gender equality in developing parts of the world like the South Asian region (Leopold and Ratcheva 2016). Increasing gender equality is not only a moral goal but is thought to be central to building strong and inclusive economies (OECD 2017, 1).

It is in this context that we explore the state of women in the judiciary of Nepal by drawing on the concept of motility capital as the capacity of actors to be mobile in social settings based on three factors: access, ability and appropriation (Kaufmann et al. 2004). For example, although the feminisation of the legal profession has increased to a certain extent in the West (Mack and Roach Anleu 2012; Kenney 2012), unequal female representation remains a prominent challenge in the judiciary amongst

---

[1] Corresponding author.

developing economies in South Asia. More importantly, the relationship between gender and judges remains an understudied topic in the region. We focus on Nepal and consider the policy and practice insights from the contemporary state of women in the judiciary in post-conflict and post-disaster Nepal. We reveal several systemic problems to advancing the prospect of women in the judiciary, including poor governance, the glass wall, the path of broken glass and the glass ceiling. We contend that addressing the issue of women's representation in the labour workforce across a variety of sectors and professions, including the judiciary, is significant from the perspective of the SDGs. We conclude by suggesting that gender sensitive judicial reforms in Nepal need to enhance the education and employability of graduates from various law schools and mitigate or minimise intra and extrajudicial corruption.

Women and Society in Nepal

The Federal Democratic Republic of Nepal is sandwiched between the two most populous nations: China and India. In administrative terms, there are seven provinces – divided into seventy-seven districts – with Kathmandu as the capital city (ECN 2017). Nepal has a population of over 29 million people, more than half (53.5 per cent) of whom are female (CBS 2018). It is one of the forty-seven least developed countries (LDC) in the world (UNCDP 2018) and is ranked 149th out of 189 countries in the Human Development Index – a composite guide made up of three key variables: life expectancy, educational achievement and income (UNDP 2018). The country has not fully recovered from the end of a decades-long armed conflict in 2006, as well as the devastation of the 2015 earthquake. The conflict that raged between the mid-1990s and mid-2000s claimed over 13,000 lives (UNOHCHR 2012, 14). On 25 April 2015, a severe earthquake struck the central parts of the country claiming nearly 9,000 lives and injuring over 22,000 people (see Dhakal 2018a). These circumstances have exacerbated gender inequality at the grass-roots. For example, it is estimated that between 40 and 60 per cent of all victims or those affected by the armed conflict were women (Thapa and Canyon 2017, 1). Furthermore, 55 per cent of the casualties and 48 per cent of those injured in the 2015 earthquake were women (Relief Web 2015). However, post-crises Nepal has witnessed several key developments that bodes well for gender equality.

First, it is a welcome coincidence that women occupied three powerful positions in the executive, legislative and judiciary branches at the same time – the president, the speaker of Parliament and the chief justice of the Supreme Court (Mawby and Applebaum 2018). In 2015, Onsari Gharti Magar became the first female speaker of Parliament and served until 2018. The former deputy speaker, who had also served as a minister for youth and sports, is affiliated with the Communist Party of Nepal (Maoist) and was elected unopposed (Kathmandu Post 2015). In the same year, Bidhya Devi Bhandari was elected as the first female president by the Parliament of Nepal. The former minister of defence, who is also a well-known women's rights campaigner is a close ally of Prime Minister Khadga Prasad Oli and is affiliated with the United Marxist Leninist (BBC News 2015). In 2016, Sushila Karki became the first female chief justice. Karki, a prominent lawyer and a permanent justice of the Nepalese Supreme Court since 2010, was recommended for the position by the Judicial Council and was unanimously endorsed by a parliamentary panel.

Second, the 2017 local elections that were held for the very first time in almost two decades, led to 40 per cent of women's representation in local governments (UNDP 2018). This was primarily because of the introduction of constitutional provisions[2] requiring that women should be at least one third of elected representatives (Article 84) (CAS 2015, 36–37).

Third, in 2019, Nepal's #MeToo moment occurred when the then sitting speaker of the House of Representatives, Krishna Bahadur Mahara, was formally charged and arrested over rape allegations (Kathmandu Post 2019). It is highly unusual for any high-profile male figure to be accused of crimes against women in Nepal. The federal Parliament employee filed a first information report accusing Mahara of attempting to rape her in her apartment in Kathmandu. Mahara was the first high-profile politician to be tried for sexual assault. Ultimately in 2020, he was acquitted by the Kathmandu District Court on the grounds of insufficient evidence to prove the charge levelled against him and was released from detention (*The Himalayan Times* 2020). It was nevertheless an important to step to have charges laid in the first place.

The legal and political system in Nepal remains marked by structural gender inequality and disadvantage (ADB 2010), and corrupt politicians and criminals have been accuses of using the judiciary as a tool of impunity and political control (Khanal 2019). Nevertheless, the fact that women held three key leadership positions and that charges of attempted

---

[2] Constitution of Nepal, Art. 84(8) for the House of Representatives, and Art. 176(9) for the provincial legislature.

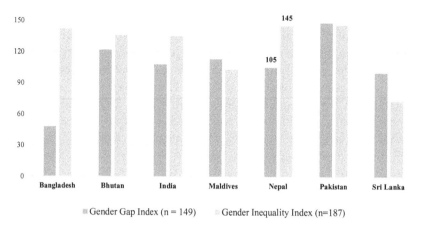

■ Gender Gap Index (n = 149)   ▪ Gender Inequality Index (n=187)

Figure 8.1   Gender gap index and gender inequality index rankings of selected South Asian countries
(*Sources*: WEF 2018; UNDP 2018)

rape were filed against a powerful male politician were indeed a watershed moment for the women's movement in Nepal. Transparency International (2018) ranks Nepal 124th out of 180 nations in the Corruption Perception Index. Political turmoil, corruption and weak governance have been identified as major barriers to policy reforms and economic progress (Dhakal and Burgess 2020). The country's overall poor performance in terms of controlling corruption is particularly problematic for gender parity. It has been shown that corruption in Nepal has a significant impact on women from low socio-economic backgrounds who have little opportunity or power to assert their rights or demand services from the state (UNDP 2020, 5).

Nonetheless, despite progress on several fronts, the state of the gender gap and inequality across South Asia suggests that Nepal's performance is below par. As Figure 8.1 indicates, Nepal is ranked 105th out of 149 nations in the Gender Gap Index (WEF 2018) and 145th out of 187 countries in the Gender Inequality Index (UNDP 2018). Comparatively, the gender gap is significantly lower in countries like Bangladesh. Sri Lanka ranks the highest in terms of gender equality at the regional level. The WEF's (2018) granulated data on economic participation and opportunity, educational attainment, health and survival, and political empowerment, suggests that, aside from political empowerment, women remain significantly behind men in terms of health, economic participation and survival. For example, despite increased political representation at the macro level, the female labour force participation rate is only 26 per cent compared to 54 per cent for males (CBS 2018, xi), which indicates lower economic prospects for women.

Gender and the Judiciary: The Literature

The literature on gender and the judiciary in Asia is small and indicates that the topic remains underexplored. For example, Siampukdee (n.d.) identifies the hidden gender bias of the merit system and discrimination towards women in the judiciary in Thailand. Zheng et al. (2017) argue that the vertical and horizontal mobility of Chinese judges in their career development fosters gender inequality and influences women's structural positions in courts. They label this phenomenon the 'elastic ceiling' (Zheng et al. 2017, 169). In South Asia, Holden (2019, 102) contends that the sustainability of female representation in the judiciary of Pakistan depends upon context-appropriate professionalism to strengthen their legitimacy and ultimately break the glass ceiling. Hoekstra (2010) suggests the need to introduce gender quotas due to the lack of diversity in the Indian judiciary. For instance, the data indicate that over a quarter (27 per cent) of judges in the Lower Courts, 11 per cent in High Courts and 9 per cent in the Supreme Court, were women (Thakur 2018). Nevertheless, studies on how women enter, navigate their career and succeed in the judicial systems across South Asia remains under the radar.

Apart from the literature specifically on gender and the judiciary, there is a broader literature on career development that can be used to gain insights into the progression of women into and through the judicial system. Patton and McMahon (2006) highlight the importance of the general theory of career development. Duffy and Dik (2009) point out that a one-size-fits-all type theory of career development has limited utility in certain circumstances. Two theoretical strands in the space of women's career development in the judiciary are noteworthy. First, the construct of self-efficacy signifies an individual's belief in their capabilities to execute actions and behaviour to manage situations and achieve desired outcomes (Bandura 1986). It is obvious that the concept of self-efficacy plays an important role in career selection and the progression of women. However, it is necessary to concede that employment decisions are not solely dependent on an employee's self-efficacy. Job characteristics and other socio-economic variables are critical in influencing intentions to enter and remain in the workforce (Maddux 1995). Second, the extent of a woman's career mobility relates to their opportunity structure, characteristics, resources, time and access to new jobs (Pindus et al. 1995; Mandel 2013). When women have the opportunity to invest in skills, this can drive career mobility.

If the judicial workforce is to be viewed from a systems perspective (Florin et al. 1992), the mobility of women to enter the profession, progress through their careers and acquire key leadership positions can be evaluated through the lens of inputs and outputs. Inputs refer to a variety of resources or capital that actors build, utilise and harness for the sake of their careers. Outputs can be results such as securing employment or advancing their career. Since mobility is not only a geographic but also a social phenomenon, Kaufman, Bergman and Joye (2004) take an integrated view of spatial and social aspects of mobility which they call 'motility capital'. The idea of motility capital is that actors have the capacity to be mobile in social settings based on three factors: access, ability and appropriation, which we explain shortly. In this chapter, we rely on innovation within the mobility paradigm that has the potential to bridge the two understandings of mobility – spatial and social – for several reasons. On the one hand, spatial mobility refers to geographic displacement, that is, the movement of actors from an origin to a destination. On the other, social mobility refers to the transformation in the distribution of resources or social position of individuals, families or groups within a given social structure or network. Kaufman et al. (2004, 752) posit that

> the main virtue of a systemic approach to mobility is the recognition that movement can take many forms, that different forms of movement may be interchangeable, and that the potentiality of movement can be expressed as a form of 'movement capital'.

Since capital is 'an investment of resources with expected returns' (Lin 2001, 3) the motility construct can be viewed as a resource or capital in light of three specific factors: access, competence and appropriation (Kellerman 2012). The first factor is 'access', which means the ability of women to enter the workforce and potential barriers to entry. Access is constrained by available options and conditions of entry to the judiciary as a profession. The second factor is 'ability', which incorporates competence and refers to people skills (soft skills) as well as technical (hard) skills of female actors in the workforce. Competence is often multifaceted and dependent on others to recognise and appreciate it. The third factor that determines motility is 'appropriation', which incorporates how actors interpret and act upon perceived or real access and skills. It is about contextual choices that female actors make in order to evaluate their mobility options against access and competences – primarily weighed by their own personal aspirations, motives and needs. All three elements of motility are fundamentally linked to socio-economic, cultural and political structures. We apply these three tenets of motility (as developed by Kaufmann et al. 2004) as part of an exploratory approach to understanding gender and the judiciary in Nepal.

Exploring the Gender and Judiciary Nexus in Nepal

The 2030 Agenda has set aspirations to achieve gender parity across the globe and in countries like Nepal (Dhakal 2018b). The question of what policy and practice insights can be generated from the current state of women in the judiciary in post-conflict and post-disaster Nepal is significant from the perspective of developing countries working towards the SDGs. Drawing on the motility framework, this chapter adopts an exploratory research approach in order to consider the state of women in the judiciary in Nepal.

One of the key distinctions between a confirmatory approach and an exploratory approach to research is that the former aims to test a hypothesis and the latter aims to develop propositions (see Davies 2006). The exploratory method is appropriate when the primary aim of the research is to scope out the magnitude or extent of a particular phenomenon or a problem (Bhattacherjee 2012, 6). In addition, while the outcomes of exploratory investigations may not always have direct and immediate impact on the decision-making processes, such an approach does offer policy insights and can inform future research agendas (Dhakal et al. 2018; Dhakal 2018c).

Since exploratory studies rely on wide-ranging evidence from multiple sources, such as documents and interviews (Rowley 2002), we adopted a two-pronged approach to examine the state of gender in the judiciary of Nepal. First, we analysed the higher education data on female enrolment in the field of law across four law schools. Second, we examined the existing and emerging gender specific opportunities and challenges in the Nepalese judiciary based on eleven informal conversations (Turner 2010) with research participants, carried out between June 2018 and May 2019 in the capital city (Table 8.1). Of these participants, two were men and nine were women. They include both sitting and retired judges

Table 8.1 *Code, occupation and gender of research participants*

Code	Current Position	Age Group	Gender
1JS	Lawyer/Development Worker (NGO)	40–50	M
2JS	Retired Law Professor (ACA)	60–70	M
3JS	Legal Professional (NGO)	20–30	F
4JS	Lawyer (FPS)	40–50	F
5AJ	Legal Professional (FPS)	20–30	F
6AJ	Legal Professional (NGO)	20–30	F
7AJ	Lawyer (GOV)	30–40	F
8RJ	Retired Judge (GOV)	70–80	F
9RJ	Retired Judge (GOV)	70–80	F
10SJ	Sitting Judge (GOV)	40–50	F
11SJ	Sitting Judge (GOV)	40–50	F

ranging in age from twenties to eighties, as well as lawyers and an academic.

The main purpose of our conversations was to gather stakeholder perspectives on gender issues within the judiciary. We instigated a thematic analysis to classify, analyse and record predominant patterns based on previously identified literature as well as new emerging themes from the collected information (Collis and Hussey 2009). Our analysis accumulated the experiences of research participants and identified and developed themes from the statements of aspiring, sitting and retired judges, as well as relevant stakeholders.

It is necessary to note here that two of the co-authors of this chapter served in the judiciary of Nepal for over five decades in various capacities and are now retired. The second co-author, Sharada Shrestha, is a retired justice of the Supreme Court of Nepal. She obtained her LLM qualifications from Lucknow University, India, and completed her BL and BSc degrees at Tribhuvan University in Nepal. In 1966, Sharada became the first woman judge in the country when she was appointed as a judge to the Land Reform Special Court. She is the current president of the Nepalese Women Judges Forum and a member of the International Association of Women Judges.

The third co-author, Gauri Dhakal, is a retired justice of the Supreme Court of Nepal. She completed MA, BL and BA degrees at Tribhuvan University. She is active in the International Association of Women Judges and is also the current vice president of the Nepalese Women Judges Forum.

We therefore drew upon our contacts within the judiciary to gain access to research participants, which would otherwise have been difficult. The design of our research has been informed and inspired by insider perspectives and experiences, as well as access to interviews with stakeholders and law education enrolment data that are otherwise not readily available to the public.

The Judicial System in Nepal

The history of the judicial system in Nepal has been discussed at length elsewhere (see Joshi and Katuwal 2014; Ghimire 2018). Our aim in this section is to provide a brief overview in order to enhance the contextual understanding of the findings. The Constitution of Nepal 2015 declares the country to be an independent, indivisible, sovereign, secular, inclusive, democratic, socialism-oriented, federal democratic republican state. The Constitution in its preamble commits to 'an independent, impartial and competent judiciary' (Government of Nepal 2015).

The administration of justice of the country is regulated by various statutes and regulations related to the judiciary, such as the Administration of Justice Act 2016, the Supreme Court Act 2016, the Supreme Court Regulations 1992, the High Court Regulations 2016 and the District Court Regulations 2016 (Supreme Court of Nepal 2018). The Judicial Administration Act 2016 makes provisions for the High Court, District Court and State Court under the Supreme Court of Nepal. At present, there are seven High Courts along with nine permanent benches and two temporary benches. There are a total of seventy-five District Courts as well as additional specialised judicial institutions like the Debt Recovery Tribunal, Revenue Tribunal, Administrative Court, Foreign Employment Tribunal and Special Courts (Supreme Court of Nepal 2018).

The Judicial Council oversees judicial governance matters in Nepal. It dates back to the 1990s, when the council was established as an independent body for the first time in the 1990 Constitution. The overall role of the council has been carried over to the 2015 Constitution in terms of making recommendations or giving advice on the appointment, transfer, disciplinary action against and dismissal of judges and other matters relating to the administration of justice (Article 183, the Constitution). More importantly, the council also formulates the code of conduct for judges and enforces it (Judicial Council Secretariat 2018). The judges of all three tiers of courts are appointed by the president on the recommendation of Judicial Council (NLC 2020). The Constitution also describes the eligibility qualifications and experiences required to be appointed as judges. To be eligible for the position of chief justice, a candidate must have served as a judge of the Supreme Court for at least three years. Any citizen of Nepal with a bachelor's degree in law who meets one of the following four conditions: who has either served as the chief judge or a judge of a High Court for at least five years; or who has constantly practiced law as a senior advocate or advocate for at least fifteen years; or who is a distinguished jurist having continuously worked for at least fifteen years in the judicial or legal field; or who has served in the post of gazetted first class or a higher post of the Judicial Service for at least twelve years will be eligible for appointment as a judge of the Supreme Court (NLC 2020, 53–54). District judges are generally appointed from a pool of civil servants belonging to the Judicial Service, although it is possible for other persons to qualify. Council members consider the integrity, capability and character of judicial candidates after consulting with the candidates' seniors and peers, and the courts in which the candidate practices (p. 57).

Nevertheless, there is a perception of a conflict of interest in terms of the composition of the council. For example, the council is headed by the chief justice, and its members include a senior-most judge of the Supreme Court, the federal minster for law and justice, one jurist recommended by the prime minister and one senior advocate recommended by the Nepal Bar Association (Judicial Council Secretariat 2018). Hence the independence and impartiality of the council can be questioned to a certain extent and women representation in the judiciary needs to be contextually examined, as some of the groups identified also serve as a pool for future judicial appointments.

In 2013, the National Judicial Academy published one of the most comprehensive reports on gender equality and social inclusion within the judiciary. In the past, the administrative and judicial systems had no deliberate and systematic inbuilt mechanisms to promote gender equality and social inclusion. It was not until after the political upheaval of 2007 that resulted in the abolition of the monarchy that changes began to be made (NJA 2013, 13).

The National Judicial Academy also highlights the fact that although judges are the ones to deliver justice, the judiciary ecosystem is comprised of various stakeholders including judges, public prosecutors and private lawyers (NJA 2013, 43). Nepal's Supreme Court has consistently lacked in diversity both in terms of gender and other socially marginalised groups, leading to the lack of legitimacy and negative public perceptions of the judicial system (Malagodi 2018). The absence of diversity in the judiciary, can however be linked to the current process of appointing judges. For example, Karki and Katuwal (2018) argue that the following are clearly in violation of the principles of natural justice: supersession of senior judges without questioning the integrity and efficiency; the appointment of candidates being informally approved by the political power centers; and the appointment of those with undue proximity and appointment based on collegial, kinship and family lineage.

Legal Education and Disputes over Enrolments

A law degree is a prerequisite for entry into the judicial service. Therefore, any effort to consider gender and judges in Nepal also needs to consider the overall legal education landscape and the enrolment trends of female law students over time. The latest publicly available data on higher education indicates that a total of 361,077 students were enrolled in tertiary education in 2017 (Ministry of Education 2018). There were more female (52.2 per cent) than male (47.8 per cent) students (Ministry of Education 2018, 52). The field of education had the highest share of female students at nearly 64 per cent and the field of engineering had the lowest share at 14 per cent. Female students accounted for over one third (33.7 per cent) of total students in the field of law.

Legal education in Nepal is offered through colleges/campuses affiliated with various universities. The two most prestigious are Nepal Law Campus and Kathmandu School of Law. The Nepal Law Campus, previously known as the Nepal Law College, is the oldest institution, established in 1954 (NLC n.d.) and affiliated with the Tribhuvan University. Although there is no tangible way to compare the quality of legal education being offered, in the global context Tribhuvan University is ranked between 801st and 1,000th in the *Times Higher Education (THE)* World University Rankings (THE 2021). Although the Kathmandu School of Law, affiliated with Kathmandu University, is not included in THE rankings, it is considered a leading private institution for legal education in the country.

In terms of student enrolment numbers, there is general scepticism about the trustworthiness of publicly available data. For instance, the seminal National Judicial Academy report on gender equality and social inclusion acknowledges the difficulty of obtaining student enrolment data from various law schools in the country (NJA 2013, 68). In order to explore granulated data on the trend of enrolment in law schools, two of the co-authors visited four law schools: (1) Nepal Law Campus,

Table 8.2 *Female enrolment in LLB and LLM in four law schools in Nepal*

	LLB Program			LLM Program		
Year	Total	Female	Female %	Total	Female	Female %
2010	1,753	507	28.90	142	42	29.58
2011	1,017	323	31.70	169	62	36.69
2012	3,105	655	21.10	134	46	34.33
2013	2,150	699	32.50	148	44	29.73
2014	1,996	650	32.50	138	62	44.93
2015	3,684	1,236	33.50	129	60	46.51
2016	4,590	1,636	35.60	254	95	37.40
2017	11,196	3,917	34.90	212	107	50.47
Total	29,491	9,623	32.60	1,326	518	39.06

Source: Authors, based on personal communication with campus chiefs from respective law schools

Tribhuvan University; (2) National Law College, Tribhuvan University; (3) Chakrabati Habi Education Academy College of Law, Purbanchal University; and (4) Kathmandu School of Law, Kathmandu University. During these visits we met with the head of departments. Based on the aggregate data we were able to obtain, the number of law students has steadily increased in law schools over the past decade (see Table 8.2). The share of female LLB students is one third of the total enrolment and nearly 40 per cent of LLM enrollments.

This student enrolment data highlight several interesting trends. First, in 2017, there was a sudden spike in enrolments. The head of the Department of Nepal Law Campus suggested to us that political interference was behind this sudden perceived growth as the newly elected politicians pressured law schools to enrol students from their constituency. This political interference in law school enrolment led not only to an intake of students solely based on membership of political parties in power or allied organisations instead of academic standings, but also a skewed a normal student–teacher ratio of 31:1 (THE 2020).

For instance, in 2017, the Nepal Law Campus had a total of fifty-five teaching staff for 10,945 LLB and LLM students that resulted in chaos in terms of learning and teaching delivery (Parajuli, conversation with author, 14 April 2019). Second, despite the lack of adequate job opportunities in the legal sector within the country, over 6,000 students were studying law, or nearly 2 per cent of the entire university population of which approximately one third are females. Although the latest data on the exact number of practising lawyers in the country are not available, the Bar Association of Nepal (2013) estimates that there are around 12,000 lawyers in the country, including senior advocates, advocates and pleaders, which is less than one third of the total law graduates in the past decade. The National Judicial Academy estimates that approximately 90 per cent of all lawyers in Nepal are men (NJA 2013). Although it is evident that the number of female law students has increased in recent years, an overwhelming majority have not entered the workforce. This may be for one of two reasons.

First, there have been concerns expressed by various stakeholders in terms of a mismatch between growth in the number of law students and the absence of sufficient job opportunities for law graduates in Nepal. For example, one of the interviewees stated that:

> Not many undergraduate students, male or female for that matter, attend the law school to be lawyers. There is an expectation in our society for females to complete bachelors' level education, and studying law is mistakenly perceived as being easy, that's all . . .
>
> (3JS).

Second, unlike other disciplines, the Bachelor of Laws (LLB) legal course is an option for the students to earn an additional qualification after completing an undergraduate course from other fields. Many do not bother to complete their extra law qualification once they secure a job in other sectors where a law qualification is not required.

Women Judges in Nepal

There are 431 judges at the Supreme, High and District Court levels.[3] Less than 5 per cent, or twenty-one, judges are women (see Figure 8.2). The low number of female judges in the country is not surprising. Of the nearly 5,000 staff in the judiciary, an overwhelming majority (86 per cent) are male (NJA 2013, 75). It is in this context that one of the

---

[3] Data from various sources including Gautam, T. – Judicial Council Secretariat, conversation with author, 13 June 2019; Subedi, I. – personal assistant of the chief justice of Supreme Court, conversation with author, 14 June 2019, and publicly available records as reported by the Judicial Council Secretariat (2017) and the Supreme Court of Nepal (2019).

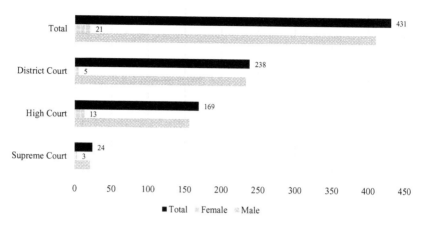

Figure 8.2   Women judges in the courts of Nepal[4]

interviewees commented on the lack of genuine political support for gender equality:

> Increasing women judges or female representation in the judiciary does not really have a political backing. [The] current political class hardly gets the basic premise of gender empowerment. For most of them, gender upliftment means establishing a unit within government ministry or department because it is lucrative in terms of finding opportunities to travel abroad or secure donor funding [1JS].

Of the eleven interviewees, two were sitting judges, two were retired judges, three were aspiring judges and the rest were judicial stakeholders (see Table 8.1). The focus of our interviews revolved around the following key topics: the contemporary changes, challenges and prospects for the judiciary generally; career opportunities and progression for women judges; and the state of gender equality in Nepalese society and how it manifests in the judiciary.

Our analysis reveals four main themes: the influence of dysfunctional governance on the judiciary, the glass wall; the path of broken glass; and the glass ceiling, which we explain in turn.

Dysfunctional Governance: 'Intra' and 'Extra' Judiciary Corruption

All interviewees raised the issue of corruption within the judiciary as a barrier for women's entrance to the courts. As mentioned earlier, this is

---

[4] Judicial Council Secretariat 2017; Supreme Court of Nepal 2019.

hardly surprising in the broader context of Nepal, which has consistently performed poorly in the global corruption index. Whether it is the influence of political parties on the judicial process (Momen 2013) or the erosion of citizens' trust in judiciary as well as courts (Askvik et al. 2010), corruption has emerged as the main cause of dysfunctional governance of the Nepalese Judiciary. Credible media reports in recent years have focused on two types of corruption–led dysfunctional governance: intra-judicial (within the judiciary) corruption and extrajudicial (outside the judiciary) corruption.

First, internationally, it has been reported that the Judicial Council Secretariat sacked the then sitting chief justice who was found to have faked his date of birth to remain in office longer (Bhandari 2018). Second, in local news outlet the *Nepali Times* magazine, Neupane (2018) highlights the phenomenon of 'justice for sale' and reports how money, power and patriarchy influence court judgments and allow criminals to avoid conviction. Third, Nepal's first female Supreme Court chief justice was suspended in the last month of her tenure after an impeachment motion was filed in Parliament accusing her of bias and interfering with the executive branch. Karki was known for her zero tolerance against corruption within and outside the judiciary, which ultimately led lawmakers of the ruling coalition to file an impeachment motion against her. She was accused of running a parallel government and abusing her powers (ANI 2017). Although the motion was withdrawn due to public pressure and lawmakers of opposing parties obstructing parliamentary affairs, one of the leading weekly newspapers in English, the Nepali Times (2017) in its editorial titled 'Lady Justice' stated:

> Clearly, Karki had ruffled a lot of feathers. It may just be that she was too honest and too impervious to threats and intimidation for the corrupt political cartel that runs this country to tolerate. The executive and legislative branches have now brought down the remaining pillar in Nepal's democracy that was still standing upright, the judiciary.

According to Dahal (2017), the unprecedented attempt to pass the impeachment motion was a way for the corrupt political class to ensure that Karki was suspended so that she would not be able to deliver her verdict on pending corruption cases linked to ruling politicians.

Fourth, in 2019, the Judicial Council recommended three lawyers and two career justices for appointment as justices to the Supreme Court and eighteen others for appointment as High Court judges. However, many of the recommended justices had direct conflicts of interest in terms of political affiliation or family ties with the ruling political class. These recommendations by the Judicial Council showed that it is not independent. The local outlet *My Republica* (2019) cited a well-respected retired judge and ex-president of the Nepal Bar Association who said:

> There is no longer an institution called the court. Even those deemed unfit to be permanent judge at High Courts have been recommended [for the Supreme Court]. Some of those recommended for the Supreme Court and high courts are corrupt middlemen. There is need of a broad discussion over some of the nominees.

These examples indicate that the judiciary in Nepal has gone backwards in terms of curtailing corruption, particularly since the 2007 Global Corruption Report (Transparency International 2007). Even in 2007, this report pointed out that Nepalese society perceived the judiciary as the institution that was the most corruption-afflicted institution among all other public institutions in the country. It is in this context, one of the interviewees said (2JS):

> the idea that there can be a pure judiciary that is completely free of corruption is naïve. However, what I can tell you is that ... the level of accountability in our judiciary has eroded drastically after the abolition of monarchy ... there is no doubt about that. The concerted efforts to undermine various institutions in the country including the judiciary are much more aggressive and visible now ... I see corruption in judiciary as a symptom of a much bigger problem in the country.

This statement reflects a common view of the judiciary in Nepal as highly corrupt. This perspective along with the growing local and international media coverage on corruption contributes to an overall impression of the judiciary in Nepal that is affected by political interference and entrenched corruption (see Stiftung 2018).

The Glass Wall: Invisible Entry Barriers

The idea that women can be fully integrated into the workforce remains under-developed in the context of Nepal. Women who are willing to enter the labour market are still considered to be defying social norms, particularly in many rural and regional parts of Nepal. This at least partially explains why female labour participation is only 26 per cent (CBS 2018, xi).

Our participants, especially the aspiring judges, perceived that this invisible glass wall in society restricts the possibilities of women to enter the legal workforce. The difficulties for women of entering the profession are further compounded by limited options and the high conditions of entry. For example, one of the interviewees [6AJ] captured the essence of this invisible barrier as the following:

> The majority of communities in Nepal are patriarchal, here women are generally subordinate to men in virtually every aspect of life. Men are considered to be the leader of the family and superior [to] women while the social norms and values at that time were also biased in favor of men … belief of our society is constructed in such a way that makes women entering the work[force] more complicated. Our deep-rooted values which still discriminates between son and daughters from very childhood. Education, opportunity and liberty for men is taken as granted and, only some women get such opportunity and access especially in the legal field dominated by men.

There was also a broader understanding amongst interviewees that the invisible glass door is almost visible in the context of the judiciary of Nepal. One of the interviewees said [3JS]:

> It is really tough to find even the basic information about job openings … so onerous. The websites are outdated and provide little useful information if any. When you do visit the office to find out more about the job, no one takes you [as a woman] seriously… they make you go around room after room … and everyone acts like they know nothing … and remember I am a lawyer, and I really don't want to pay a bribe. The other issue is that senior women in the office are not particularly helpful either, how can we expect gender equality in the society when women don't assist or promote other women … it is really frustrating … no wonder hundreds of law graduates go abroad each year for studies or jobs.

This statement is not necessarily surprising, as it is common to have to pay bribes simply to access basic public services in South Asia (Transparency International 2018). However, these accounts also relate to the access factor of motility and indicate the systemic problem of corruption and associated dysfunctional governance. Biased social attitudes towards women, combined with the lack of adequate opportunities are the main barriers in terms of access for women to the judiciary. The combined judicial and legal workforce is approximately no more than 15,000 positions – there are hardly any new opportunities for new law graduates. Consequently, graduates may go abroad for jobs and higher education. Dhakal (2018b) reports that the lack of quality education and jobs in the country mean that every year nearly 400,000 youth leave the country for foreign employment and over 25,000 youth leave the country to pursue higher education abroad.

The Path of Broken Glass: Career Progression Challenges

In countries like Nepal, women face challenges in progressing their career every step of the way – which is what we call 'the path of broken glass'. To walk on a path of broken glass is difficult and dangerous. This metaphor is more appropriate than the sticky floors, which describes how some jobs thwart men and women to get ahead in certain positions (Laabs 1993). In many cases, women in the judiciary of Nepal are held back because of the gender-specific barriers that make it difficult to enter the profession or slow their career journey. For example, one of the interviewees identified corruption as a key challenge that held her back:

> The idea that there is very little corruption within our judiciary is a hoax. Let me tell you something, when I was serving as one of the first few women judges in the country, I was transferred to a court in [a] regional area. It became difficult for me, as an indigenous of Kathmandu Valley, to balance between my career aspirations and family commitments. So, when I approached a reputed person with significant influence in order to discuss my options the person initially began to question my capacity as a woman judge and indicated that I did not have appropriate skills to succeed as a judge in the valley. Later on, he blatantly changed his tune and indicated that if I can arrange a payment of large sum in cash, it would be possible for me to be transferred ... he instructed me to drop the bribe at this particular hotel in Kathmandu. Back then such corruption remained under the radar, now we hear more about it in the news ... but it has always been there [8RJ].

The fact that professional capacity was a question, just because one is a woman, on top of the demand for a bribe, suggests yet another layer of difficulty on the path to career progression for women in the judiciary. The biased gender-specific perception of the judge and judicial authority is not unique to Nepal and it has been a recurring theme in studies of the judiciary in the West as well (see Rackley 2002). However, women in the judiciary of Nepal have little time and resources to invest in skills development and/or develop capacity due to societal expectations around family commitments. For example, one of the interviewees [10SJ] said:

> As soon as my responsibilities at work wrapped up, my family responsibilities commenced. I had to go home, prepare dinner, look after my kid, and [make] him ready for school the next day. While my male colleagues enjoyed social events over drinks or playing cards and expanded their networks with high-ranking officials. It was during these gatherings many of the important office matters such as who gets selected for upcoming professional development opportunities or who gets recommended for

the promotion were informally decided. Needless to say, I was never recommended nor was I informed about such opportunities during an entire first decade of my career.

These sentiments reflect on the structural disadvantage that impedes gender equality in the judiciary as the recognition and appreciation of competence is often associated with male social capital such as their informal networks and associations (Dhakal 2014), making it difficult for women to progress in their career.

The Glass Ceiling

The 'glass ceiling' is a useful metaphor to describe transparent or artificial barriers that prevent women from reaching high-level leadership positions (see Guy 1994). The metaphor of the glass ceiling in the context of motility equates to the appropriation factor, which refers to institutional processes that lead to policies and plans. One of our interviewees [9RJ] spoke to us against the backdrop of the historic election in 2016 of the first female president, the first female speaker of Parliament and the first female chief justice of the Supreme Court:

> Nepal is yet to have [a] woman as a Minister for Legal Affairs and an Attorney General . . . and men in power have been able to create artificial barriers for women in judiciary in my opinion. It is not that I expect having women in these positions will improve gender equality overnight . . . but I do feel that having women in such positions can be seen as a proxy indicator of progress and hope for gender equality at the institutional level. Let me share this with you, there was a clause in the old constitution that prevented people without at least seven years' judiciary experiences to be nominated as a Supreme Court justice. The Constitution was later amended so that only three years of experiences would be adequate, primarily to benefit men. This change had an adverse impact on long-serving and highly qualified women being nominated as a Chief Justice. So, my point is, having a women minister or an Attorney General could impact policy in a more meaningful way.

Some of the interviewees also implied that the country aspires to achieve gender equality but that these aspirations are only on paper or for the benefit of foreign donor agencies. The point being, without recalibrating social values, paper reforms alone are inadequate to improve the status of women in the country, especially in the judiciary. One of the interviewees [11SJ] stated:

> Our judiciary has been without a vision or a mission in relation to gender equality. Those with decision-making authority never made an attempt to

learn from other countries and apply in the context of our judiciary. In recent years, political leaders have exerted excessive political interference in order to ensure that the judges remain in their pocket and potentially rule in their favor when there is such a need. I also feel that the inept leadership in the judiciary is unwilling to acknowledge that there is not a level playing field for women.

These sentiments reflect the lack of appropriation aspects of motility, as the policies and rules were amended just to give preference to men over women in the judiciary rather than enabling women to evaluate their mobility options.

Conclusion

The nexus between women's empowerment and sustainable development is a global priority. In light of this, our chapter explored the policy and practice insights from the contemporary state of women in the judiciary in post-conflict and post-disaster Nepal. The chapter posited that gender on the bench matters for fulfilling sustainable development aspirations. The opportunities and challenges for women in the Nepalese judiciary have not been well-studied from a gendered point of view, and this is also true of the broader South Asia region. The framework of motility has enabled us to examine gender inequality in terms of access, ability and appropriation within the judiciary of Nepal.

Our findings reveal that contemporary student enrolments for women in legal education appear to be encouraging, although four specific systemic problems exist in advancing the prospect of women in the judiciary. These problems relate to poor governance, the glass wall, the path of broken glass and the glass ceiling. The issues that arise include corruption in the judiciary, entry barriers to the profession, career progression hurdles and the lack of appropriation that have adverse impacts on the motility of women judges in Nepal.

The gender issue clearly has not been a priority of the political class. On the rare occasions when gender is a priority, it is often superficial and marred by short-term vested interests. This is hardly a surprise as the evidence indicates that Nepal still lags behind in terms of meaningful representation for women in the political, social, economic and educational sphere. The constitutional provision that requires a 33 per cent quota for women has increased political representation of women in some sectors. And yet, the constitutional provision has still attracted criticism for putting emphasis on quantity over quality (see Rai 2019).

The chapter contends that the issue of women's representation in the Nepalese judiciary is significant from the perspective of accomplishing gender specific SDGs and recommends that gender sensitive judiciary reforms of the future need to pay attention to education and employability of women graduates from various law schools, and mitigation of intra and extrajudicial corruption. If women representation in the broader legal workforce, and within the judiciary, are to be increased, the relevance of legal education and the employability of graduates from various law schools need serious attention. What this requires is substantial state investment that takes a systematic approach to the entire legal workforce. In addition, law schools need to collect longitudinal data on the quality of legal education, as well as experiment with work-integrated learning such as internships in the private sector or at different tiers of government branches. A broader emphasis on increasing the quality of legal education will indirectly benefit women who are studying and/or planning to study law.

What is most concerning is the magnitude and scope of intra and extrajudicial corruption that has hindered the motility of women in terms of selection, appointment, promotion and transfer. Since the judiciary has a vital role to play as an anchor of the integrity governance infrastructure in Nepal, implementing good governance within the judiciary by setting up independent institutional mechanisms to keep it free from political interference is necessary. Meanwhile, the issues raised in this chapter are a reminder that post-conflict and post-disaster sustainable development in Nepal looks much more sanguine with concerted policy efforts and investment in law education and removing gender-specific barriers in judiciary, than without them.

References

ADB (2010) *Overview of Gender Equality and Social Inclusion in Nepal.* Manila: Asian Development Bank.

ANI (2017) 'Nepal Politicians to Allow Chief Justice Sushila Karki to Superannuate with Grace', 29 May, https://indianexpress.com/article/world/nepal-politicians-to-allow-chief-justice-sushila-karki-to-superannuate-with-grace-4679018

Askvik, Steinar, Ishtiaq Jamil and Tek Nath Dhakal (2011) 'Citizens' Trust in Public and Political Institutions in Nepal'. *International Political Science Review* 32(4): 417–437.

Bandura, A. (1986) 'The Explanatory and Predictive Scope of Self-Efficacy Theory'. *Journal of Social and Clinical Psychology* 4(3): 359–373.

Bar Association of Nepal (2013) 'Information Sheet – Nepal Bar Association', www
.nichibenren.or.jp/library/ja/bar_association/word/data/Nepal.pdf.

BBC News (2015) 'Bidhya Devi Bhandari Elected Nepal's First Female President',
29 October, www.bbc.com/news/world-asia-34664430

Bhandari, R. (2018) 'Nepal's Chief Justice Sacked after He Is Accused of Faking
Date of Birth', *New York Times*, 14 March, www.nytimes.com/2018/03/14/
world/asia/nepal-court-gopal-parajuli.html

Bhattacherjee, A. (2012) *Social Science Research: Principles, Methods, and Practices,*
2nd ed. Tampa: University of South Florida.

CBS (2018) 'Report on the Nepal Labour Force Survey 2017/18', Kathmandu,
Central Bureau of Statistics (CBS).

Collis, J. and Hussey, R. (2009) *Business Research: A Practical Guide for
Undergraduate and Postgraduate Students.* New York: Palgrave Macmillan.

Cybermetrics Lab (2019) 'Ranking of Universities, Nepal', www.webometrics.info/
en/About_Us

Dahal, B. (2017) 'Unimpeachable Evidence', https://archive.nepalitimes.com/regu
lar-columns/Legalese/unimpeachable-evidence,901

Davies, P. (2006) 'Exploratory Research'. In *The SAGE Dictionary of Social
Research Methods,* edited by V. Jupp, London: SAGE, 110–111.

Dhakal, S. P. (2014) 'A Methodological Framework for Ascertaining the Social
Capital of Environmental Community Organisations in Urban Australia'.
International Journal of Sociology and Social Policy 34(11/12): 730–746.

(2018a) 'Analysing News Media Coverage of the 2015 Nepal Earthquake Using
a Community Capitals Lens: Implications for Disaster Resilience'. *Disasters*
42(2): 294–313.

(2018b) 'Cooperative Enterprises and Sustainable Development in Post-Crisis
Nepal: A Social Responsibility Perspective on Women's Employment and
Empowerment'. *Contemporary Issues in Entrepreneurship Research* 8:
185–200.

(2018c) 'The State of Higher Education and Vocational Education and Training
Sectors in Nepal'. In *Transitions from Education to Work: Workforce Ready
Challenges in the Asia Pacific,* edited by R. Cameron et al., London:
Routledge.

Dhakal, S. P. and Burgess, J. (2020) 'Decent Work for Sustainable Development in
Post-Crisis Nepal: Social Policy Challenges and a Way Forward'. Social
Policy & Administration. 55(1): 128–142.

Duffy, R. D. and Dik, B. J. (2009) 'Beyond the Self: External Influences in the
Career Development Process'. *The Career Development Quarterly* 58(1):
29–43.

ECN (2017) 'Overview of Elections in Nepal'. Election Commission of Nepal
[ECN], Kathmandu, www.election.gov.np/election/np

Florin, P., Chavis, D., Wandersman, A. and Rich, R. (1992) 'A Systems Approach to Understanding and Enhancing Grassroots Organisations the Block Booster Project'. In *Analysis of Dynamic Psychological Systems*, edited by R. L. Levine and H. E. Fitzgerald, 215–243. New York: Plenum Press.

Ghimire, R. (2018) *Improving Access to Justice through Embracing a Legal Pluralistic Approach: A Case Study of Nepal*. Doctor of Philosophy thesis, School of Law, University of Wollongong, https://ro.uow.edu.au/theses1/467

Government of Nepal (2015) *Constitution of Nepal 2015.*

Guy, M. E. (1994) 'Organisational Architecture, Gender and Women's Careers'. *Review of Public Personnel Administration* 14(2): 77–90.

Hoekstra, V. (2010) 'Increasing the Gender Diversity of High Courts: A Comparative View'. *Politics & Gender* 6(3): 474–484.

Holden, L. (2019) 'Women Judges in Pakistan'. *International Journal of the Legal Profession* 26(1): 89–104.

Joshi, D. R. and Katuwal, R. K. (2014) 'Nepali Legal and Judicial System: An Overview'. *National Judicial Academy Law Journal* 8(2014): 63–81.

Judicial Council Secretariat. (2018) 'About Judicial Council'. Kathmandu, Judicial Council Secretariat, http://jcs.gov.np

Kathmandu Post (2015) 'Onsari Gharti Magar Elected First Woman Speaker', 17 October, https://kathmandupost.com/valley/2015/10/16/onsari-elected-first-woman-speaker

(2019) 'Police Arrest Krishna Bahadur Mahara over Rape Allegations', *Kathmandu Post*, 6 October. https://kathmandupost.com/national/2019/10/06/police-arrest-krishna-bahadur-mahara-for-rape-charges

Kaufmann, V., Bergman, M. M. and Joye, D. (2004) 'Motility: Mobility as Capital'. *International Journal of Urban and Regional Research* 28(4): 745–756.

Kellerman, Aharon (2012) 'Potential Mobilities'. *Mobilities* 7(1): 171–183.

Kenney, S. J. (2012). 'Choosing Judges: A Bumpy Road to Women's Equality and a Long Way to Go'. *Michigan State. Law Review* 5: 1499–1528.

Khanal, B. (2018) 'Unwholesome Tendencies in the Judicial Appointment: A Nepali Perspective'. *Kathmandu University School of Law Review* 6: 53–67.

Laabs, J. (1993) 'The Sticky Floor beneath the Glass Ceiling'. *Personnel Journal* 72 (5): 35–39.

Leopold, T. and Ratcheva, V. S. (2016) 'Why It Could Take 1,000 Years for Men and Women to be Equal in South Asia', Geneva, The World Economic Forum, www.weforum.org/agenda/2016/10/1000-years-till-gender-equality-south-asia

Lin, N. (2001) *Social Capital A Theory of Social Structure and Action*. London: Cambridge University Press.

Mack, K. and Roach Anleu, S. (2012) 'Entering the Australian Judiciary: Gender and Court Hierarchy'. *Law & Policy* 34(3): 313–347.

Maddux, J. E. (1995) 'Self-Efficacy Theory'. In *Self-Efficacy, Adaptation, and Adjustment: Theory, Research and Application*, edited by J. E. Maddux, Boston: Springer, 3–33.

Malagodi, M. (2018) 'Challenges and Opportunities of Gender Equality Litigation in Nepal'. *International Journal of Constitutional Law* 16(2): 527–551.

Mandel, H. (2013) 'Up the Down Staircase: Women's Upward Mobility and the Wage Penalty for Occupational Feminization, 1970–2007'. *Social Forces* 91 (4): 1183–1207.

Mawby, B. and Applebaum, A. (2018) *Rebuilding Nepal: Women's Roles in Political Transition and Disaster Recovery*. Washington, DC: Georgetown Institute for Women, Peace and Security.

Ministry of Education (2018) *Education in Figures 2017 (At a Glance)*. Kathmandu: Government of Nepal.

Momen, Md. (2013) 'Influence of Political Parties on the Judicial Process in Nepal: Asian Studies'. *Journal of Critical Perspectives on Asia*. 49: 150–152.

My Republica (2019) 'Controversy Flares over Court Nominees', 4 April, https://myrepublica.nagariknetwork.com/news/controversy-flares-over-court-nominees

Nepali Times (2017) 'Editorial Lady Justice', Issue # 857, 5–11 May, https://archive.nepalitimes.com/article/editorial/lady-justice-sushila-karki,3693

Neupane, T. (2018) 'Justice for Sale', *Nepali Times*, 24 August, www.nepalitimes.com/banner/justice-for-sale.

NJA. (2013) *Gender Equality and Social Inclusion Analysis of the Nepali Judiciary*. Lalitpur: National Judicial Academy [NJA].

NLC (2020) Constitution of Nepal. Kathmandu, Nepal Law Commission.

(n.d.) 'A Brief History of Legal Education in Nepal'. Kathmandu: Nepal Law Campus (NLC). www.nlc.edu.np

OECD (2017) 'Gender Equality', www.oecd.org/gender/Gender-equality-flyer.pdf,

Ozkazanc-Pan, B. (2019) 'On Agency and Empowerment in a #MeToo World'. *Gender, Work & Organization* 26(8): 1212–1220.

Patton, W. and McMahon, M. (2006) 'The Systems Theory Framework of Career Development and Counseling: Connecting Theory and Practice'. *International Journal for the Advancement of Counselling* 28(2): 153–166.

Pindus, N. M., Flynn, P. and Nightingale, D. S. (1995) *Improving the Upward Mobility of Low-Skill Workers: The Case of the Health Industry*. Washington, DC: The Urban Institute.

Press Trust of India (2016) 'Sushila Karki Confirmed as Nepal's First Woman Chief Justice', *Times of India*, 11 July, https://timesofindia.indiatimes.com/world/south-asia/Sushila-Karki-confirmed-as-Nepals-first-woman-chief-justice/articleshow/53145026.cms

Rackley, E. (2002) 'Representations of the (Woman) Judge: Hercules, the Little Mermaid, and the Vain and Naked Emperor'. *Legal Studies*: 22(4): 602–624.

Rai, R. (2019) 'Gender Equality in Nepal: At a Crossroads of Theory and Practice', www.idea.int/news-media/news/gender-equality-nepal-crossroads-theory-and-practice

Relief Web (2015) 'Response to the Nepal Earthquake'. New York: UN Office for the Coordination of Humanitarian Affairs, https://reliefweb.int/sites/reliefweb.int/files/resources/gender_equality_bulletin_no_1_-_21_may_2015.pdf

Rowley, J. (2002) 'Using Case Studies in Research'. *Management Research News* 25 (1): 16–27.

Siampukdee, U. (n.d.) 'Status of Women Profession: Gender Equality of Judicial Occupation in Thailand'. In *Globalisation and Regionalism: 'The Present Day of Globalisation – Current Status and Issues'*, edited by T. Shinoda et al., Kyoto: Ochanomizu Shobo. www.ritsumei.ac.jp/acd/re/k-rsc/hss/book/pdf/vol03_10.pdf

Stiftung, B. (2018) 'Country Report Nepal'. Gütersloh, Germany, www.bti-project.org/fileadmin/files/BTI/Downloads/Reports/2018/pdf/BTI_2018_Nepal.pdf

Supreme Court of Nepal (2019) 'Judiciary in Nepal'. Kathmandu, Supreme Court of Nepal, www.supremecourt.gov.np/web/index.php/index

Thakur, P. (2018) 'Just 27% of Judges in Lower Courts Women, Reveals Study', *Times of India*, 13 August, https://timesofindia.indiatimes.com/india/just-27-of-judges-in-lower-courts-women-reveals-study/articleshow/65380343.cms

Thapa, L. and Canyon, D. V. (2017) 'The Advancement of Women in Post-Conflict Nepal'. Occasional Paper. Daniel K. Inouye:Asia Pacific Centre for Security Studies, April, http://apcss.org/wpcontent/uploads/2010/03/17-Thapa-The-advancement-of-women-in-post-conflict-Nepal.pdf.

THE (2020) Nepal Tribhuvan University. www.timeshighereducation.com/world-university-rankings/tribhuvan-university

Transparency International (2007) *Global Corruption Report 2007*. Cambridge: Cambridge University Press.

(2018) *Corruption Perceptions Index 2018*, www.transparency.org/files/content/pages/2018_CPI_Executive_Summary.pdf.

Turner, D. W. (2010) 'Qualitative Interview Design: A Practical Guide for Novice Investigators'. *The Qualitative Report* 15(3): 754–760.

UN (2015) *Transforming Our World: The 2030 Agenda for Sustainable Development*. A/RES/70/1. New York: United Nations [UN], https://sustainabledevelopment.un.org/post2015/transformingourworld

UNDP (2010) *Corruption, Accountability and Gender: Understanding the Connections*. New York: United Nations Development Program (UNDP).

(2018) *Researching Women's Political Inclusion in the 2017 Local Elections: Some Comments and Findings*. Kathmandu: United Nations Development Programme [UNDP]. www.np.undp.org/content/nepal/en/home/blog/

2018/researching-women-s-political-inclusion-in-the-2017-local-elections-some-comments-and-findings.html

UNOHCHR (2012) *Nepal Conflict Report*. Geneva: United Nations Office of the High Commissioner for Human Rights (UNOHCHR).

UNSRIJAL (n.d.) *UNDP: Promoting Gender Equality in the Judiciary*. New York: United Nations Special Rapporteur on the Independence of Judges and Lawyers (UNSRIJAL), viewed 1 October 2019, https://independence-judges-lawyers.org/gender-in-the-judiciary-and-the-legal-profession

WEF (2018) *Gender Gap Report 2018*. Geneva: World Economic Forum [WEF]. www3.weforum.org/docs/WEF_GGGR_2018.pdf.

Zheng, C., Ai, J. and Liu, S. (2017) 'The Elastic Ceiling: Gender and Professional Career in Chinese Courts'. *Law & Society Review* 51(1): 168–199.

9

Feminising the Indian Judiciary

The Gender Gap and the Possibilities of Objectivity

SIMASHREE BORA

In the last decade, gender diversity within the Indian judiciary has been a matter of concern. However, the challenges of representation and the gender gap remain largely unexplored. Feminists have embarked upon a critical quest to fight for gender equality and reform of the law (Agnes 1999). A critical perspective sees law as a tool of the powerful elite. In many ways, law has emerged as a dominant institution, but at the same time it is used as a mode of resistance. However, women's access to law is compromised.

Feminists point out the gendering of work and how the production of power is masculine in spheres like medicine, technology, politics and so forth (Hacker 1989; Kirkup and Keller 1992; McDowell 1997). Within the legal profession in India, women's position is governed by societal norms. This chapter argues for increased attention to women's position in terms of the intersections of culture, class, caste and religion, and the way this affects their ability to access the law. Carol Smart argues that the law is deaf to core concerns of feminism and so feminists should be extremely cautious of how and whether they resort to law (Smart 1989, 2).

There is no doubt that since independence, various law reform efforts in India have aimed to protect and enhance women's rights.[1] Despite this, institutional disparity and the lack of equal opportunity for women within the legal domain are still a matter of concern that has an impact on judging and judgments. The judicial structure itself exhibits gender

---

[1] Dowry prohibition Act, 1961, The Commission of Sati (Prevention Act), 1987, Protection of Women from Domestic Violence Act, 2005, The Sexual Harassment of Women at Workplace (Prevention, Prohibition and Redressal) Act, 2013, The Criminal Law Amendment Act, 2013 and most recently the Supreme Court's ordinance of Triple Talaq as deemed constitutional are worth mentioning.

disparity and a lack of diversity, and not all states have their own High Court.[2]

Studies of women's entry, position and representation in the judiciary are a contemporary phenomenon. My chapter builds upon these studies to consider the sociological position of women in the judiciary in India, particularly in the High Courts. The findings from my field work observations inform this chapter. The first section outlines the history of women in the Indian judiciary and the legal profession followed by a detailed statistical account of women judges and chief justices of various High Courts since India's independence. I profile women who have been able to make an impact by contributing to landmark judgments in the highest order of the judiciary. The next section looks at challenges posed by structural norms governing women's position in the profession, judicial thinking and, finally, the legal decision-making process. I consider how women judges construe the idea of gendered performances within the court, the attributes of structural hierarchies in the highest order of the judiciary and how gender roles determine courtroom behaviour. I suggest that legal socialisation still matters to the overall growth of women within the highest courts in India.

Studying Women in the Judiciary: Methods

This chapter brings a feminist perspective to the gender gap and the mobility of women within the upper judiciary. I do so from the lens of sociology. Sociologists from India have studied the legal domain through studies of the legal profession and the structure of the legal system in society (Sharma 1984; Oommen 1986; Gandhi 1987, 1994). As part of the modernisation process of the state, the legal system has been depicted as the vehicle of social change (Singh 1978). The gender composition of the judiciary has received insufficient attention. Today, in both the lower and upper judiciary, women are a small proportion of the total number of judges. In the lower judiciary, only 27.6 per cent are women judges compared to 71.4 per cent male judges (Gosh et al. 2018). The percentage of women judges remains below 40 per cent in all states, with a few exceptions of smaller states like Goa, Meghalaya and Sikkim. In a study on women in the lower judiciary from 2007 to 2017, Chandrashekaran et al. (2020) observe that there has been a considerable increase of

---

[2] I used the term 'diversity' as a broad category to include gender, caste, religion and the issue of reservation in the lower courts.

women in the junior division of civil judges, where women make up 36.45 per cent of the state lower judiciary. On the other hand, at the district level it is a dismal story, with women comprising only 11.75 per cent of district judges (Chandrashekaran et al. 2020, 36). There has been an increase in the entry of women into the cadre of civil judges (junior division) because of the recruitment method focused on attracting fresh law graduates, many of whom are women (Chandrashekaran et al. 2020, 39).

In addition to the judiciary, some sections of legal practice have seen an increase of women. Swethaa Ballakrishnen (2013) argues that the position of women lawyers in private law firms in India has undergone profound change. The overarching growth in the number of women and their success in private firms creates the opportunity for 'gender egalitarian workspaces' (Swethaa Ballakrishnen 2013, 1264). Ballakrishnen finds that in big law firms, women do not experience discrimination in comparison to their male colleagues. She also points out the relative privilege of these women based on their class status and education, as graduates of elite and competitive National Law Universities of India. Her research is consistent with my observations while teaching at Maharashtra National Law University Mumbai,[3] where more than 50 per cent of students were female and most are from upper-class and well-educated families.

I begin by charting the historical journey of women within the Indian judiciary in order to make an assessment of the process of entry, career progression and mobility of women as judges within the system. With that focus, I demonstrate when and how women judges enter the highest courts of law, identifying factors such as the establishment of the courts and the variations of women's presence in those courts. I use statistical data to categorise women's representation and positions in various High Courts of India. This chapter looks specifically at women in the upper judiciary and to do this I have compiled lists of women who were judges in the High Courts and the Supreme Courts since the establishment of these courts up until 2019. I collected narratives of women lawyer, advocates, senior councillors, mediators and judges in order to gain a

---

[3] I taught sociology to the students of (B.A.) LLB programme as a part of the graduate programme. At the outset, simply by looking at the high fee structure one can make a cursory observation of the economic status of the students, most of whom come from strong economic backgrounds. This also implies that National Law Universities (NLUs) cater to a specific class and reproduce class behaviour within the institutional structure. The gender ratio varies in various NLUs.

thematic perspective on the process of gendering the judiciary. The diverse groups of women, particularly from the Bombay High Court, represent the social world of women legal professionals and the lawmaking process.

As part of my research, I experienced difficulties securing appointments and permissions to interview sitting judges due to various protocols, time limitations and at times their unwillingness to be involved in the study. I faced a series of denials and failed attempts at the judge's office until an opportunity came to meet a (male) judge; his obvious hesitation to discuss gender and the judiciary made me rethink the underlying incongruity of non-acceptance of matters pertaining to gender within the judiciary.

My research and observations of the judiciary as a social space are derived from my frequent visits to the Bombay High Court. The social universe of the judiciary and the judicial structure varies depending on its origins, location and the overall composition of personnel in the institution. The everyday life of the court is defined by its culture of work, professionalism and how different meanings are constructed around various social settings. I take seriously the call of anthropologists to observe the everyday activities of the courts, affirming Malinowski's call for close observation of phenomena that cannot otherwise be studied through questioning or data compilation (Malinowski 1922, 18).

My first interview with one of the senior advocates was arranged inside the High Court Library. In that location, the majority of legal professionals present were men, while the presence of women who were sitting, conversing and reading was much less visible.[4] Likewise, the lack of visibility of women at public events or in public spaces was marked. For example, in April 2019, the Honorable Judge of Bombay High Court Justice Bharati Dangre delivered a public talk on 'social context judging'. Organised by the Bar Council of Bombay High Court, I noticed that the participants were all female lawyers, advocates, councillors, young

---

[4] The interview was arranged by a colleague, so I could begin a deep conversation. Ten minutes into our conversation, I felt that our discussion was being interrupted by other parallel questioning and conversations between the interviewee and her colleagues. Although it seemed like a friendly intervention in the beginning, later the ongoing commenting on our conversations seemed to me a way of controlling her responses. The accidental informant was concerned about the authenticity of my interviewee's information on issues on women and judiciary. Social science researchers in India are often presumed to be a journalist or a reporter, so I was cautioned to make entry of correct and valid data into my 'article'.

students and so on. The absence of men at this public talk on feminism was noticeable.

Women in India: Historicising the Indian Judiciary

Under the shadow of patriarchy, Indian women have been fighting battles on many fronts. It is extremely difficult to define exactly who Indian women are considering the complex composition of society. Critical studies on women's position and status in Indian society show that they occupy a subordinated, gendered role and discrimination. An ideal representation of women has been called into question. In terms of work and labour, many women work outside of the home and contribute to economic activities. Yet the professional workplace is often construed as a men's domain. Moreover, women are at the bottom of the hierarchy in many professions.

The entry of women into certain professions related to science and technology, administration, law, governance, sports and politics is a modern phenomenon. For a long time, law remained an exclusive male-dominated area. Law in ancient and medieval India was practiced in traditional courts of the kings under the precincts of religion. The term 'Wakil' or 'Vakil', meaning lawyers in India, used to refer to specialists known for negotiations or bargaining in Muslim India (Calkins 1968–1969; Sharma 1984). The Indian legal system underwent significant changes during the colonial period. In 1773, with the establishment of the Supreme Court in Calcutta, and later with the introduction of formal legal education in India, Sharma (1984, 47) argues that the legal system became 'professional' in nature. But even then, the Indian upper class and castes dominated the legal profession along with the Europeans.

In the late nineteenth century, Cornelia Sorabji became the first Indian women lawyer who went to London to study law. Her life and experience both in England and India is illustrative of the path of early women in the legal field but to a great extent enables us to understand the trajectory of women in law. Comparative studies have considered the lives of first women lawyers around the world to understand various challenges faced by them within the legal profession and how they tried to break away from male exclusivity (Mossman 2006). There are several prominent women who have broken the glass ceiling in the judiciary in India. For example, in 1959 Lily Thomas (1928–2019) was the first Indian woman to complete an LLM and joined the Madras High Court. She then moved to the Supreme Court in 1960 as the first female senior lawyer. In the same year as Lily Thomas became a High Court judge, Justice Ana Chandy became the first woman appointed to the Kerala High Court. The first woman to be elevated and appointed as a judge of the Supreme Court of India was Justice Fatima Beevi. The first woman to achieve the position of chief justice of a High Court was Justice Leila Seth, who presided as chief justice of the Himachal Pradesh High Court.

Colonial and post-colonial India presents a diverse array of social scenarios for women's entry into and involvement in the legal domain. The number of women entering the legal profession during colonial times is unknown. What we do have is the life and writings of Cornelia Sorabji, whose work as a lawyer reveals women's struggles in the social, political and legal arena in colonial India (see Gooptu 2010). Along with the first women lawyers of the world, her life story has found place in international scholarship because of her long connection with the West (Mossman 2006).

During the colonial era, the attitudes of colonial legislatures and the British Parliament differed in their treatment of the judicial appointments of women. For example, as early as 1896, Cornelia Sorabji was given special permission by a British Court to provide legal representation (Mossman 2006, 19). However, Britain was reluctant to permit women's entry to the legal profession more broadly, as was evident when Cornelia was required to take the B.C.L. Examination (of Oxford University) separately from the men sitting the exam (Sorabji, 27–28).[5] Not only that, as Cornelia wrote

> it was June 1892 that I did my B.C.L. Examination. It was not till after the War that women were admitted to degrees. I took my degree of B.C.L., formally, in the Convocation of 1922 – the earliest moment at which I could get back from my work in India to take it
>
> (Sorabji, 30).

While she was in London, Cornelia was warned that as a woman it would not be easy to enter into the legal profession in Bombay (Sorabji 2010). In fact, she was told that male clients would not want to explain their disputes to a woman and that a legal clerk would also object. Later, her prospective job with an English solicitor was opposed by the chief justice of Bombay High Court (Sorabji 2010, 70).

---

[5] On her refusal to do so, a decree was passed by the university vice chancellor allowing Cornelia to be allowed to sit for the B.C.L. Examination (pp. 27–28).

There is insufficient scholarly work on women judges in the High Courts in India, with a few exceptions. George H. Gadbois, Jr (2011) has profiled ninety-three judges. He asks crucial questions related to their socio-economic backgrounds, life experiences and judicial appointments. Following the footsteps of Gadbois, Abhinav Chandrachud (2018) discusses the internal politics of the Supreme Court through interviews and conversations of judges that took place in the 1980s. While these works focus on rivalries, executive influence on the judiciary and the overall politics of the judicial system, gender-based politics within the judiciary was not considered. Both studies also do not include the small number of women judges of the Supreme Court of India.

Some biographical works focus on the struggle of women judges and their contributions to women's rights and liberation. In 1971, Anna Chandy's important autobiographical work named *Atmakatha* was published. Anna Chandy is one of the first-generation Malayalee feminists (Devika 2005) who during her time fought for proportional reservation in government jobs for women and demanded that they be recognised with the status of a depressed community (Devika and Sukumar 2006). Chandy's own writings on equal inheritance rights of Christian women also provided a space for feminist thinking in early twentieth century India which many see in conjunction with cultural pluralism and women's liberation (Damodaran and Visvanathan 1995). In a much later intervention, feminist discourse includes women from the legal professions, along with other women. These movements pointed out the gendered construction of social reforms that were led by men. Women in the legal professions contributed immensely to the legalisation of women's rights by fighting against customary practices prevalent in various communities.

In the 1990s, it was still rare for a woman to serve as judge on a High Court. In the early 1990s, Justice Leila Seth, who presided as chief justice of the Himachal Pradesh High Court, had the opportunity to swear in another women judge. Reflecting on this occasion, she wrote (Seth 2003, 329–330)

> 23 March 1992 was a very special day. Justice Kamlesh Sharma, who was an additional judge of the Himachal Pradesh High Court, was appointed as a permanent judge; I had the honour of giving her the oath of the office – a woman Chief Justice swearing in a woman judge. This had not ever happened in India before... This was quite unusual, considering that out of about four hundred permanent High Court judges in all of the eighteen High Courts at that time, only about ten were women.

This account is one example of the impact that the appointment of a new woman judge to a High Court had at the time. I turn next to analyse the composition of the High Courts in India over time in terms of gender.

An Overview of Women in the High Courts of India

The twenty-five High Courts of India include seventy-five women judges on the bench in comparison to 585 male judges. This means women constitute only 11 per cent of the judges of the High Courts in India. In November 2016, women judges constitute 16 per cent of the total number of judges, with sixty-four women judges against 397 male judges. From 2016 to 2019, there was a decrease in the total representation of women judges in the High Courts. The Supreme Court of India has thirty judges including three women judges,[6] and so far since its inception in 1950 only eight women were elevated as a judge.[7] There have been forty-six chief justices of the Supreme Court of India, yet no woman has ever held that position. The High Courts of Himachal Pradesh, Manipur, Meghalaya, Telangana, Tripura and Uttarakhand do not have women sitting as judges at present. The states of Bombay, Calcutta Delhi, Madras, Punjab and Haryna have the highest number of women judges. Jammu and Kashmir and Madras Courts are currently headed by women chief justices.[8]

Table 9.1 *Composition of the bench of the High Courts by gender*[9]

Gender of Judges	Total Number	%
Male	585	88.63
Female	75	11.36
Total	660	100

The number of women on the bench of the High Courts needs to be considered in light of the growth in the establishment of High Courts over many years. From a historical perspective, under the Indian High Court Acts of 1861, the Calcutta High Court came into existence in 1862,

---

[6] R. Bhanumathi (2014–2020), Indu Malhotra (2018–2021), Indira Banerjee (2018–2022).

[7] Fatima Beevi (1989–1992), Sujata Manohar (1994–1999), Ruma Pal (2000–2006), Gyan Sudha Misra (2010–2014), Ranjana Prakesh Desai (2011–2014), R. Bhanumathi (2014–2020), Indu Malhotra (2018–2021), Indira Banerjee (2018–2022).

[8] Hon'ble Justice Miss Gita Mitta (Jammu and Kashmir), Hon'ble Justice Smt. V. K. Tahilramani (Madras). The percentage of women chief justices is 8 per cent.

[9] Table 9.1 current as of 1 May 2019.

followed in the same year by Madras and Bombay. Allahabad and Karnataka High Courts were established in 1866 and 1884 respectively. From the beginning of the twentieth century up until India's independence in 1947, only three High Courts were established.[10] Immediately after independence, the total number of High Courts grew to eight with the establishment of the High Courts of Punjab (1947), Guwahati (1948), Orissa (1948), Rajasthan (1949) and Kerala (1956).

The next four decades (1960s–1900s) only saw four new High Courts come into existence: Gujarat (1960), Himachal Pradesh (1971), Sikkim (1975) and Delhi (1986). Andhra Pradesh needs special mention. In 1954, Andhra Pradesh formed a new state after separating from the Madras presidency. In 1956, it merged with Hyderabad state and since then the High Court of Andhra commenced with its principle seat at Hyderabad. This was the situation until 2014 when the state of Andhra bifurcated and formed the new states of Andhra Pradesh and Telangana. It was only in 2019 that separate High Courts were founded for the newly formed states.[11] The twenty-first century witnessed major shifts coupled with the formation of some new states in India. A total of eight High Courts were established, namely Chattisgarh (2000), Jharkhand (2000), Uttarakhand (2006), Manipur (2013), Meghalaya (2013), Tripura (2013) and Andhra Pradesh and Telengana (2019). Some states such as Arunachal Pradesh, Mizoram, Nagaland and Goa still do not have their own independent High Courts, despite the fact that the Constitution mentions that there shall be a High Court for each state (Article 214).

This timeline of the High Courts offers an overview of the entry and appointment of women judges. In this context, Table 9.2 demonstrates women's entry and their representation in the upper judiciary since the establishment of various High Courts in India.[12] From 1970 to 2019, there have been ninety-one women appointed to the High Courts in total.

The data show that some of the oldest High Courts have some of the lowest numbers of women judges. The High Courts of Allahabad, Calcutta, Jammu and Kashmir, Karnataka and Orissa, despite being the oldest High Courts, show an extremely low number of women. Delhi High Court has the highest representation of women.

---

[10] Patna High Court (1916), Jammu and Kashmir (1928) and Madhya Pradesh (1936).

[11] The data for the High Court of State of Andhra Pradesh (AP) are based on two timelines, 1954 to 2014 (for the old state of AP, and 2019 onwards (for the states of Andhra and Telangana).

[12] As of 30April 2019.

Table 9.2 *The entry of women judges to the High Courts*[a]

Year of Establishment	High Court	1970–1980	1981–1990	1991–2000	2001–2010	2011–2019	Total
1862	Bombay	1	0	3	4	3	11
1862	Madras[b]	0	1	3	3	2	9
1862	Calcutta	0	0	0	3	1	4
1884	Karnataka	0	1	0	0	2	3
1886	Allahabad	0	0	1	0	2	3
1916	Patna	0	0	0	2	0	2
1928	Jammu and Kashmir	0	0	0	0	0	0
1936	Madhya Pradesh	0	0	1	5	0	6
1947	Punjab and Haryana	0	0	1	2	3	6
1948	Orissa	0	1	0	1	0	2
1948	Guwahati[c]	–	–	–	1	1	3
1949	Rajasthan	1	1	1	1	4	8
1954	Andhra Pradesh	1	0	2	1	0	4
1956	Kerala	1	1	1	1	0	4
1960	Gujarat	0	0	2	1	1	4
1971	Himachal Pradesh	0	1	0	1	0	2
1975	Sikkim	0	0	0	0	0	0

1996	Delhi	1	3	1	7	4	16
2000	Chhattisgarh	0	0	0	0	0	0
2000	Jharkhand	0	0	0	2	0	2
2006	Uttarakhand	0	0	0	1	0	1
2013	Manipur	0	0	0	0	0	0
2013	Meghalaya	0	0	0	1	0	1
2013	Tripura	0	0	0	0	0	0

[a] The timeline does not include the newly formed High Courts of Andhra and Telangana. Judges of these two HCs are listed under current (sitting) judges. See Appendix I for a detailed profile of the former women judges.

[b] The Madras High Court online site does not hold any official record of the former judges. Therefore the number of women entered at various periods is unknown except the nine women among 315 judges whose names were extracted from www.hcmadras.tn.nic.in/formerjudges.pdf.

[c] No record is available of Justice Smt. Meera Sharma to determine the period of her service in the Guwahati High Court.

Table 9.3 *Total number of judges of the High Courts by gender*

Year of Establishment	High Court	Total Number of Judges since Establishment	Number of Women Judges	%
1862	Bombay	405	11	2.71
1862	Calcutta	107	4	3.73
1862	Madras[13]	315	unknown	unknown
1884	Karnataka	125	3	2.4
1886	Allahabad	584	3	0.51
1916	Patna	234	2	0.85
1928	Jammu and Kashmir	70	0	0
1936	Madhya Pradesh	182	6	3.29
1948	Orissa	80	2	2.5
1954	Andhra Pradesh	177	4	2.25
1956	Kerala	56	4	7.1
1947	Punjab and Haryana	212	6	2.83
1948	Guwahati	69	3	4.34
1949	Rajasthan	170	8	4.70
1960	Gujrat	141	4	2.83
1971	Himachal Pradesh	35	2	5.7
1975	Sikkim	11	0	0
1996	Delhi	158	16	10.12
2000	Chhattisgarh	22	0	0
2000	Jharkhand	18	2	11.11
2006	Uttarakhand	19	1	5.26
2013	Manipur	2	0	0
2013	Meghalaya[14]	3	2	66.66
2013	Tripura	2	0	0

Table 9.3 shows the total number of judges that have sat on a High Court and the percentage of women judges since the establishment of that court.

The High Court of Allahabad, with the highest number of judges over time (584), has in fact had the lowest proportion of women judges (0.51 per cent),

[13] The list of 315 former judges wascollected from www.hcmadras.tn.nic.in/formerjudges .pdf, accessed 9 April 2019. I extracted the names of nine female judges from this list and their detailed profiles are listed in Appendix I.

[14] The list does not include judges who presided at the Shillong Bench of Gauhati HC before Meghalaya HC was established in 2013. Those are included in Gauhati High Court.

Table 9.4 *Composition of the bench of the High Courts by gender in 2019*[15]

High Court	Total Number of Sitting Judges	Total Female Sitting Judges	% of Female Judges
Allahabad	108	6	8.69
Andhra Pradesh (2019)	10	3	10.34
Bombay	70	10	14.08
Calcutta	41	7	18.42
Chattisgarh	14	2	14.28
Delhi	35	7	18.91
Guwahati	19	1	5
Gujarat	27	4	14.28
Himachal Pradesh	7	0	0
Jammu and Kashmir	8	1	12.5
Jharkhand	19	1	5
Karnataka	31	3	9.67
Kerala	34	5	13.88
Madhya Pradesh	32	3	9.37
Madras	58	10	17.24
Manipur	3	0	0
Meghalaya	2	0	0
Orissa	14	1	7.14
Patna	30	2	6.66
Punjab and Haryana	51	7	13.72
Rajasthan	25	1	4
Telangana	10	0	0
Sikkim	2	1	50
Tripura	2	0	0
Uttarakhand	8	0	0

followed by the High Court of Patna with just 0.85 per cent women judges. Five High Courts, mostly ones that have recently been established, have not yet had women judges on the bench. The High Courts of Andhra, Bombay, Calcutta, Gujrat, Karnataka, Madhya Pradesh, Punjab and Haryana, and Rajasthan, which had the highest number of judges in total, also had the lowest number of women with an average of 2.85 per cent. In general, women make up less than 3 per cent of the higher judiciary in India.

[15] The data on sitting (current) judges arebased on their presence at various courts on 1 May 2019, accessed at https://doj.gov.in/appointment-of-judges/list-high-court-judges.

Table 9.5 *List of former women chief justices of the High Courts*

High Court	Total Number of Chief Justices since Establishment	Total Women Chief Justices (CJ)	% of Women CJs
Allahabad	43	0	0
Andhra Pradesh	36	0	0
Bombay	45	2	4.44
Calcutta	14	2	14.28
Chattisgarh	12	0	0
Delhi	32	2	6.25
Guwahati	31	0	0
Gujarat	25	0	0
Himachal Pradesh	23	1	4.34
Jammu and Kashmir	30	0	0
Jharkhand	12	2	16
Karnataka	29	0	0
Kerala	49	3	6.12
Madhya Pradesh	23	0	0
Madras	47	2	4.25
Manipur	4	1	25
Meghalaya	5	1	20
Orissa	29	0	0
Patna	39	1	2.56
Punjab and Haryana	62	0	0
Rajasthan	35	0	0
Sikkim	19	0	0
Tripura	3	0	0
Uttarakhand	9	0	0

Overall, these figures show that women are still under-represented in the judiciary in India, although the level of under-representation varies from state to state.

Structural Challenges and Social Hierarchies: A Gendered View of the Judiciary

Aside from the criteria in the Constitution of India, the process of becoming a judge in the higher courts is influenced by social processes. The legal requirements to be a judge of the High Courts as set out in the Constitution suggest that appointments are an objective process.

However, I show that judicial appointments are also conditioned by social context. This is true not only for whether women are appointed as a judge, but also for how women are treated and assessed once they are in office. On being the first woman chief justice of a High Court, Justice Leila Seth writes

> I knew that, being a woman, I would be critically watched and that any mistakes or misjudgments that I made would be highlighted and would reflect on other women who followed. I needed to be conscientious and diligent
>
> (Seth 2003, 320).

Seth's reflections demonstrate her consciousness of the social processes that influenced how she was perceived as a judge. In this section, I consider the influence of various social processes on judicial appointments and career progression. This includes the relevance of family connections to judicial appointment success, the challenges for women to overcome gender obstacles such as experience in legal practice even before they can be appointed as a judge, the lack of diversity within the judiciary and the persistent influence of tradition on the role of women.

Nexus of Family and Legal Institutions

In the 1970s, women from urban areas slowly started entering the legal profession. It became apparent that these women mostly came from a family with a legal background, such as fathers, grandfathers, uncles, brothers or cousins who practice in the High Courts in India.[16] This familial affiliation with the profession resonates with comparative studies that show the importance of male family members to gaining entrance to the profession.

Family and family history remain a factor affecting whether a woman is able to gain entry to the legal profession. Occasionally the stories of former judges, chief justices and senior advocates only briefly mention a few women lawyers who appear before the court. These women lawyers faced challenges because of the strict gender dynamics within the court. The court as a site of work and life experience produced a gendered

---

[16] Leila Seth writes, 'the issue of women judges being appointed to the High Courts had been under discussion for a while. It became even more prominent in 1975, which was Women's International Year' (pp. 251–252).

space, making it difficult for women lawyers to break into the 'old boys club'.

Women who come from a family with connections to the legal profession continue to have an advantage and a means to overcome the challenges with entering the legal profession. This was emphasised by several of my respondents:

> As a female judge, long hours away from commitments like social, family, religious etc. define your position in the judicial authority. Commitments and absence from playing certain roles has to be honoured, accepted and supported. The very understanding of the family as a support system is more available if one comes from or enters into a family being in the same profession. In that case, the struggles need not be in terms of exposure, rather in terms of understanding, acceptance, and expectations. Preparedness and legal socialisation help in dealing with judges
>
> (Respondent A).

Socialisation into the legal profession through family connections is essential for women to enter the legal profession, as it is the only way for women to learn in detail about how the legal profession works and the skills required. In this regard, acquisition of such skills and class privileges can be regarded as 'cultural capital' (Bourdieu 1986). In particular, in the legal profession confidence is a quality required in the court room. Confidence as a quality is gendered and often associated with men rather than with women.

> The confidence it gives you to deal with the judges, the confidence to answer queries put by the judges and even the confidence to tell the judges you are wrong (clearly just because one is a judge does not always necessarily mean they are right) along with the pressure of making a presentation in the open court and making a statement
>
> (Respondent B).

The need for confidence in court affects women's position within the system. This subjective understanding of court behaviour is part of the informal criteria for selecting judges. Opportunity due to family or socio-economic factors and life chances based on certain privileges are often what enables a person to become a legal professional, particularly for women. Further, proficiency in the English language, essential when arguing before the higher courts, is considered an essential requirement. Historically, Indian judges or justices belonged to a privileged background (Chandrachud 2015). This has slowly changed, and today there is a more diverse group of women coming into the legal domain, although the issue of diversity remains critical.

While family with legal connections may be a source of privilege and support for some women, it can also be a site of gender discrimination. Traditional family norms and conservative behaviour cautions women against breaking barriers. 'Breaking into the old boys club means more than just creating opportunity to enter into the legal profession', says a senior advocate (Respondent C).

Customary practices prevented women from fulfilling certain professional requirements. For instance, many women were not allowed by their families to practice law as they were required to wear white (most of them wore a *saree* during that time). In various parts of India, mostly among Hindus, as a part of customary practice and to observe mourning, widows are required to wear white clothes. Such dress codes restrict unmarried or married women from the legal profession. This practice also affects women in other professions such as *nursing*.

This symbolic discrimination and violation of women's aspirations has reduced women's roles in public. Women who wore odd colours were looked down upon by their peers. For the longest time, feminists have been fighting against gender stereotyping that serve to uphold patriarchal values. The elimination of women in the first phase of their professional career further contributes to the under-representation and unequal opportunities of women in the legal field. The notion of legal socialisation explains the nurturing of professional aspirations, although this is separate from domestic socialisation, which is guided by complex value systems. Women who do enter the legal profession often feel the cultural gap allied with their transition from family to the professional world. Many women find it challenging because legal spaces embody normative ideas of masculinity or heterosexuality.

Gender disparity within the judicial system must be contextualised, keeping in mind the rural–urban divide. The High Courts are located in the urban centres of the cities. Women in the High Court are mostly selected from urban settings, mostly practising lawyers or advocates of High Courts. Women practising in the district courts rarely make their ways to be judges in the High Courts. This disparity drawn between judicial service and practitioners is very much evident in the process of judicial appointments. It is often claimed that preference for appointment to the High Court is mostly given to the people at the Bar, rather than to those in the judicial service. This has been a major disparity in judicial appointments in general. At present only twenty-seven women judges of various High Courts were recruited from the judicial service, while the rest came from the Bar.

It has been observed that judicial appointments are primarily determined by the government of the day and so appointments are affected by
politics (Raksht 2004, 2960). Along with executive influence, Raksht also
identifies the communal and regional considerations in the decision-
making process in appointing judges in India. Justice Leila Seth (2003)
in her autobiography explains the political and ideological influence in
decisions of appointing judges in the late 1980s when there were only a
handful of women judges in the High Courts. Lobbying, networks and
most importantly the political negotiations between governments and the
judiciary further complicate judicial independence. Writing about her
contemporary, Justice Fatima Beevi, Seth comments on the political
process of selecting candidates:

> A couple of Supreme Court judges told me that she had lobbied for the
> position on the grounds that she would be the first Muslim woman in the
> world to be a judge of a Supreme Court, and that there was at the time no
> Muslim judge in the Supreme Court in India...Many people knew that
> her brother-in-law was a prominent local politician and believed that the
> Congress government had been assured that they would get the Kerala
> Muslim votes in the forthcoming elections if she were made a judge
>
> (Seth 2003, 317).

This was also looked upon as breaking the norms of merit required to be
a judge in India. This in some ways also reveals professional rivalries of
the time. Explaining her disappointment, Seth writes

> when her appointment was actually announced and she was sworn in on 6
> October, I felt terribly upset, both for the system and for myself. It showed
> that lobbying worked. It showed that politics worked. It showed that the
> misuse of religion worked. Above all, it showed that every decent conven-
> tion could be broken and that merit was no consideration
>
> (Seth 2003,318).

This shows that appointments may be less to do with gender and more
related to other factors.

The Natural Filtration of Women into the Judiciary

There remains a much more subtle process of the exclusion and elimination of women in the judiciary. The women respondents in my study
point out additional requirements, in addition to their professional
degree and the license to practise, that are necessary to be appointed as
a judge. The judiciary as an institution has developed informal conditions

for fulfilling judicial rules and regulations. For instance, a lawyer can practise at various tribunals, the High Courts, the Magistrate Courts and the Railway Courts. To be successful and experienced in the field of law requires women lawyers to be able to attract potential litigants, which requires social connections and networking. According to one of my respondents, 'As merit is still considered the most important factor for a lawyer to be elevated as a judge, it requires diligence, powerful connections to establish such a career' (Respondent G). The notion of merit is debated and critiqued by many women because of its social implications. In this profession, the visibility of women often leads to questions about the 'merit' of their appointment. One of my respondents observed that 'Merit cannot be just a personal trait; rather it needs complex attributes, such as intelligence to networking skills that may seem to transpire into your persona.'

The appointment of women can depend on the client–lawyer relationship. However, within the legal professional, women are perceived to be the lesser gender. Sometimes clients show a preference for male lawyers. There is an inherent reluctance for clients to reach out to women lawyers or advocates. This tendency to treat female professionals as less capable than their male counterparts needs sociological explanation and therefore requires contextualisation within the realm of culture and family. The subordinate nature attributed to women, which restricts their standing in society, means that women lawyers may have fewer clients than male lawyers. Therefore, women lawyers find it harder to gain work experience and build fewer networks. This leads to reduced appearances before various magistrates and judges, which is required to enhance their visibility if they wish to apply to become a judge. The visibility and preparedness of a lawyer in presenting their cases is considered an important criteria and skill. Therefore, beginning with their time working as a lawyer, there is a filtration process that leads to the reduction in the number of women who are appointed as judges.

Similarly, various social roles assigned to women determine the possibility of becoming a judge. The prospects of a lawyer becoming a judge are based on the amount of time spent with clients, time on case law research and time preparing papers to present before the court. According to one judge:

> Family and culture are considered as the most important factors in shaping the structure within which various roles as legal professionals can be carried on. Do I have the time to work uninterruptedly and not

[be] distracted by other responsibilities? Do I have some sort of support
system within the family when it comes to sharing roles and responsibilities with other members of the family?

(Respondent A).

These questions are more frequently posed by women lawyers and
advocates than men. Women in higher positions acknowledge the competing role performances within family, such as the roles of daughter,
wife, sister, daughter-in-law and mother. Women within the profession
express a similar conundrum of differential gender norms perpetuated
within the domestic sphere. Among their social roles, motherhood stands
out as a crucial one for women. As explained by another respondent:

What happens if there is a sick child at home? The lady who happens to
be an advocate has to either sacrifice her professional role or being a
mother. A woman is only in a position to sacrifice her role as a mother
only if there be [sic] a support system. How much of that support
system looks upon the role of the mother is as important as the professional part of it

(Respondent E).

Adding to such social conundrums, women have the desire to fulfil their
responsibilities to their professional career and the home. Gender roles
can be redefined only if the support system for women gives equal weight
to both professional and personal life. Family responsibilities may place
professional responsibilities at risk.

These challenges may decline as more women enter the profession.
Former Acting Chief Justice of Kolkata High Court, Hon'ble Smt. Justice
Nishita Mhatre opines that without any doubt the justice system would
be different if there are more women judges. Sharing her own experience,
Justice Mhatre says that judgments, judges and therefore, the justice
system, function based on cultural attributes and it is very apparent both
in the poor treatment of women litigants and women legal professionals.
Citing many instances of gendered behaviour, she recalls hearing sexist
and snide remarks about female colleagues. The private life of female
colleagues often becomes a matter of public discussion and Justice
Mhatre suggests that this has direct impact on decision-making.

During the process of appointment, according to her, 'women's personal life is torn into shreds before consideration for elevation' to the
court as a judge. Cultural morality thus constructs a masculine idea of the
judicial system and that is because of the inherent tendency to exert
gender-based norms. Similarly, reflecting on gendered behaviour of the

judicial system, Justice Ruma Pal points out how women litigants are stereotyped within the courts. In her opinion, there are advantages of having women on the bench. But often there is a concern that men do not see women as individuals. Men are still influenced by the stereotype of a women in need of protection.[17]

Historically, it took a long time to reform the laws pertaining to women, despite the fact that constitutional rights were given equally to both men and women. Up until now, for instance, what constitutes marital rape is a matter of contestation. Justice Ruma Pal observes that the idea of consent within marriage needs more clarity because 'a rape remains a rape if the wife says "No"'[18]. The rights of woman should only correspond with her individual constitutional rights, which suggests the need for the democratisation of gender relations. The ongoing movement for women's rights therefore questions both the patriarchal family structure and its corresponding relations with law.

In terms of gender, the impartiality and neutrality of the judiciary is a myth. Representing a masculine culture, the judiciary produces a hegemonic version of heterosexual femininity. The use of overt sexist language is commonly witnessed in court. One lady judge recalls

> When I was the acting Chief Justice, I was sending names of advocates to the Supreme Court for elevation from bar to the bench. My two male colleagues in the collegiums were against elevation of a particular woman advocate. The chief reasons cited by them were her inability to listen, lack of humility and aggressive disposition, for which she was considered a cantankerous woman. With similar qualities, a man would be regarded as a good and assertive lawyer who represents his clients very well and can persuade the judges. As a lawyer she had appeared several times before me in the court. Considering her eligibility, I persistently questioned the reasons cited against her, and eventually she was elevated as a judge
>
> (Respondent F).

The structure of the judicial system reflects patriarchal gendered norms, as viewed by both male and female legal professionals. However, women judges' point out the 'double disadvantage' of being part of the judicial system. Most of the time collegiums[19] are dominated by men. Even

---

[17] This is based on a lecture entitled 'Gender Justice and Constitutional Law' given by Justice Ruma Pal at the Indian Institute of Technology Bombay, 18 September 2018.

[18] 'Gender Justice and Constitutional Law' given by Justice Ruma Pal at the Indian Institute of Technology Bombay, 18 September 2018.

[19] A collegium is an extrajudicial authority invented by Justice J. S. Verma in October 1998.

regular interaction between the lower and upper judiciary is affected by sexual politics. As has been noted by one respondent, 'Merely because you become a judge, you don't forget about your biases' (Respondent F). Justice Felix Frankfurter of the United States Supreme Court has noted that a person 'brings his whole experience, his training, his outlook, his social, intellectual and moral environment with him when he takes a seat on the supreme bench' (Elman 1956, 40–41). This is also true in India. Within the judicial structure, masculine politics excludes women and thereby women become the 'other' within the judicial authority (Berns and Baron 1994).

Diversity in the Judiciary

Legal professionals, especially judges, are often largely homogeneous groups. Critical scholarship reveals that the judiciary as an institution needs to be viewed atthe intersections of class, race, ethnicity, religion and gender to unmask the ways that the judiciary preserves existing social hierarchies and power relations. Some scholars place emphasis on policies to reform judicial appointments as an essential means to bring diversity in the judicial system in general and most importantly to see its impact on judicial decisions and judging. Despite this, little has changed in the composition on the bench. Baroness Hale (2006) argues that a diverse judiciary is an indispensable requirement of any democracy.

For example, in the Indian context, Dalits form only 3 per cent of judges on the Higher Courts. Measures to enhance diversity are required to address this under-representation and discrimination against the lower castes, such as calls for reservations in the higher judiciary (Kumar 2016).[20] Like other professions, there had been a growing demand for reservations in the legal professions as well. Some of the states like Bihar, Andhra Pradesh and Tamil Nadu opted for reservations for Scheduled Castes, Scheduled Tribes, Other Backward Classes, the disabled and women. This was implemented in the lower judiciary but not in the High Courts and the Supreme Court of India. Along with reservations for various socially backwards and discriminated castes, reservation for women in the lower judiciary is part of these demands

---

[20] See, *The Wire*, https://thewire.in/law/annual-diversity-statistics-judiciary. See, Special Report (in English) on Reservation in Judiciary submitted to the president of India December 2013, laid in Parliament on 11.12.2014.

for diversity. For example, it was only recently that the state of Bihar introduced a 35 per cent reservation for women in the lower judiciary.[21] Before that in 1996, Andhra Pradesh applied reservation rules for women, along with all backwards castes.[22] These are examples of local measures to diversify the judiciary and include more women.

The Contemporary Shift in Culture

The contemporary shift in culture emphasises the individuality of women and their constitutional rights as citizens or persons of equal importance rather than setting them against men. At present, various lawmakers argue for eradicating stereotypes or discrimination based on such stereotypes. Women judges, lawyers, advocates and councillors, as part of movements against gender-biased laws and regulations, are focused on advocating for change within the legal domain as well as in the functioning of the judiciary.

For example, Mahila Courts in India are specialised courts for women fighting various legal cases.[23] Mahila Courts are headed by a woman judge and deal exclusively with cases pertaining to offences against women. In 1987, the first court for women was established in Andhra Pradesh and later many were formed in Delhi. In addition, the National Commission for Women has provided specific recommendations concerning family and women's disputes in the Family Courts.[24]

Women judges have often prioritised matters of marital rape, domestic violence, property rights, divorce and maintenance. It is only when women hold positions as a judge that they can challenge the structural

---

[21] According to the Bihar Reservation of Vacancies in post and Services (for Scheduled Caste, Scheduled Tribe and other Backward Classes) Act, 1991 as amended from time to time. See, the Bihar Superior Judicial Services (Amendments) Rules, 2016.

[22] Section 7: 'Reservation: Rules 22 and 22 A of the Andhra Pradesh State and Subordinate Service Rules, 1996 in so far as they relate to Scheduled Castes, Scheduled Tribes, Backward Classes, Women and one percent for Physically Handicapped persons shall apply to appointments to be made by direct recruitment.'

[23] Granting of maintenance under section 125 of Criminal Procedure Code, cases under sections 354 and 509 of Indian Penal Code (assault and criminal force with intent to outrage modesty, by exhibiting objects and gestures) are looked after under these courts. Similarly, cases of kidnapping under Section 363 I.P.C., procuring minor girls for the purpose of prostitution, rape under Section: 376 I.P.C. and cruelty by husband or in-laws Section 498-A I.P.C. are dealt at Session Level Courts. See, Vatuk's (2013) study on Mahila Courts as an alternative dispute resolution body in India.

[24] See Family Courts – (Report on Working of Family Courts and Model Family Courts), National Commission for Women.

discriminations within the courts. Women judges have been able to provide landmark judgments on gender justice and redefine laws. Sujata Mahohar was part of the landmark Vishaka judgment which dealt with sexual harassment of women in the workplace.[25] Justice Ruma Pal offered a crucial and critical analysis of 'what constitutes mental cruelty in a marriage' and 'cruelty as a ground for divorce'.[26] In the 2017 judgment on the Nirbhaya Rape case (Delhi), an incident that sparked nationwide protest, Justice R. Bhanumati writes,

> crimes against women not only affects women's self-esteem and dignity but also degrades the pace of societal development. I hope that this gruesome incident in the capital and death of this young woman will be an eye-opener for a mass movement 'to end violence against women' and 'respect for women and her dignity' and sensitizing public at large on gender justice. Every individual, irrespective of his/her gender must be willing to assume the responsibility in fight for gender justice and also awaken public opinion on gender justice. The public at large, in particular men, are to be sensitized on gender justice. The battle for gender justice can be won only with strict implementation of legislative provisions, sensitization of public, taking other pro-active steps at all levels for combating violence against women and ensuring widespread attitudinal changes and comprehensive change in the existing mind set.[27]

These issues of gender and judging were raised in a contemporary judgment on the entry of women to the Sabarimala Temple in Kerala. Justice Indu Melhotra, the lone female judge in the five-member bench in the Supreme Court of India gave a dissenting judgment, while the majority verdict allowed women to enter. Melhotra writes, 'in a secular polity, issues which are matters of deep religious faith and sentiment must not ordinarily be interfered with by Courts'.[28] This case sparked significant public debate. Singh and Roy (2018) suggest that

---

[25] See, *Vishaka& ORS. v. State of Rajasthan & ORS*. Date of Judgment: 13/08/1997. The Bench was composed of Justice J. S. Verma (CJI), Sujata V. Manohar and B. N. Kirpal.

[26] 'Cruelty can be physical or mental. Cruelty which is a ground for dissolution of marriage may be defined as willful and unjustifiable conduct of such character as to cause danger to life, limb or health, bodily or mental, or as to give rise to a reasonable apprehension of such a danger. The question of mental cruelty has to be considered in the light of the norms of marital ties of the particular society to which the parties belong, their social values, status, environment in which they live.' See, *A. Jayachandra v.Aneel Kaur* on 2 December 2004, Supreme Court of India. The bench was composed of Ruma Pal, Arijit Pasayat and C. K. Thakker.

[27] See judgment, *Mukesh & Anr. v. State for NCT of Delhi & Ors*, p. 429.

[28] See judgment by Justice Indu Malhotra, *Indian Young Lawyers Association & Ors. v. State of Kerala & Ors*, p. 22.

Justice Malhotra's understanding of the 'essentiality' of religious practices in Ayyappa community is flawed, because it is not formulated in isolation, but is influenced by patriarchal structures which establish an ideological hegemony within the religious group. The rationality of any religion or a particular ritual is mostly determined and propagated by the male leaders and members in the group. In order to perpetuate their domination, they tend to devise customs, often by the irresponsible interpretation of traditional texts, which consequently results in the subordination of women.

Their view is common amongst groups seeking to enhance gender justice and reduce discrimination for women in India.

Conclusion

The representation and position of women in the High Courts and the Supreme Court of India remains extremely low, raising questions about the discriminatory nature of these institutions. This chapter argues that the idea of an objective judgment by a judge is predetermined by a gendered interpretation that is biased against women and is deeply rooted in a patriarchal system.

Since independence, only a limited number of women have held the position of judge in India. Feminists have regularly questioned the judiciary in terms of its role in sexual discrimination and the need for the protection of women's rights. Within the judicial structure, as I show from various narratives, sexual politics and hierarchical power remain a barrier to entry to and progression in the profession.

For the judiciary to function in an unbiased manner, there is a need for a cultural shift in subjectivity that would enable lawmakers to see beyond the cultural realm. Women judges, lawyers or advocates are also capable of offering an objective outlook towards the laws, litigants and citizens in general, or at least they bring to the bench a perspective that is not dominated by patriarchal attitudes. In the present context, it is essential to continue the campaigns for the protection of constitutional rights, and to support an approach to legal interpretation that is unbiased by gender norms. One significant contemporary step forward has been the appointment of the first transgender judge of Lok Adalat, alternative dispute resolution mechanisms and the first transgender registered lawyer at Bar Council of Tamil Nadu. Equal gender representation and equal opportunity for women in the judiciary remain a work in progress.

Appendix 1:

List of Names of Former Women Judges since Establishment (30 April 2019)

Allahabad
(1) Hon'ble Ms. Shobha Dikshit (27/11/1991 – 24/03/1998)
(2) Hon'ble Dr. Justice Vijay Laxmi (07/04/2016 – 30/06/2017)
(3) Hon'ble Ms. Ghandikota Sri Devi (2/11/2018 – 14/05/2019)

Andhra
(1) Smt. Justice K. Amareswari (1977 – 1990)
(2) Ms. Justice O. R. Maruthi (1992 – 1999)
(3) Smt. Justice T. Meena Kumari (1998 – 2010)
(4) Ms. Justice Rohini (2001 – 2014)

Bombay
(1) Justice Sujata V. Manohar (1978)
(2) Mrs. R.K. Baam (1994 – 2202)
(3) Mrs. Dr. P.D. Upasani (1996 – 2002)
(4) Smt. Ranjana Prakash Desai (1996 – 2011)
(5) Nishita Mhatre (2001 – 2017)
(6) Smt. R.S. Dalvi (2005 – 2015)
(7) R. P. Sondurbaldota (2008 – 2017)
(8) Smt. Vasanti A. naik (2015 – 2018)
(9) Smt. V.K. Tahilramani (2001 – 2018)
(10) Smt. Sangitrao S. Patil (2016 – 2018)
(11) Dr. (Mrs.) shalini Shashank Phansalikar (2015 – 2019)

Calcutta High Court
(1) Justice Shukla Kabir Singha (2010 – 2013)
(2) Justice Anindita Roy Saraswati (2012 – 2013)
(3) Justice Indira Banerjee (2002 – 2016)
(4) Justice Nandira Patherya (2006 – 2018)

Delhi High Court
(1) Justice Leila Seth (1978 – 1991)
(2) Justice Smt. Sunanda Bhandare (1984 – retirement not known)
(3) Justice Mrs. Santosh Duggal (1988 – 1993)
(4) Justice Usha Mehra (1990 – 2003)

(5) Justice Sharda Aggarwal (2000 – 2002)
(6) Justice Gita Mittal (2004 – 2006)
(7) Justice Manju Goel (2004 – 2007)
(8) Justice Aruna Suresh (2006 – 2010)
(9) Justice Rekha Sharma (2006 – 2011)
(10) Justice Reva Khetrapal (2006 – 2014)
(11) Justice Veena Birbal (2007 – 2014)
(12) Justice Indermeet Kaur (2009 – 2018)
(13) Justice Indira Banerjee (2016 – 2017)
(14) Justice Sunita Gupta (2013 – 2016)
(15) Justice Pratibha Rani (2011 –2018)
(16) Justcie Deepa Sharma (2013 – 2018)

Guwahati
(1) Justice Meera Sharma
(2) Justice Anima Hazarika (01/01/2005 – 01/05/2006)
(3) Justice Indira Shah (02/03/2012 – 08/06/2016)

Gujarat
(1) Hon'be Miss Justice Sugnya Kamalashanker Bhatt (1994 – 1995)
(2) Hon'ble Miss Justice Rekha Maharlal Doshit (1995 – 1997)
(3) Hon'ble Ms. Justice Bela Mandhurya Trivedi (19/02/2011 – 27/06/2011)
(4) Hon'be Smt. Justice Abhilasha Kumari (2006 – 2018)

Himachal Pradesh
(1) Justice Kamlesh Sharma (25/06/1990 – 31/08/2003)
(2) Justice Abhilasha Kumari (02/12/2005 – 04/01/2006)

Jharkhand
(1) Hon'ble Mrs. Justice Jaya Roy (30/07/2008 – 07/08/2013)
(2) Hon'ble Mrs. Justice Poonam Srivastava (28/10/2010 – 25/04/2012)

Karnataka
(1) Manjula Chellur (20/02/2000 – 25/09/2012)
(2) Justice B.S. Indrakala (24/02/2012 – 18/11/2013)
(3) Justice Mrs. Rathnakala (24/10/2013 – 04/03/2016)

Kerala
(1) Smt. Justice Anna Chandy (09/02/1956 – 05/04/1967
(2) Kumari Justice P. Janaki Amma (30/05/1974 – 22/12/1983)
(3) Kumari Justcie M. Fatima Beevi (04/08/1983 – 30/04/1989)
(4) Mrs. Justice K.K. Usha (25/02/1991)

Madhya Pradesh
(1) Justice Smt. Sarojini Saxena (27/09/1994 – 28/09/1994)
(2) Justice Smt. Manjusha Namjoshi (18/10/2005 – 21/08/2009)
(3) Justice Smt. Sushma Shrivastava (15/05/2006 – 12/11/2011)

(4) Justice Smt. Indrani Datta (01/07/2008 – 16/11/2011)
(5) Justice R. Mala (2009 –2017
(6) Justice Smt. Vimla Jain (13/09/2010 – 11/06/2014)

Madras
(1) Mrs. Padmini Jesudurai (1986 – 1992)
(2) Justice Smt. Kanta Kumari (15/06/1992 – 14/11/1992)
(3) Toom Meenakumari (1998 – 2001)
(4) Prabha Sridevan (2000 – 2010)
(5) R. Bhanumathi (2003 – 2013)
(6) Chitra Venkataraman (2005 – 2014)
(7) Aruna Jagadeesan (2009 – 2015)
(8) Smt. S. Vimala (2013 – 2019)
(9) Justice Smt. Indira Banerjee (05/04/2017 – 06/08/2018)

Meghalaya
(1) Hon'ble Mrs. Justice Anima Hazaraika (01/01/2005 – 01/05/2006)

Orissa
(1) Justice Smt. Amiya Kumari Padhi (18/04/1988 – 14/09/1995)
(2) Justice Smt. Aruna Suresh (28/10/2010 – 18/02/2012)

Patna
(1) Justice Rekha Kumari (24/01/2005 – 08/07/2008)
(2) Justice T. Meena Kumari (2010

Punjab and Haryana
(1) Hon'ble Mrs. Justice Bakshish Kaur (14/05/1999 – 06/07/2002)
(2) Justice Nirmal Yadav (05/11/2004 – 11/02/2010)
(3) Justice Mrs. Justice Sabina (12/03/2008 – 10/04/2016)
(4) Justice Anita Chaudhry (20/06/2013 – 30/12/2018)
(5) Justice Mrs. Raj Rahul Garg (25/09/2014 – 04/07/2016)
(6) Mrs. Justice Sneh Prashar (25/09/2014 – 20/07/2017)

Rajasthan
(1) Justice Kumari Kanta Bhatnagar (26/09/1978)
(2) Justice Mrs. Mohini Kapoor (13/07/1985 – 17/11/1995)
(3) Justice Mrs. G.S. Mishra (21/04/94 – 12/07/2008)
(4) Justice Mrs. Meena V. Gomber (29/09/2009 – 30/07/2013)
(5) Justice Mrs. Nisha Gupta (28/04/2011 – 12/09/2015)
(6) Justice Ms. Bela Trivedi (17/02/2011 – 08/02/2016
(7) Justice Ms. Jaishree Thakur (05/01/2015 – 05/10/2016)
(8) Justice Kumari Nirmaljit Kaur (09/07/2012 – 20/11/2018)

Uttarakhand High Court (2006)
(1) Hon'ble Mrs. Justice Nirmal Yadav (11/02/2010 – 03/03/2011)

References

Agnes, Flavia. 1999. *Law and Gender Inequality: The Politics of Women's Rights in India*. New Delhi: Oxford University Press.

Ballakrishnen, Swethaa. 2013. 'Why Is Gender a Form of Diversity: Rising Advantages for Women in Global Indian Law Firms'. *Indiana Journal of Global Legal Studies*, Vol. 20, Issue 2, pp. 1261–1289.

Berns, Sandra S. and Paula Baron. 1994. 'Bloody Bones: A Legal Ghost Story and Entertainment in Two Voices to Speak as a Judge'. *Australian Feminist Law Journal*, Vol. 2, Issue 1, pp. 125–149.

Bourdieu, P. 1986. The Forms of Capital. In J. Richardson (ed.) *Handbook of Theory and Research for Sociology of Education*. New York: Greenwood. pp. 241–258.

Calkins, P. B. 1968-1969. 'A Note on Lawyers in Muslim India'. *Law and Society Review*, Vol. 3, Issues 2/3, pp. 403–406.

Chanda, Sangita. 2014. *Women and Legal Profession: In Reference to Indian Context*. New Delhi: Satyam Law International.

Chandrachud, Abhinav. 2015. *An Independent, Colonial Judiciary: A History of the Bombay High Court During the British Raj, 1862-1947*. New Delhi: Oxford University Press.

2018. *Supreme Whispers: Conversations with Judges of the Supreme Court of India, 1980-1989*. Gurgaon: Penguin Books India.

Chandrashekaran, Sumathi, Diksha Sanyal, Shreya Tripathy andTarika Jain. 2020. 'Breaking through the Old Boys' Club: The Rise of Women in the Lower Judiciary'. *Economic and Political Weekly*, Vol. LV, Issue 4, pp. 33–40.

Damodaran, A. K. and Susan Visvanathan. 1995. 'Cultural Pluralism'. *India International Centre Quarterly*, Vol. 22, Issues 2/3, pp. 1–15.

Devika, J. 2005. *Her-Self: Gender and Early Writings of Malayalee Women*. New Delhi: Popular Prakashan.

Devika, J. and Mini Sukumar. 2006. 'Making Space for Feminist Social Critique in Contemporary Kerala'. *Economic and Political Weekly*, Vol. 41, Issue 42, pp. 4469–4475.

Elman, Philip, ed. 1956. *Of Law and Men: Papers and Addresses of Felix Frankfurter, 1939-1956*. New York: Harcourt Brace.

Gadbois, George Harold. 2011. *Judges of the Supreme Court of India: 1950-1989*. New Delhi: Oxford University Press.

Gandhi, J. S.1987. *AtukV*. New Delhi: Gian Publishing House.

(ed.) 1994. *Professions, Law and Social Change*. New Delhi: Har –Anand Publications.

Gosh, Arijeet, Diksha Sanyal, Nitika Khaitan and Sandeep Reddy. 2018. 'Tilting the Scale: Gender Imbalance in the Lower Judiciary'. New Delhi: Vidhi Centre for Legal Policy.

Gooptu, Suparna. 2010. *Cornelia Sorabji: India's Pioneer Woman Lawyer: A Biography.* New Delhi: Oxford University Press.

Hacker, Sally. 1989. *Pleasure, Power, and Technology.* Boston: Unwin Hyman.

Hale, Baroness. 2006. *The Appointment and Removal of Judges: Independence and Diversity.* International Association of Women Judges Conference 8th Biennial, 3–7 May 2006, Sydney.

Kirkup, Gill and Laurie Smith Keller, eds.1992. *Inventing Women: Science, Technology and Gender.* Cambridge: Polity.

Kumar, Alok Prasanna. 2016. 'Absence of Diversity in the Higher Judiciary'. *Economic and Political Weekly,* Vol. 51, Issue 8, pp. 10–11.

Malinowski, Bronislaw. 1922. *Argonauts of the Western Pacific: An Account of Native Enterprise and Adventure in the Archipelagoes of Melanessian New Guinea.* London: Routledge and Kegan & Paul.

McDowell, Linda. 1997. *Capital Culture: Gender at Work in the City.* Oxford: Blackwell.

Mitchell, J. Clyde, ed. 1969. *Social Networks in Urban Situations.* Manchester: Manchester University Press.

Mossman, Mary Jane. 2006. *The First Women Lawyers: A Comparative Study of Gender Law and the Legal Professions.* Oxford: Hart Publishing.

Seth, Leila. 2003. *On Balance.* New Delhi: Penguin India.

Oommen, T. K. 1986. 'The Legal Profession in Independent India: A Sociological Overview'. *Indian Bar Review,* Vol. 13, Issues 3/4, p. 377.

Raksht, Nirmalendu B. 2004. 'Judicial Appointments'. *Economic and Political Weekly,* Vol. 39, Issue 27, pp. 2959–2961.

Sharma, K. L. 1984. *Sociology of Law and Legal Profession* (A Study of Relation between Lawyers and Their Clients). Jaipur: Rawat Publications.

Sharma, S. L. 2010. 'Status of Research on Legal Profession in India'. In S. K. Verma and M. Afzal Wani (eds.), *Legal Research and Methodology* (2nd edition). New Delhi: Indian Law Institute, pp. 184–195.

Singh, Prakhar and Pragya Roy. 2018. 'Questioning the Dissenting Voice in the Sabarimala Verdict'. *Economic and Political Weekly,* Vol. 53, Issue 44.

Singh, Yogendra. 1978. 'Legal System, Legitimation and Social Change'. In *Essays on Modernization in India.* Delhi: Manohar Book Service, pp. 137–157.

Smart, Carol. 1989. *Feminism and Power of Law.* London: Routledge.

Sorabji, Cornelia. 1934. *India Calling: The Memories of Cornelia Sorabji.* London: Nisbet, reprint. Oxford University Press, Delhi, 2001, Trent editions, Nottingham 2004.

Sorabji, Richard. 2010. *Opening Door: The Untold Stories of Cornelia Sorabji, Reformer, Lawyer and Champion of Women's Right in India.* London: I. B. Tauris & Co. Ltd.

Vatuk, Sylvia. 2013. 'The "Women's Court" in India: An Alternative Dispute Resolution Body for Women in Distress'. *The Journal of Legal Pluralism and Unofficial Law,* Vol. 45, Issue 1, pp. 76–103.

10

Concluding Remarks

ULRIKE SCHULTZ

The chapters in this volume on the feminisation of the judiciary in the Asia Pacific provide a rich picture of the situation for women judges in the Pacific Islands, Sri Lanka, Thailand, Indonesia, Nepal, India, the Philippines and Malaysia. This research is significant and empirically grounded. There has been little international comparative work on these countries to date, and the contributions offer in-depth accounts of women judges in light of the specific political and judicial systems in the respective countries. This edited volume by Melissa Crouch adds new empirical insights to the flourishing work on gender issues in judging all around the world.

Global Work on Gender and Judging

In the past fifteen years, mainly feminist authors have increasingly focused on gender and judging, dealing with issues of women and gender in the legal profession: lawyers, prosecutors, notaries and judges. The topic was whether women could get into socially – and economically – important positions in adequate numbers to give them an equal share of power, financial success and influence, and what to do if this was not yet the case. In 2006, an international research collaborative started its work. Ever since, at every international socio-legal meeting, sessions on gender and judging have been organised. Initially socio-legal scholars, jurists and sociologists contributed, then as in this collection, scholars from cultural studies joined in, opening the door to scholars from other disciplines and other countries. *Gender and Judging*, the first edited book dealing with nineteen countries, was edited by Ulrike Schultz and Gisela Shaw in 2013; others followed on women in the judiciary in sub-Saharan countries (Bauer, Dawuni 2015): *Women Judges in the Muslim World* (Lindbekk, Sonnefeld 2017) and *Gender and Judging in the Middle East and Africa*

(Lindbekk, Maktabi 2021).[1] There is little work on East Asia and the Pacific to date.

It is difficult to find colleagues from countries around the world, particularly the Global South, who could contribute. This partly explains why the first volumes primarily had authors from the Global North. Crouch has assembled an impressive group of scholars to explore jurisdictions that up until now have received little attention. This is a reflection of the fact that in the past two decades, not only has women's share in the legal academy grown (Schultz 2021a) as the number of women studying law has increased, but also the participation of women academics in conferences of all parts of the world, including scholars from the Global South, has gone up.[2] With the use of videoconferences during the Covid-19 pandemic, as bad as it is, the worldwide exchange on the subject has intensified.[3]

The Importance of and Interest in Gender and Judging

I first want to address why it is important to deal with this topic of gender and judging, and then explain why the topic has generated such intensive interest globally. The topic of gender and judging is highly complex and diverse and does not lend itself to monocausal explanations.[4] Each of the contributions helps feminist and sociological theory building by adding new knowledge of the situation of women in the judiciary, of women in higher positions and decision-making in general, and women's rights. Although we have a global women's movement and although there are global factors influencing women's professional success, the development

---

[1] In addition, numerous national studies, almost uncountable articles and monographs on women in the judiciary in many countries of the world have been published; biographies and autobiographies of eminent female judges and films have been produced (Schultz 2021a). Women also appear more frequently as judges in popular culture, for example in TV series.

[2] A current research project (2016–2021) deals with 'women on the bench in five fragile states', giving details on Afghanistan, Haiti, Guatemala, Angela und Uganda. www.cmi.no/projects/2122-women-on-the-bench

[3] A new project on gender in customary and indigenous law and proceedings has benefitted from it and deals, amongst other things, with women in judging in traditional courts.

[4] Chapters on women and judging have also been included in the collection *Women in the World's Legal Professions* (Schultz and Shaw 2003) and in special issues of the *International Journal of the Legal Profession* on *Women in the Judiciary* (Schultz and Shaw 2008/2012), *Gender and Judicial Education* (Dawson, Schultz and Shaw 2014) and *Women and Judicial Appointment* (Mesengu and Schultz 2020).

in each country has to be seen and evaluated in the context of the judicial system, the political regime, culture, religion, the economic situation, ethnicity, colonial influence and the strong historical roots on which the systems are based (as chapters in this volume attest, for example Chapter 6). This makes this work both rewarding as well as demanding.

Interest in this topic remains high because judges in most countries are in high, (ideally) independent, positions with considerable influence and power. In democracies, the judiciary is one of the three pillars of the state, which guarantees the balance of powers and the application of and adherence to the rule of law. Even in autocratic societies the judiciary is vested at least with symbolic power to defend the law. The question of whether the influx of women is changing the judiciary is therefore of great importance and almost explosive power.

Comparing Structural Differences and Gender Effects

The divide between civil and common law countries still plays a role because of the difference in the structure of the judiciary between these two systems (see Chapter 1). Civil law countries have career systems where judges start at an early age after legal education and are hired based on their examination results. In common law countries, most of which have the split between solicitors and barristers, judges are nominated from experienced practitioners and are appointed for their perceived professional success and qualification in their professional work. Therefore, the feminisation of the judiciary in civil law countries often started earlier when the first waves of women were qualified and knocked at the door of legal institutions.

Some countries have an interesting mixture of systems, meaning that each country had and has its own trajectory of development in terms of the entrance of women judges. Also socialism and communism have left traces as shown in chapters in this volume and also reports on Eastern Europe. The programme of socialism and communism deprives higher occupations, including the legal and judicial functions, of their special importance, which devalues these professions and leads to a loss in income and prestige. This has facilitated women's access to the judiciary, as the positions become less desirable for male competitors.[5]

---

[5] Worldwide a decline in status and prestige of lawyers is experienced due to the meanwhile high academisation of the population and the enormous increase in lawyers over the past decades which has led to a growing gap between lawyers on the top and at the bottom.

The number of judges per head of the populations differs significantly between the countries. Generally speaking, in the common law world, magistrates are in charge of minor judicial cases, and judges sit in High Courts and may go on circuit through the country, whereas in civil law countries there are just judges in charge of judicial proceedings and courts are in all cities. Another point which matters in comparing is whether there are different judicial branches or specialised courts, which may show different patterns of female participation (Schultz 2013). This is of importance in Muslim countries which have religious Shari'a courts mainly for family matters (see for example Chapter 7). Some still do not permit women judges, others now allow them. In the Global North family law has always been regarded as a classical field for women to deal with.

Finally, in common law countries the personality of the individual judge may have greater significance than in civil law systems. As a result, the subject of women in the judiciary has often been accompanied by greater media and political attention in common law than in civil law countries, where judgments in most cases do not identify the judges' names and a specific court decision is not attributed to any one judge but rather to the bench at large.

In the following part I will try to further embed the findings of this volume into the results of the research we have so far had.

Entry of Women to the Judiciary

The story of women in the judiciary is short, in Europe only going back not much more than 100 years. Women had to fight their way step by step over decades, first for admission to academic studies at universities, then for admission to legal education, to practical training and finally for entrance to the profession and the judiciary. The image of a jurist was of an important male.[6] Women were considered unsuitable for legal work, and particularly for judicial work, due to gendered perceptions of their character (Schultz 2017). Women were seen as too emotional, therefore unable to judge objectively, and too soft for the difficult cases judges must deal with. But they also were unwanted competitors in the legal field. It was therefore a big step for societies to open the doors of legal practice to these Others. In most countries, as is also reflected in chapters in this

---

[6] Emphasised by the professional dress they wear, particularly the pompous wig and gown in common law countries.

volume, it was easier for women to gain access to the legal profession than to the judiciary. In some places this was because women needed as a precondition full civil rights including the right to vote for public office. This was not coupled with full gender equality in other fields of law, which took much longer to achieve, also step by step over decades (for Germany, e.g. Schultz 2016a), especially in family law where in some of the countries in this volume women today still experience inequality that requires ongoing struggles and action for equality by the local female jurists.

After World War II, as constitutions increasingly provided for equal rights for women, they were gradually able to overcome the obstacles to entering the legal field. Progress however was slow. In France, women got the right to vote only after World War II; the first female judge was admitted in 1946; in Italy in 1965; in Portugal, only at the end of the Salazar regime in 1978. But just these countries became leading in the feminisation of the profession, France seems to be the first country where women outnumbered men which happened already in the course of the 1990s (Schultz, Shaw 2013b). Some of the countries in this volume that still lag behind were ironically amongst the first countries to admit a female judge. The explanation lies in the intersection of gender and class. In countries with aristocratic or oligarchic structures, women from leading influential families gained privileges which could override legal barriers. All in all, in the countries assembled in this collection, the chronological sequence in women's entry and career in the judiciary was not so different from the Western world. Overall, women's entry and career in the judiciary, whether in the Global South or Global North, differs from country to country depending on certain factors. A special case is Myanmar where the military regime favoured the increase of women in the judiciary to weaken it (see Chapter 1).

It is interesting to compare where the first women obtained their legal education. When women could not get access to legal education in their countries, they went to neighbouring countries, where it was possible. This was quite common in Europe at the end of the nineteenth century (Schultz 2021). In countries with a colonial history women and men had to go to the 'metropole', the colonial power, because in their home countries no law faculties had been set up for the new law imposed by the ruling force. As this required funding to travel, women had to stand back behind their brothers, and had more problems than men to obtain scholarships. When faculties were finally founded in their home countries, the question was whether women were allowed in or still had to go abroad.

In almost all countries of the world, the proportion of women judges has increased significantly over the past three decades. Drivers of success were not necessarily the inclusion of gender equality in constitutions, but mere economic reasons. In a neo-liberal economy, women are needed in the workforce, and also in higher occupations. In February 2021, even Saudi Arabia nominated its first woman judge as commercial arbitrator. Religion was and is an impeding factor. In many Muslim countries, there is still a tension between constitutional rights of gender equality and religious law. Women are still (to differing extents) legally dependant on men who may even have custody over them, remain in charge of the matrimonial financial regime and have custody over the children, and family matters are dealt with in the special religious Shari'a courts which have no or few female judges and where in many countries women cannot be represented by women lawyers, as those are not allowed to appear there (Maktabi 2017). In contrast, Pakistan has a considerable proportion, about a third, of female judges, and Turkey, due to the former secular regime, almost has gender equality on the bench. In Syria, the authorities pushed for the recruitment of women in the judiciary as women proved to be less corrupt (Cardinal 2013).

Careers in the Judiciary

In all countries, women gain entry to the lower courts but have more difficulty moving up to higher courts, described as attrition rate. In this book, the images of the glass wall, the path of broken glass and the glass ceiling are used to stand for 'in other words, corruption, entry barriers, career hurdles and policy' (Chapter 8). In my research on Germany, some women judges have described a 'clay ceiling' between the local and regional courts of first instance. The local courts however give the women flexibility to combine family and professional work, therefore judges have informed me that the judiciary is a mothers' paradise, also due to the generous possibilities for part-time work, matrimonial and parental leave.

Family work may impede professional careers, to different degrees. Some families may have household staff - in the Global South more often than in the Global North, while other women cannot afford such help. The ideas of what constitutes a good mother, how much housework a woman takes on and if children should go to day care differ enormously, partly independent of the political system and economic situation, rather the result of cultural patterns and religion. Many countries demand mobility from judges who may have to work at courts far away from their home, which conflicts with their family duties.

In most civil law countries, judges are career judges and they can move up from first instance courts to appeal courts. But the nomination procedure to supreme or constitutional courts tends to follow a different path with more political influence. In Germany, there is gender parity at the Federal Constitutional Court, due to political motions for gender equality. However, the high federal courts have gender gaps.

The Impact of Women on the Judiciary: Do Women Judge Differently?

The contributions in this volume provide different perspectives not only on the increase of women judges (called thin feminisation) but also on their particular contribution to judging (called thick substantive feminisation). Thin feminisation may be considered a crucial preliminary step for gendered judging (see Chapter 1). But do women add substance, pass morally superior judgment or overall judge differently? Asking the question may be poisonous as it leads immediately towards the so-called patriarchal dilemma. Notions of difference tend to reinforce stereotypes that 'women are different' or fail to meet the dominant (male) concept of objectivity as a judge. This may be a reason why women had been excluded from the legal profession. On the other hand, it is desirable to have a high quality of justice and the question is whether women enhance it. And can women judges be expected to judge differently to safeguard women's interests and follow a feminist agenda? (Hunter 2008).

I have been collecting evidence in the worldwide research on women in the judiciary. Some patterns are discernible and highlighted in the contributions in this book. They cannot be generalised across the board because the subject matter of cases and special features of the legal and procedural systems are important. There are, however, areas of law that are 'gender-coded', such as family law (Bessières, Mille 2014) and criminal law, in which the personality and life circumstances of the parties involved play a special role. But gender can also influence decisions in other areas of law, and it is not only the sex/gender of the judge that is important but also that of the parties, lawyers and witnesses (Schultz 2017).

Women have different living conditions and personal experiences than men which may lead to different gendered sympathies and behaviour apart from any stereotypical notions of femininity and essentialist claims. The chapters in this book, from Chapter 3 on Sri Lanka to Chapter 6 on the Philippines – add fresh evidence to findings collected a decade ago. In what follows I provide a few examples of findings from the past two decades that have become the basis for comparison (Schultz 2016b).

In a number of countries, it was reported that in family law in custody cases, women tended to show more empathy towards women who wanted to obtain custody of a child. In alimony cases, female judges were less generous to housewives than were male judges. The obvious explanation is that female judges, as 'working women', feel less sympathy for women who rely financially on their husbands (Schultz and Shaw 2013b).

In immigration cases in the United States, women judges granted asylum to female petitioners more often than their male colleagues did (Menkel-Meadow 2010). Brenda Hale, the first female president of the Supreme Court in the United Kingdom, argued in a House of Lords decision that the right of asylum for victims of political persecution should be extended to cases of threatened female genital mutilation (Rackley 2008), a view clearly informed by feminist empathy. These are examples of 'pro-woman' decisions.

In the USA, there is extensive research on the gender impact of sexual harassment in the workplace (Boyd, Epstein and Martin 2010). A so-called panel effect was discovered: male judges tended to favour female complainants if at least one female judge was on the panel. An all-male court reduced the complainant's chances. Similar results were reported in cases of racial discrimination. African American judges and white judges perceive racial harassment differently (Chew and Kelley 2009). These are not only cases of gendered sympathy, but they also show that male judges delegated the gender competence in these cases to their female colleagues. It was obvious that the more diverse the backgrounds and experiences of the judges, the greater the range of ideas and information contributing to the institutional process.

At the European Court of Justice, the female German advocate general advocated for uniform premiums in health insurance policies for men and women, whereas previously women had to pay higher contributions (due to costs caused by longer life expectancies),[7] a clear case of trying to achieve gender justice.

In criminal law, there were the expectations that women might in general show a deeper understanding of wrongdoers and pass milder sentences and that they might work towards offering them more psycho-social assistance.

---

[7] In Germany, uniform premiums were introduced at the end of 2012. The potentially higher costs caused by pregnancy and childbirth had already been compensated in 2006 after the Equal Treatment (Anti-Discrimination) Act had been passed.

But it was also expected that they would pass stricter sentences in cases of violence, in particular sexual violence, to possibly counterbalance a male tendency to downplay these cases because of male preconceived opinions and male solidarity. In our comparative work, we found mixed evidence of gender differences in cases of violence and sexual abuse. In some countries, it was reported that women in general passed milder sentences, also in cases of sexual violence, which could be an indication that they did not want to run the risk of seeming to be biased towards the offender.

They more often than men tended to take a more interdisciplinary approach, and avoided rigid application of universal rules and narrow doctrinal decisions and showed a tendency to 'redraw the line between the law and the social', reached more balanced decisions and avoided contentious solutions, rather searched for win/win solutions contributing to more substantive justice in the Weberian sense (Schultz 2017).

We have received strong evidence from several countries over many years that female judges are less corrupt than their male colleagues (Syria, Kenya, Uganda, Pakistan, Bulgaria and others). One explanation may be that many of them are not the principal family breadwinners; a more convincing reason could be that they have gained higher morals through an education geared towards female virtues. Many of the chapters in this volume raise the issue of corruption as one inherent in the judiciary. This is also proof of the fact that parties can never rely on how an individual judge decides due to all the differences in family origin, ethnicity, polit-ical stance, experiences and economic conditions, and of course the – in most cases still male dominated – socialisation they receive during their legal studies and training. Also, the male culture at the law courts frames their minds (Böning and Schultz 2018).

The chapters show how important it is to have women with their particular life experience at supreme and constitutional courts because there they have the chance to directly influence legal change towards more gender equality. Likewise, research in Canada showed that women at the Supreme Court were the great dissenters in cases which dealt with women's or gender issues, an effect which weakened over time when gender imbalances and discriminatory regulations disappeared (Belleau and Johnson 2008).

Working as a communication trainer for lawyers and the judiciary, I have also cast a closer look at the communication behaviour of men and women at court[8] which may influence the outcome of cases. This topic is

---

[8] Also Gleeson, Jones and McBean 2019 with many further references.

not dealt with in this volume and is an area ripe for future research. I found some empirical research confirming my own perceptions that women judges' style of interrogation could be friendlier, more responsive to people at court. I also found examples of men who showed less respect for other female actors in court in order to undermine their authority[9] and who were less attentive to women in the proceedings.

Dealing with these gender perceptions and description of differences also proves how important it is to include gender issues in all kinds of legal university and practical training (Schultz, Shaw and Dawson 2014).

Epilogue

This leads to the final question of why it is important to have women on the bench, which all chapters in this book deal with and answer with different emphases. I interviewed a female appeal court president for my research on women in leading positions in the judiciary in Germany (Schultz 2013) who in response to this question said: 'Women make the judiciary more colourful', meaning that women not only bring in a different spectrum of life experience but also change the face of the judiciary.

To sum it up and put it in my words: equal participation is an inherent feature of democracy, a demand of the gender equality principle in the constitution.[10] Equal participation enhances legitimacy and public confidence in the judiciary, and therefore the judiciary will better reflect society and represent the diversity of the litigants.

The increasing visibility of women in the courtroom potentially attracts more women to a career in the judiciary and diversifies the role models for women's careers in the judiciary. Particularly in countries that still have strong patriarchal cultures, seeing women judges in court will also potentially give women the confidence that they do have access to justice and may raise the comfort level of women appearing in court (Cowan 2013, 321, also cited in Chapter 3).

---

[9] In the United States, courses for criminal defence lawyers address how to influence women – and men – at court, in particular as members of the jury, playing along with gender stereotypes.

[10] In Europe not only a demand of national constitutions but also of the EU regulations and directives resulting in national anti-discrimination legislation (Schultz 2019).

By providing these empirical accounts of women judges in the Global South – from the Pacific Islands to Southeast Asia and South Asia – Melissa Crouch enables a new generation of scholarship to emerge and inspire new thinking on the role of women in the judiciary in the Asia-Pacific.

References

Bauer, Gretchen and Jarpa J. Dawuni (2016) *Gender and the Judiciary in Africa: From Obscurity to Parity?* (New York, Routledge).

Belleau, Marie-Claire and Rebecca Johnson (2008) 'Judging Gender: Difference and Dissent at the Supreme Court of Canada' 15/1–2 *International Journal of the Legal Profession* 57–71.

Bessière, Céline and Muriel Mille (2014) 'The Judge Is Often a Woman: Professional Perceptions and Practices of Male and Female Family Court Judges in France' 56/Supplement 1 *Sociologie du Travail* e43–e68.

Bogoch, Bryna (2003) 'Lawyers in the Courtroom: Gender, Trials and Professional Performance in Israel' in Ulrike Schultz and Gisela Shaw (eds.) *Women in the World's Legal Professions* (Oxford, Hart) 247–268.

Böning, Anja and Ulrike Schultz (2018) 'Juristische Sozialisation' in Christian Boulanger and Julia Rosenstock (eds.) *Studienbuch Interdisziplinäre Rechtsforschung* (Baden-Baden, Nomos).

Boyd, Christina L., Lee Epstein and Andrew D. Martin (2010) 'Untangling the Causal Effects of Sex on Judging' 54/2 *American Journal of Political Science* 389–411.

Cardinal, Monique (2013) 'The Impact of Women on the Administration of Justice in Syria and the Judicial Selection Process' in Ulrike Schultz and Gisela Shaw (eds.) *Women in the World's Legal Profession* (Oxford, Hart) 191–211.

Chew, Pat und Robert Kelley (2009) 'Myth of the Color-Blind Judge: An Empirical Analysis of Racial Harassment Cases' 86 *Washington University Law Review* 1117–1166.

Dawson, Brettel, Ulrike Schultz and Gisela Shaw, eds. (2016) *Gender and Judicial Education* (London, Routledge).

Hunter, Rosemary (2008) 'Can Feminist Judges Make a Difference?' 15/1–2 *International Journal of the Legal Profession* 7–36.

Lindbekk, Monika and Nadia Sonneveld, eds. (2017) *Women Judges in the Muslim World* (Leiden, Brill).

Maktabi, Rania (2017) 'Enfranchised Minors: Women as People in the Middle East after the 2011 Arab Uprisings' 6/1 *Laws. Evolving Challenges: An International Retrospective on Feminist Legal Theory*, special issue edited by Rosemary Auchmuty. https://doi.org/10.3390/laws6010004, 1–25.

Menkel-Meadow, Carrie (2009) 'Asylum in a Different Voice: Judging Immigration Claims and Gender' in Jaya Ramji-Nogales, Andrew I. Schoenholz and Philip G.

Schrag (eds.) *Refugee Roulette: Disparities in Asylum Adjudication and Proposals for Reform* (New York, New York University Press).

Rackley, Erika (2008) 'What a Difference Makes: Gendered Harms and Judicial Diversity' 15/1–2 *International Journal of the Legal Profession* 37–56.

Schultz, Ulrike (2003a) 'Women in the World's Legal Professions: Overview and Synthesis' in Ulrike Schultz and Gisela Shaw (eds.) *Women in the World's Legal Profession* (Oxford, Hart) XXV–LXII.

(2003b) 'Women Lawyers in Germany: Perception and Construction of Femininity' in Ulrike Schultz and Gisela Shaw (eds.) *Women in the World's Legal Professions* (Oxford, Hart) 295–321.

(2013) '"I Was Noticed and I was Asked . . ." Women's Careers in the Judiciary: Results of an Empirical Study for the Ministry of Justice in Northrhine-Westfalia, Germany' in Ulrike Schultz and Gisela Shaw (eds.) *Gender and Judging* (Oxford, Hart) 145–166.

(2016a) 'Equal Rights for Men and Women in Germany: How a Constitutional Principle Was Transformed into Reality' in Heinrich Boell Stiftung South Caucasus (ed.) *Fight for the Public Space: When Personal is Political* (Tiflis) S. 85–96.

(2016b) 'Sexism in Law and the Impact of Gender Stereotypes in Legal Proceedings' in Heinrich Boell Stiftung South Caucasus (ed.) *Fight for the Public Space: When Personal is Political* (Tiflis) 97–108.

(2017) 'Do Female Judges Judge Better?' in Monika Lindbekk and Nadia Sonneveld (eds.) *Women Judges in the Muslim World* (Leiden, Brill) 23–50.

(2019) 'The Gender and Judging Project: Equity in Germany: Diversity and the Courts' in Susann Sterett and Lee Walker (eds.) *Research Handbook on Law and Courts* (Northampton, Elgar Publishing).

(2020b) 'Gender in Socio-Legal Teaching and Research' 21/7 *German Law Journal* 1345–1361.

(2021a) 'Introduction: Gender and Careers in the Legal Academy: Overview and Synthesis' in Ulrike Schultz, Gisela Shaw, Margaret Thornton and Rosemary Auchmuty (eds.) *Gender and Careers in the Legal Profession* (Oxford, Hart) 1–36.

(2021b) 'Gender and Its Impact on Decision-Making in (International) Arbitration: A View from Germany' *International Journal of the Legal Profession*, forthcoming.

Schultz, Ulrike and Gisela Shaw, eds. (2003) *Women in the World's Legal Professions* (Oxford, Hart).

(eds.) (2012) *Women in the Judiciary* (London: Routledge) (reprint of Special Issue: Gender and Judging, *International Journal of the Legal Profession* 15/1–2.

Schultz, Ulrike and Gisela Shaw, eds. (2013a) *Gender and Judging* (Oxford, Hart).

(2013b) 'Introduction: Gender and Judging: Overview and Synthesis' in Ulrike Schultz and Gisela Shaw (eds.) *Gender and Judging* (Oxford, Hart) 3–47.

INDEX